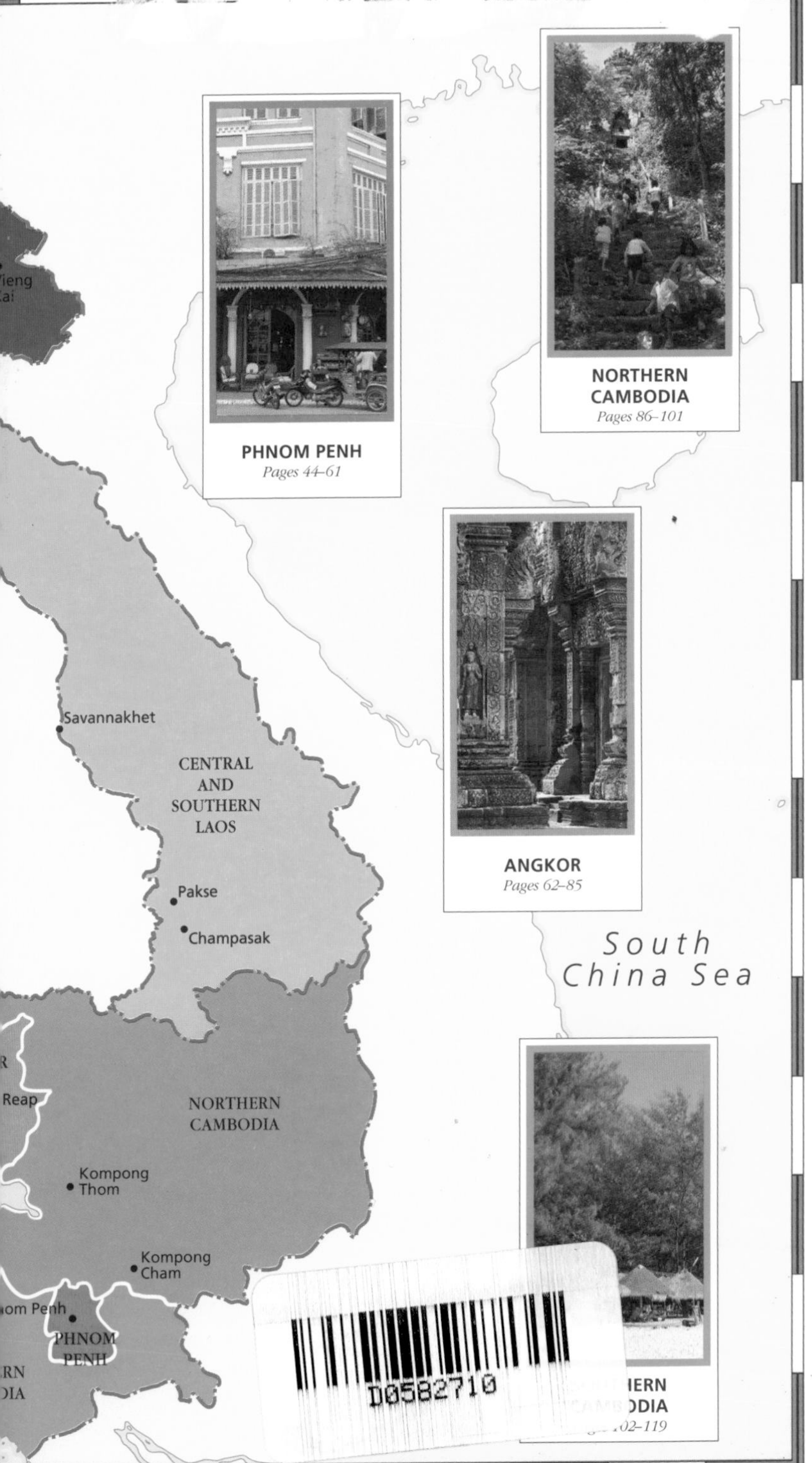

ieng
ai
Savannakhet
CENTRAL AND SOUTHERN LAOS
Pakse
Champasak
Reap
NORTHERN CAMBODIA
Kompong Thom
Kompong Cham
om Penh
PHNOM PENH
RN
DIA
South China Sea
PHNOM PENH
Pages 44–61
NORTHERN CAMBODIA
Pages 86–101
ANGKOR
Pages 62–85
HERN
CAMBODIA
102–119
D0582710

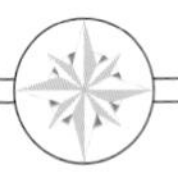

EYEWITNESS TRAVEL

CAMBODIA AND LAOS

EYEWITNESS TRAVEL
CAMBODIA AND LAOS
DK

LONDON, NEW YORK,
MELBOURNE, MUNICH AND DELHI
www.dk.com

MANAGING EDITOR Aruna Ghose
SENIOR EDITORIAL MANAGER Savitha Kumar
SENIOR DESIGN MANAGER Priyanka Thakur
PROJECT EDITOR Smita Khanna Bajaj
PROJECT DESIGNER Amisha Gupta
EDITORS Karen Faye D'Souza, Shreya Sarkar
DESIGNER Neha Sethi
SENIOR CARTOGRAPHIC MANAGER Uma Bhattacharya
CARTOGRAPHER Schchida Nand Pradhan
DTP DESIGNER Rakesh Pal
SENIOR PICTURE RESEARCH COORDINATOR Taiyaba Khatoon
PICTURE RESEARCHER Sumita Khatwani
MAIN CONTRIBUTORS David Chandler, Peter Holmshaw, Iain Stewart, Richard Waters
PHOTOGRAPHERS Demetrio Carrasco, Linda Whitwam
ILLUSTRATORS
Chingtham Chinglemba, Sanjeev Kumar, Surat Kumar Mantoo, Arun Pottirayil, Gautam Trivedi

Printed and bound in Malaysia by Vivar Printing Sdn Bhd

13 14 15 16 10 9 8 7 6 5 4 3 2 1

First published in UK in 2011
by Dorling Kindersley Limited
80 Strand, London WC2R 0RL

Reprinted with revisions 2013

A CIP CATALOGUE RECORD IS AVAILABLE FROM THE BRITISH LIBRARY.

ISBN 978-1-4093-8647-6

FLOORS ARE REFERRED TO THROUGHOUT IN ACCORDANCE WITH AMERICAN USAGE, IE THE "FIRST FLOOR" IS AT GROUND LEVEL.

Front cover main image: A view of majestic Angkor Wat across a pond of beautiful lotus flowers, Cambodia

Visitors kayaking down the Nam Song, Vang Vieng

CONTENTS

Monks enjoying a quiet moment amid the stone sculptures, the Bayon

◁ Vast, green paddy fields near Boun Neua, Phongsali province

CAMBODIA AREA BY AREA

View of French-style shophouses, Savannakhet

LAOS AREA BY AREA

Detail of carving, Wat Xieng Men

A busy roadside café near Nam Phu Square, Vientiane

TRAVELERS' NEEDS

SURVIVAL GUIDE

Wat Xieng Thong, Luang Prabang

HOW TO USE THIS GUIDE

This guide helps you to get the most from your visit to Cambodia and Laos. It provides detailed practical information and expert recommendations. *Introducing Cambodia and Laos* maps the two countries and sets them in their historical and cultural context. *Cambodia Area by Area* and *Laos Area by Area* are the main sightseeing sections. They cover all the important sights with maps, photographs, and illustrations. Information on hotels, restaurants, shops and markets, and entertainment is found in *Travelers' Needs*. The *Survival Guide* has advice on everything from travel and medical services to telephones and post offices.

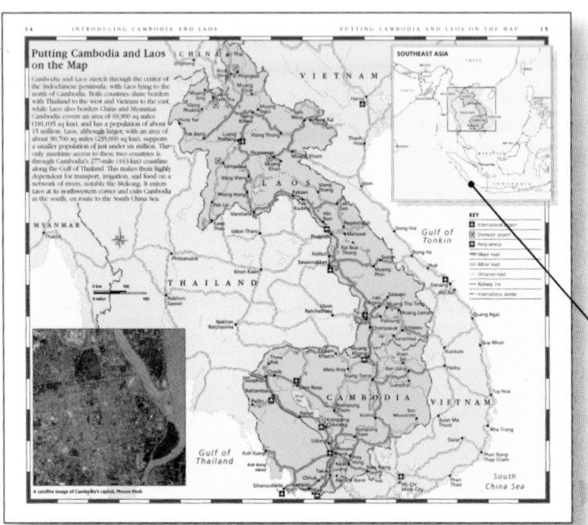

PUTTING CAMBODIA AND LAOS ON THE MAP

The orientation map shows the location of Cambodia and Laos in relation to their neighboring countries. Each country has been divided into four main sightseeing areas. These eight sections form the separate chapters.

A locator map shows where Cambodia and Laos are in relation to other Southeast Asian countries.

CAMBODIA AND LAOS AREA BY AREA

Each of the eight sections starts with an introduction and a map. The best places to visit have been numbered on a *Regional Map* at the beginning of each chapter. The key to the map symbols is on the back flap.

1 Introduction

The history, landscape, and character of each area is outlined here, showing how the area has developed over the centuries and what it has to offer the visitor today.

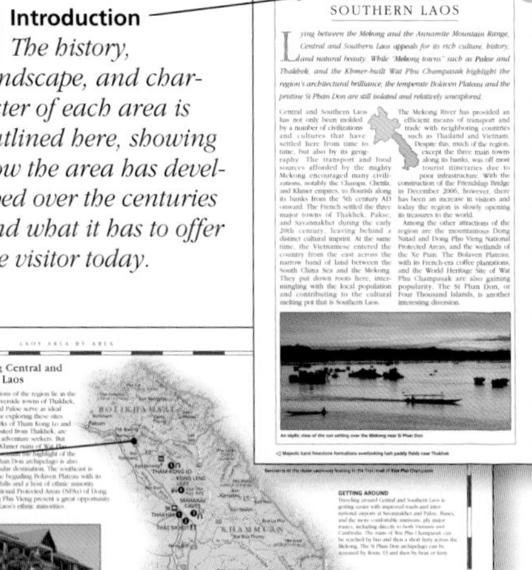

Each region can be quickly identified by its color coding. A complete list of color codes is shown on the inside front cover.

2 Regional Map

This map shows the road network and gives an illustrated overview of the region. All the sights are numbered and there are also useful tips on getting around.

Sights at a Glance lists the chapter's sights by category: Places of worship, National parks, Museums, and Markets.

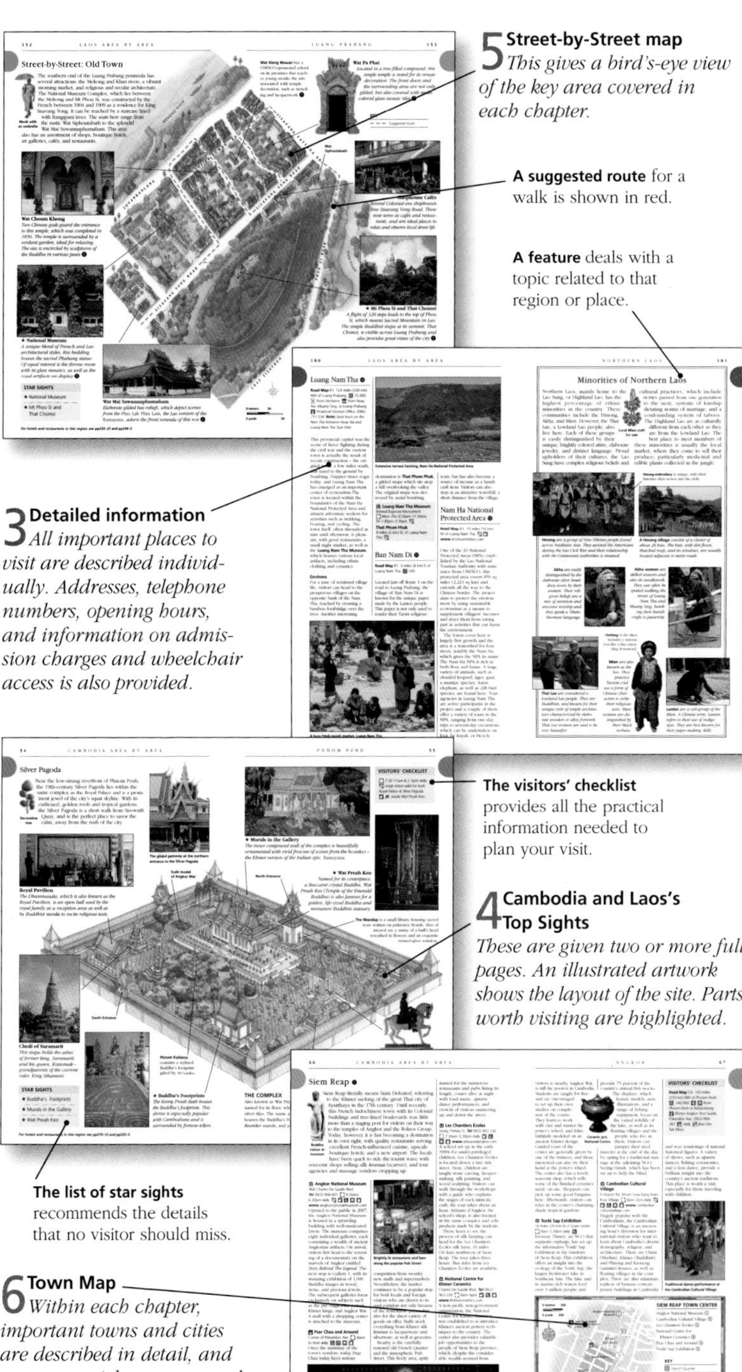

5 Street-by-Street map
This gives a bird's-eye view of the key area covered in each chapter.

A suggested route for a walk is shown in red.

A feature deals with a topic related to that region or place.

3 Detailed information
All important places to visit are described individually. Addresses, telephone numbers, opening hours, and information on admission charges and wheelchair access is also provided.

The visitors' checklist provides all the practical information needed to plan your visit.

4 Cambodia and Laos's Top Sights
These are given two or more full pages. An illustrated artwork shows the layout of the site. Parts worth visiting are highlighted.

The list of star sights recommends the details that no visitor should miss.

6 Town Map
Within each chapter, important towns and cities are described in detail, and numerous sights recommended. A handy map locates the main sights and transport hubs in the town.

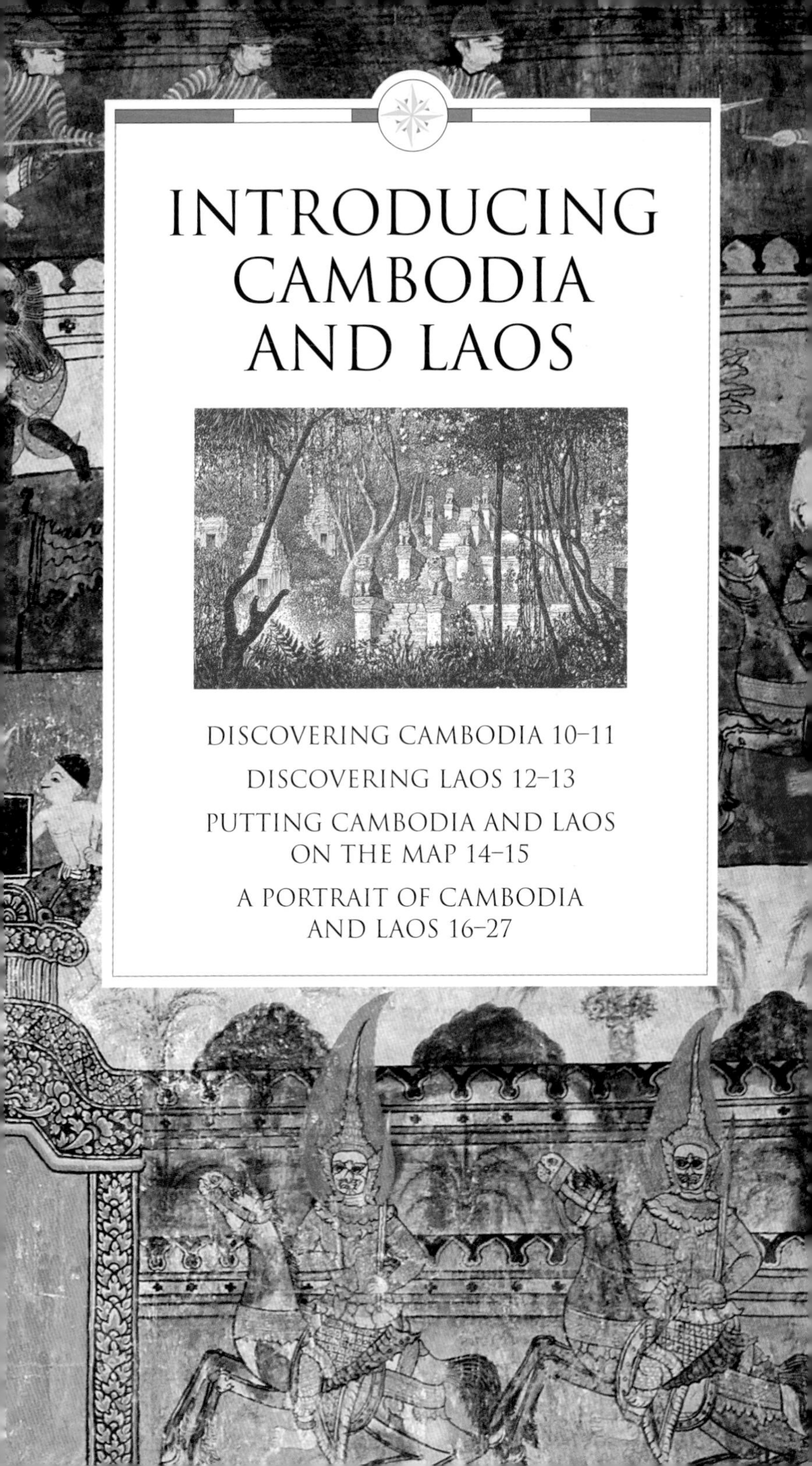

INTRODUCING CAMBODIA AND LAOS

DISCOVERING CAMBODIA

Cambodia is a compact country, sharing borders with Thailand, Laos, and Vietnam. It is flanked by mountains to the north and the southeast, while the Tonlé Sap Lake dominates the central region. The Mekong River cuts through the country from the north en route to the Mekong Delta in Vietnam, bringing rich nutrients into the Tonlé Sap Lake and flooding it during the monsoon. To the south, the 277-mile (443-km) long coastline is dotted with unspoiled islands, some of which are still undeveloped. Despite being decimated by war during the 1970s, the country's burgeoning capital, Phnom Penh, and cities such as Siem Reap are exhilarating destinations.

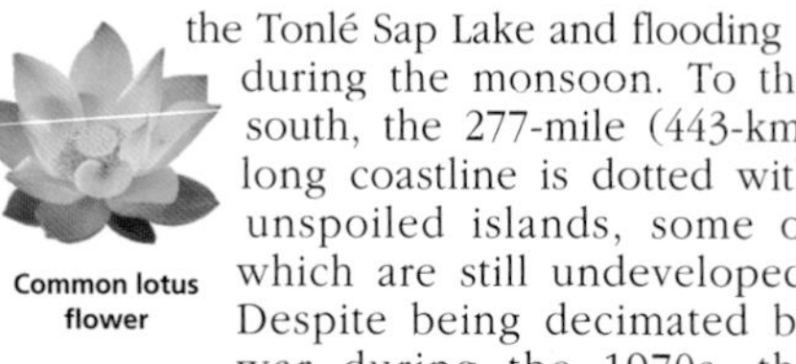

Common lotus flower

Inner courtyard of the National Museum of Cambodia, Phnom Penh

PHNOM PENH

- **Colonial architecture**
- **Artifacts from Angkor**
- **Bustling markets**

Once hailed as the Pearl of the Orient, Phnom Penh still retains some of its former French charm: in its Gallic cuisine and in the shuttered townhouses that line many of its streets. Built under French administration, the **Royal Palace and Silver Pagoda** *(see pp52–5)* are quintessentially Khmer, housing fabulous Buddhist treasures. Nearby is the riverfront area of Sisowath Quay, the heart of Phnom Penh, and the **National Museum of Cambodia** *(see p50)*, which shelters a vast array of artifacts from the Angkorian period. To the southwest lies the **Tuol Sleng Genocide Museum** *(see p51)*, where thousands were tortured en route to the **Killing Fields of Choeung Ek** *(see p58)*. The city's busy markets are packed with everything from *kramas* (scarves) to pirated DVDs.

ANGKOR

- **Temples of Angkor**
- **Floating villages**
- **Vibrant nightlife**

The temples of Angkor, the chief highlight of this region, are among the most celebrated ancient buildings in the world. They offer visitors a glimpse of Cambodia's greatest period – culturally and architecturally. The ideal way to visit these magnificent temples is via the riverside town of **Siem Reap** *(see pp66–7)*. Fast becoming a favorite of glossy lifestyle magazines with the growth of upscale boutique hotels, quality shops, and spa treatments, Siem Reap has much to offer. Among the town's attractions is **Psar Chaa** *(see p66)*, an old market selling everything from fresh produce and souvenirs to clothes and jewelry. The town's vibrant nightlife, centered around the lively Pub Street, adds to its ever increasing charm.

However, most visitors head to the Hindu-Buddhist temples of Angkor. The temples' surviving statuary, which has endured civil war and looting, and the vast *barays* (reservoirs) that cleverly diverted rivers to the rice fields of Angkor have captured the imagination of millions of visitors. Perhaps the best known of these temples is **Angkor Wat** *(see pp68–9)*, which is the world's largest religious complex, and best viewed at sunrise or sunset. **Ta Prohm** *(see pp80–81)*, among the most atmospheric of the Angkorian ruins, still remains engulfed by the encroaching jungle and was featured in

Monks sitting among the enigmatic stone faces of Bayon, Angkor Thom

◁ Vibrant mural detailing military scenes in the 19th century on an interior wall of a *wat*, Luang Prabang

Atmospheric ruins of Sambor Prei Kuk, surrounded by dense forest

the movie *Lara Croft: Tomb Raider* (2001), starring Angelina Jolie. The majestic city of **Angkor Thom** *(see pp72–5)*, with the Bayon and its 216 smiling faces, said to be of Avalokitesvara, a Bodhisattva, is enigmatic and otherworldly.

Located a short distance south of Siem Reap is the natural wonder of the Tonlé Sap Lake and the **Prek Toal Bird Sanctuary** *(see p84)*, regarded as the most important breeding ground for large waterbirds in Southeast Asia. The floating village of **Kompong Khleang** *(see p85)*, the largest permanent settlement on the Tonlé Sap, provides an authentic experience of traditional rural life in Cambodia.

Painted stork

NORTHERN CAMBODIA

- **Jungle temples**
- **Sightings of the endangered Irrawaddy dolphin**
- **Lush paddy fields**

Northern Cambodia is a mesmerizing region, with a varied landscape comprising fertile paddy fields and thick forests teeming with wildlife. To the west of the Tonlé Sap Lake is **Battambang** *(see p90)*, the second largest city in the country. Known as the "rice bowl of Cambodia," the city is dotted with fertile paddy fields and derelict, rarely visited Khmer temples. The **Killing Caves of Phnom Sampeau** *(see p91)*, a short distance from Battambang, are another grim reminder of Cambodia's violent past. The rice plains and tiny villages finally give way to the spectacular remains of **Prasat Preah Vihear** *(see pp94–5)*, an Angkorian temple lying close to the border with Thailand. The 7th-century pre-Angkorian ruins of **Sambor Prei Kuk** *(see p98)* are also among Cambodia's ancient wonders. The town of **Kratie** *(see p100)*, located on the Mekong River, is perhaps the best place for spotting the rare Irrawaddy dolphin. Beyond Kratie begins the vast wilderness of the northeast, with forests, plantations, and ethnic hill tribes. **Sen Monorom** *(see p101)*, the capital of Cambodia's largest province, is referred to as "the Switzerland of Cambodia" for its cool climate and rolling hills.

SOUTHERN CAMBODIA

- **Sunbathing on beautiful beaches**
- **Coastal national parks**
- **Sumptuous seafood**

Flanked to the west by the Cardamom Mountains and to the east by Vietnam, Southern Cambodia is a picturesque region fringed by turquoise bays, powder-fine beaches, and a largely undeveloped archipelago of verdant islands. The town of **Sihanoukville** *(see pp106–7)* is the gateway to the stunning white beaches of Otres and Occheuteal, among others. The nearby islands of **Koh Rong Samloem** and **Koh Ta Kiev** *(see pp108–9)* are delightfully quiet, if basic, and offer great diving and jungle treks respectively. Covering an area of 58 sq miles (150 sq km), the relatively unexplored **Ream National Park** *(see p108)* is home to endangered birds of prey and butterflies, and is a great place for organized jungle treks. Inland, within the **Bokor National Park** *(see p115)*, home to the Asiatic tiger, lies the deserted Bokor Hill Station, a former French outpost, and the location for numerous films. Farther south, **Kep** *(see p116)*, once a fashionable retreat for French Colonialists, is famed for its sunsets and seafood.

Dazzling waters off Koh Rong Samloem, near Sihanoukville

DISCOVERING LAOS

Sharing borders with five other nations, Laos's location lends it great diversity, both in its landscape and its people. The mighty Mekong River, which cuts through the country, is a vital lifeline in an otherwise landlocked nation. The misty jungles of the north are inhabited by a large number of ethnic minorities with their own distinct cultures and languages. The sun-baked plains of the south are home to Lao-speaking rice farmers, while the urban elite dwell in the capital city of Vientiane and in Luang Prabang, the former abode of the monarchy. Numerous Buddhist *wats* (temples) and relics of French Colonial architecture greatly add to the charm of these cities.

Buddha head souvenir

VIENTIANE

- **Pha That Luang**
- **Sunset drinks beside the Mekong**
- **Eclectic statuary at Xieng Khuan (Buddha Park)**

Laos's somewhat somnolent capital, Vientiane, is refreshingly free of the traffic jams that plague many other Asian capitals and most sights of interest are easily accessible. A pilgrimage to the Buddhist stupa of **Pha That Luang** *(see p143)* can help visitors understand the spirit of Lao nationhood, which, even in today's technically atheist Communist state, remains tied to the Buddhist faith. Busloads of visitors from other parts of the country arrive here, making it a good place to mingle with Lao people. The influence of the French Colonial period is still visible in the buildings near the central Nam Phu Square, not far from the riverside restaurants along the Mekong. **Xieng Khuan** *(see p146)*, a park by the river, has a huge collection of statues. At the head of Lan Xang Avenue lies the **Patuxai** *(see p142)*, or Victory Gate, clearly inspired by the Parisian Arc de Triomphe. Several Buddhist *wats,* including **Wat Si Saket** *(see p141),* and **Haw Pha Kaew** *(see p140),* which is now a museum of Buddhist art, can be seen all over the city.

View of the setting sun from the Mekong, Luang Prabang

Monks in front of Laos's national monument, Pha That Luang

LUANG PRABANG

- **Buddhist architecture at Wat Xieng Thong**
- **National Museum Complex**
- **Boat trips on the Mekong**

The former royal capital, declared a World Heritage Site by UNESCO in 1995, is the high point of many visitors' trip to Laos. Located at the confluence of the Mekong and Khan rivers, Luang Prabang's landscape is dotted with a mixture of superb Buddhist architecture and 19th-century French Colonial villas, many of which have now become stylish hotels. Among the best-known sites in Luang Prabang is **Mt Phou Si** *(see p154)*, which offers excellent views of the city and its surroundings. The dozens of Buddhist temples, including **Wat Xieng Thong** *(see pp160–61)*, **Wat Xieng Mouan** *(see p157),* and **Wat Choum Khong** *(see p157)* that line the streets, often one after another, are well worth a visit. The Old Town area of Luang Prabang is surprisingly small and can easily be covered on foot in a few hours. This is a fascinating area, with several examples of French Colonial architecture and many elegant restaurants serving delicious local and international dishes. Visitors may also get to interact with jovial young monks eager to practice their English. Among the city's other attractions is the popular **Night Market** *(see pp156–7)* on Sisavang Vong Road, where visitors will find handicrafts made by the local Hmong people.

Close by is the **National Museum Complex** *(see p156)*, which was the residence of the Lao royal family until the Communist takeover in 1975.

NORTHERN LAOS

- **Enigmatic Plain of Jars**
- **Historically significant caves in the Vieng Xai valley**
- **Pristine forests and rivers of Luang Nam Tha**

The mountainous and isolated area spanning the wide north is vastly different from the rest of the country. This region is home to a variety of Highland Lao ethnic minorities such as the Akha, Hmong, Mien, and Khamu, who are ethno-linguistically distinct from the Lowland Lao, as well as various Tai groups who speak languages related to the national tongue. In the northwest, the town of **Luang Nam Tha** *(see p180)* has emerged as a jumping-off point for a variety of outdoor activities in the nearby **Nam Ha National Protected Area** *(see p180)*. Trekking, mountainbiking, and white-water rafting are ideal ways to experience this mountainous environment. Another option is to take a boat tour on the Mekong River from Luang Prabang to the border town of Huay Xai. In the northeast, the **Plain of Jars** *(see p175)* boasts megalithic sites still not completely explained by archaeologists. Farther east, toward the Vietnamese border, lies the remote **Vieng Xai** valley *(see p174)*, where Communist revolutionary cadres sought shelter from intense American bombing during the 1960s and 70s. The adventurous can explore the caves, waterfalls, and tubing opportunities in the Nam Song in the well-known backpacker haven of **Vang Vieng** *(see pp172–3)*.

Site 1 of the megalithic Plain of Jars, Xieng Khuang province

CENTRAL AND SOUTHERN LAOS

- **Wat Phu Champasak**
- **Boat trip through the Tham Kong Lo**
- **Si Phan Don**

Vast plains, which are home to traditional rice farmers, flank the Mekong River south of the capital. The charming towns of **Thakhek** *(see p190)*, **Savannakhet** *(see pp192–3)*, and **Pakse** *(see p194)*, nestled along the Mekong, are worth a visit. Pakse in particular forms the gateway to the magnificent, though crumbling, pre-Angkorian ruins of **Wat Phu Champasak** *(see pp196–7)*. In the south lies the inland archipelago of **Si Phan Don** *(see pp202–3)*, or Four Thousand Islands. This unique environment of waterfalls and deep pools offers sanctuary to a variety of birds as well as the endangered Irrawaddy dolphin. Farther inland from the Mekong plain, majestic limestone mountains are dotted with a plethora of caves such as the famous **Tham Kong Lo** *(see p191)*, which is negotiated by a 4-mile (6-km) boat trip through its length. In the southeast of the country, the **Bolaven Plateau** *(see p198)*, home to several ethnic minorities, is a rich agricultural region specializing in coffee. Also seen here are remnants of the **Ho Chi Minh Trail** *(see p191)* used by the Vietnamese during the Vietnam War (1954–75).

The ruins of Wat Phu Champasak reflected in the waters of one of its *barays* (reservoirs)

Putting Cambodia and Laos on the Map

Cambodia and Laos stretch through the center of the Indochinese peninsula, with Laos lying to the north of Cambodia. Both countries share borders with Thailand to the west and Vietnam to the east, while Laos also borders China and Myanmar. Cambodia covers an area of 69,900 sq miles (181,035 sq km), and has a population of about 15 million. Laos, although larger, with an area of about 90,700 sq miles (235,000 sq km), supports a smaller population of just under six million. The only maritime access is through Cambodia's 277-mile (443-km) coastline along the Gulf of Thailand. Historically this made both countries dependent for transport, irrigation and food on a network of rivers, notably the Mekong. It enters Laos at its northwestern corner and exits Cambodia in the south, en route to the South China Sea.

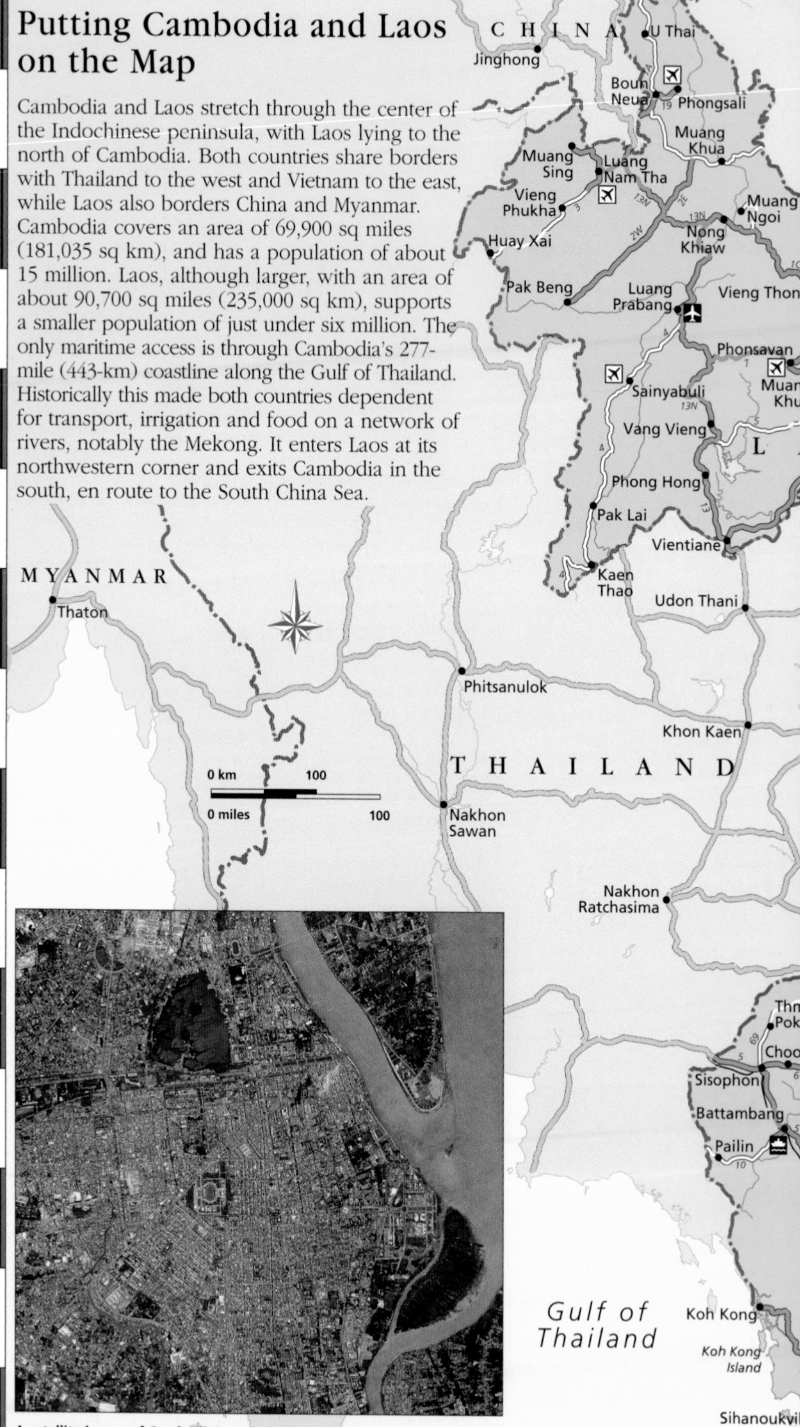

A satellite image of Cambodia's capital, Phnom Penh

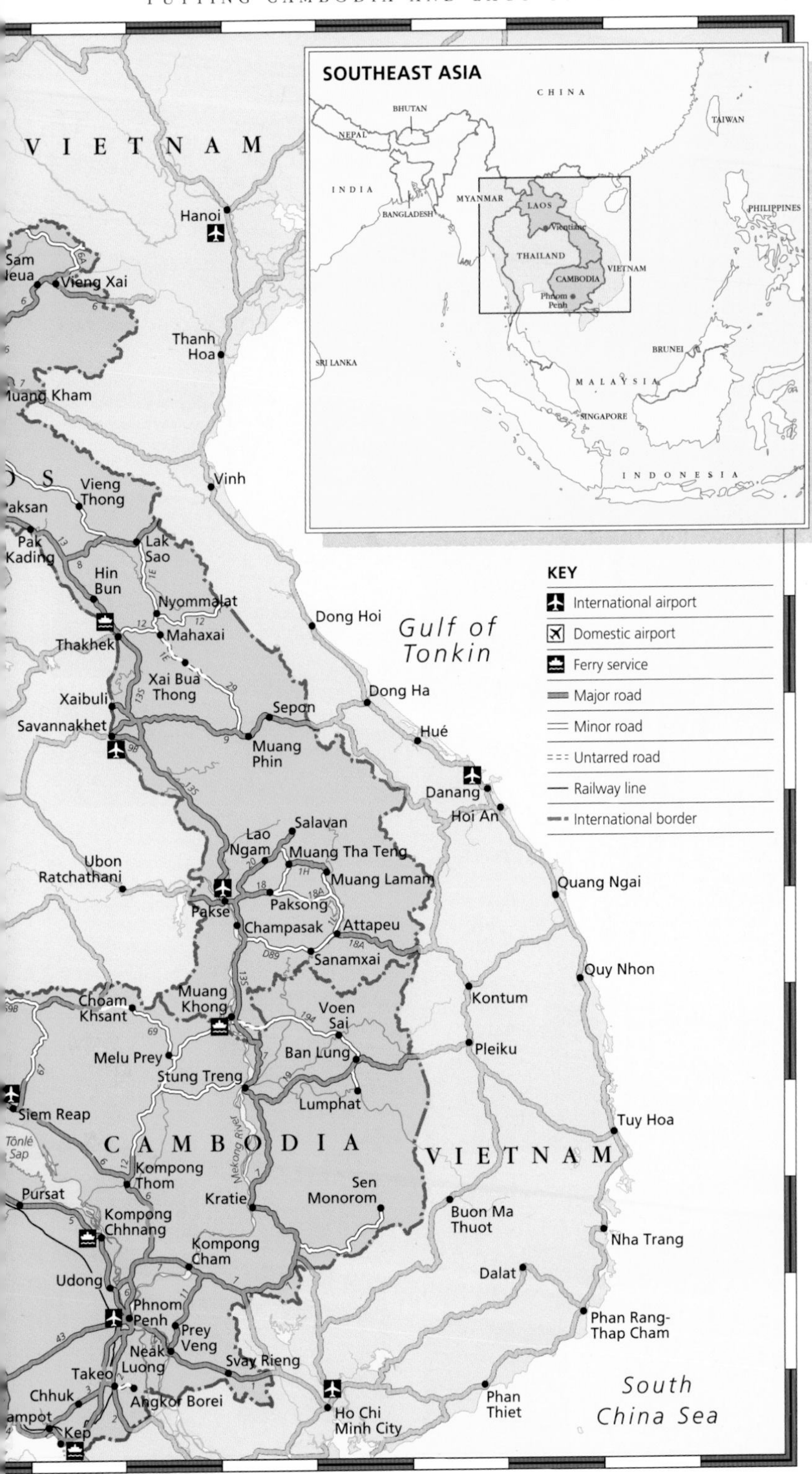
SOUTHEAST ASIA
CHINA
BHUTAN
NEPAL
TAIWAN
INDIA
MYANMAR
BANGLADESH
LAOS
Vientiane
PHILIPPINES
THAILAND
VIETNAM
CAMBODIA
Phnom Penh
SRI LANKA
BRUNEI
MALAYSIA
SINGAPORE
INDONESIA
KEY
International airport
Domestic airport
Ferry service
Major road
Minor road
Untarred road
Railway line
International border
VIETNAM
Hanoi
Sam
Vieng Xai
Thanh Hoa
Vinh
Vieng Thong
Pak Kading
Lak Sao
Hin Bun
Nyommalat
Dong Hoi
Gulf of Tonkin
Thakhek
Mahaxai
Xai Bua Thong
Dong Ha
Xaibuli
Sepon
Savannakhet
Muang Phin
Hué
Danang
Hoi An
Salavan
Lao Ngam
Muang Tha Teng
Ubon Ratchathani
Muang Lamam
Quang Ngai
Paksong
Pakse
Champasak
Attapeu
Sanamxai
Quy Nhon
Choam Khsant
Muang Khong
Kontum
Voen Sai
Melu Prey
Ban Lung
Pleiku
Stung Treng
Lumphat
Siem Reap
Tuy Hoa
Tônlé Sap
CAMBODIA
Mekong River
VIETNAM
Kompong Thom
Sen Monorom
Pursat
Kratie
Buon Ma Thuot
Kompong Chhnang
Nha Trang
Kompong Cham
Dalat
Udong
Phnom Penh
Phan Rang-Thap Cham
Prey Veng
Neak Luong
Svay Rieng
Takeo
South China Sea
Chhuk
Angkor Borei
Phan Thiet
Ho Chi Minh City
Kep

Landscape and Wildlife

Common red hibiscus

With some of the best-preserved rain forests in Asia, Cambodia and Laos are home to rich biological diversity. Laos's mountainous and rugged landscape is typified by soaring outcrops of karst limestone, fecund river valleys, and emerald-green paddy fields. Much of central Cambodia is flat, with the terrain defined by the fertile influence of the Tonlé Sap and Mekong rivers. The abundant wildlife in the region includes a number of endangered animals such as the Asian elephant and the tiger. New species such as the antelope-like saola and the kha nyou are also found here. The region's rain forests, however, are being steadily depleted by illegal and state-sanctioned logging.

Majestic karst limestone mountains in Vang Vieng, Laos

RAIN FOREST PRESERVES
Covering thousands of square miles, the rain forests of the two countries include outstanding national parks such as Nam Ha in Laos and Botum Sakor in Cambodia. These largely inaccessible forests harbor a stunning array of wildlife, including various species of birds, mammals, and reptiles.

The clouded leopard *is known to inhabit the rain forests of Asia. One of the most agile cats, it is a superb tree climber.*

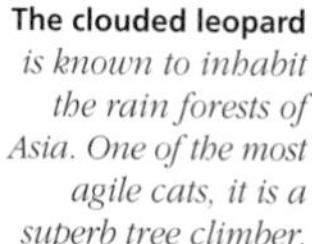
The Siamese crocodile *is a freshwater reptile typically found around rivers in rain forests. It is critically endangered in the wild.*

The Malayan porcupine *is a common resident of Asian rain forests. A nocturnal species, it is one of the largest rodents in the region.*

MEKONG RIVER
Forming an entire border between Laos and Cambodia, the 2,710-mile (4,361-km) long Mekong is the world's 12th longest river. It is home to a variety of big fish, including the giant Mekong stingray, measuring up to 14 ft (4 m) across, and the world's largest catfish.

Irrawaddy dolphins *number fewer than 100 in the Mekong. They live in brackish waters near coasts, and river mouths, as well as estuaries.*

Frangipani *trees, cultivated in tropical and subtropical countries, have evergreen leaves and a strong perfume.*

The dugong, *also known as the sea cow, is a marine mammal that is found off the coast of Cambodia.*

TONLE SAP

A combined lake and river system, the Tonlé Sap is not only Cambodia's most intriguing natural feature and its greatest natural resource, it is also the largest lake in Southeast Asia. This floodplain, with its rich biodiversity, is a perfect habitat for waterbirds, aquatic animals, and fish.

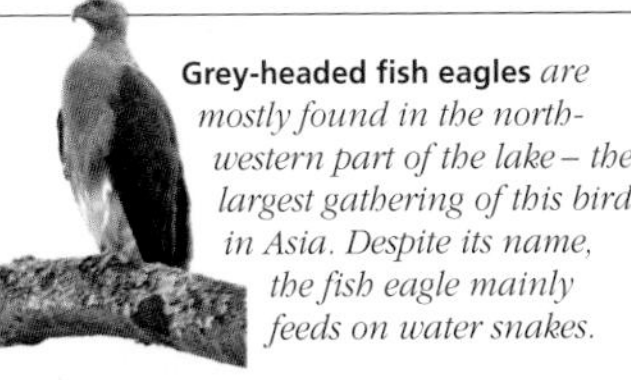

Grey-headed fish eagles *are mostly found in the north-western part of the lake – the largest gathering of this bird in Asia. Despite its name, the fish eagle mainly feeds on water snakes.*

The black-headed ibis *often feeds on the banks of the Tonlé Sap. This exotic wader's existence is now under threat due to drainage and loss of habitat.*

Fishing cats *are common in the lake and depend on its wetlands for prey. They mainly eat freshwater fish, but also catch rats and birds.*

MANGROVE FOREST

The region's mangrove wetlands are vital in protecting its coastline. A nursery for juvenile fish, the mangroves are home to marine organisms, as well as birds. The Peam Krasaop Nature Reserve in Southern Cambodia has some of the best mangroves in the country.

Crab-eating macaques *are widespread in the region. Known at times as the "crop raider," their main diet consists of fruit and seeds.*

The loris *is found in tropical habitats in Southeast Asia. It is poached for Chinese traditional medicine and the pet trade.*

Storks, *especially the milky stork and lesser adjutant, are quite rare, but still found in Cambodia's mangrove forests.*

COASTAL FOREST

Many of Cambodia's most important forest preserves lie along its coastline. These preserves, which include the Botum Sakor and Ream National Park, are home to a wide variety of animals, reptiles, and marine organisms, including pileated gibbons, pythons, king cobras, and dugongs.

The blue-eared kingfisher, *one of the ten different species of kingfishers found in Cambodia, lives in coastal forests and hunts for small fish and insects.*

The hawksbill turtle *is common around the coast of Cambodia. It has a distinctive beaked mouth and a beautifully patterned shell.*

Bantengs *were probably the ancestors of domestic cattle. Large and graceful, they live in herds and prefer open, dry, deciduous forests.*

Peoples of Cambodia

Ethnic Khmers constitute almost 95 percent of Cambodia's population, making it the most homogenous country in the world. At the same time, the country is also home to a number of ethnic minorities, principal among them the Cham, the Chinese, and the Vietnamese. There are at least 20 distinct hill tribes, such as the Kavet, the Tompuon, and the Phnong, who inhabit the mountainous northeast provinces. The majority of the country's population lives in rural areas.

A Phnong woman with her baby, Mondulkiri province

Traditional Khmer *apsara* dance performers

ETHNIC KHMERS

The Khmers are the dominant ethnic group in Cambodia and are proud to proclaim themselves the descendants of the great civilization of Angkor, the symbol of the nation. They once controlled a large chunk of Southeast Asia that extended into modern-day Thailand and Vietnam. The impact of classic Khmer culture in Cambodia is evident in the revival of several ancient arts such as the *apsara* (celestial dancing girl) dance and the music that accompanies these dances, both of which go back to the glorious traditions of Angkor.

ETHNIC VIETNAMESE

Although official records state that there are only about 100,000 Vietnamese in Cambodia, the actual number may be much higher, making them the largest non-Khmer group in the country. Settled in southeast and central Cambodia, they form the numerous fishing communities around Takeo and the Tonlé Sap Lake. Many Vietnamese are also rice farmers. Phnom Penh has a large population of Vietnamese, many of whose ancestors had been brought over from Vietnam by the French as civil servants.

A Vietnamese man selling vegetables from his boat

Chinese shopkeepers in Phnom Penh

ETHNIC CHINESE

Cambodians of Chinese or mixed Chinese and Cambodian descent are known as the Khmer Chen. The Chinese controlled businesses and economic interests in Cambodia before the 1975 revolution, but the community was brutally persecuted by the Khmer Rouge, and thousands emigrated. Today, half a million Khmer Chen live in Cambodia and they continue to dominate commerce in the urban centers, particularly banking, moneylending, and the import and export of food products.

ETHNIC CHAM

Originally from the Champa Kingdom of Central Vietnam, the Cham people, who number at least 250,000, have lived in Cambodia for over 500 years. More than 90 percent of the Cham are Muslims, and are referred to as the Khmer Islam *(see p21)*. Most live in Cham-only villages along the banks of the Mekong River and the Tonlé Sap Lake. Apart from fishing, they are also involved in farming, raising cattle, and growing rice. Cham men wear a sarong called a *batik* and the women usually cover their heads with a scarf or turban.

Cham men socializing after prayers

Peoples of Laos

Laos is one of the most sparsely populated countries in Asia, with only six million inhabitants in a landmass larger than the United Kingdom. The population is broadly divided into two groups – the Lowland Lao and the Highland Lao – although there are as many as 160 recognized ethnic minorities. There are also small communities of ethnic Vietnamese, numbering around 140,000, and Chinese, constituting between 2 and 5 percent of the population, including rapidly expanding numbers of migrant workers.

Devout Chinese offering prayers at a temple

LOWLAND LAO

Forming an estimated 68 percent of the population, most Lao Loum, or Lowland Lao, can trace their ancestry back to the Thai tribe that originated in southern China. They live along the Mekong River and in river valleys across the nation. Their language comprises five major dialects, all mutually intelligible. Although nearly all Lowland Lao practice Theravada Buddhism, they still retain a few rituals related to animism. They are the most affluent group in the nation, dominating both government and commerce.

The Lao Loum *are known to be expert silversmiths, creating intricate pieces of jewelry that are in great demand.*

Skilled wet-rice farmers, *the Lao Loum build houses raised on wooden stilts in order to protect them from flooded rice paddies. Rice granaries are often built next to the houses.*

HIGHLAND LAO

Ethnic minorities in Laos can be categorized into two groups: the Lao Theung, or Upland Lao, who account for around 23 percent of the population, and the Lao Sung, or Highland Lao, who comprise 9 percent of the population. These groups tend to have lower living standards compared to the Lao Loum, and suffer from discrimination. While the Upland Lao, such as the Katu, are primarily of Mon-Khmer ancestry, the term Highland Lao loosely describes ethnic groups such as the Yao and the Hmong who live at high altitudes.

The Hmong, *who number around 475,000, are the biggest minority group in Laos. Hmong men traditionally wear a black tunic and black wide-legged pants, while the women's clothing differs with each subgroup.*

The Katu *live in heavily forested mountains near the Vietnamese border and depend on the forests for their food and livelihood. Katu women often have facial tattoos. However, this is a dying tradition.*

Religions of Cambodia and Laos

A Buddhist shrine

Buddhism is by far the most widespread religion in both Cambodia and Laos, with a majority of the people practicing this faith. Virtually every village has a *wat* (temple), the spiritual heart of the community, where the monks reside. Animist beliefs also remain very strong and most followers believe that the world is influenced by an array of spirits, guardians, and ghosts. Although these traditions are strongest in rural areas, many city dwellers also consult a shaman. There are some followers of Islam in Cambodia and both countries also have a considerable Christian population.

A young monk reading scriptures at a *wat* in Laos

BUDDHISM

Theravada Buddhism defines most cultural practices in Cambodia and Laos, and entering monkhood is thought to accrue many benefits. Most men become monks for a short period in their lives, typically between three months and three years, living under a set of strict monastic rules. Women are also allowed to become monks, although it is usually later in life, often after the death of their husbands.

Pha That Luang *is one of the most revered Buddhist sites in Laos. The original temple is said to have been built by missionaries sent by King Ashoka in the 3rd century BC, and was rumored to contain a piece of the Buddha's breastbone. The Boun That Luang festival is held here each year.*

Buddhism in Cambodia *is influenced by Hinduism and animism. These influences are visible not just in rituals and ceremonies, but also in temples such as the Bayon in Angkor Thom* (see pp72–5), *where statues of the Buddha coexist with those of Hindu gods.*

ANIMIST BELIEFS

Animism is practiced by the 50 or so ethnic minorities in Laos, who follow varied forms of its rituals and customs. Several Lowland Lao also retain a belief in *phi* (spirits), which are associated with numerous aspects of day-to-day life, including health, the house, and nature. Believers show respect to all spirits, except the *mneang phteah* and *mrenh kongveal*, who are considered troublemakers and also capable of causing serious illness.

Animist customs *among ethnic minorities include leaving offerings of food and burning incense sticks to placate spirits. Ancestor worship is important for a number of groups such as the Lao Theung, the Lao Sung, and the hill tribes of Cambodia, including the Khmer Leu.*

Spirit houses *are shrines to animist spirits. Virtually every household, office, and shop has one since they are believed to act as a safeguard against malevolent forces.*

ISLAM

A majority of Muslims, numbering about 250,000 in Cambodia and some 500 in Laos, are of Cham origin, although a few are ethnic Malays. Belonging to the Sunni sect of Islam, the Cambodian Chams, who suffered terribly under the Khmer Rouge, live on the coast of Cambodia in fishing communities. The Cham of Laos live mostly in Vientiane.

Islamic places of worship *were ransacked under the Khmer Rouge and an estimated 132 mosques were destroyed. Today, however, many new mosques are being built along the coast of Cambodia.*

Khmer Islam, *the name given to the Muslims in Cambodia, traditionally practiced a syncretic form of the religion, incorporating animist beliefs. In recent years, however, they have become more orthodox.*

Headscarves are worn by most Cham women.

Cham villagers *on the coast of Cambodia are experiencing a resurgence in Islamic culture and pride.*

OTHER RELIGIONS

Christianity, Confucianism, and the Baha'i faith are among the other religions practiced in Cambodia and Laos. There is a substantial, and expanding, Christian population in both countries, along with small numbers of followers of the Baha'i and Confucian faiths. Evangelical and Mormon churches are active in Cambodia, but proselytizing was officially banned in 2007, after missionary groups were accused of trying to convert people by offering free food and clothing.

Abdu'l-Bahá *was the eldest son and successor of Bahá'u'lláh, the founder of the Baha'i faith. There are around 8,000 followers of this faith in Laos, and Vientiane, the capital, houses a National Spiritual Assembly, or elected council, which leads the faith.*

Confucianism *is practiced by many ethnic Chinese in the region. The religion is based on the teachings of the highly revered Chinese sage and philosopher Confucius (551–479 BC), who outlined a code of moral, social, and political ethics that includes loyalty to the state and to the family.*

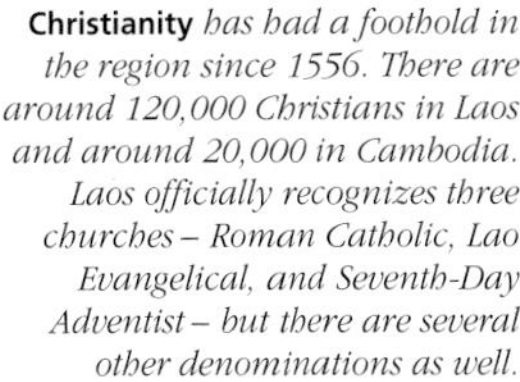

Christianity *has had a foothold in the region since 1556. There are around 120,000 Christians in Laos and around 20,000 in Cambodia. Laos officially recognizes three churches – Roman Catholic, Lao Evangelical, and Seventh-Day Adventist – but there are several other denominations as well.*

Buddhism in Cambodia and Laos

For many centuries, both Buddhism and Hinduism coexisted in this region. While the early Funan Kingdom was primarily Hindu, it was influenced by Buddhism, which became a secondary religion between the 1st and 6th centuries AD. During the Angkor period in Cambodia, Buddha images flourished alongside representations of Hindu gods such as Shiva and Vishnu. Today, Buddhism is the primary religion in both Laos and Cambodia. A majority of the population follows the Theravada Buddhist sect, which belongs to the Hinayana, or Lesser Wheel School, and is said to closely mirror the original form of the religion. In Laos, the religion continues to be influenced by animist beliefs, and spirit and ancestor worship.

Statue of Seated Buddha at Wat Ong Teu Mahawihan, Laos

PRACTICE OF BUDDHISM

Religious rituals form part of the daily life of most Cambodians and Lao. Visits to *wats,* the giving of alms, and merit-making – the performance of good deeds as mentioned in the Buddhist doctrine – are performed by all devout Buddhists. Many men also enter monkhood, at least for a brief period.

Traditional saffron robes worn by monks.

Feeding monks forms an important part of the Buddhist New Year celebrations.

Burning incense sticks *accompanies virtually all prayer ceremonies. This ritual has been in practice for thousands of years and links prayer with meditation and ritual purification.*

Bowing and prostrating *before an image of the Buddha, or before a monk, is believed to be an act of humility in Buddhist culture. The act is thought to bring good fortune.*

The offering of alms *is an ancient Buddhist tradition, born in the early days when monks were wanderers whose only possessions were a robe and a begging bowl. The tradition continues today and is a meritorious act, thought to bring good* karma *(fate). Solemn almsgiving is conducted at dawn every day when monks leave their monasteries to seek sustenance.*

The New Year *is a special occasion marked by rituals and* baci sukhuan *ceremonies* (see p124). *Celebrations last for several days; on the third day, statues of the Buddha, kept in* wats, *are cleansed with perfumed water. This ritual is said to bring happiness and good fortune.*

Banana leaves and flowers, *used as offerings in* wats, *are often artistically molded into forms such as that of a stupa.*

Colorful bunting is used to decorate *wats* during the New Year celebrations.

Prayers being offered

The Phabang *is the most sacred image of the Buddha in Laos and is currently housed in the National Musuem Complex in Luang Prabang. On Buddha Day, the image is cleansed with holy water and taken out in a procession to Wat Mai.*

BUDDHIST CELEBRATIONS

Visits to *wats*, thanksgiving ceremonies, prayers, and other offerings are an essential part of Buddhist celebrations. Most festivals are connected to the Buddhist calendar and may be specific to a particular tradition or ethnic group.

Visak Bochea, *or Buddha Day, is held on a full moon night, usually in May. It is celebrated with traditional processions, among other activities.*

BUDDHIST SYMBOLS

There are several religious symbols in Buddhism, each representing different aspects of the religion. Most of them can be seen in *wats*, stupas, and other religious sites. Symbols such as the Wheel of Law are said to have been used by the Buddha himself.

The Bodhi tree *is the tree under which the Buddha achieved enlightenment.*

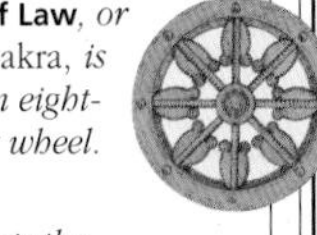

The Wheel of Law, *or* Dharmachakra, *is symbolized as an eight-spoked chariot wheel.*

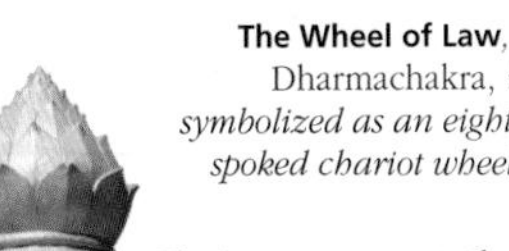

The Lotus *represents the progress of the soul.*

Naga, *or serpent, is a dragon-like figure representing wisdom and a protective force for the Buddha.*

Architecture of Cambodia and Laos

Over the centuries, architectural styles in Laos and Cambodia have been shaped by myriad influences, most notably Buddhist and Hindu temple-building traditions and French Colonial construction techniques. In urban areas, a degree of Soviet influence is also evident in the concrete municipal buildings, marketplaces, and apartment blocks. In the countryside, however, tried-and-tested designs have been maintained, and rural buildings continue to use locally sourced materials, such as timber, bamboo, and palm leaves, which are well suited to the tropical monsoon climate.

Floating houses on the Tonlé Sap

TEMPLE ARCHITECTURE

Up until the 10th century, temples in Laos and Cambodia were made mainly with brick. Khmer ceremonial buildings after this time were constructed using sandstone, usually with a lower section of laterite (moist clay blocks that harden over time). Their elaborate decorative designs, created by expert stone masons, incorporate religious and spiritual themes, and also reflect historical, military, and dynastical events. Many features of classic Khmer architecture, such as *nagas* (serpents), elaborate pediments, and lintels, were later incorporated into Buddhist buildings in the region. Modern temples in both countries are more similar to contemporary Thai designs, featuring a pointed roof, front veranda, and an elaborate gateway.

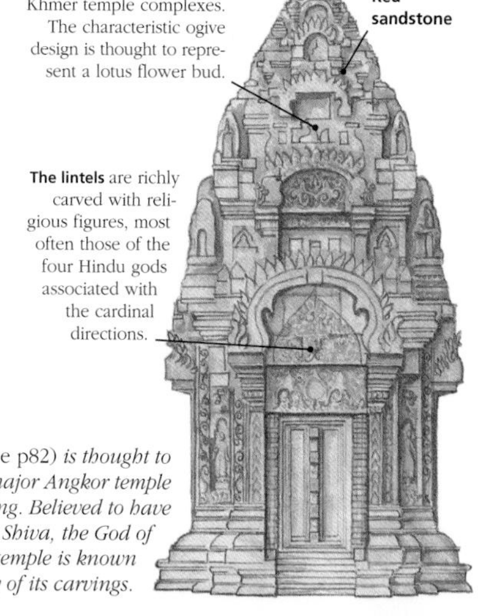

A central tower, or a number of towers, crown Khmer temple complexes. The characteristic ogive design is thought to represent a lotus flower bud.

Red sandstone

The lintels are richly carved with religious figures, most often those of the four Hindu gods associated with the cardinal directions.

Banteay Srei (see p82) *is thought to be the only major Angkor temple not built by a king. Believed to have been dedicated to Shiva, the God of Destruction, the temple is known for the intricacy of its carvings.*

Bas-relief on a brick wall, Prasat Kravan

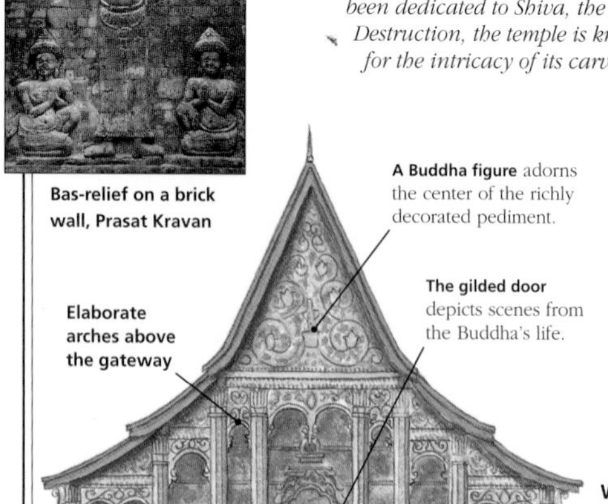

A Buddha figure adorns the center of the richly decorated pediment.

The gilded door depicts scenes from the Buddha's life.

Elaborate arches above the gateway

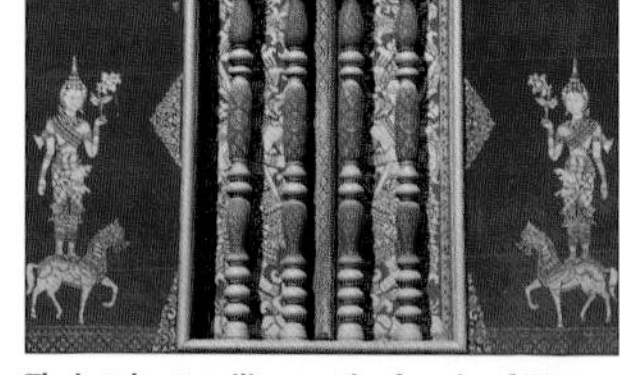

Thai-style stenciling on the façade of Wat Sene, Luang Prabang

Wat Manolom (see pp164–5) *was originally built in the 14th century on the site of an early Khmer Buddhist mission. The main ordinance hall was reconstructed in 1972 and is a good example of modern Lao temple architecture. Inside the* wat *is a huge bronze Buddha that dates from the 1370s.*

RURAL ARCHITECTURE

Houses in rural areas are traditionally wood and bamboo structures, built on stilts to raise the home above seasonal flood waters. The main living quarters of each rectangular two-story building is divided into sections for sleeping and cooking, with a storage area above.

House on stilts near the Mekong River

Space below the house is used to keep livestock.

Tiled roof

Wooden houses *on stilts are usually built with a steep staircase. The roofs are tiled, thatched, or made from corrugated metal.*

COLONIAL ARCHITECTURE

The most important architectural reminders of French rule are found in 19th- and 20th-century buildings in Phnom Penh, Vientiane, Battambang, Siem Reap, Luang Prabang, and Kampot. Kep has a fascinating number of Modernist seaside villas, some restored, but most in ruins.

Two-story brick and stucco villas *are one of the enduring legacies of Colonial rule, although many have been poorly maintained since independence. Phnom Penh boasts a particularly fine collection of French villas.*

Shuttered windows shade the interior from direct sunlight while the slats allow a breeze to circulate and cool the house.

The Presidential Palace *in Vientiane showcases a grand Neo-Classical façade and elegant colonnaded balconies. It was once the home of the French governor of Laos but is now used for official ceremonies.*

MODERN KHMER ARCHITECTURE

Influenced by the clean lines and simplicity of the Modernist movement, New Khmer Architecture, at its height from 1955 to 1972, draws heavily on ancient Khmer temple designs. The National Sports Complex in Phnom Penh, for example, was laid out on an east-west axis, mirroring classic Khmer buildings with *barays* (reservoirs). The most influential architect of this period, Vann Molyvann, created structures such as the startling library at Phnom Penh's Teacher Training College, with its radial roof resembling a farmer's hat. The sharply geometrical building of the National Bank of Cambodia and St Michael's Church in Sihanoukville are also striking examples.

A stupa-like spire emerges from the roofline.

Fan-shaped roof

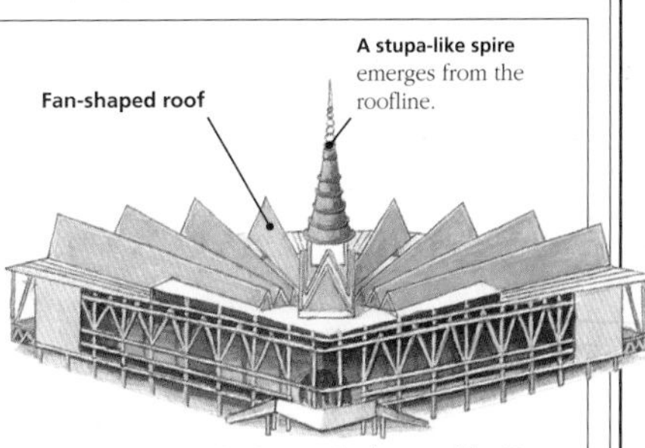

Chaktomuk Conference Hall, *designed by Vann Molyvann and completed in 1961, has a stunning façade that is supported by concrete stilts. Renovated in 2000, the Chaktomuk Conference Hall now hosts conferences and performances of traditional music and dance.*

The French Legacy

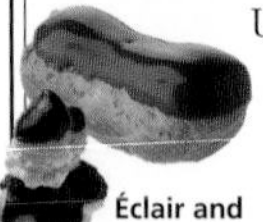
Éclair and profiterole

Until the mid-19th century, Colonial interest in Cambodia and Laos was minimal, mainly consisting of sporadic forays by Catholic missionaries in search of conversions. However, continued aggression by Thailand and Vietnam caused King Norodom of Cambodia to invite the French to establish a protectorate in 1863, who eventually made it into a French colony. Laos, too, was steadily absorbed into Indochina. Although the French withdrew from the region in 1954, their legacy remains in the boulevards and Neo-Classical buildings of Phnom Penh, and in the streets of Laos, where coffee is served as *café au lait*.

Pastry shops *selling French delights, such as éclairs and profiteroles, were common in the main towns, and some survive even today. In Colonial times they were owned mainly by ethnic Vietnamese.*

FRENCH CUISINE

The French culinary influence is most evident in popular snacks such as baguettes and croissants. Locals usually eat them for breakfast or as a quick bite, often with a thick layer of pâté, or luncheon meat, and some sliced salad, vegetables, or pickles. Phnom Penh, Vientiane, and other tourist centers have trendy French restaurants, bistros, and brasseries where the partaking of apéritifs, digestifs, and classic French wine continues to thrive.

Baguettes *are the most visible reminders of French cuisine. Every town still has a bakery producing these quintessentially French loaves. Vientiane baguettes, made in traditional French style, are particularly good.*

The first railway line *in Cambodia was laid by the French between 1930 and 1940. It extended from Phnom Penh right up to Poipet on the Thai border.*

ECONOMY

French Colonialists concentrated on exploiting the rich natural resources of the region with timber, rubber, corn, and rice being the main items of export. They were also responsible for installing the first roads, railway line, and rubber plantations. Apart from imposing a more efficient taxation system, the French did little to transform the village-based economies of these countries.

Rubber plantations, *first established by the French, remain a significant industry in Cambodia even today.*

LANGUAGE AND CULTURE

A French theater artiste

French heritage also lingers in the language and culture of these countries. There are French-language schools in all major cities and private institutions offer classes in French. French-language newspapers such as *Le Rénovateur* and *Cambodge Nouveau* are still popular, and establishments such as the Centre Culturel Français (CCF) continue to flourish. In the field of sports, soccer, which was first introduced by the Colonialists, continues to be the most popular game.

The Centre Culturel Français *in Phnom Penh, Vientiane, and Luang Prabang attempts to revive interest in French culture. It organizes film screenings, exhibitions, and other cultural events.*

FRENCH ARCHITECTURE

Perhaps the most prominent feature of the French legacy is seen in the Neo-Classical architecture of major towns. Although many of the once-grand buildings are now crumbling due to neglect, fiscal constraints, or local distaste for what they once represented, cities such as Phnom Penh, Siem Reap, Battambang, and Kampot have an impressive array of chic Modernist villas, lovely old French quarters, and Colonial façades. The National Museum Complex and the Centre Culturel Français in Luang Prabang represent French-Lao-style architecture.

Serene riverside boulevards, *such as Sisowath Quay in Phnom Penh, lined with tall, swaying palms and other foliage, are typically Parisian. They add to the Colonial charm of cities such as Vientiane, Battambang, and Kampot.*

Louvered windows not only allow ventilation, but also provide shade from the tropical sun.

Roofs usually boast European-style terra-cotta tiles.

Verandas lined with double doors extend from the front of the house.

Colonial villas, *some of the best examples of which are in Phnom Penh, formed cooling tropical retreats for the French. Most of them, however, have now been abandoned.*

The interior of the Foreign Correspondents' Club *in Phnom Penh is classically French Colonial in design, with a mahogany bar, slim columns, and elegant seating overlooking the Mekong River.*

Elaborate stucco detailing adorns many French Colonial buildings.

Official buildings *of the Colonial era are recognized by their imposing Neo-Classical façades, which embody the authority of the bygone administration.*

Multiple-arch design

Shophouses *in Kampot's French quarter, in Cambodia, are typically Colonial. They have shuttered windows with rectangular transoms over the opening, and multiple arches. Most of them, however, are now quite dilapidated and in desperate need of repair.*

CAMBODIA AREA BY AREA

A PORTRAIT OF CAMBODIA

Emerald paddy fields, a rich diversity of wildlife, powder-fine beaches, and the magnificence of the temples of Angkor – Cambodia has an alluring mix of romantic escapes and exhilarating outdoor pursuits, as well as world-renowned archaeological wonders. All this, combined with the warmth of its people, have helped put the country firmly on the tourist map.

LAND AND ECOLOGY

Covering an area of 69,900 sq miles (181,035 sq km), Cambodia is bordered by Laos to the north, Thailand to the north and west, and Vietnam to the east. To the southwest lie the Cardamom Mountains, rising to almost 5,787 ft (1,764 m), while in the north are the dramatic 1,804-ft (550-m) high Dangkrek Mountains. The most dominant feature of the country, however, is the mighty Mekong River, which runs its course from Tibet and floods the Tonlé Sap during the monsoon, swelling its waters to make it the largest freshwater lake in Southeast Asia. The northeast lays claim to being the wildest and most remote region, with forests and mountains inhabited by tigers and wild elephants. In the northwest, fertile Battambang enjoys the sobriquet "the rice bowl of Cambodia." The south, with its archipelago of deserted islands and perfect beaches, is a pleasant tropical retreat and is well worth visiting.

The endangered wild Asian elephant

Cambodia's pristine landscape, forests, and wildlife, however, are under threat from oil-drilling companies and logging. The habitats of the Asian tiger and other endangered species such as the banteng, wild Asian elephant, and Asian golden cat are visibly shrinking. Deforestation is also contributing to the flooding of the Mekong, while gradual siltation threatens the existence of the Tonlé Sap Lake. Fortunately, the government has adopted a number of conservation proposals and set up several national parks and other areas to protect wildlife and forest cover.

POLITICS AND THE ECONOMY

Cambodia was ranked 164 (out of 182) in the 2011 Corruption Perceptions Index, providing evidence of the limited transparency of its government and the execution of democracy. Official positions are usually achieved not on merit, but on the power of wealth and nepotism. This is also reflected in the fact that

Visitors relaxing on the beautiful beach at Koh Russie, Sihanoukville

◁ Crumbling ruins of the once magnificent Phnom Bakheng, Angkor

Hun Sen, leader of the Cambodian People's Party (CPP), has been at the helm of political affairs since 1993, making him the longest-serving prime minister in Southeast Asia. Although a multiparty democracy on paper, there was very little opposition in the way the CPP won 72 percent of the seats in parliament in the June 2012 elections. Criticism of Hun Sen is seldom heard, especially since dissident media has been silenced.

Despite such pitfalls, the country is making steady headway, with economic growth at around 5 percent. While oil, rubber, and the availability of cheap labor are fueling this growth, Cambodia has also found a niche as an international garment producer, and tourism remains one of its highest foreign exchange earners.

Angkor Wat, Cambodia's most popular attraction

SOCIETY AND RELIGION

According to official records, Cambodia is the most homogenous country in Southeast Asia, with almost 95 percent of its 15 million people ethnic Khmer. In reality, however, the population also includes 100,000 Vietnamese, about half a million Chinese and around 250,000 Cham Muslims, as well as the Khmer Lue, the ethnic minorities that live in the northeast.

Khmer society lays stress on the importance of the family. While elders are respected and obeyed, women are expected to be models of restraint and to treat their husbands with deference. Nevertheless, women are dominant figures in society, providing moral and financial succor to the family. Although fidelity is a given for them, it is normal for husbands to have extramarital affairs – a problem that has led to the country having the highest incidence of HIV infection in Southeast Asia.

A traditional Khmer *apsara* dancer

While a majority of Khmers today are Buddhists – the religion came from India during the 13th and 14th centuries – Hinduism was the dominant state religion during the Angkor period. Most men spend at least a few weeks in a *wat* (temple) as a monk, learning the teachings of Theravada Buddhism. Most ethnic minorities, however, practice animism, while the Chams are followers of Islam.

CULTURE AND THE ARTS

Although all traces of Cambodia's culture were erased during the years of the Khmer Rouge, the country now seems to have rediscovered its artistic edge, with exiled artists returning to their roots. Traditional dance, particularly ballet, is also making a glorious return through the University of Fine Arts. Musical instruments such as *khsae muoy* (single-stringed bowed instrument) and *tro khmae* (three-stringed fiddle), used by *apsara* dancers in Angkor, are popular even today. Cambodia is also renowned for its fine silk weaving, silver-smithing, sculpting, wood carving, and ceramics made in traditional kilns in Siem Reap.

CAMBODIA THROUGH THE YEAR

Cambodians love a good celebration and festivals provide the opportunity for family members scattered across the country to reconnect and reassert their sense of togetherness. Many of Cambodia's festivals, such as Bon Chol Vassa and Meak Bochea, are based on lunar cycles. Thus, dates for these festivals change from year to year. While most secular holidays follow the Gregorian calendar, a few, such as Bon Om Tuk, or the Water Festival, date back to the days of Angkor. Apart from being solemn religious occasions, these festivals present rural Khmers with an excuse to return home to visit family. Celebrations are often followed by partying, funfairs, and fireworks. Cambodia has three seasons – hot, rainy, and cool – which influence several festivals, especially in rural areas since agriculture is the main livelihood for a majority of the population.

Firecrackers for Chinese New Year

Revelers celebrating Chinese New Year

HOT SEASON

Temperatures ratchet up in February, which is the start of the hot season, and keep rising till April, which is the hottest month. April also marks the end of the harvest. The sweltering heat and high humidity can test visitors' endurance. However, areas such as Ratanakiri and Mondulkiri provinces in the northeast, which have the advantage of higher elevations, enjoy cooler weather.

JANUARY–FEBRUARY

Victory Day *(Jan 7)*, nationwide. This holiday commemorates the victory of the Vietnamese over the Khmer Rouge's bloody regime. Celebrations are marked by exhibitions and remembrance services.

Chinese New Year *(end Jan/early Feb)*, Phnom Penh. This exciting, vibrant festival sees the city's streets thronging with colorful dragon dancers and processions, along with firework displays at every corner. Although this is not a national holiday, it is a widely celebrated festival and many Chinese commercial businesses shut down for its duration. There is a large population of Chinese in Phnom Penh, along with a significant number of Vietnamese who also celebrate Tet (New Year) at the same time. Wealthy families eager to flaunt their fortunes organize elaborate private firework displays.

Meak Bochea *(end Jan/early Feb full moon)*, nationwide. The name of this festival means Big Prayer and it is one of the holiest and most important ceremonies in the Buddhist religion. Candlelit processions commemorate the 1,250 disciples who gathered to witness the last sermon delivered by the Buddha before his death in northern India 2,500 years ago. Families visit their local *wat* (temple) during the full moon to venerate the five precepts of Buddhism and the great teacher himself, lighting candles and making offerings of food and money in order to gain merit.

MARCH–APRIL

Women's Day *(Mar 8)*, nationwide. Celebrating the role of women in modern society and highlighting issues such as rape, domestic violence, and inequality, this is a vital festival in a country where women are often abused and subjugated. UNESCO Phnom Penh has supported this important day over the past few years by sponsoring the Ministry of Women's Affairs of Cambodia. Parades are held in various parts of the country and T-shirts highlighting women's rights and messages against domestic violence are distributed. Drama shows and workshops are organized, which are often attended by the prime minister.

Cambodian New Year *(April 14–16)*, nationwide. This festival is better known as Chaul Chnam Thmey and lasts for a period of three days. Khmers see it as a time to go wild in a nationwide water fight as well as applying talcum powder to each other's faces. The festival has its roots

Dancer, Cambodian New Year

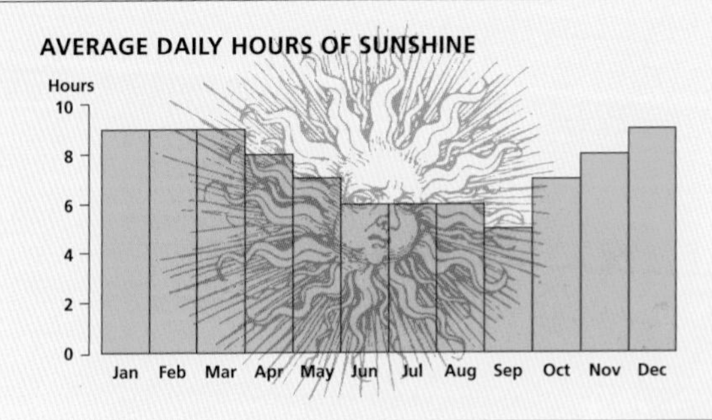

Sunshine Chart
Even during the rainy season the sun is hot, particularly in the middle of the day. It is wise to carry bottled water and eat plenty of fruit to keep energy levels high. The heat and humidity can be debilitating, especially for those not used to tropical weather. A hat and sunscreen are strongly recommended.

in Hinduism, the country's primary religion before the arrival of Buddhism. The best place to be is Wat Phnom *(see pp50–51),* where free concerts are held at night. The last day of the festival involves worshipers bathing Buddha statues with water and apologizing to monks, elders, and grandparents whom they may have offended during the year. This ritual is known as *pithi srang*. It is also celebrated in a similar fashion in Laos. Visitors are likely to have water thrown at them during this period.

RAINY SEASON

This season is characterized by short, intense bursts of rain, which leave the land glistening and remote roads impassable. This is a good time to explore temples as there are relatively fewer people around.

MAY–JUNE

Visak Bochea *(May full moon)*, nationwide. The Buddha's birthday, his enlightenment, and admission to Nirvana are celebrated with candlelit processions to the local *wat*, most notably at Angkor Wat *(see pp68–9).*
International Labor Day *(May 1)*, nationwide. Traditionally a day when workers march for their rights, such as the improvement of minimum wages. Their achievements are also celebrated.
Genocide Day *(May 9)*, nationwide. This day commemorates the many lives lost to the Maoist-driven Khmer Rouge. It is a pensive occasion for every Khmer. Without exception, every family was torn asunder by the bloody regime of the Khmer Rouge.
King Sihamoni's Birthday *(May 13)*, nationwide. Although there are no mass celebrations or processions on this day, firework displays take place at the Tonlé Sap lakefront late at night.
Royal Ploughing Ceremony *(late May)*, Phnom Penh. Also known as Bon Chrat Preah Nongkol, this festival celebrates the first planting of rice for the coming harvest. Locals dress up in colorful traditional attire and participate in a lively procession. The procession is led by the king and other royals outside the National Museum *(see p50),* where a sacred ox is fed with a selection of food and drink. A Brahmin priest then predicts the kind of harvest that can be expected, according to what the ox has eaten. This is a significant festival for many Cambodians as their fortunes are linked to the land that they farm. The presence of the king also reaffirms the importance of this ceremony.

Monks walking with lit candles at the Bayon during Visak Bochea

Oxen heading the procession during the Royal Ploughing Ceremony

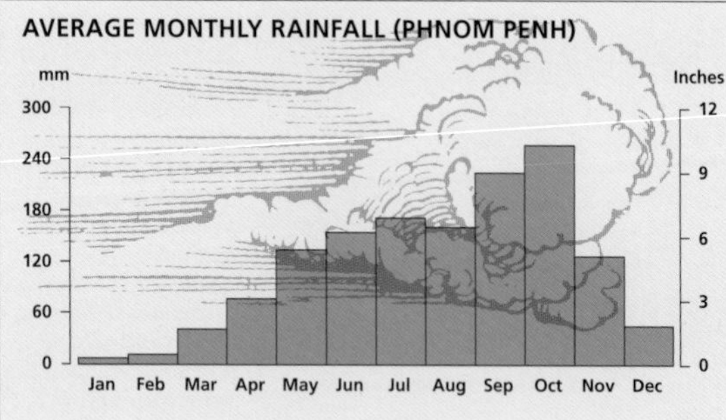

Rainfall Chart
During the monsoon, rains may last for a few hours per day followed by bright sunshine. The heaviest rainfall occurs in the mountains along the coast and in the southwest where precipitation varies from between 2,500 mm (98 inches) to more than 5,000 mm (197 inches).

JULY–AUGUST

Bon Chol Vassa *(Jul full moon)*, nationwide. Held to coincide with the eighth full moon of the lunar calendar, this festival marks the beginning of the three-month Buddhist Lent, a time of fasting and strict meditation. This is also the time for young men to be ordained as monks. Traditionally, the newly ordained monks would spend the entire rainy season within the temple, but nowadays this period can be as little as three weeks.

COOL SEASON

As the rains retreat toward the end of October and early November, a cool breeze sweeps over the land. The Tonlé Sap, having been rejuvenated, abounds with fish. The best time to visit the country is between November and January, when humidity levels are lower than usual.

SEPTEMBER–OCTOBER

Bon Dak Ben *(Sep–Oct full moon)*, nationwide. Dedicated to the spirits of the dead, this is one of the most traditional of Khmer festivals. Influenced by elements of animism, the festival is celebrated over a period of 15 days, beginning on the full moon. Food and drink are offered to monks so that they may assist people in blessing the souls of their ancestors. People throng to temples to listen to sermons and make offerings of respect to their ancestors. They believe it is vital to keep the spirits of the dead appeased; these spirits are believed to protect the living.

Bon Pchum Ben *(Sep/Oct)*, nationwide. This festival of the dead is equivalent to All Souls' Day. Khmers make offerings of boiled eggs, paper money, food, and drink to the dead in order to avoid being haunted.

Monk collecting alms, Bon Dak Ben

Bon Kathen *(variable)*, nationwide. Starting at the end of the Buddhist Lent and continuing for a month until the next full moon, this festival marks the emergence of monks from their retreat with offertory robes and slow public processions to the local *wat*. Donations are given in order to receive merit, thereby improving *karma* (fate) for the next life.

King Sihanouk's Birthday *(Oct 31)*, nationwide. This day celebrates the country's influential and mercurial leader, the former king, Sihanouk, who managed to endure both Colonialism – eventually achieving Cambodian independence – as well as the Khmer Rouge. It is believed that understanding his psyche is the key to comprehending the complex soul of Cambodia and the compromises it has had to make in order to survive. Processions take place in front of the Royal Palace *(see p52–5)* and many loyal followers of the former king return to Phnom Penh to celebrate.

NOVEMBER–DECEMBER

Independence Day *(Nov 9)*, nationwide. Cambodia's independence from France is marked by processions of elaborate floats in front of

Colorful float parades in front of the Royal Palace, Independence Day

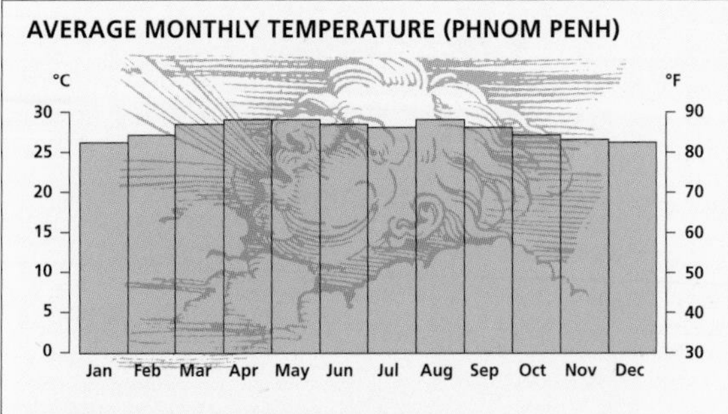

Temperature Chart
The rainy season, which lasts from May to late October, turns the land an emerald green. This is followed by the cool season in November. Coastal and mountainous areas can get very cool at this time. Temperatures start rising in February and peak in April, which is the hottest month of the year.

Dance performance in front of Angkor Wat, Angkor Festival

the Royal Palace. A special day for all Khmers, fireworks and parades are arranged across the country and bunting strung across narrow streets. The main festivities, however, take place at the famous Independence Monument at the junction of Norodom and Sihanouk boulevards in Phnom Penh.

Bon Om Tuk *(Nov)*, nationwide. This three-day event, also known as the Water Festival, celebrates the victory of Angkor over the Chams in the 12th century. It also observes the natural phenomenon of the Tonlé Sap reversing its flow and emptying back into the Mekong River, thus marking the end of the rainy season. (It is the only waterway in the world to reverse its flow at different times of the year.) Along with the Cambodian New Year, it is the most important festival in the Cambodian calendar. Boat races and a carnival atmosphere on the Tonlé Sap attract millions from across the country. More than 400 boats take part in the boat race of Bon Om Tuk, with oarsmen and their vessels coming from far and wide and bringing with them thousands of supporters from their villages. A smaller festival also takes place around Angkor Wat, but the real heart of the celebration lies in Phnom Penh, on the Mekong.

Boat crews getting ready for the race, Bon Om Tuk

Legends of Angkor Wat Festival *(variable)*, Angkor Wat. This festival of performing arts is held at Angkor Wat. Epic stories of Khmer myth are enacted, accompanied by traditional dances, costumes, and musicians, with the temple providing a stunning backdrop. The royal family often attends the event, which makes for a truly memorable evening.

PUBLIC HOLIDAYS

New Year's Day (Jan 1)

Victory Day (Jan 7)

Meak Bochea (Jan/Feb)

Women's Day (Mar 8)

Cambodian New Year (Apr 14–16)

Visak Bochea (May)

International Labor Day (May 1)

Royal Ploughing Ceremony (May)

King Sihamoni's Birthday (May 13)

Queen Mother's Birthday (Jun 18)

Constitution Day (Sep 24)

Bon Pchum Ben (Sep/Oct)

Coronation Day (Oct 29)

King Sihanouk's Birthday (Oct 31)

Independence Day (Nov 9)

Bon Om Tuk (Nov)

Human Rights Day (Dec 10)

THE HISTORY OF CAMBODIA

From the splendor of the Khmer Empire to the chilling brutality of the Khmer Rouge, Cambodia has had a tumultuous past. For nearly six centuries, between the fall of Angkor and the rise of Communism, the kingdom lay buried in obscurity, forgotten by the rest of the world. Recent years, however, have seen the nation overcome its former misfortunes and become a developing economy.

It is likely that the Khmers originated in China and arrived in what is now Cambodia several millennia ago. Archaeologists have discovered evidence of stone-working people in northwestern Cambodia around 4000 BC. They date the first rice cultivation in the region to around 2000 BC, and bronze working to perhaps a millennium later. At that time, many Cambodians lived in fortified, circular villages, eating rice and fish, and raising domestic animals. Bronze artifacts, found in places such as Kg Chhnang in the heart of present-day Cambodia, prove that they possessed advanced metalworking skills.

The first urban civilization in Cambodia, and what is now southern Vietnam, sprang up both inland and along the coast, where excavations of a port-city have been carried out near the Vietnamese town of Oc-Eo. The rulers of this civilization, known to the Chinese as Funan, established their capital at Angkor Borei and built an extensive canal system, probably used for drainage and transportation. They traded with China and India and coins from the Roman Empire have been found at Oc-Eo. Unfortunately, no reliable written records from this era have survived.

Statue of a Hindu deity, Angkor Borei

Between 500 BC and AD 500, Cambodia experienced the process referred to as "Indianization." During this time, elements of Indian culture, such as the Hindu pantheon, Buddhism, language (Sanskrit), a writing system, a centralized administration, and the idea of universal kingship, were absorbed by the Khmer and blended with local customs such as ancestor worship.

The earliest inscriptions in the Khmer language date from the 7th century AD. Between the 5th and 8th centuries AD, several small city-states flourished in central Cambodia and northeastern Thailand. These were known collectively as Chenla. Stone inscriptions from this period reveal the slow unification of principalities under a smaller group of rulers. This was to culminate, in the early 9th century, in the consolidation of power near the present-day city of Siem Reap, by the mysterious "universal monarch" known as Jayavarman II, who established the Khmer Empire.

TIMELINE

4200 BC–AD 700 Caves in northwestern Cambodia occupied by stone-working people

200 BC Kingdom of Funan established in southern Cambodia

Roman coin used for trading

AD 600–AD 700 The Chenla period

4000 BC | 2000 BC | AD 1 | AD 200 | AD 400 | AD 600 | AD 800

2000 BC Cultivation of rice begins in the region

1000 BC Bronze casting begins

500 BC–AD 500 "Indianization" of Cambodia

Jayavarman II

802 Jayavarman II establishes the Khmer Empire

◁ **A lithograph by Louis Delaporte, dated 1873, depicting a French expedition into Angkor**

RISE OF ANGKOR

Angkor, derived from the Khmer word for city, dominated much of mainland Southeast Asia between 802 and 1431. At the end of the 9th century, King Yasovarman I moved the capital closer to Siem Reap, where it remained for the next 500 years. He named the new city Yasodharapura after himself. Successive kings expanded the empire, building more temples honoring themselves, their forebears, and Hindu deities such as Shiva, the God of Destruction.

Between 1130 and 1150, King Suryavarman II built the spectacular Angkor Wat, which served as an astronomical observatory, his tomb, and a monument to Vishnu, the Hindu Protector of Creation. The might of the Khmer Empire steadily increased and by the mid-12th century, its rule stretched beyond present-day Cambodia to what is now northeastern Thailand, southern Laos, and southern Vietnam. The powerful empire had trade links with China, but trade was conducted on a barter basis, because Angkor never used currency of any kind.

Successive kings, such as Jayavarman VII (r.1178–1220), a Mahayana Buddhist, added to the architectural magnificence of Angkor. He built the walled city of Angkor Thom inside Yasodharapura, and several impressive temples, including the Bayon. But the days of Hindu influence were numbered and in the 13th century, most Cambodians converted to Theravada Buddhism, the relatively ascetic religion of the country today, and the construction of stone temples ended.

Bayon-style statue of Jayavarman VII

DECLINE AND FALL OF ANGKOR

In the 14th century, several Theravada kingdoms broke away from the empire and in 1431, Thai armies attacked Yasodharapura. As a result, the city was partially abandoned and the royal capital was moved south, close to Phnom Penh.

The next five centuries, often referred to as the Middle Period, were marked by frequent wars with Thailand and by the slow, informal expropriation of Cambodian territory in the Mekong Delta by the Vietnamese. Vietnam established a protectorate in Phnom Penh in the 1830s and fought Thai forces sent from Bangkok to dislodge them. In 1848, however, a fragile peace was established between the two warring states.

THE COLONIAL ERA

In 1863, France, which had colonized southern Vietnam, offered its protection to Cambodia in exchange

A 19th-century lithograph depicting French scholars removing precious artifacts from Angkor

TIMELINE

Angkor Wat

1130–50 Angkor Wat built

1200–50 Conversion of Khmer people to Theravada Buddhism

1431 Thais attack; Angkor partially abandoned

1010 | 1130 | 1250 | 1370 | 1490

Bas-relief, the Bayon

1178–1220 Jayavarman VII builds the Bayon and the walled city of Angkor Thom

Bas-relief depicting Thai mercenaries, Angkor Wat

Prince Norodom Sihanouk at a ceremony celebrating the victory of his political party

for certain economic privileges. The French protectorate evolved into complete control after an anti-French rebellion was suppressed in the 1880s.

The French record in Cambodia, however, was mixed. On the one hand, they established towns, roads, and institutions; the economy flourished, the population doubled, and Cambodia was at peace for the first time in centuries. France also forced Thailand to return the annexed territory, and French scholars restored the Angkorian temples, reconstructing the history of Angkor. On the other hand, France did little to improve education or health and also imposed high taxes on the locals.

INDEPENDENCE AND REVOLT

In 1941, the French crowned 19-year-old Prince Norodom Sihanouk as king of Cambodia. They also allowed Japanese troops to be stationed in Cambodia during World War II. In March 1945, the Japanese imprisoned French officials throughout Indochina (Cambodia, Laos, and Vietnam) and urged local leaders to declare independence. Sihanouk did so reluctantly, welcoming back the French when they returned to power in October 1945. But in 1952, he launched a royal crusade, forcing the French to grant Cambodia its independence the following year. In 1955, however, Sihanouk abdicated the throne to become a full-time politician, founding a political party, Sangkum Reastr Niyum, that won several elections unopposed. The Communist Party, led by Pol Pot (1925–98), had a small following at that time and had little chance of coming to power.

In 1968, the war in Vietnam began to spill over into Cambodia as the US Army bombed Communist supply bases in the country. By this time, local and international pressure had weakened Sihanouk's control and in March 1970, the National Assembly voted to depose him. A pro-American regime, led by Lon Nol, came to power. This event precipitated the Cambodian Civil War. Sihanouk vowed to return, accepting support from North Vietnam, China, and Cambodian Communists. Months of fighting and heavy bombing ensued between Communist and US-backed forces until the former occupied the capital, ending the war in April 1975.

Communist soldiers during the Cambodian Civil War, 1975

French in Cambodia

1593 Thais sack Cambodian capital at Longvaek

1610

1730

1794 Thais annex northwestern quarter of Cambodia

1830–49 Wars between Thailand and Vietnam over Cambodia

1850

1863 Imposition of French protectorate

1941 Norodom Sihanouk crowned king by the French

1945 French return to power

1953 France grants Cambodia independence

1968 War begins between US-backed South Vietnam and Communist North Vietnam

1970

1970 Sihanouk overthrown in bloodless, pro-American coup

1970–75 Cambodian Civil War

POL POT'S KHMER ROUGE

On April 17, 1975, Cambodian Communist forces occupied Phnom Penh, welcomed by a population exhausted by five years of civil war. Within 48 hours, however, the victors forcibly evacuated the city, driving over two million people into the countryside to take up agricultural work. The Communists, under Pol Pot, established the government of Democratic Kampuchea (DK) and in order to form a new society "with no oppressors and no oppressed," abolished money, personal property, schools, laws, religious practices, markets, and freedom of movement.

Pol Pot (1925–98) led the Khmer Rouge

Pol Pot, the prime minister of DK, remained hidden during this time, denying DK's Communist affiliations. He wanted the revolution to be seen as uniquely Khmer. In reality, he borrowed many policies and slogans directly from Maoist China.

In 1975, the regime executed thousands of former soldiers and ex-civil servants. Paranoid about unidentified enemies destroying DK, they also began indiscriminate executions the next year. In the countryside, where the regime irrationally sought to triple rice production overnight, thousands died of malnutrition, overwork, and disease.

When fighting broke out between DK and Vietnam in September 1977, Pol Pot finally came into the open, traveling to China to seek military aid. In a speech delivered before the visit, he claimed that the Communist Party of Kampuchea (CPK), which until then had been hidden to all but its members, had ruled Cambodia since April 1975. As the fighting with Vietnam expanded into a full-scale war, thousands of inhabitants from the eastern parts of Cambodia, suspected of being pro-Vietnamese, were executed. Several DK cadres, including a 25-year-old regimental commander called Hun Sen, sought refuge in Vietnam, where the Vietnamese began recruiting refugees into a "liberation army."

Khmer Rouge fighters celebrating their victory as they enter Phnom Penh, April 17, 1975

A DEMOCRATIC STATE

In December 1978, Vietnam invaded DK with a force of over 100,000 men. Phnom Penh fell in January 1979, and Pol Pot, his colleagues, and thousands of DK troops fled to Thailand. The "three years, eight months, and twenty days" of tyranny, as Cambodians commonly refer to this period, were over, but not before over 1.5 million people had met with unexpected, and often violent, deaths. The Vietnamese established a friendly regime in Phnom Penh that called itself the People's Republic of

TIMELINE

Khmer Rouge soldier

1975 Cambodian Communists come to power

1976 Democratic Kampuchea (DK) established, with Pol Pot as prime minister

1977 War breaks out between DK and Vietnam

1979 Vietnamese topple DK, establish pro-Vietnamese regime

1984 Hun Sen becomes prime minister

1989 Vietnamese withdraw military support

1991 Paris Peace Conference establishes UN protectorate over Cambodia

1993 Coalition government takes office after UN-sponsored elections

1975 | 1980 | 1985 | 1990 | 1995

Paris Peace Conference, 1991

Kampuchea (PRK). Hun Sen; at 27, he was named foreign minister, the youngest in the world to hold the post.

Protected by 200,000 Vietnamese troops, the PRK moved cautiously to stabilize the country. It re-opened schools, re-introduced money, and allowed the revival of Buddhism. Unfortunately, although the horrors of the Khmer Rouge regime had now become widely known, DK retained Cambodia's seat at the UN, because China, the US, and their allies vigorously opposed the Vietnamese "invasion." This isolated PRK from all except the former Soviet Bloc. As a result, most of the assistance the country needed to recover never arrived.

Coronation ceremony of King Norodom Sihamoni, October 29, 2004

PEACE AT LAST

Vietnam withdrew its troops from Cambodia in 1989, and the PRK renamed itself the State of Cambodia (SOC), rejecting Marxism-Leninism. The PRK party structures remained in place, and political opposition was dealt with severely. Over the next two years, Cambodia's fate hung in the balance.

Cambodian soldiers holding portraits of Norodom Sihanouk

A major international conference held in Paris in 1991, however, decided to establish a temporary UN protectorate over Cambodia to disarm the three Cambodian factions that opposed the PRK – Sihanouk's Funcinpec party, the Khmer Rouge, and the Khmer People's National Liberation Front – repatriate over 300,000 Khmer from Thailand, and prepare the country for general elections. The United Nations Transitional Authority in Cambodia (UNTAC) was the most expensive UN operation to date and accomplished mixed results. They held fresh elections in July 1993, won by the royalists. Sihanouk was crowned king for the second time, with Hun Sen serving as prime minister. Initially, the SOC and DK factions refused to disarm, which forced the victors into an uneasy coalition that lasted until 1997, when the Khmer Rouge finally collapsed.

In the new millennium, foreign investment and assistance poured in, as did millions of tourists. King Sihanouk retired in 2004, succeeded by his son, Norodom Sihamoni. In 2007, the UN established the Extraordinary Chambers in the Courts of Cambodia (ECCC) to try leaders of the Khmer Rouge. Pol Pot was never tried by the tribunal as he died in 1998. Hun Sen's Cambodian People's Party has tightened control over politics and for the first time, the kingdom is at peace and part of the globalized world.

Norodom Sihamoni at his coronation

1997 Hun Sen deposes his coalition partners; Khmer Rouge movement finally collapses

2007 International tribunal to try leaders of DK opens in Phnom Penh. Boeung Kak Lake government land-grab in Phnom Penh spurns years of protest

2012 US Secretary of State Hillary Clinton attends ASEAN conference in Phnom Penh

2000 | **2005** | **2010** | **2015**

1998 Cambodia joins ASEAN

2004 Sihanouk retires as king and is replaced by his son, Sihamoni

Prime Minister Hun Sen in Phnom Penh

2010 Kang Kek Lew (Comrade Duch) sentenced to 35 years in prison for crimes against humanity by the Khmer Rouge Tribunal

Cambodia at a Glance

Dominated by the Mekong River and the Tonlé Sap Lake, Cambodia's central plains are an incredibly fertile area. The majestic Dangkrek Mountains in the north and the Cardamom Mountains in the southwest form secure habitats for a variety of endangered plants and animals. The country's 277-mile (443-km) long coastline is marked with fine powdery beaches, while the warm tropical waters are dotted with thousands of islands, making a rich contrast to the rugged north. Although the temple complexes of Angkor continue to be Cambodia's primary attraction, towns such as Ban Lung, Battambang, and Sihanoukville also have much to offer.

Siem Reap (see pp66–7) *serves as an ideal base for exploring the magnificent temples of Angkor, as well as the Tonlé Sap, Southeast Asia's largest freshwater lake.*

Angkor Wat (see pp68–9) *was built by King Suryavarman II in the early 12th century and rediscovered by the French during the 1860s. It is the biggest and best preserved of the numerous temples that were built in and around the ancient city of Angkor Thom.*

Kbal Chhay Cascades (see p109), *situated on the scenic Prek Toeuk Sap River, is a favorite picnicking and swimming spot among locals and also visitors, particularly during the rainy season.*

Sihanoukville (see pp106–7) *is a bustling town that serves as a gateway to an archipelago of verdant islands and a number of splendid beaches. Boat trips, snorkeling, scuba diving, and windsurfing are on offer here.*

Prasat Preah Vihear (see pp94–5), *another temple from the Angkor period, was built by seven different Khmer kings. Dramatically located atop the cliffs of the Dangkrek Mountains, this complex is 2,625 ft (800 m) long, with a majestic stairway that ascends through four exquisitely carved* Gopuras *(gateway towers) before reaching the sanctuary.*

Kratie *(see p100)* is a great place to spot the endangered Irrawaddy dolphin, which is found in the muddy waters of the Mekong River.

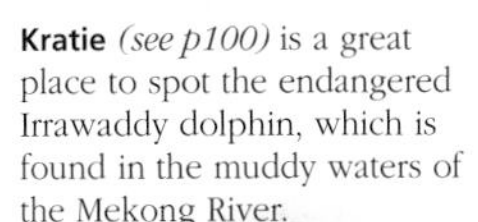

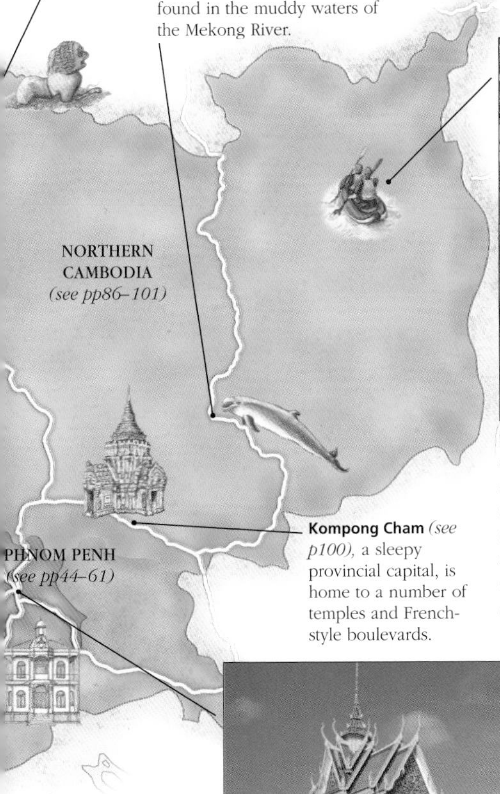

NORTHERN CAMBODIA *(see pp86–101)*

Ban Lung (see pp100–101), *capital of the remote province of Ratanakiri in the northeast, awes visitors with its waterfalls, bamboo forests, and crater lakes. An emerging hub for ecotourism, it offers exciting activities such as trekking, kayaking, and elephant rides.*

Kompong Cham *(see p100),* a sleepy provincial capital, is home to a number of temples and French-style boulevards.

PHNOM PENH *(see pp44–61)*

0 km 50

0 miles 50

The Royal Palace and Silver Pagoda (see pp52–5) *are the most striking landmarks in Phnom Penh. The Royal Palace, built in 1866, is the official residence of the king of Cambodia. The adjoining Silver Pagoda, named for the 5,000 silver tiles that cover its floor, is the most important structure in the complex. Also known as Wat Preah Keo, it houses the sacred Emerald Buddha.*

Happy Hour
4pm-6pm
Angkor
&
Anchor
Viva

PHNOM PENH

Cambodia's capital city is a sprawling metropolis, abuzz with scooters, tuk-tuks, and luxury 4WDs. A study in contrasts, Phnom Penh has vibrant, colorful markets, which thrive alongside sleek new malls, designer boutiques, shuttered French villas, and Parisian-style cafés dating from Colonial times. The city is also an excellent springboard for visits to other parts of the country.

Due to its strategic position at the confluence of the Tonlé Sap and Mekong rivers, Phnom Penh became the capital of the Khmer Empire in the mid-15th century after it was relocated from Angkor. Phnom Penh, meaning Hill of Penh, derives its name from the legend of an old lady, Penh, who found four Buddha statues washed up on the shore of the Mekong River and set them on a hill. The city traded with Laos and China until the 17th century, when it was reduced to a buffer state between the warring Vietnamese and Thais. The Thais eventually razed the city in 1772. In 1863, Phnom Penh found itself under French rule, which lasted till 1953, when King Sihanouk finally declared independence.

Phnom Penh fell to Pol Pot's black-clad forces on April 17, 1975; the city was emptied of its population, who were driven to the infamous Killing Fields of Choeung Ek. Cambodia was liberated by the Vietnamese in 1979 but it was another ten years before Phnom Penh was finally free to manage its own affairs. Having moved past the uncertainties of the 1980s, the city has reinvented itself with a growth in public works and considerable foreign aid.

Once known as the Pearl of the Orient, the capital is regaining some of its former luster, offering a selection of world-class boutique hotels and international cuisine. Local specialties include *amok* (fish cooked in coconut milk), *kari* (curry), and rice noodle soup. The atmospheric Sisowath Quay, which overlooks the Tonlé Sap River, harbors a wealth of French restaurants, bookshops, and stylish boutiques, as well as dozens of local eateries. Sights well worth a visit include the Royal Palace and Silver Pagoda, the National Museum, and the Tuol Sleng Genocide Museum.

Scenic view of the Mekong River from the tree-lined riverfront, Sisowath Quay

◁ **Parisian-style roadside café in a French Colonial building, Phnom Penh**

Exploring Phnom Penh

A vibrant city, far removed from its harrowing past, Phnom Penh attracts a steady flow of visitors. Designed around a grid system, the capital does not have a distinct city center. The 3-mile (2-km) sweep of the riverfront known as Sisowath Quay is arguably the most attractive area in the city. Lined with popular boutiques and myriad restaurants and bars, the area is liveliest at night. The city's best-known landmarks, the beautiful and sprawling Royal Palace and Silver Pagoda, lie across from the flag-studded promenade of the Tonlé Sap River. A little farther ahead are the terra-cotta pavilions of the National Museum. To the west lies the well-known Central Market with its Mediterranean-style dome and bustling shops. The southern part of the city is home to the Tuol Sleng Genocide Museum and Psar Tuol Tom Pong.

SIGHTS AT A GLANCE

Places of Worship
Wat Ounalom ❸
Wat Phnom ❹

Palaces and Museums
Killing Fields of Choeung Ek ❽
National Museum of Cambodia ❷
Royal Palace and Silver Pagoda pp52–5 ❶
Tuol Sleng Genocide Museum ❻

Markets
Central Market ❺
Psar Tuol Tom Pong ❼

Areas of Natural Beauty
Koki Beach ❾
Phnom Chisor ⓬
Phnom Tamao Wildlife Rescue Center ⓫
Tonlé Bati ❿

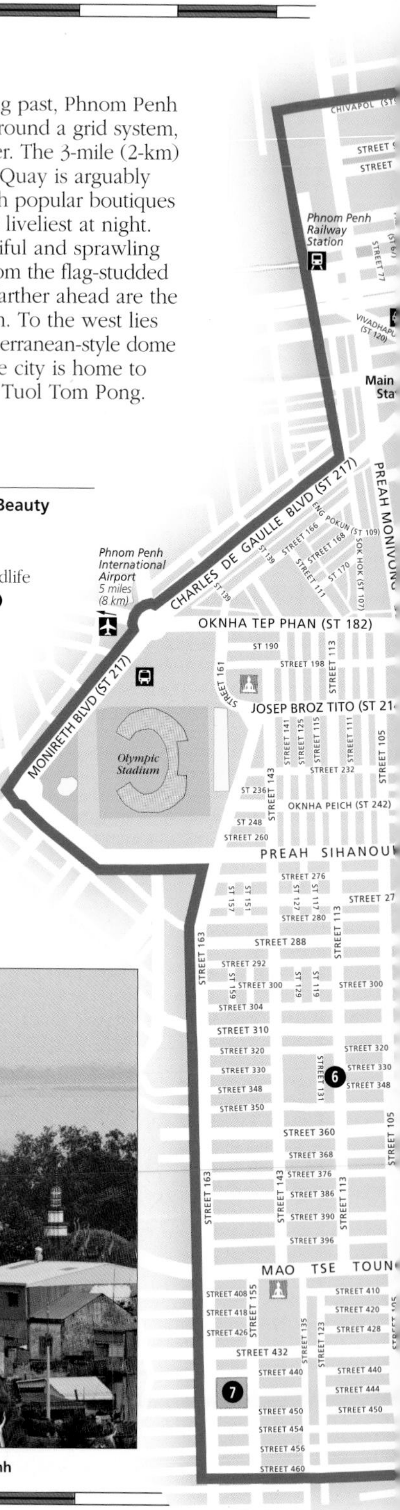

The Royal Palace dominating the skyline, central Phnom Penh

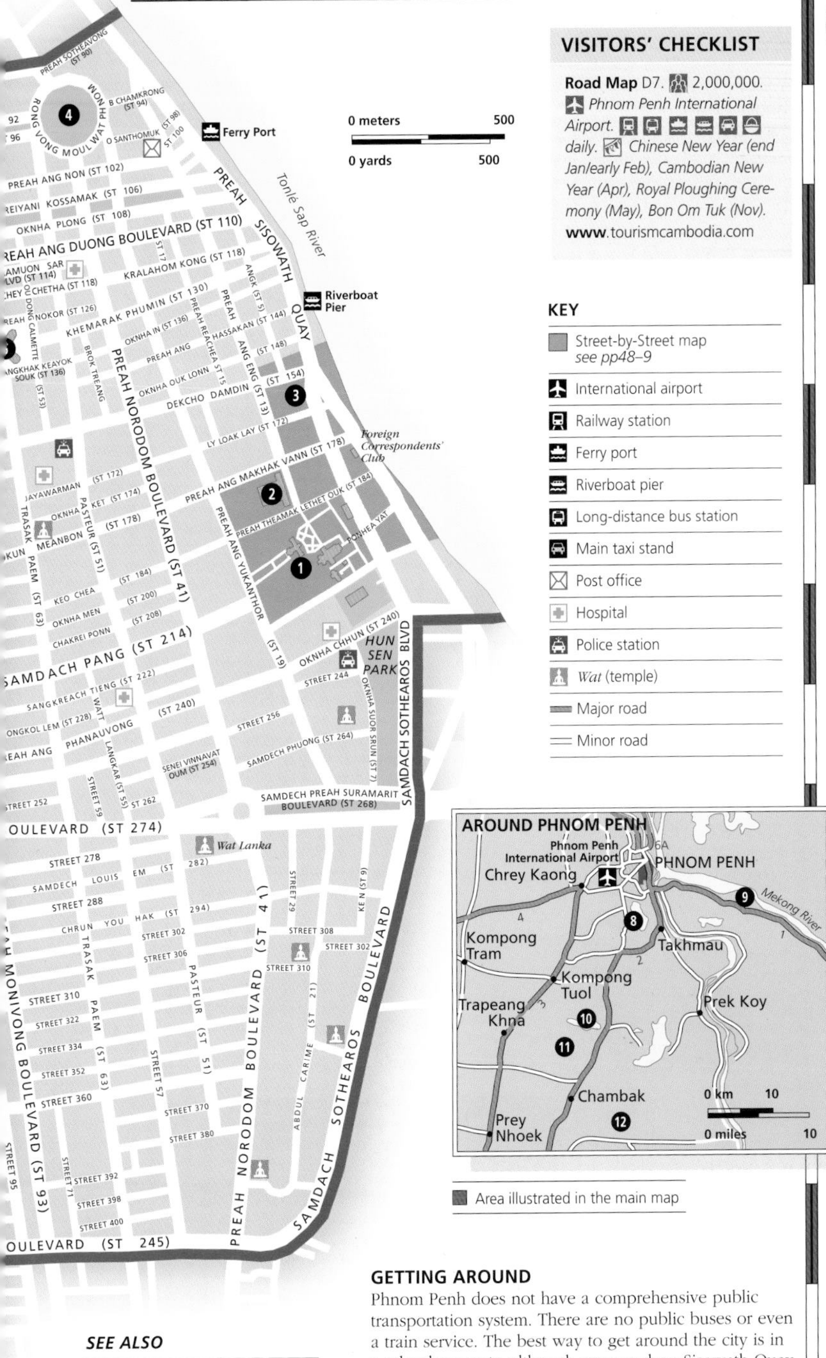

Area illustrated in the main map

VISITORS' CHECKLIST

Road Map D7. 2,000,000. *Phnom Penh International Airport.* *daily.* *Chinese New Year (end Jan/early Feb), Cambodian New Year (Apr), Royal Ploughing Ceremony (May), Bon Om Tuk (Nov).* **www**.tourismcambodia.com

KEY

- Street-by-Street map *see pp48–9*
- International airport
- Railway station
- Ferry port
- Riverboat pier
- Long-distance bus station
- Main taxi stand
- Post office
- Hospital
- Police station
- *Wat* (temple)
- Major road
- Minor road

GETTING AROUND

Phnom Penh does not have a comprehensive public transportation system. There are no public buses or even a train service. The best way to get around the city is in a tuk-tuk or *moto*, although areas such as Sisowath Quay are best explored on foot. Metered taxis, a relatively recent addition to the city, are reasonably priced, though not always easy to find. Those who like to cycle can also move around the city on a hired bicycle.

SEE ALSO

- ***Street Finder*** pp60–61
- ***Where to Stay*** pp210–12
- ***Where to Eat*** pp232–5

Street-by-Street: Riverfront

Phnom Penh's riverfront is distinguished by its Gallic architecture – stucco-fronted, ocher-colored villas, and shuttered townhouses – while the surrounding area is home to many embassies, a number of old municipal buildings built under the French in the 19th and early 20th centuries, and several Chinese-style shophouses. The capital's scenic riverside promenade, Sisowath Quay, is the hub of the city's nightlife, with a variety of restaurants, lively bars, and boutiques. Other interesting places in the area include the Royal Palace and Silver Pagoda, the National Museum, and Psar Kandal, all within walking distance.

Visitors enjoying a quiet meal at one of the riverside restaurants

The palace's grounds and ornamental gardens are studded with stupas and statues of the royal family.

ST 184

★ Royal Palace and Silver Pagoda
Built in the mid-19th century with French assistance, the Royal Palace is home to the current monarch, King Norodom Sihamoni. The adjoining Silver Pagoda houses the highly revered statue of the Emerald Buddha ❶

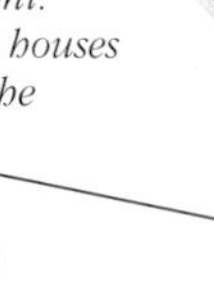

KEY

Suggested route

SAMDA

Silver Shops
Owned by Cham Muslim silversmiths, who are noted for their fine filigree work, the silver shops sell exquisite belts, jewelry, betel pots, and other souvenirs.

Foreign Correspondents' Club (FCC)
The FCC's walls are adorned with atmospheric war photographs. Comfortable leather sofas line the walls of the elegant bar and restaurant, which offers excellent food and impeccable service. The views of the river from the club are spectacular.

STAR SIGHTS

- ★ Royal Palace and Silver Pagoda
- ★ National Museum
- ★ Sisowath Quay

For hotels and restaurants in this region see pp210–12 and pp232–5

Wat Ounalom
The seat of Buddhism in Cambodia, Wat Ounalom has had a tragic history. Today, its attractions include a statue of its murdered religious leader, Samdech Huot Tat, and the stupa behind the main building, which contains a hair from the Buddha's eyebrow ❸

0 meters 100

0 yards 100

Silver shops

Psar Kandal is a dry goods market selling everything from electronics to pirated DVDs. Visitors will also find vendors offering fried crickets, a local delicacy.

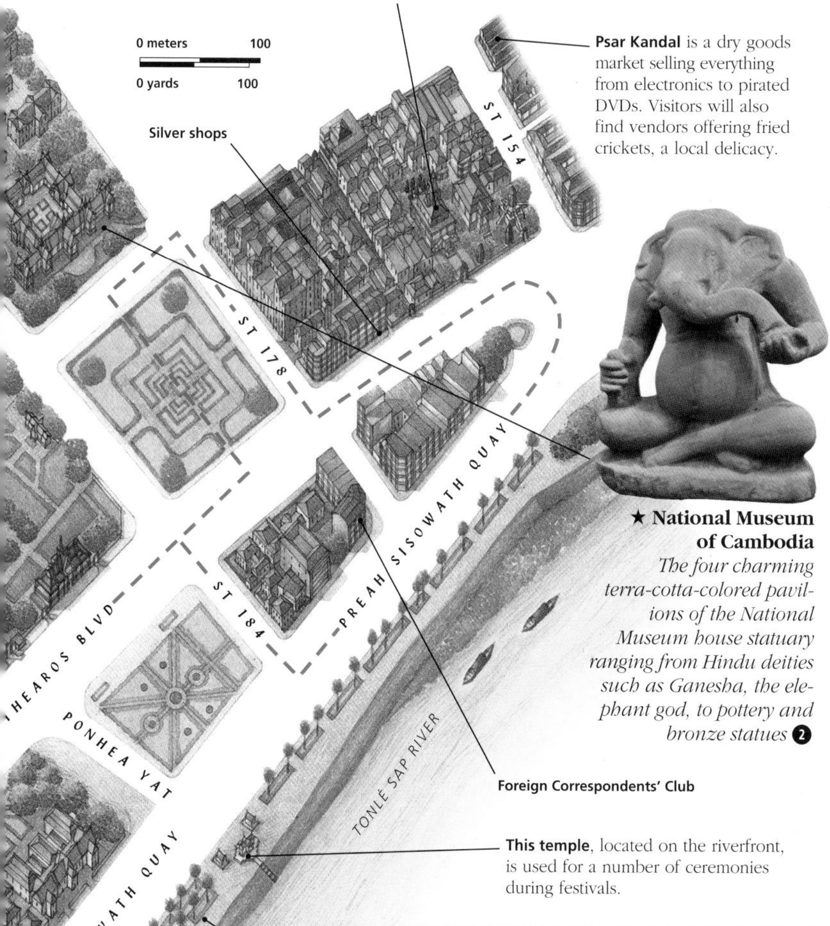

ST 154

ST 178

ST 184

PREAH SISOWATH QUAY

PONHEA YAT

HEAROS BLVD

TONLÉ SAP RIVER

★ National Museum of Cambodia
The four charming terra-cotta-colored pavilions of the National Museum house statuary ranging from Hindu deities such as Ganesha, the elephant god, to pottery and bronze statues ❷

Foreign Correspondents' Club

This temple, located on the riverfront, is used for a number of ceremonies during festivals.

PREAH SISOWATH QUAY

★ Sisowath Quay
An enchanting area, Sisowath Quay is favored by visitors for its lively bars and the wide variety of international cuisine on offer. It also serves as a starting point for river festivals and boat cruises down the Tonlé Sap River.

Imposing terra-cotta exterior of the National Museum of Cambodia, Phnom Penh

Royal Palace and Silver Pagoda ❶

See pp52–5.

National Museum of Cambodia ❷

Sts 178 and 179. **City Map** E2. *8am–5pm daily.* *last ticket sold at 4:30pm.* *inside the museum.* **www**.cambodiamuseum.info

Housed in four majestic terra-cotta pavilions enclosing an enchanting, landscaped courtyard, the National Museum of Cambodia has the country's greatest display of Khmer statuary. Exhibits range from prehistoric to present-day items and include Indian sculptures such as a striking eight-armed statue of Vishnu, a Hindu god, and a magnificent cross-legged sandstone statue of the 12th-century king, Jayavarman VII. In the courtyard is a stone statue of Yama, the God of Death. The museum also has an enviable collection of local pottery and bronze statues from the Funan as well as the Chenla periods *(see p37)*.

A small shop is located at the entrance; it sells a variety of books on Cambodian history and archaeology, as well as an assortment of souvenirs.

Stone statue of a *garuda*

Wat Ounalom ❸

Samdech Sothearos Blvd. **City Map** E2. *dawn to dusk daily.*

Built in 1943, Wat Ounalom is the headquarters and home of the Buddhist *sangha* (order) in Cambodia. In the early 1970s, over 500 monks lived here. Tragically, the Khmer Rouge murdered the then leader, Samdech Huot Tat, for his religious convictions and threw a statue of him into the Tonlé Sap River. The statue was recovered after the expulsion of the Khmer Rouge and is now on view on the second floor of the temple. Outside is a beautifully detailed stupa said to contain a hair from the Buddha's eyebrow. There is also an extensive Buddhist library in the main temple, although the building is currently under renovation. Visitors to the temple should be wary of self-styled guides who insist on showing them around for a price.

Wat Phnom ❹

Norodom Blvd, N of St 102. **City Map** D1. *dawn to dusk daily.* *Cambodian New Year.*

Built in 1373 to house the Buddha statues found by Duan Penh – who laid the foundations of the shrine – on the shores of the Tonlé Sap River, this temple, at a modest 89 ft (27 m), is the highest point in the city. Today, it has something of a carnivalesque atmosphere with flashing altar lights and elephant rides.

Visitors enter this vibrant house of worship through an easterly *naga* stairway, passing beggars, hawkers, and dogs

Sculptured *nagas* flanking the staircase leading to Wat Phnom

and cats fed by the monks. The temple's walls are adorned with *Jataka* (stories from the former lives of the Buddha) murals, although many have been blackened by smoke from the incense offerings. There is a shrine dedicated to Duan Penh behind the *vihara* (temple sanctuary). Nearby, a couple of shrines of Taoist goddesses are popular with the locals, who make offerings of cooked chicken and raw eggs here.

Central Market ❺

E of Monivong Blvd, N of St 63. **City Map** D2. *dawn to dusk daily.*

Known locally as Psar Thmei, which actually means New Market, this fabulous ocher-hued Art Deco building was erected by the French in 1937 on former swamp ground. Its immense central dome is on a scale similar to Hadrian's Pantheon in Rome. Offering a variety of products under one roof, this one-stop shop is any visitor's delight.

The food section here is packed with fresh fruits and vegetables, as well as delicacies such as peeled frogs and fried insects. Four wings radiate from the main building where vendors hawk gold and silver jewelry, watches, electronic goods, Buddha statues, clothes, and fresh flowers. The market is comfortable to visit at midday as the corridors of merchandise are surprisingly cool.

Imposing design of the dome at Central Market, Phnom Penh

Locally made cotton clothes on sale at Psar Tuol Tom Pong

Tuol Sleng Genocide Museum ❻

St 113. **City Map** C4. *8am–5:30pm daily.*

Hidden down a peaceful side street bordered with bougainvillea, this memorable, if disturbing, museum was originally a school that was turned into the Khmer Rouge torture headquarters. Tuol Sleng Prison, also known as S-21, was the largest detention center in the country and subjected 17,000 men, women, and children to torture en route to the Killing Fields of Choeung Ek *(see p58)*; most did not get that far. When Vietnamese forces liberated Phnom Penh in 1975, they found only seven people still alive at S-21, each having survived because of their skills as artist or photographer.

The prison has now been converted into a museum; its former cells and gallery are covered with thousands of haunting photographs of subjects before and after torture. There is an interesting exhibition on the second floor of the main building, which gives important details on the main instigators of the murderous regime, as well as photos and diaries, and poems written by those affected. The balconies on the upper floors are still enclosed with the wire mesh that prevented prisoners from jumping to an early death. Despite allegedly being haunted, today the place plays host to young footballers on its lawns and a colony of bats in one of the stairwells.

Psar Tuol Tom Pong ❼

S of Mao Tse Toung Blvd. **City Map** C5. *dawn to dusk daily.*

Also known as the Russian Market because of the many Russians who shopped here during the 1980s, this market is perhaps the best place for visitors looking for good bargains. Under the sweltering tin roofs is a smorgasbord of handicrafts, fake antiques, silk scarves, and musical instruments. Also on sale is a huge selection of fake designer clothing, as well as genuine items made in local factories. They are sold here at a fraction of their international prices.

Wire mesh enclosing the balconies, Tuol Sleng Genocide Museum

Royal Palace and Silver Pagoda ❶

Built in the mid-19th century in the classic Khmer style, the Royal Palace is the official residence of Cambodia's reigning monarch, King Sihamoni. Bearing a striking resemblance to the Grand Palace in Bangkok, Thailand, the Royal Palace, with its gilded, pitched roofs framed by *nagas* (serpents), is one of the most prominent landmarks of Phnom Penh. Known as Preah Barom Reachea Vaeng Chaktomuk in the Khmer language, the palace was built with French assistance on the site of a former temple, on the western bank of the Tonlé Sap River, and is designed to face the rising sun. Parts of the complex are closed to the public.

Column detail, Royal Offices

Main Entrance

A tour of the Royal Palace begins at the main entrance, situated in the eastern part of the complex. The ticket counters are located here and visitors can also hire English-speaking guides for a few dollars. Visitors should be dressed in clothes that cover the arms, shoulders, and legs. Suitable items of clothing can also be hired from here.

Silver Pagoda

See pp54–5.

Pavilion of Napoleon III

A former French villa, this pavilion was built in Giza, Egypt, by Napoleon III for his wife, Empress Eugénie. Presented to King Norodom I (r.1860–1904) in 1876, it was entirely dismantled, shipped to Phnom Penh, and re-erected in the grounds of the Royal Palace. The pavilion stands out from all other structures in the complex on account of its Colonial design and the exquisite iron fretwork of its balconies.

The pavilion was refurbished in 1991 with assistance from the French government. Today, photographic exhibits, as well as a collection of royal memorabilia such as busts, gifts from visiting dignitaries, glassware, and royal clothing are on display inside.

Intricately detailed façade of the Throne Hall

Pavilion of Napoleon III in the grounds of the Royal Palace

Royal Treasury

A tall, narrow pavilion, whose upper story, or Hor Samritvimean, houses regalia that was used in royal coronation ceremonies. Its highlights include the Great Crown of Victory and the Victory Spear, as well as the Sacred Sword. The lower floor is home to some minor regalia and utensils.

Throne Hall

Built in 1917 and inaugurated by King Sisowath in 1919, the Throne Hall is known locally as Preah Thineang Dheva Vinnichayyeaah, meaning the Sacred Seat of Judgement. Its design is heavily influenced by Bayon-style architecture *(see p71)*, evident from its cruciform shape and triple spires. The central spire is crowned by an imposing 194-ft (59-m) high tower. The roof is adorned with *nagas* (serpents) and *garudas* (mythical beasts, half-man, half-bird). Today, the Throne Hall is used for extending a formal welcome to visiting diplomats, and coronations.

The Throne Room, accessed from a door to the east, is painted in white and yellow to symbolize Hinduism and Buddhism respectively. It is an excellent example of the harmonious fusion of the two religions, which was encouraged by the 12th-century monarch, King Jayavarman VII. Its ceiling is adorned with a beautiful mural depicting the *Reamker*, the Khmer version of the Hindu epic, *Ramayana*. A lotus-patterned carpet, donated by China in 1933, perfectly complements

ROYAL PALACE AND SILVER PAGODA

LIST OF SITES

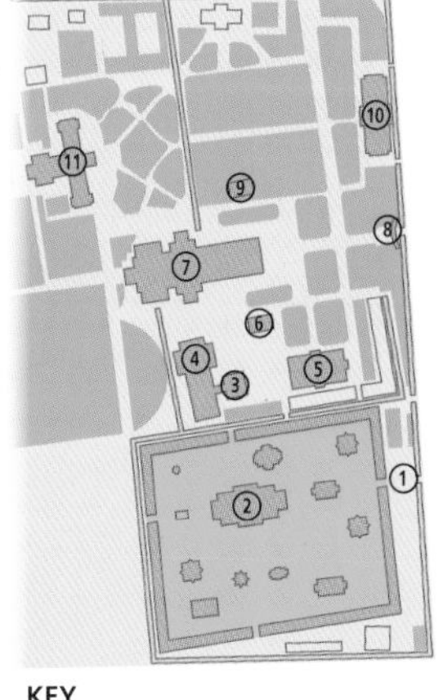

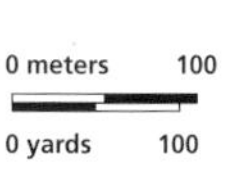

KEY

Area illustrated (*see pp54–5*)

VISITORS' CHECKLIST

City Map E2. Samdach Sothearos Blvd. *Main entrance.* *7:30–11am & 2–5pm daily.* *hired at main entrance.* *Throne Hall.* **Note**: *Royal Residence is closed to the public; Throne Hall is closed during royal receptions.*

the lotus bud floor tiles in the room. The Throne Room also houses the majestic thrones of the king and queen of Cambodia. While the king's throne is small and sits at the front, the queen's is taller and built on a golden stage adorned with *nagas*. There are three stairways running from the queen's throne – two for the Brahmin priests who tend to her during the king's coronation, and the third for the queen herself.

Victory Gate

Set on the eastern end of the complex, the Victory Gate leads directly to the Throne Hall. Once used only by the king and queen, it is now also used by visiting dignitaries.

Royal Waiting Room

Situated to the right of the magnificent Throne Hall, Hor Samranphirum, or the Royal Waiting Room, is used by the king and queen while waiting for their ceremonial elephants on coronation day. Posts to tether the beast are visible on the east side of the building, as are the platforms used by the king and queen to mount the elephants for the coronation procession.

Dancing Pavilion

Located near the Victory Gate, the Dancing Pavilion, or Chan Chaya Pavilion, was originally built in 1914 with wood. It was traditionally used by Cambodian kings to view parades and to enjoy performances of classical Khmer dances. A balcony to the east of the pavilion was used for viewing parades along Sothearos Boulevard, beyond the royal grounds.

Today, the Dancing Pavilion is used for royal celebrations, and royal as well as state banquets. The building was memorably used to celebrate the coronation of King Sihamoni in 2004.

Royal Residence

Built in the mid-20th century, during the reign of King Sisowath Monivong, by well-known Khmer architect Oknha Tep Nimith Khieu, the Royal Residence is also known as the Khemarin Palace, or the Palace of the Khmer King. It currently houses the present monarch, King Sihamoni, whose presence in the capital is indicated by the blue royal flag, which flits at full mast. The Royal Residence is off limits for visitors.

Next to this beautiful building stands the royal guesthouse known as Villa Kantha Bopha, which was built in 1956 and is only used to house foreign guests.

View of the elegantly lit exterior of the Dancing Pavilion at night

Silver Pagoda

Decorative tree

Near the low-strung riverfront of Phnom Penh, the 19th-century Silver Pagoda lies within the same complex as the Royal Palace and is a prominent jewel of the city's squat skyline. With its curlicued, golden roofs and tropical gardens, the Silver Pagoda is a short walk from Sisowath Quay, and is the perfect place to savor the calm, away from the rush of the city.

The gilded gateway at the northern entrance to the Silver Pagoda

Royal Pavilion

The Dhammasala, which is also known as the Royal Pavilion, is an open hall used by the royal family as a reception area as well as by Buddhist monks to recite religious texts.

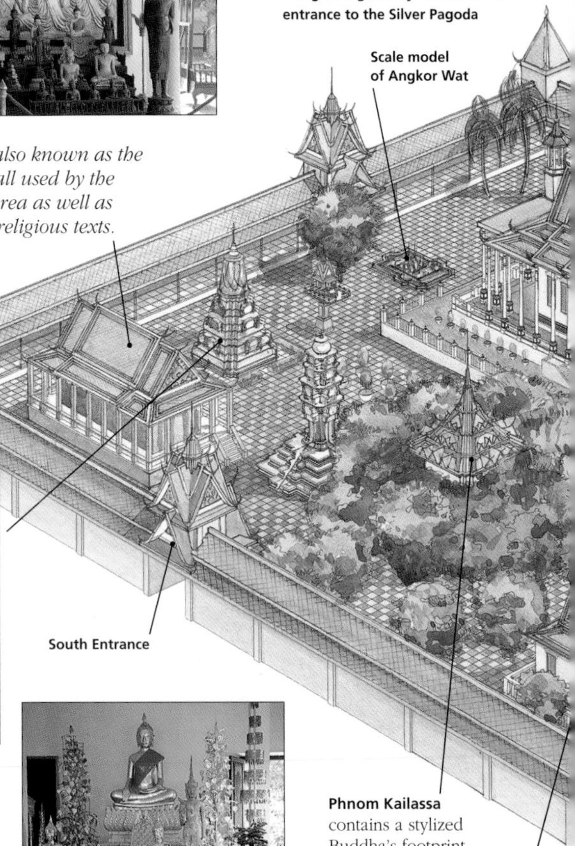

Scale model of Angkor Wat

South Entrance

Chedi of Suramarit

This stupa holds the ashes of former king, Suramarit, and his queen, Kossomak – grandparents of the current ruler, King Sihamoni.

Phnom Kailassa contains a stylized Buddha's footprint gifted by Sri Lanka.

★ Buddha's Footprints

The Keong Preah Bath houses the Buddha's footprints. This shrine is especially popular with Cambodians and is surrounded by fortune-tellers.

STAR SIGHTS

- ★ Buddha's Footprints
- ★ Murals in the Gallery
- ★ Wat Preah Keo

For hotels and restaurants in this region see pp210–12 and pp232–5

★ Murals in the Gallery
The inner compound wall of the complex is beautifully ornamented with vivid frescoes of scenes from the Reamker – *the Khmer version of the Indian epic,* Ramayana.

VISITORS' CHECKLIST

7:30–11am & 2–5pm daily. single ticket valid for both Royal Palace & Silver Pagoda. inside Wat Preah Keo.

★ Wat Preah Keo
Named for its centerpiece, a Baccarat crystal Buddha, Wat Preah Keo (Temple of the Emerald Buddha) is also famous for a golden, life-sized Buddha and miniature Buddhist statuary.

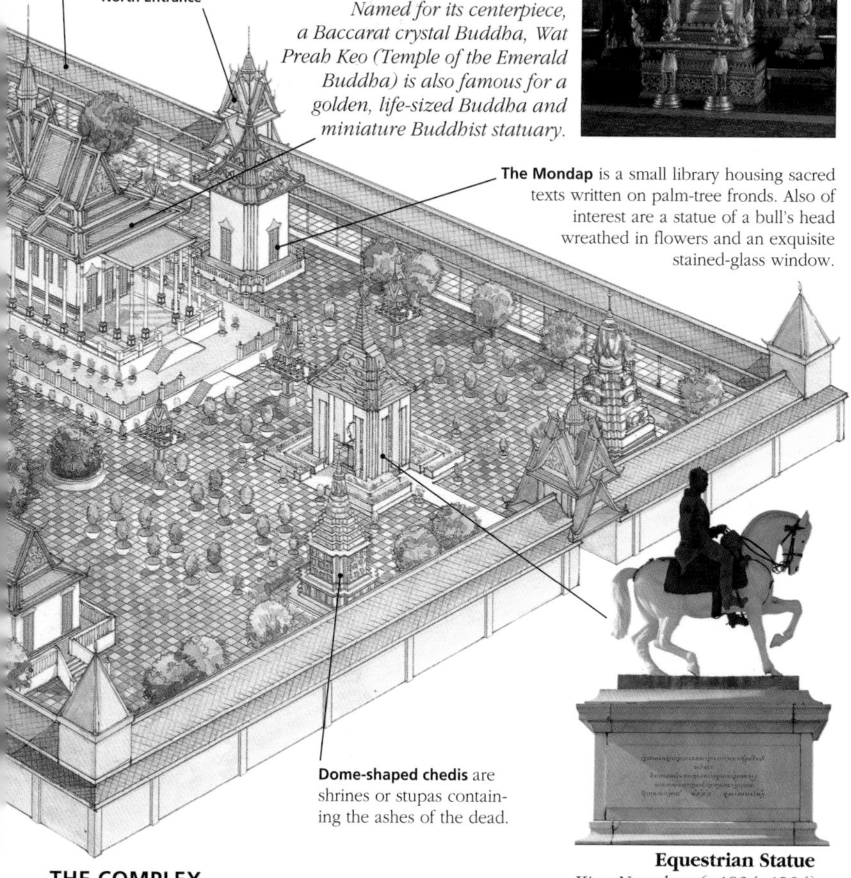

North Entrance

The Mondap is a small library housing sacred texts written on palm-tree fronds. Also of interest are a statue of a bull's head wreathed in flowers and an exquisite stained-glass window.

Dome-shaped chedis are shrines or stupas containing the ashes of the dead.

Equestrian Statue
King Norodom (r.1834–1904) and Napoleon III were firm friends – this statue of Norodom in full Napoleon III regalia is a parody of the French emperor on his steed.

THE COMPLEX

Also known as Wat Preah Keo, the Silver Pagoda is named for its floor, which is inlaid with over 5,000 solid silver tiles. The name also describes the complex that houses the Buddha's Footprints, the Mondap library, the *Reamker* murals, and a number of royal family shrines.

Façade of the Pavilion of Napoleon III and Throne Hall in the Royal Palace complex ▷

Killing Fields of Choeung Ek ❽

5 miles (8 km) S of Phnom Penh. *7am–5:30pm daily.*

A former longan orchard, this deceptively peaceful setting was the scene of one of the most disturbing acts of violence in contemporary history. Some 17,000 men, women, and children kept as prisoners in the torture chambers of Tuol Sleng Prison, also known as S-21 *(see p51)*, were brought here to be killed, often by blunted hoes to conserve bullets. Of the 129 communal graves, 49 have been left intact, and it is still possible to chance upon bone fragments and bits of clothing. Signposts close to the graves tell visitors about the number of people buried there; another one marks a macabre tree against which babies were flung by their ankles and killed.

In 1988, however, a fittingly dignified pavilion was erected within the complex in memory of the 9,000 people found here. Through the glass panels of the pavilion one can see some 8,000 skulls arranged according to age and sex. A museum in the corner of the grounds offers detailed background information not only on the founders of the Khmer Rouge, but also its victims, who included doctors, politicians, and actors.

Signpost identifying the tree against which babies were killed, Killing Fields of Choeung Ek

Koki Beach ❾

Off National Hwy 1, 9 miles (14 km) E of Phnom Penh. *from Central Market.* *dawn to dusk daily.*

A romantic picnic spot on a tributary of the Mekong River, Koki Beach is popular with young Khmers, who come here on weekends. The clean sands, stilted huts with thatched roofs, and calm setting make it an ideal place to relax and unwind. Visitors can venture on inexpensive boat trips along the river or swim close to the sandy beach, where a few people can usually be found braving the waters. There is always plenty of food to be bought from the local vendors who sell a selection of grilled fish, chicken, and fresh coconuts. The beach is also lined with makeshift restaurants specializing in local food. However, it is best to agree on the price of dishes before settling down to eat.

JUSTICE FOR VICTIMS OF THE KHMER ROUGE

Conceived in 1997 and finally set up in 2007, the Extraordinary Chambers in the Courts of Cambodia (ECCC) is a UN-backed tribunal located near Phnom Penh's airport. The first organization of its kind to bring the leaders of Khmer Rouge to justice, the ECCC is an independent tribunal comprising international monitors. Designed to be fair and open, these trials aim to relieve the burden still felt by survivors of the holocaust. The proceedings have been affected by lack of funding and alleged corruption, along with some resistance by Prime Minister Hun Sen, who fears that reopening the wound could spark a fresh civil war.

The first accused to be tried by the tribunal *was "Duch," head warden of Tuol Sleng Prison. On July 26, 2010, Duch was sentenced to 35 years in prison for war crimes and crimes against humanity. Only senior leaders of the Democratic Kampuchea, the state formed by the Khmer Rouge, are being tried.*

Trials in the Extraordinary Chambers in the Courts of Cambodia *are usually not on camera, and can be witnessed by the public except in some special cases. The courtroom is designed to provide additional seating for onlookers, with a glass partition separating them from the area where the accused and judges are seated.*

Tonlé Bati ⓾

Off National Hwy 2, 19 miles (30 km) S of Phnom Penh. *dawn to dusk daily.*

Another popular weekend haunt, Tonlé Bati is a peaceful lake with stilted huts bordering its acacia-shaded shoreline. It is frequented by locals who find it an ideal spot for a quiet picnic or fishing trip. Adding further appeal are the nearby ruins of **Ta Prohm** and **Yeay Peau**, two beautifully preserved temples built in the late 12th century under King Jayavarman VII.

Ta Prohm's main sanctuary has five chambers, each containing a Shiva *lingam* (phallic symbol), as well as a number of bas-reliefs depicting several *apsaras*. On weekends, the temple grounds play host to musicians and fortune-tellers catering to visitors. Located a short distance from Ta Prohm, Yeay Peau is named after King Ta Prohm's mother. Both sites show signs of damage by the Khmer Rouge.

Crumbling ruins of Phnom Chisor, overlooking the plains below

Phnom Tamao Wildlife Rescue Center ⓫

Off National Hwy 2, 25 miles (40 km) S of Phnom Penh. *from Central Market, then tuk-tuk.* *8:30am–5pm daily.*

Opened in 1995, the Phnom Tamao Wildlife Rescue Center is the largest zoo in the country. Covering 10 sq miles (26 sq km) of protected forest, of which only a small part is in use, the zoo serves as a rehabilitation center for animals, many of them endangered, rescued from the illegal wildlife trade. A haven for wildlife enthusiasts, the center cares for and protects several rare birds and animals that usually inhabit inhospitable parts of the country and are therefore almost impossible to observe in the wild.

These well-nurtured animals are kept in a variety of enclosures, the largest of which houses a group of Malayan sun bears who willingly accept fresh coconuts from visitors. Other exotic species found here include the world's greatest collection of pileated gibbons and the Siamese crocodile. The center also has several elephants that have been taught to paint, and many fully grown Asiatic tigers. These are best viewed in the afternoon, when they usually come out.

Asiatic tiger, Phnom Tamao

Phnom Chisor ⓬

31 miles (50 km) S of Phnom Penh. *from Central Market, then tuk-tuk.* *dawn to dusk daily.*

An 11th-century sanctuary formerly known as Suryagiri, the temple of Phnom Chisor is set upon the eastern side of a solitary hill affording wonderful views of the plains below. Within its crumbling interior stand a few surviving statues of the Buddha, while the carvings on the wooden doors depict figures standing on pigs. Best visited in the early morning or late afternoon, when it is cooler, the temple is reached by climbing almost 400 stairs – the path taken by the king of Cambodia 900 years ago. Directly below the summit is the sanctuary of Sen Ravang, the pond of Tonlé Om, and beyond it the Sen Ravang temple, all forming a symbolic straight line to sacred Angkor.

Nearby stand two deteriorating brick *prasats* (towers) of the 10th-century temple Prasat Neang Khmau. Beside them is an active pagoda where another ancient *prasat* may once have stood.

Bas-relief depicting *apsaras* in various postures at Ta Prohm, Tonlé Bati

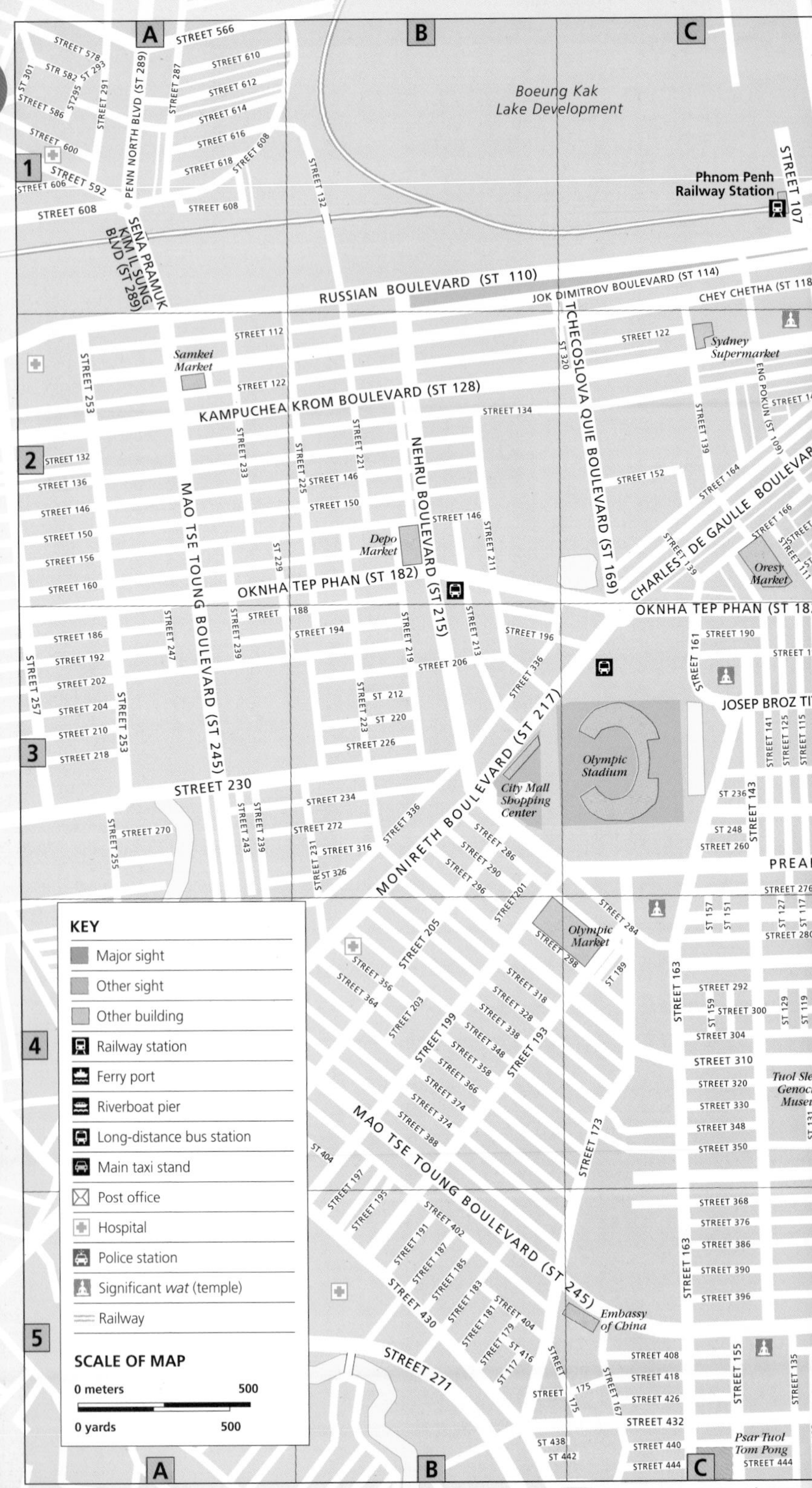

A
B
C
1
2
3
4
5
Boeung Kak
Lake Development
Phnom Penh
Railway Station
STREET 107
STREET 566
STREET 578
STR 582
ST 293
ST 301
ST295
STREET 586
STREET 600
STREET 592
STREET 606
STREET 608
STREET 291
PENN NORTH BLVD (ST 289)
STREET 287
STREET 610
STREET 612
STREET 614
STREET 616
STREET 618
STREET 608
SENA PRAMUK
KIM IL SUNG
BLVD (ST 289)
STREET 132
RUSSIAN BOULEVARD (ST 110)
JOK DIMITROV BOULEVARD (ST 114)
CHEY CHETHA (ST 118)
STREET 112
Samkei
Market
STREET 122
STREET 253
KAMPUCHEA KROM BOULEVARD (ST 128)
STREET 134
ST 320
TCHECOSLOVA QUIE BOULEVARD (ST 169)
STREET 122
Sydney
Supermarket
ENG POKUN (ST 109)
STREET 139
STREET 132
STREET 136
STREET 146
STREET 150
STREET 156
STREET 160
STREET 233
STREET 225
STREET 221
STREET 146
STREET 150
NEHRU BOULEVARD (ST 215)
STREET 146
STREET 211
Depo
Market
ST 229
MAO TSE TOUNG BOULEVARD (ST 245)
STREET 152
STREET 164
CHARLES DE GAULLE BOULEVARD
STREET 166
STREET 139
Oresy
Market
OKNHA TEP PHAN (ST 182)
OKNHA TEP PHAN (ST 182)
STREET 188
STREET 186
STREET 192
STREET 202
STREET 204
STREET 210
STREET 218
STREET 257
STREET 253
STREET 247
STREET 239
STREET 194
STREET 219
STREET 213
STREET 196
STREET 206
STREET 336
STREET 190
STREET 161
JOSEP BROZ TITO
ST 212
ST 220
STREET 223
STREET 226
MONIRETH BOULEVARD (ST 217)
Olympic
Stadium
City Mall
Shopping
Center
STREET 141
STREET 125
STREET 115
ST 236
STREET 143
ST 248
STREET 260
STREET 230
STREET 270
STREET 255
STREET 243
STREET 239
STREET 234
STREET 272
STREET 316
STREET 231
ST 326
STREET 336
STREET 286
STREET 290
STREET 296
STREET 201
STREET 276
STREET 284
Olympic
Market
STREET 298
ST 157
ST 151
ST 127
ST 117
STREET 280
STREET 205
STREET 356
STREET 364
STREET 203
STREET 199
STREET 318
STREET 328
STREET 338
STREET 348
STREET 358
STREET 366
STREET 374
STREET 374
STREET 388
STREET 193
ST 189
STREET 163
STREET 292
ST 159
STREET 300
ST 129
ST 119
STREET 304
STREET 310
STREET 320
STREET 330
STREET 348
STREET 350
Tuol Sleng
Genocide
Museum
ST 131
STREET 173
ST 404
MAO TSE TOUNG BOULEVARD (ST 245)
STREET 197
STREET 195
STREET 402
STREET 191
STREET 187
STREET 185
STREET 183
STREET 430
STREET 181
STREET 179
STREET 404
ST 416
ST 117
STREET 271
STREET 368
STREET 376
STREET 386
STREET 390
STREET 396
STREET 163
Embassy
of China
STREET 408
STREET 418
STREET 426
STREET 432
STREET 440
STREET 444
STREET 155
STREET 135
STREET 175
STREET 167
ST 438
ST 442
Psar Tuol
Tom Pong
STREET 444
KEY
Major sight
Other sight
Other building
Railway station
Ferry port
Riverboat pier
Long-distance bus station
Main taxi stand
Post office
Hospital
Police station
Significant wat (temple)
Railway
SCALE OF MAP
0 meters 500
0 yards 500

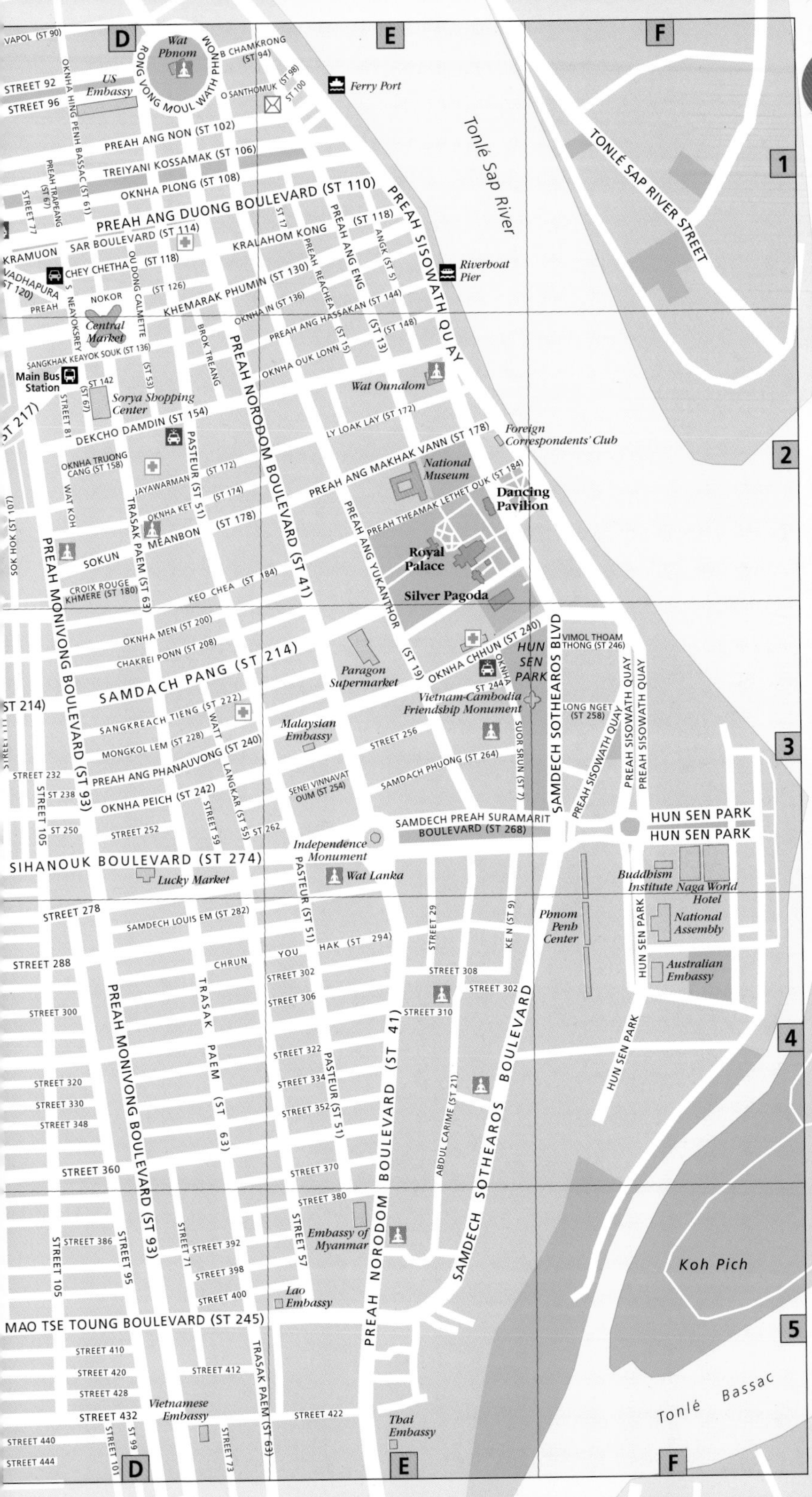
D
E
F
1
2
3
4
5
Wat Phnom
US Embassy
Ferry Port
Tonlé Sap River
TONLÉ SAP RIVER STREET
STREET 92
STREET 96
RONG VONG MOUL WATH PHNOM
OKNHA HING PENH BASSAC (ST 61)
B CHAMKRONG (ST 94)
O SANTHOMUK (ST 98)
ST 100
PREAH ANG NON (ST 102)
TREIYANI KOSSAMAK (ST 106)
OKNHA PLONG (ST 108)
PREAH ANG DUONG BOULEVARD (ST 110)
PREAH SISOWATH QUAY
PREAH TRAPEANG (ST 67)
STREET 77
SAR BOULEVARD (ST 114)
KRAMUON
CHEY CHETHA (ST 118)
(ST 118)
KRALAHOM KONG
PREAH ANG ENG
PREAH REACHEA
ANGK (ST 5)
ST 17
Riverboat Pier
VADHAPURA (ST 120)
NOKOR
PREAH
S. NEAYOKSREY
OU DONG CALMETTE
(ST 126)
KHEMARAK PHUMIN (ST 130)
OKNHA IN (ST 136)
PREAH ANG HASSAKAN (ST 144)
(ST 148)
(ST 13)
(ST 15)
Central Market
SANGKHAK KEAYOK SOUK (ST 136)
(ST 53)
BROK TREANG
PREAH NORODOM BOULEVARD (ST 41)
OKNHA OUK LONN
Main Bus Station
ST 142
(ST 67)
Sorya Shopping Center
Wat Ounalom
ST 217)
STREET 81
DEKCHO DAMDIN (ST 154)
LY LOAK LAY (ST 172)
PASTEUR (ST 51)
Foreign Correspondents' Club
OKNHA TRUONG CANG (ST 158)
JAYAWARMAN
(ST 172)
(ST 174)
PREAH ANG MAKHAK VANN (ST 178)
National Museum
Dancing Pavilion
WAT KOH
OKNHA KET
MEANBON
(ST 178)
PREAH THEAMAK LETHET OUK (ST 184)
SOK HOK (ST 107)
PREAH MONIVONG BOULEVARD (ST 93)
TRASAK PAEM (ST 63)
SOKUN
PREAH ANG YUKANTHOR (ST 19)
Royal Palace
Silver Pagoda
CROIX ROUGE KHMERE (ST 180)
KEO CHEA (ST 184)
OKNHA MEN (ST 200)
CHAKREI PONN (ST 208)
SAMDACH PANG (ST 214)
Paragon Supermarket
OKNHA CHHUN (ST 240)
HUN SEN PARK
OKNHA
ST 244
VIMOL THOAM THONG (ST 246)
SAMDECH SOTHEAROS BLVD
ST 214)
SANGKREACH TIENG (ST 222)
WATT
Vietnam-Cambodia Friendship Monument
LONG NGET (ST 258)
Malaysian Embassy
MONGKOL LEM (ST 228)
STREET 256
PREAH SISOWATH QUAY
PREAH SISOWATH QUAY
PREAH ANG PHANAUVONG (ST 240)
STREET 232
ST 238
LANGKAR (ST 55)
SENEI VINNAVAT OUM (ST 254)
SAMDACH PHUONG (ST 264)
SUOR SRUN (ST 7)
OKNHA PEICH (ST 242)
STREET 59
STREET 105
ST 250
STREET 252
ST 262
SAMDECH PREAH SURAMARIT BOULEVARD (ST 268)
HUN SEN PARK
HUN SEN PARK
Independence Monument
SIHANOUK BOULEVARD (ST 274)
Lucky Market
PASTEUR (ST 51)
Wat Lanka
Buddhism Institute
Naga World Hotel
STREET 278
SAMDECH LOUIS EM (ST 282)
STREET 29
KE N (ST 9)
Phnom Penh Center
National Assembly
YOU HAK (ST 294)
STREET 288
CHRUN
STREET 302
STREET 306
STREET 308
STREET 302
HUN SEN PARK
Australian Embassy
STREET 300
TRASAK PAEM (ST 63)
STREET 310
SAMDECH SOTHEAROS BOULEVARD
STREET 322
STREET 334
STREET 352
PASTEUR (ST 51)
STREET 320
STREET 330
STREET 348
ABDUL CARIME (ST 21)
STREET 360
STREET 370
STREET 380
PREAH NORODOM BOULEVARD (ST 41)
STREET 386
STREET 95
STREET 71
STREET 392
STREET 398
STREET 400
STREET 57
Embassy of Myanmar
Koh Pich
Lao Embassy
MAO TSE TOUNG BOULEVARD (ST 245)
STREET 410
STREET 420
STREET 428
STREET 432
STREET 412
TRASAK PAEM (ST 63)
Vietnamese Embassy
STREET 422
Thai Embassy
Tonlé Bassac
STREET 440
STREET 444
STREET 101
ST 99
STREET 73

ANGKOR

The ancient capital of the great Khmer Empire, Angkor is without doubt one of the most magnificent wonders of the world and a site of immense archaeological significance. Located in dense jungle on the hot and torpid plains of northwestern Cambodia, its awe-inspiring temples transport visitors back to an enchanting and mysterious ancient world of grandeur and glory.

Often referred to as the eighth wonder of the world, Angkor, the ancient capital of Cambodia, is a remarkable place. For nearly six centuries, between AD 802 and 1432, it was the political and religious heart of the Khmer Empire, an empire that extended from the South China Sea almost to the Bay of Bengal.

The Khmer Empire was founded at the beginning of the 9th century AD Jayavarman II (r.802–850), who proclaimed himself *devaraja* (god-king) of the land. He built a gigantic, pyramidal temple-mountain representing Mount Meru, the sacred mythical abode of the Hindu gods. This structure laid the foundations of Angkor's architecture. In the following centuries, his successors shifted the capital from Roluos to Angkor, built magnificent temples such as Phnom Bakheng, Angkor Wat, Banteay Kdei, and Ta Prohm, as well as the bustling city of Angkor Thom. Today, the remains of the metropolis of Angkor occupy 77 sq miles (200 sq km) of northwest Cambodia, and although its wooden houses and magnificent palaces decayed centuries ago, the impressive array of stone temples still stand. Set between two *barays* (reservoirs), Angkor today contains around 70 temples, tombs, and other ancient ruins. Among them is the splendid Angkor Wat, the world's largest religious complex.

One of the most important archaeological sites in the world, Angkor attracts millions of visitors each year, providing a substantial boost to Cambodia's economy. Other sites in the area include the rapidly developing town of Siem Reap. With its tree-lined boulevards and gentle pace, Siem Reap is the gateway to the temples of Angkor, which lie only 4 miles (6 km) north of town.

Monks enjoying the stunning sunset over Angkor Wat atop Phnom Bakheng

◁ **Elaborate carvings on walls and doorways at Banteay Srei, Siem Reap province**

Exploring Angkor

Set among dense green forests and neat rice paddies, the massive monuments of Angkor are the most remarkable architectural masterpieces in Southeast Asia. Located north of Siem Reap town, in Siem Reap province, the vast Angkor Wat complex, with its imposing towers, and the great city of Angkor Thom, with its impressive causeway and the gigantic smiling faces of the Bayon, are breathtaking sights, especially at sunrise or sunset. Farther north are the smaller yet unique temples of Preah Khan and Preah Neak Pean. To the east of Angkor Thom is the magical Ta Prohm, with large trees growing through the temple walls. Farther out, the pink sandstone structure of Banteay Srei lies to the northeast, while to the southeast are the temples of the Roluos Group, the oldest in Angkor.

SIGHTS AT A GLANCE

Towns, Cities, and Villages

Chong Kneas 15
Kompong Khleang 18
Kompong Phhluk 17
Siem Reap pp66–7 1

Historical Sites

Angkor Wat pp68–9 2
Angkor Thom pp72–5 3
Banteay Kdei 10
Banteay Srei 13
East Baray 7
Phnom Bakheng 4
Prasat Kravan 12
Preah Khan 5
Preah Neak Pean 6
Pre Rup 8
Roluos Group 14
Srah Srang 9
Ta Prohm pp80–81 11

National Parks and Preserves

Prek Toal Bird Sanctuary 16

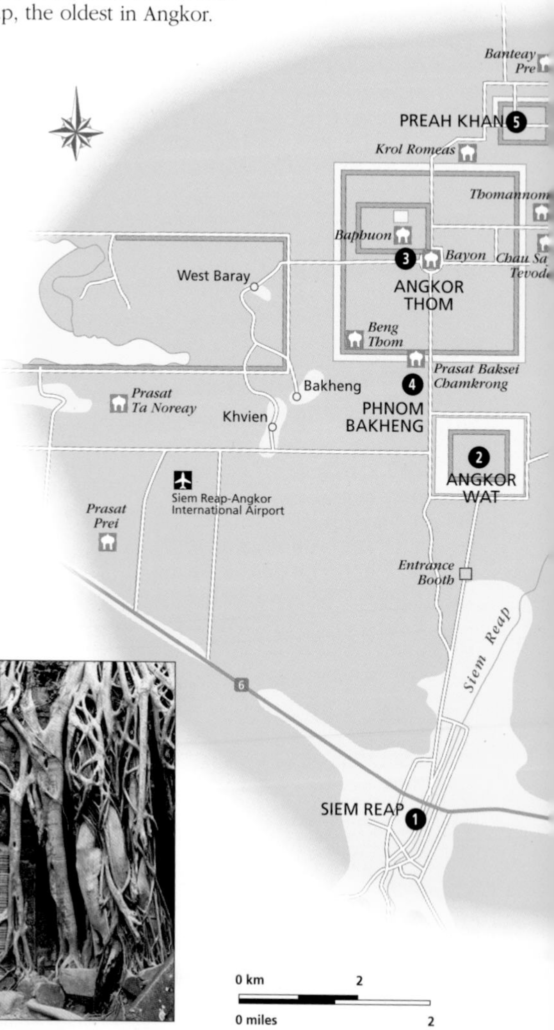

Banteay Pre
PREAH KHAN 5
Krol Romeas
Thomannom
Bapbuon
3 Bayon
Chau Sa Tevoda
West Baray
ANGKOR THOM
Beng Thom
Prasat Baksei Chamkrong
Bakheng
4 PHNOM BAKHENG
Prasat Ta Noreay
Khvien
2 ANGKOR WAT
Siem Reap-Angkor International Airport
Prasat Prei
Entrance Booth
Siem Reap
6
SIEM REAP 1
0 km 2
0 miles 2

The tree featured in the film *Lara Croft: Tomb Raider*, Ta Prohm

Tuk-tuks plying the road between Siem Reap and Angkor

GETTING AROUND

The temples at Angkor require both time and motorized transport to visit. It is possible to visit the main sites by motorcycle, but the most comfortable way to travel in this hot and dusty area is in an air-conditioned car with a driver. In Colonial times, the French defined two circuits, both starting at Angkor Wat, which are still used today. The 11-mile (18-km) "small circuit" takes at least a day and covers the central temples of the complex, continuing to Ta Prohm, before returning to Angkor Wat by way of Banteay Kdei. The "great circuit," a 17-mile (27-km) route, takes in the small circuit as well as the outer temples, going past Preah Neak Pean to Ta Som before turning south to Pre Rup. This takes at least two full days.

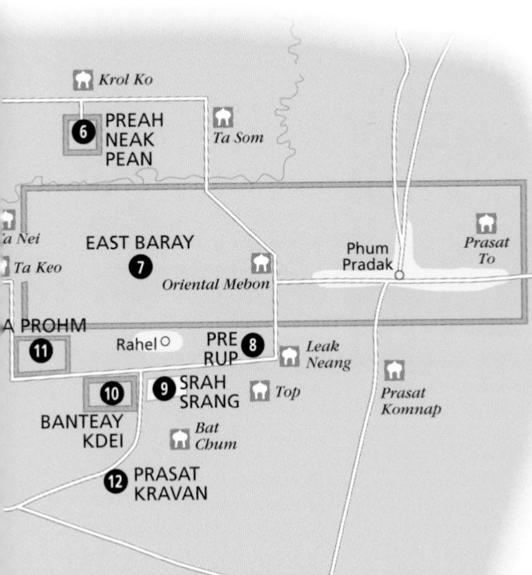

Exquisite carvings of *apsaras* at the Bayon, Angkor Thom

SEE ALSO

- ***Where to Stay*** pp212–14
- ***Where to Eat*** pp235–8

Siem Reap ❶

Buddha statue at museum

Siem Reap literally means Siam Defeated, referring to the Khmer sacking of the great Thai city of Ayutthaya in the 17th century. Until recently, this French Indochinese town with its Colonial buildings and tree-lined boulevards was little more than a staging post for visitors on their way to the temples of Angkor and the Roluos Group. Today, however, it is fast becoming a destination in its own right, with quality restaurants serving excellent French-influenced cuisine, upscale boutique hotels, and a new airport. The locals have been quick to ride the tourist wave with souvenir shops selling silk *kramas* (scarves), and tour agencies and massage vendors cropping up.

Angkor National Museum

968 Charles De Gaulle Blvd. **Tel** *(063)-966-601.* *8:30am–6:30pm daily.*
www.angkornationalmuseum.com

Opened to the public in 2007, the Angkor National Museum is housed in a sprawling building with well-manicured lawns. The museum comprises eight individual galleries, each containing a wealth of ancient Angkorian artifacts. On arrival, visitors first head to the screening of a documentary on the marvels of Angkor entitled *Story Behind The Legend.* The next stop is Gallery 1, with its stunning exhibition of 1,000 Buddha images in wood, stone, and precious jewels. The subsequent galleries focus exclusively on subjects such as the pre-Angkorian period, Khmer kings, and Angkor Wat. A mall with a shopping center is attached to the museum.

Psar Chaa and Around

Corner of Pokambor Ave. *dawn to dusk daily.*

Once the mainstay of the town's vendors, today Psar Chaa today faces serious

Brightly lit restaurants and bars along the popular Pub Street

competition from boutique shops lining surrounding streets. Nevertheless, the market continues to be a popular stop for both locals and foreign visitors who are drawn to its cool corridors not only because of the reasonable prices, but also for the sheer variety of goods on offer. Stalls stock everything, from wood carvings to lacquerware and silverware, to groceries.

Nearby is the carefully restored old French Quarter and the atmospheric Pub Street. This lively area, aptly named for the numerous restaurants and pubs lining its length, comes alive at night with loud music, *apsara* dance performances, and crowds of visitors sauntering up and down the street.

Les Chantiers Écoles

Stung Thmey St. **Tel** *(063)-963-330.* *7am–5pm daily.*
www.artisansdangkor.com

A school set up in the early 1990s for under-privileged children, Les Chantiers Écoles is located down a tiny side street. Here, children are taught stone carving, lacquer-making, silk painting, and wood sculpting. Visitors can walk through the workshops with a guide who explains the stages of each intricate craft; the tour takes about an hour. Artisans d'Angkor, the school's shop, is also located in the same complex and sells products made by the students.

Those keen to see the process of silk farming can head for the Les Chantiers Écoles silk farm, 10 miles (16 km) northwest of Siem Reap. The tour takes three hours. Bus rides from Les Chantiers Écoles are available.

National Centre for Khmer Ceramics

Charles De Gaulle Blvd. **Tel** *(063)-963-330.* *8am–6pm.*
www.khmerceramics.com

A non-profit, non-government organization, the National Centre for Khmer Ceramics was established to re-introduce Khmer's ancient pottery techniques to the country. The center also provides valuable job opportunities to the people of Siem Reap province, which, despite the considerable wealth accrued from

Outstanding display of Buddha images in Gallery 1, Angkor National Museum

visitors to nearby Angkor Wat, is still the poorest in Cambodia. Students are taught for free and are encouraged to set up their own studios on completion of the course. They learn to work with clay and master the potter's wheel, and kilns faithfully modeled on an ancient Khmer design. Guided tours of the center are generally given by one of the trainees, and those interested can also try their hand at the potter's wheel. The center also has a lovely souvenir shop, which sells some of the finished ceramics made on-site. Shoppers can pick up some good bargains here. Afterwards, visitors can relax in the center's charming, shady tropical gardens.

Ceramic pot, National Centre

Tonlé Sap Exhibition

16 miles (26 km) N of town center. *8am–5:30pm daily.*

Krousay Thmey, an NGO that supports orphans, has set up the informative Tonlé Sap Exhibition in the outskirts of Siem Reap. This exhibition offers an insight into the ecology of the Tonlé Sap, the largest freshwater lake in Southeast Asia. The lake and its marine-rich waters feed over 3 million people and provide 75 percent of the country's annual fish stocks. The displays, which feature models, nets, illustrations, and a range of fishing equipment, focus on the varied wildlife of the lake, as well as its floating villages and the people who live in them. Visitors can pamper their tired muscles at the end of the day by opting for a traditional massage at the adjoining NGO, Seeing Hands, which has been set up to help the blind.

Cambodian Cultural Village

6 Airport Rd, Khum Svay Dang Kum, Krus Village. ***Tel** (063)-963-098.* *8am–7pm daily.*
www.cambodianculturalvillage.com

Hugely popular with the Cambodians, the Cambodian Cultural Village is an interesting hour's diversion for international visitors who want to learn about Cambodia's diverse demography, religion, and architecture. There are Cham (Muslim), Khmer (Buddhist), and Phnong and Kroueng (animist) houses, as well as floating villages in the complex. There are also miniature replicas of famous contemporary buildings in Cambodia and wax renderings of national historical figures. A variety of shows, such as *apsara* dances, fishing ceremonies, and a lion dance, provide a brilliant insight into the country's ancient traditions. This place is worth a visit, especially for those traveling with children.

VISITORS' CHECKLIST

Road Map C6. 155 miles (250 km) NW of Phnom Penh. *140,000.* *from Phnom Penh or Battambang.* *Khmer Angkor Tour Guide, Pokambor Ave, (063)-964-347.* *daily.* *Bon Om Tuk (Nov).*

Traditional dance performance at the Cambodian Cultural Village

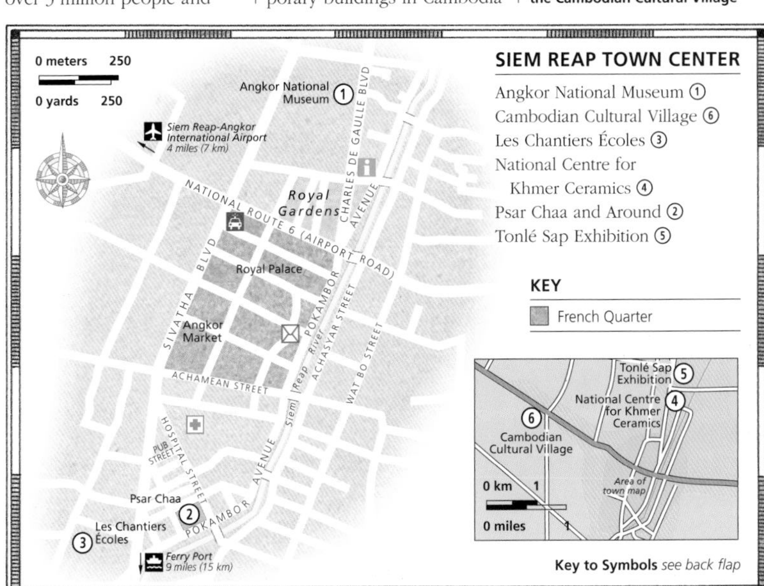

Angkor Wat ❷

The largest religious monument in the world, Angkor Wat literally means the City which is a Temple. Built during the 12th century by King Suryavarman II, this spectacular complex was originally dedicated to the Hindu god, Vishnu. The layout is based on a *mandala* (sacred design of the Hindu cosmos). A five-towered temple shaped like a lotus bud, representing Mount Meru, the mythical abode of the gods and the center of the universe, stands in the middle of the complex. The intricate carvings on the walls marking the temple's perimeter are outstanding and include a 1,970-ft (600-m) long panel of bas-reliefs, and carvings of *apsaras* (celestial dancing girls). The outermost walls and the moat surrounding the entire complex symbolize the edge of the world and the cosmic ocean, respectively. Angkor Wat, unusual among Khmer temples, faces the setting sun, a symbol of death.

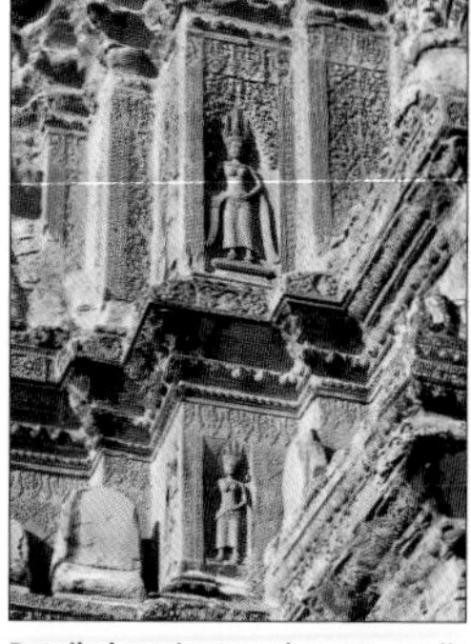

Detailed carvings on the outer walls of the central sanctuary

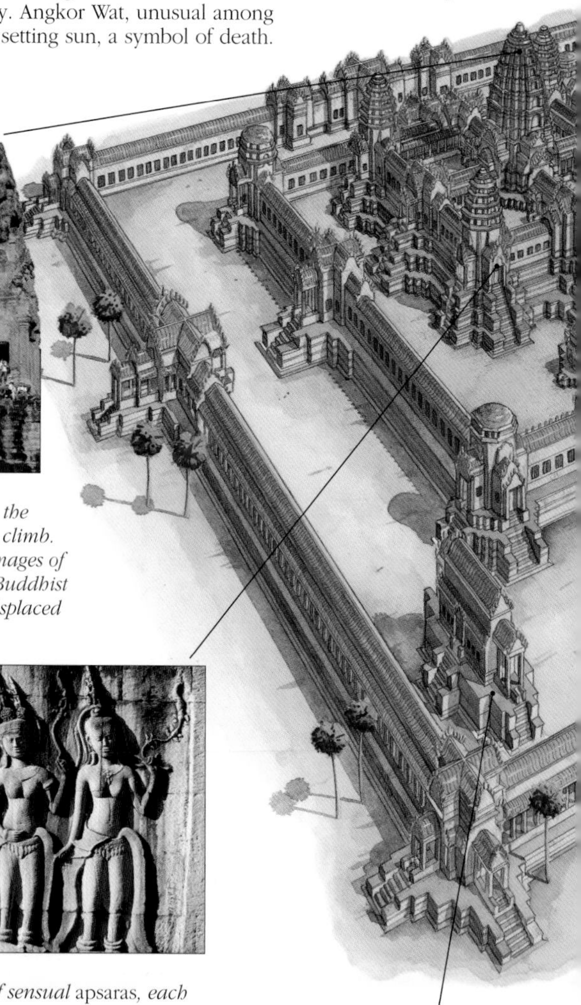

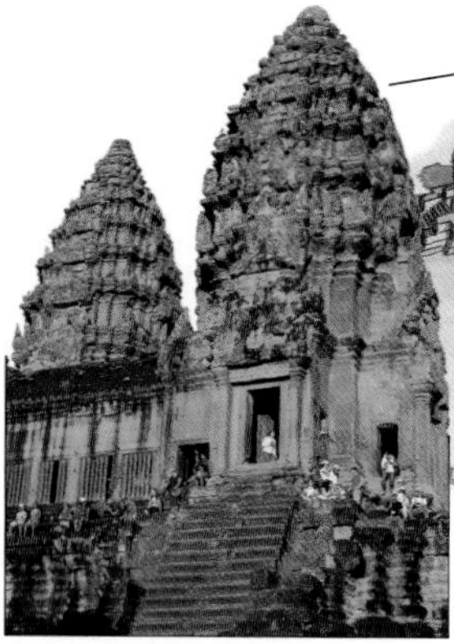

★ Central Sanctuary
Towering over the complex, the central sanctuary is a steep climb. Its four entrances feature images of the Buddha, reflecting the Buddhist influence that eventually displaced Hinduism in Cambodia.

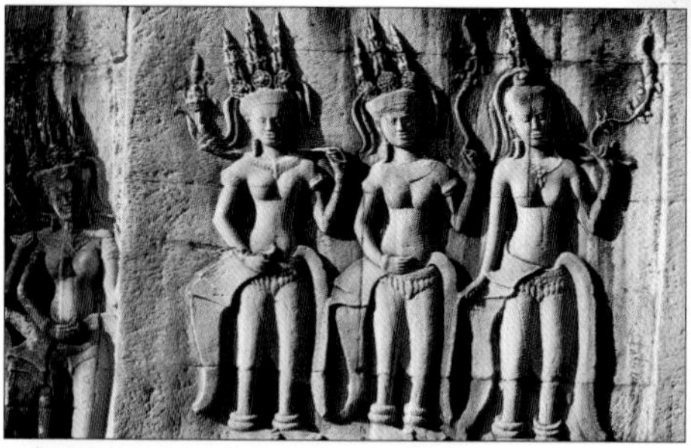

★ Apsaras
The carvings of hundreds of sensual apsaras, *each one different from the next, line the walls of the temple. Holding alluring poses, they are shown wearing ornate jewelry and exquisite headgear.*

The library provides views of the upper levels of Angkor Wat.

For hotels and restaurants in this region see pp212–14 and pp235–8

View of Towers

The five towers of Angkor Wat rise through three levels to a grand central shrine. The entire complex is surrounded by thick walls. The view of the temple from the giant pool to the left of the causeway is stunning – particularly at sunrise – with its five towers reflected in the still water.

VISITORS' CHECKLIST

Road Map C6. 4 miles (6 km) N of Siem Reap. *Siem Reap.* *from Siem Reap.* *Khmer Angkor Tour Guide Association, Siem Reap, (063)-964-347.* *5am–6pm daily.* *general Angkor ticket.* **www**.khmerangkortourguide.com

★ Gallery of Bas-Reliefs

The southern section of the western gallery depicts several scenes from the Hindu epic Mahabharata. *The intricate bas-reliefs here feature images of hundreds of brave, weapon-bearing warriors engaged in furious combat during the Battle of Kurukshetra.*

Bas-reliefs in the southern gallery depict images of King Suryavarman II, who initiated the construction of Angkor Wat.

Hall of Echoes

The Terrace of Honor was used by the king to receive ceremonial processions and foreign dignitaries.

The Causeway

The wide pathway leading to the temple's main entrance on the west side affords a spectacular view of Angkor Wat's grand exterior. Balustrades carved in the form of nagas *(serpents) once lined both sides of the avenue.*

STAR FEATURES

- ★ Central Sanctuary
- ★ Apsaras
- ★ Gallery of Bas-Reliefs

Architecture of Angkor

Devada sculpture at Angkor Thom

Angkor-period architecture generally dates from Jayavarman II's establishment of the Khmer capital near Roluos in the early 9th century AD. From then until the 15th century, art historians identify five main architectural styles. The earliest, Preah Ko, is rooted in the pre-Angkorian traditions of Sambor Prei Kuk *(see pp98–9)*, to Angkor's east, and the 8th-century temple style of Kompong Preah, relics of which are found at Prasat Ak Yum by the West Baray. Khmer architecture reached its zenith during the construction of Angkor Wat.

Pink sandstone library building in the inner enclosure of Banteay Srei

PREAH KO (AD 875–890)

The Preah Ko style was characterized by a simple temple layout, with one or more square brick towers rising from a single laterite base. The Roluos Group *(see pp82–3)* saw the first use of concentric enclosures entered via the *gopura* (gateway tower). Another innovation was the library annex, possibly used to protect the sacred fire.

This well-preserved guardian figure *is carved from sandstone and set in the outer brick wall of a sanctuary tower at the 9th-century Lolei Temple.*

The eastern causeway of Bakong *runs straight from the main* gopura *to the high central tower. This structure is raised on a square-based pyramid, rising to a symbolic temple-mountain.*

BAKHENG TO PRE RUP (AD 890–965)

The temple-mountain style, based on Mount Meru, evolved during the Bakheng period. Phnom Bakheng *(see p78)*, Phnom Krom, and Phnom Bok all feature the classic layout of five towers arranged in a quincunx – a tower on each side, with a fifth at the center. The Pre Rup style developed during the reign of Rajendravarman II (r.944–68). It continues the Bakheng style, but the towers are higher and steeper, with more tiers.

Phnom Bakheng *impressively exemplifies the Bakheng style. It was the state temple of the first Khmer capital at Angkor, and dates from the late 9th century. It rises majestically through a pyramid of square terraces to the main group of five sanctuary towers.*

Pre Rup*'s carved sandstone lintels are more finely detailed than in earlier styles. Distinguished by its size and the abrupt rise of its temple-mountain through several levels to the main sanctuary, it is speculated that the structure may have served as a royal crematorium –* pre rup *means turn the body.*

BANTEAY SREI TO BAPHUON (AD 965–1080)

Represented by the delicate and refined Banteay Srei *(see p82)*, this eponymous style is characterized by ornate carvings of sensuous *apsaras* and *devadas* (dancers). By the mid-11th century, when Khmer architecture was reaching its majestic apogee, this style had evolved into the Baphuon style, which is distinguished by vast proportions and vaulted galleries. The sculpture of the period shows increasing realism and narrative sequence.

The five-tiered Baphuon (see p72) *was the state temple of Udayadityavarman II (r.1050–66). The structure was described by 13th-century Chinese traveler Zhou Daguan as "a truly astonishing spectacle, with more than ten chambers at its base."*

Banteay Srei, *constructed between AD 967 and 1000, is known for its fine craftsmanship, evident in the exquisite detail of the bas-reliefs and carved stone lintels.*

ANGKOR WAT (AD 1080–1175)

Art historians generally agree that the style of Angkor Wat *(see pp68–9)* represents the apex of Khmer architectural and sculptural genius. The greatest of all temple-mountains, it also boasts the finest bas-relief narratives. The art of lintel carving also reached its zenith during this period.

Bas-reliefs of Suryavarman II *in the west section of the southern gallery portray the king seated on his throne, surrounded by courtiers with fans and parasols. Below him, princesses and women of the court are carried in palanquins. In another fine bas-relief, the king is shown riding a great war elephant.*

An aerial view of Angkor Wat *makes the vast scale and symbolic layout of the complex very clear. Every aspect of Angkor is rich with meaning, the most apparent being the central quincunx of towers rising to a peak, representing the five peaks of the sacred Mount Meru.*

BAYON (AD 1175–1240)

Considered a synthesis of previous styles, Bayon – the last great Angkor architectural style – is still magnificent, but also characterized by a detectable decline in quality. There is more use of laterite and less of sandstone, as well as more Buddhist imagery and, correspondingly, fewer Hindu themes.

Bas-reliefs depicting scenes of battle *at the temple of the Bayon in Angkor Thom* (see pp72–5) *provide a remarkable record of contemporary wars between the Khmer Empire and the Kingdom of Champa; resulting in the victory of Khmer King Jayavarman VII in 1181.*

The South Gate of Angkor Thom *is surmounted by a large, four-faced carving of the* devaraja *(god-king), Jayavarman VII. He is depicted as the Bodhisattva Avalokitesvara, gazing somberly in the four cardinal directions for eternity.*

Angkor Thom ❸

Figure from Terrace of the Leper King

Remarkable in scale and architectural ingenuity, the ancient city of Angkor Thom, which means Great City in Khmer, was founded by King Jayavarman VII in the late 12th century. The largest city in the Khmer Empire at one time, it is protected by a wall 26 ft (8 m) high, about 7.5 miles (12 km) long, and surrounded by a wide moat. The city has five gates – four facing the cardinal directions and an extra one on the east side – all bearing four giant stone faces. Within the city are several ruins, the most famous of which is the Bayon, an atmospheric temple at the center of this complex.

Exploring the complex

The fortified city of Angkor Thom is spread over an area of nearly 4 sq miles (10 sq km). Of the five gateways into the city, the most commonly used is the South Gate, from which a pathway leads straight to the Bayon temple. Beyond this lie the ruins of many other striking monuments, including Baphuon and Phimeanakas.

South Gate

The imposing South Gate is the best preserved of the five gateways into Angkor Thom. Its approach is via an impressive causeway flanked by 154 stone statues – gods on the left side, demons on the right – each carrying a giant serpent.

The South Gate itself is a massive 75-ft (23-m) high structure, surmounted by a triple tower with four gigantic stone faces facing the cardinal directions. The gate is flanked by statues of the three-headed elephant Erawan, the fabled mount of the Hindu god, Indra.

The Bayon

See pp74–5.

Massive smiling stone face gazing into the distance, South Gate

Baphuon

Believed to be one of the grandest of Angkor's temples, Baphuon was built by King Udayadityavarman II in the 11th century. A Hindu temple, its pyramidal mountain form represents Mount Meru, the mythical abode of the gods. A central tower with four entrances once stood at its summit, but has long since collapsed.

The temple is approached via a 656-ft (200-m) long raised causeway and has four gateways decorated with bas-relief scenes from Hindu epics such as the *Mahabharata* and *Ramayana* (*Reamker* in Khmer). Inside, spanning the western length of Baphuon, is a huge Reclining Buddha. As the temple was dedicated to Hinduism, this image was probably added later, in the 15th century. The temple has undergone intensive restoration, and is now fully open to the public.

Phimeanakas

This royal temple-palace was built during the 10th century by King Rajendravarman II and added to later by Jayavarman VII. Dedicated to Hinduism, it is also known as the Celestial Palace, and is associated with the legend of a golden tower that once stood here, and where a nine-headed serpent resided. This magical creature would appear to the king as a woman, and the king would couple with her before going to his other wives and concubines. It was believed that if the king failed to sleep with the serpent-woman, he would die, but by sleeping with her, the royal lineage was saved.

The pyramid-shaped palace is rectangular at the base, and surrounded by a 16-ft (5-m) high wall of laterite enclosing an area of around 37 acres (15 ha). It has five entranceways, and the stairs, which are flanked by guardian lions, rise up on all four sides. There are corresponding elephant figures at each of the four corners of the pyramid. The upper terrace offers great views of the Baphuon to the south.

Preah Palilay and Tep Pranam

Two of the lesser, yet still impressive, structures at Angkor Thom, Preah Palilay and Tep Pranam are located a short distance to the northwest of the Terrace of the Leper King.

Preah Palilay dates from the 13th or 14th century and is a small Buddhist sanctuary set within a 164-ft (50-m) square laterite wall. The sanctuary, which is partially collapsed, is entered via a single gateway, and rises to a tapering stone tower. A 108-ft (33-m) long causeway leads to a terrace

Visitors climbing the stairs leading to the top of Phimeanakas

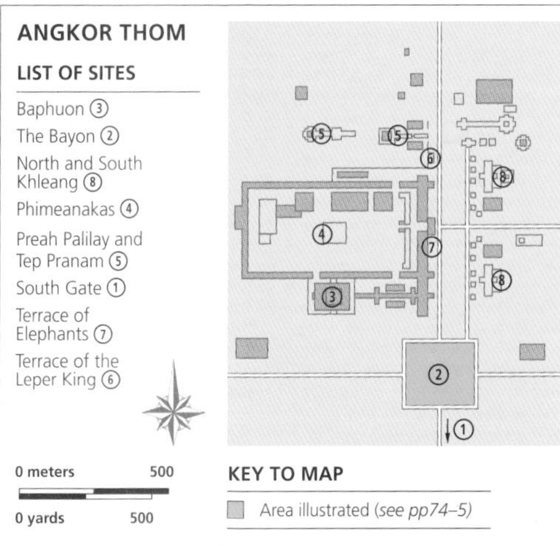

VISITORS' CHECKLIST

Road Map C6. 1 mile (2 km) N of Angkor Wat; 5 miles (8 km) N of Siem Reap. *from Angkor Wat.* *Khmer Angkor Tour Guide Association, Siem Reap, (063)-964-347.* *5am–6pm daily.* *general Angkor ticket.*

to the east of the sanctuary, which is distinguished by fine *naga* (serpent) balustrades. Nearby, to the east, lies Tep Pranam, a Buddhist sanctuary built in the 16th century. This was probably originally dedicated to the Mahayana school. Used as a place of Theravada worship now, it features a big sandstone Buddha image, seated in the "calling the earth to witness" *mudra* (posture).

Terrace of the Leper King

This small platform dates from the late 12th century. Standing on top of this structure is a headless statue known as the Leper King. Once believed to be an image of King Jayavarman VII, who, according to legend, had the disease, it is in fact a representation of Yama, the God of Death. This statue is, however, a replica, as the original was taken to Phnom Penh's National Museum *(see p50).*

Restoration in progress at the Terrace of the Leper King

The terrace is marked by two walls, both beautifully restored and decorated with exquisite bas-reliefs. Of the two, the inner one is more remarkable, and is covered with figures of underworld deities, kings, celestial females, multiple-headed *nagas*, *devadas*, *apsaras*, warriors, and strange marine creatures.

The exact function of this terrace, which appears to be an extension of the Terrace of Elephants, is not clear. It was probably used either for royal receptions or cremations.

Terrace of Elephants

Built by King Jayavarman VII, this structure is over 950 ft (300 m) long, stretching from the Baphuon to the connecting Terrace of the Leper King. It has three main platforms and two smaller ones. The terrace was primarily used by the king to view military and other parades. It is decorated with almost life-sized images of sandstone elephants in a procession accompanied by mahouts. There are also images of tigers, serpents, and Garuda, the eagle mount of Vishnu.

North and South Khleang

These two essentially similar buildings are located to the east of the main road running past the Terrace of Elephants. The North Khleang was built by King Jayavarman toward the end of the 10th century, and the South Khleang was constructed by King Suryavarman I during the early 11th century. The main architectural feature of the Khleangs are their sandstone lintels as well as elegant balustered stone windows. Unfortunately, the original function of the buildings is as yet unknown. Khleang, which means storehouse, is a modern designation and considered misleading.

Intricately carved and sculpted bas-reliefs and elephant figures, Terrace of Elephants

The Bayon

Located in the heart of Angkor Thom, the Bayon is one of the city's most extraordinary structures, epitomizing the "lost civilization" of Angkor. Shaped like a pyramid, this symbolic temple-mountain rises on three levels, and features 54 towers bearing more than 200 huge, yet enigmatic stone faces. It is entered through eight cruciform towers, linked by galleries that were once covered and which are gradually being restored. These galleries have some of the most striking bas-reliefs found at Angkor, showcasing everyday scenes as well as images of battles, especially those against the Cham.

Row of gods lining the path to Angkor Thom's South Gate

★ Enigmatic Faces
The temple's central towers are decorated with four massive, mysteriously smiling faces gazing out in the cardinal directions. These are believed to represent the all-seeing and all-knowing Bodhisattva Avalokitesvara, as personified by Jayavarman VII himself.

Outer Enclosure

Central Tower

The Western Gallery
A statue of the Hindu god Vishnu, thought to date from the time of the founding of the temple, is installed in the southern section of the western gallery, one of the many galleries surrounding the Bayon. Devotees burn incense sticks before this statue.

South Gate

★ Bas-Reliefs in the Southern Gallery
Carved deep into the walls, the bas-reliefs in the southern gallery feature images from everyday life in 12th-century Angkor. These include depictions of a cockfight, meals being cooked, festival celebrations, and market scenes.

Library

STAR FEATURES

- ★ Enigmatic Faces
- ★ Bas-Reliefs in the Southern Gallery
- ★ Southern View of the Bayon

For hotels and restaurants in this region see pp212–14 and pp235–8

★ Southern View of the Bayon
From a distance, the Bayon appears to be a complicated, almost erratically structured temple. On closer inspection, however, its 54 majestic towers and 216 eerie stone sculptures take a more definite shape – their architectural grandeur inspiring the visitor with a sense of awe.

Bas-reliefs of a Khmer circus

Detail of *Devada*
The devada *(dancer) differs from the sensual* apsara *and could be either male or female. A* devada *is portrayed in less alluring poses.*

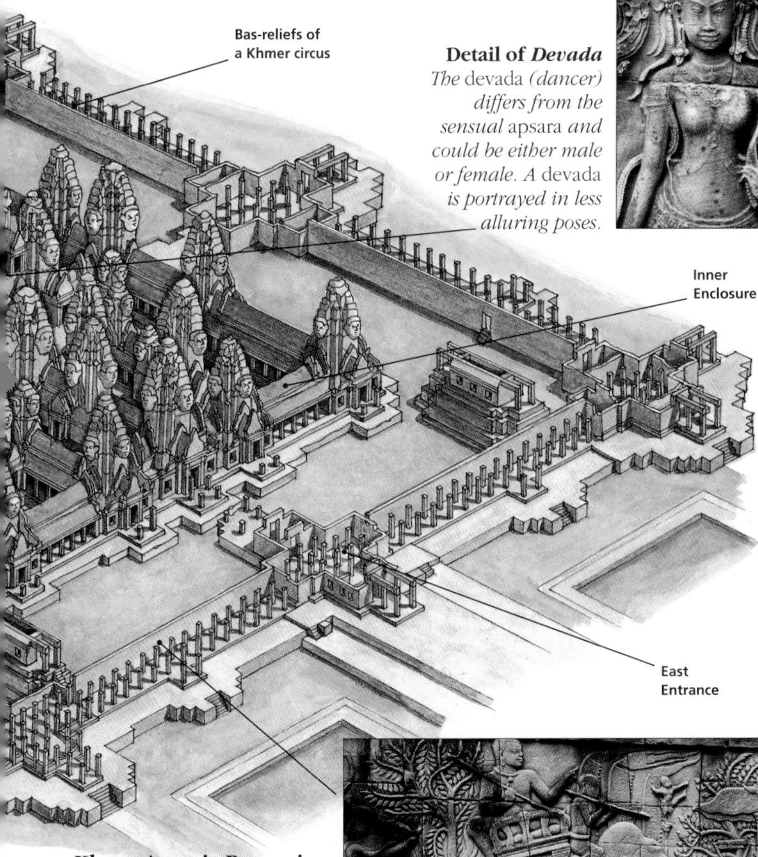

Inner Enclosure

East Entrance

Khmer Army in Procession
The bas-reliefs in the eastern gallery provide scenes from the struggle between the Khmers and the Cham, which has been recorded in painstakingly fine detail. Here, the Khmer king, seated on an elephant, leads his army into battle.

The fascinating stone faces adorning the towers of the Bayon, Angkor Thom ▷

Visitors waiting to see the sunset over Angkor Wat, Phnom Bakheng

Phnom Bakheng ❹

Road Map C6. 550 yards (500 m) S of Angkor Thom. *dawn to dusk daily. general Angkor ticket.*

Famous for its sunset views of Angkor Wat, the Tonlé Sap, and the Bayon, the ancient Hindu temple of Phnom Bakheng surveys the surrounding plains from the top of a 220-ft (67-m) high hill. Built by King Yasovarman I, the Bakheng complex is one of the region's first examples of Mount Meru-style temple architecture. The complex was once surrounded by 109 towers spread around its six tiers; however, most of them are now missing.

Preah Khan ❺

Road Map C6. 0.5 miles (1 km) NE of Angkor Thom. *dawn to dusk daily. general Angkor ticket.*

Named for the sacred sword owned by the 9th-century King Jayavarman II, the Preah Khan temple complex was built by Jayavarman VII (r.1181–1215). It is believed to have functioned as his temporary capital while Angkor Thom was being restored after it was sacked by the Cham in 1177. It also served as a monastery and religious college with over 1,000 teachers. An inscribed stone stela found here in 1939 indicates that the temple was based at the center of an ancient city, Nagarajayaciri – *jayaciri* means sword in Siamese. Originally dedicated to the Buddha, this temple was later vandalized by Hindu rulers who replaced many Buddha images on the walls with carvings of numerous Hindu deities.

Today, the complex extends over a sprawling 2 sq miles (5 sq km), and is surrounded by a 2-mile (3-km) long laterite wall. The central sanctuary is accessible through four gates set at the cardinal points. One of the main highlights is the Hall of Dancers, named for the *apsara* bas-reliefs that line the walls. The premises also has a massive *baray* (reservoir). The most notable temple in the complex is the Temple of the Four Faces. Similar to Ta Prohm *(see pp80-81)*, Preah Khan is studded with great trees whose roots cover and, in places, pierce the laterite and sandstone structures over which they grow. Unlike Ta Prohm, however, the temple has undergone restoration by the World Monuments Fund, and many of the trees have now been cut down.

Statue of a hermit in prayer, Preah Khan

Preah Neak Pean ❻

Road Map C6. 3 miles (5 km) NE of Angkor Thom. *dawn to dusk daily. general Angkor ticket.*

This monument – a shrine dedicated to Avalokitesvara – is set within the center of a cruciform arrangement of sacred ponds. Around the shrine's base coil a couple of snakes, giving the temple its name – Entwined Serpents. Located in the now dry North Baray, the temple is built around a central artificial square pond measuring 230 ft (70 m), which is surrounded by four smaller ponds. The central pond represents the mythical Lake Anvatapta, which is located at the summit of the universe and is responsible for giving birth to the four great curative rivers, each represented by a different gargoyle at each corner of the central pool. The east head is that of a man, the south a lion, the west a horse, and the north an elephant. When the temple was functioning, sacred water would be diverted through their mouths into the smaller pools and used to heal devotees.

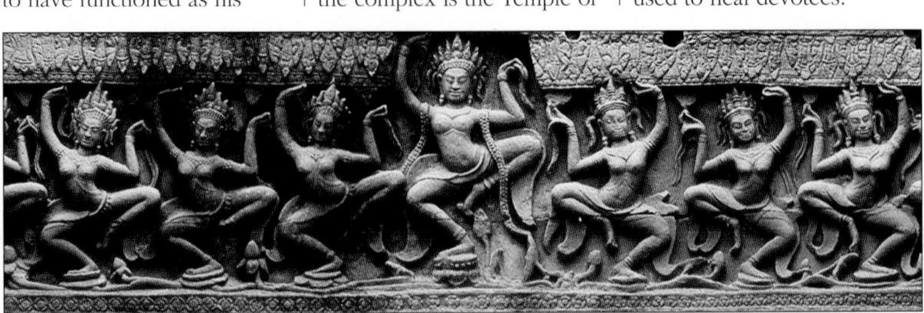

Intricately detailed bas-relief of *apsaras* in the Hall of Dancers, Preah Khan

East Baray 7

Road Map C6. 1 mile (2 km) E of Angkor Thom. *dawn to dusk daily. general Angkor ticket.*

The second largest of Angkor's *barays*, East Baray measures 4 miles by 1 mile (6 km by 2 km) and was built by King Yasovarman I in the 9th century. Watered by the Stung Treng, it held close to 13 billion gal (50 million cu m) of water and may have been 10 ft (3 m) deep. While some believe that its purpose was symbolic, representing the sea surrounding Mount Meru, others contend its purpose was for irrigation – with a population of about one million, it would have been essential to produce three rice harvests a year.

On an island in the middle of the *baray* is the **Oriental Mebon** temple, built by Rajendravarman II in honor of his parents. Surrounded by three laterite walls, the temple gradually rises to a quincuncial arrangement of towers dotted with holes that would have supported stucco decorations.

Picturesque view of the lake from the landing platform, Srah Srang

Towering lotus-shaped structures, Pre Rup

At ground level its stairways are flanked by sandstone lions and at its corners are four well-preserved sandstone elephants.

Pre Rup 8

Road Map C6. 3 miles (5 km) E of Angkor Thom. *dawn to dusk daily. general Angkor ticket.*

Dedicated to the Hindu god Shiva, Pre Rup has five lotus-shaped towers. Thought to have been a crematorium, its name means Turning of the Body, relating to a religious rite of tracing the deceased's outline in their ashes.

Srah Srang 9

Road Map C6. 3 miles (5 km) E of Angkor Thom. *dawn to dusk daily. general Angkor ticket.*

To the west of Pre Rup lies the great reservoir of Srah Srang or Royal Bath. Built in the 7th century and measuring 1,312 ft by 2,625 ft (400 m by 800 m) it was used exclusively by King Jayavarman V and his wives. On the western side of the lake is a landing platform flanked by two sandstone lions and balustrades bearing a large *garuda* on the back of a three-headed serpent. The lake is best visited at sunrise, when water buffalo graze in its shallows and local children congregate for a swim.

Banteay Kdei 10

Road Map C6. 3 miles (5 km) E of Angkor Thom. *dawn to dusk daily. general Angkor ticket.*

Built in the late 12th century, Banteay Kdei, meaning Citadel of the Cells, lies west of Srah Srang. This Buddhist temple has four entrances, each guarded by *garudas*. One of the highlights of this temple is the Hall of Dancers located in the central corridor.

BARAYS

Integral to Khmer architecture, the *barays* provided a twofold function: firstly, as a religious symbol of the Sea of Creation, and secondly, as a vital means of irrigation to ensure a bounteous crop. The most notable reservoirs in Angkor are the East Baray and West Baray. The latter was built in the 11th century and covered an area of 7 sq miles (18 sq km), making it the largest *baray* ever constructed. With a maximum depth of 23 ft (7 m), it could contain 32 billion gal (123 million cu m) of water and still supports several species of fish. Both reservoirs feature man-made islands with temples.

Vast expanse of water channels, West Baray

Ta Prohm ⓫

Perhaps the most evocative and mysterious of all the temple structures at Angkor, Ta Prohm, which means Ancestor of Brahma, was a wealthy Buddhist monastery built during King Jayavarman VII's reign (r.1178–1220). During the Colonial period, the French started their archaeological restoration of the temple, making a deliberate attempt to maintain the structure as they found it by limiting restoration and cutting down little of the surrounding dense jungle. As a result, the temple buildings remain smothered by the roots of giant banyan trees, preserving the atmosphere that 19th-century explorers must have experienced.

Bas-reliefs depicting dancing *apsaras* at the eastern entrance

Waterfall Tree
Named for the cascading appearance of its roots down the wall of the inner gallery, this strangler fig tree has encompassed its host and dominates the temple's masonry.

★ Face Tower
The four stone faces on Gopura 5 are believed to represent Jayavarman VII. Seen above the west entrance, they are reminiscent of the huge faces carved into the Bayon (see pp74–5).

Dinosaur Carving
A narrow stone column in the complex has ornate circles that enclose various animal reliefs. One such carving depicts what seems to be a stegosaurus. No one has been able to explain the presence of this mysterious carving.

STAR SIGHTS

- ★ Face Tower
- ★ Crocodile Tree
- ★ Tomb Raider Tree

VISITORS' CHECKLIST

Road Map C6. 0.5 miles (1 km) E of Angkor Thom. *Khmer Angkor Tour Guide Association, Siem Reap, (063)-964-347.* *dawn–dusk daily.* *general Angkor ticket.*

★ **Crocodile Tree**
On the easternmost gopura of the central enclosure is the strangler fig known as the Crocodile Tree. Every year its roots spread further across the complex.

To East Entrance

The Hall of Dancers, located in a sandstone building, features rows of intricate *apsara* bas-reliefs.

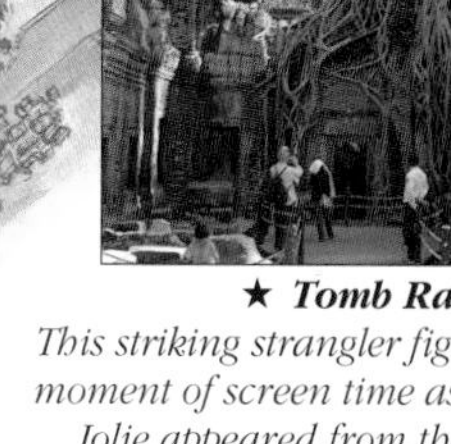

★ ***Tomb Raider* Tree**
This striking strangler fig enjoyed a moment of screen time as Angelina Jolie appeared from the doorway below it in one of the most dramatic scenes of Lara Croft: Tomb Raider.

Galleries, many of which are crumbling and not suitable for exploration, are linked by narrow passageways and in turn connect the *prasats* of the structure.

Angelina Jolie in *Tomb Raider*

LARA CROFT: TOMB RAIDER

Long before she became half of a Hollywood power couple, Angelina Jolie was delighting teenagers who played the seminal strategy game, *Tomb Raider*. With her sultry looks, passable English accent, and lithe figure, she seemed the perfect choice to bring the long-running video game character to the screen. A couple of scenes in the movie were shot in Cambodia and it is here that Jolie's global social conscience seems to have been sparked. She remains a firm patron of Cambodia, a UN ambassador, and a champion of children's causes.

Painted storks nesting among the trees, Prek Toal Bird Sanctuary

Chong Kneas 15

Road Map C6. 9 miles (15 km) S of Siem Reap. *Gecko Environment Centre (063)-832-812.* *dawn to dusk daily.*

By far the most accessible floating village from Siem Reap *(see pp66–7)*, and the most commercial, Chong Kneas is typical of the villages found on the Tonlé Sap Lake. Inhabited by a mix of Vietnamese and Khmer people, this atmospheric settlement can be reached either by road from Siem Reap or on a boat. The road trip, passing lush paddy fields and an ancient temple atop Phnom Krom, takes about 30 minutes from the town center. Although less intriguing than the Kompong Khleang, Chong Kneas is worth a visit for its floating market, clinic, catfish farm, school, and restaurants. Also an exciting highlight is the Gecko Environment Centre's educating exhibition on the ecology and problems relating to the management of the Tonlé Sap's biodiversity.

Boats to Chong Kneas and other distant villages can be hired from Siem Reap, but prices are usually quite high.

Passenger ferry, Chong Kneas

Prek Toal Bird Sanctuary 16

Road Map C6. 19 miles (31 km) S of Siem Reap. *from Chong Kneas.* *dawn to dusk daily.*

Widely regarded as the most important breeding ground for large waterbirds in Southeast Asia, Prek Toal Bird Sanctuary covers 120 sq miles (311 sq km) on the northwest tip of the Tonlé Sap Lake. Of the three designated biospheres on the lake, Prek Toal is the best known and is easily accessible from Siem Reap. The seasonally flooded forest abounds with numerous endangered birds such as the lesser and greater adjutants, milky and painted storks, black-headed ibis, spot-billed pelican, and grey-headed fish eagle. An ideal day trip for ornithologists and wildlife enthusiasts, Prek Toal is best visited during the dry season (Feb–Apr) – the time when migratory birds congregate in this preserve in large numbers.

Visiting the sanctuary can be an expensive proposition, although the price includes transport to and on the lake, entrance to the biosphere, meals, and guided tours. Trips can be arranged usually through a guesthouse or a tour operator. Visitors can also make their own arrangements, which would include hiring a taxi to the Chong Kneas dock, from where a boat to the Prek Toal Environmental Research Station can be hired. Those keen on witnessing the spectacular sunrises and sunsets can stay overnight at the research station, although they will have to pay for accommodations and food.

Locals ferrying goods to and fro at the floating market, Chong Kneas

For hotels and restaurants in this region see pp212–14 and pp235–8

LAKE ECOSYSTEM

Situated in the very heart of the country, the dumb-bell shaped Tonlé Sap is Cambodia's most prominent feature and the largest freshwater lakes in Southeast Asia. During the dry season, the lake withers to a diminutive 965 sq miles (2,500 sq km), but when the monsoon arrives it swells to a colossal 4,633 sq miles (12,000 sq km). The lake's ecosystem supports the surrounding floodplain with more than 200 species of fish, several types of waterbirds, and reptiles such as crocodiles and turtles. Thousands of fishermen and their families live in floating villages dotted around the lake. The Tonlé Sap provides Cambodia with more than half of its annual supply of fish.

Inhabitants of a floating village in their boats

Kompong Phhluk ⑰

Road Map C6. 10 miles (16 km) SE of Siem Reap. *from Chong Kneas.* *dawn to dusk daily.*

The atmospheric journey through the wetlands of the Tonlé Sap Lake to reach this village on stilts is a memorable experience. With its floating tethered animal pens, pagoda, fishermen, and gentle pace of life, Kompong Phhluk offers an authentic insight into life on the great lake. Visitors can take in the activities of a typical village – local women selling vegetables on the decks of long-tail boats and school children returning home with the aid of a paddle and boat; tired sightseers can stop for refreshments at a stilted restaurant that serves local food. It is also possible to visit the vast blue of the Tonlé Sap Lake on a boat, and follow up with a swim in the gnarled, flooded forest – an eerie but exhilarating experience as swimmers must wade through inky darkness. Alternatively, visitors can go out on to the lake in a canoe on their own. The village can be reached either from Roluos, 3 miles (5 km) to the north, or Chong Kneas, although it is easier to take an organized tour.

Kompong Khleang ⑱

Road Map C6. 22 miles (35 km) E of Siem Reap. *20,000.* *from Chong Kneas.* *from Dam Dek.* *dawn to dusk daily.*

Despite being the largest floating settlement on the Tonlé Sap Lake, Kompong Khleang receives only a small number of visitors, giving

Picturesque stilted pagoda and houses, Kompong Khleang

those who do venture here an authentic experience of waterside living. In the wet season, the water levels of the lake swell to within a few feet of the 33-ft (20-m) high houses on stilts, before receding back into the marshy ground.

Similar to Kompong Phhluk, Kompong Khleang is a permanent community, its economy wholly dependent on fishing. In several ways, however, this floating village is even more astounding than Kompong Phhluk – everything floats here, from the school and the general store to the pharmacy, and even the petrol station.

An island situated in the center of the village has a small, brightly painted pagoda with a macabre depiction of heaven and hell. There is also a flooded forest located next to the village. Kompong Khleang can usually be reached by boat from Chong Kneas. During the dry season, however, visitors are advised to hire a taxi or *moto* from nearby Dam Dek.

Visitors taking a tour of the flooded forest, Kompong Phhluk

NORTHERN CAMBODIA

The geographically diverse and remote region of Northern Cambodia shares borders with Thailand to the north and Laos to the northeast. Today, improved highways allow visitors to reach previously unexplored regions. From the spectacular UNESCO-protected temple of Prasat Preah Vihear to the endangered Irrawaddy dolphin in Kratie, a visit to the north will delight any traveler.

The earliest known evidence of human settlement in the region dates back to 4300 BC, when hunter-gatherers inhabited caves in the northwest. Between the 6th and 7th centuries, Chenla rulers built several temples in the region. Northern Cambodia was overrun by invading Thai forces on numerous occasions during the 16th and 17th centuries. The Thai armies used the region as a gateway to the rest of the country in their quest to pillage the Khmer Empire. In the late 18th century, parts of the northwest were annexed by the Thais, and finally returned to Cambodia in 1946. In the 20th century, Khmer Rouge forces passed through the region as they retreated north from Phnom Penh, ahead of the Vietnamese Army.

Battambang, the country's second-largest city, is fast emerging as a popular tourist destination. Known for producing the nation's finest rice and oranges, the city also has crumbling French Colonial villas, shophouses, and a riverfront promenade. The nearby ruins of Wat Banan and Banteay Chmmer make for excellent day trips.

The remote northeastern provinces of Ratanakiri and Mondulkiri, where tourism is still in its infancy, receive few visitors. However, both have many ethnic minority villages, scattered wild elephants, waterfalls, and beautiful grassy landscapes. Yaek Lom Lake, a beautiful crater lake with inviting verdigris water, is a perfect picnic spot.

The northeast has a few excellent ecolodges and eco-trekking organizations, while farther south the town of Kratie is renowned for its sunsets and the Irrawaddy dolphin. The temple ruins of Sambor Prei Kuk and Koh Ker are well worth a visit. The region is also known for its stone handicrafts, and silk items such as *kramas* (scarves) and shirts.

Rich woodlands bordering the Mekong River on the sandbar island of Koh Trong, Kratie

◁ **Steep stone steps leading to the mountain-top temple of Wat Banan**

Exploring Northern Cambodia

Although some provincial roads in Northern Cambodia remain dusty and unpaved in parts, the region's natural beauty more than makes up for this drawback. The city of Battambang, renowned for its unique, one-track bamboo train, can be reached by improved highways or a picturesque boat ride from Siem Reap. The temple ruins of Prasat Preah Vihear, Koh Ker, and Sambor Prei Kuk make for interesting diversions, while the province of Kompong Thom, with its emerald paddy fields, is home to the unusual Phnom Santuk and the Santuk Silk Farm. A visit to the far-flung provinces of Ratanakiri and Mondulkiri, which offer rolling hills, volcanic lakes, and lush green forests, is also a rewarding experience.

A statue of Buddha carved into rock, Phnom Santuk

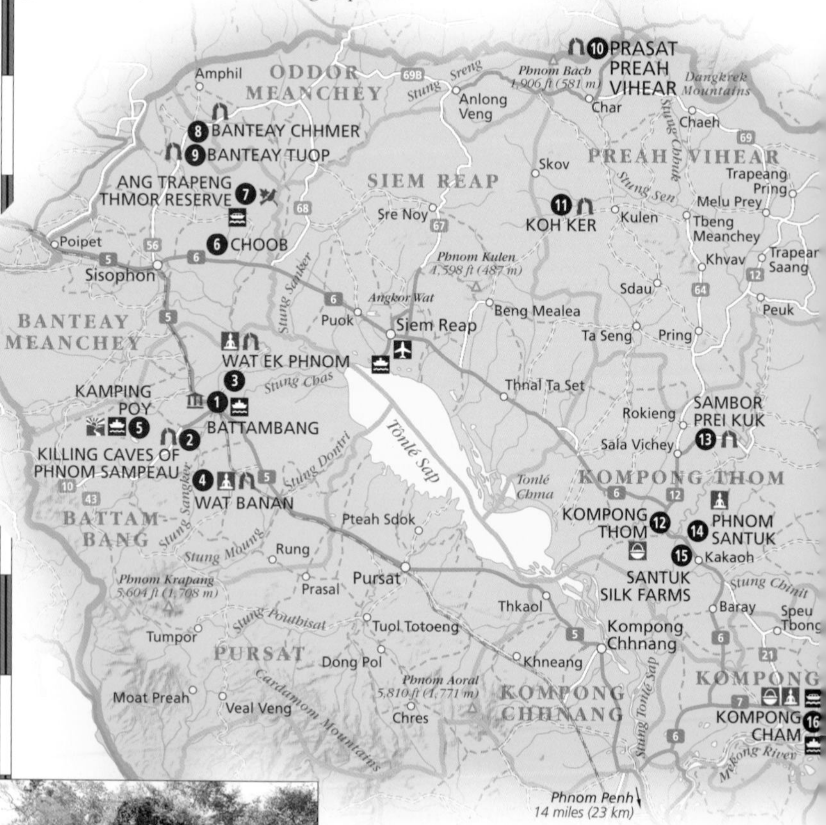

1 BATTAMBANG
2 KILLING CAVES OF PHNOM SAMPEAU
3 WAT EK PHNOM
4 WAT BANAN
5 KAMPING POY
6 CHOOB
7 ANG TRAPENG THMOR RESERVE
8 BANTEAY CHHMER
9 BANTEAY TUOP
10 PRASAT PREAH VIHEAR
11 KOH KER
12 KOMPONG THOM
13 SAMBOR PREI KUK
14 PHNOM SANTUK
15 SANTUK SILK FARMS
16 KOMPONG CHAM

ODDOR MEANCHEY
SIEM REAP
PREAH VIHEAR
BANTEAY MEANCHEY
BATTAMBANG
KOMPONG THOM
PURSAT
KOMPONG CHHNANG
KOMPONG

Amphil
Stung Sreng
Anlong Veng
Phnom Bach 1,906 ft (581 m)
Char
Dangkrek Mountains
Stung Chhuk
Chaeh
Skov
Stung Sen
Trapeang Pring
Melu Prey
Kulen
Tbeng Meanchey
Sre Noy
Poipet
Sisophon
Stung Sangker
Phnom Kulen 1,598 ft (487 m)
Khvav
Trapear Saang
Sdau
Angkor Wat
Beng Mealea
Peuk
Puok
Siem Reap
Ta Seng
Pring
Stung Chas
Thnal Ta Set
Rokieng
Sala Vichey
Tonlé Sap
Stung Dontri
Tonlé Chma
Pteah Sdok
Rung
Stung Moung
Pursat
Kakaoh
Phnom Krapang 5,604 ft (1,708 m)
Prasal
Stung Chinit
Thkaol
Baray
Speu Tbong
Stung Poutbisat
Tuol Totoeng
Tumpor
Kompong Chhnang
Dong Pol
Khneang
Phnom Aoral 5,810 ft (1,771 m)
Moat Preah
Veal Veng
Cardamom Mountains
Chres
Stung Tonlé Sap
Mekong River
Phnom Penh 14 miles (23 km)

Jungle-covered ruins of Koh Ker

GETTING AROUND

Traveling in the north can be difficult, particularly in the northeast. It is best to avoid visiting this region during the rainy season since road conditions can never be guaranteed. However, in the northwest, highways have improved dramatically. Taxis and tuk-tuks can be hired to reach sights that are off the beaten track. Ferries and riverboats ply rivers such as the Stung Sangker and Mekong. Dirt-bike tours are gaining popularity in the north and are a great way to tackle demanding roads.

For additional map symbols *see back flap*

SIGHTS AT A GLANCE

Towns and Cities

Ban Lung 19
Battambang 1
Choob 6
Kompong Cham 16
Kompong Thom 12
Kratie 17
Sen Monorom 21
Stung Treng 18

Sites of Interest

Santuk Silk Farms 15

Places of Worship

Phnom Santuk 14
Wat Banan 4
Wat Ek Phnom 3

Historical Sites

Banteay Chhmer 8
Banteay Tuop 9
Kamping Poy 5
Killing Caves of Phnom Sampeau 2
Koh Ker 11
Prasat Preah Vihear pp94–5 10
Sambor Prei Kuk 13

National Parks and Preserves

Ang Trapeng Thmor Reserve 7

Areas of Natural Beauty

Bonsraa Waterfalls 22
Yeak Lom Lake 20

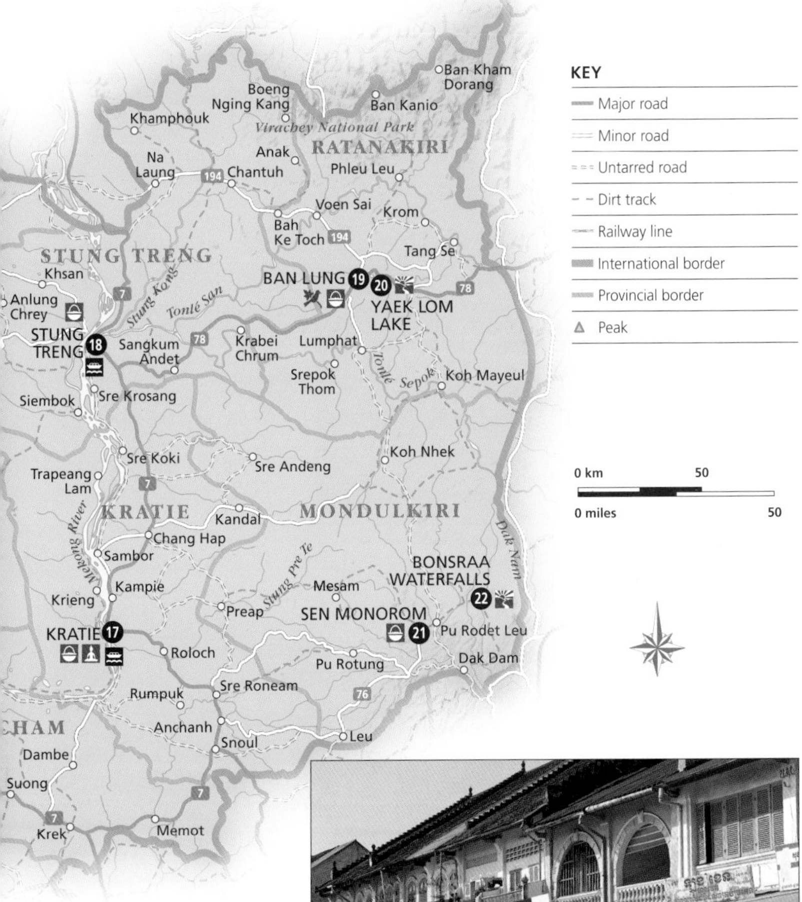

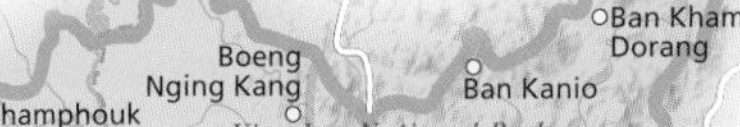

KEY

- Major road
- Minor road
- Untarred road
- Dirt track
- Railway line
- International border
- Provincial border
- Peak

0 km 50
0 miles 50

SEE ALSO

- ***Where to Stay*** pp214–15
- ***Where to Eat*** pp238–9

A row of French Colonial shophouses, Battambang

Battambang ❶

Road Map C6. 180 miles (290 km) NW of Phnom Penh. 140,000.

Cambodia's second largest city and a provincial capital, Battambang lies a short distance southwest of the Tonlé Sap Lake. Sitting by the Stung Sangker and surrounded by beautiful, verdant countryside, the city has been under Thai influence for much of its history and was returned to Cambodia only in 1907.

The impact of the French Colonial administration on the city is evident from the number of Colonial villas and shophouses still surviving today, hidden down side streets and by the riverside. In the center of town stands Psar Nath, a sprawling mustard-hued Art Deco market that was built in 1936 and is well worth a visit. The most charming area of the city is by the river, south of this bustling market. The **Battambang Provincial Museum** located here houses an eclectic Angkorian and pre-Angkorian collection of statuary, pottery, and traditional musical instruments. Battambang is only now finding an identity as a tourist destination, with a number of excellent cafés and Colonial-style hotels starting to open up. The natural beauty of the rural countryside surrounding the city must not be missed.

A row of statues at the Provincial Museum, Battambang

French Colonial buildings on the riverfront, Battambang

Environs

One mile (2 km) northwest of the city, **Phare Ponleu Selpak** is a multi-arts center for orphans and disadvantaged children. A visit to its circus school offers a glimpse into the salvaged lives of these children, many of whom become performers with the troupe. Evening performances take place five times a week.

Battambang Provincial Museum
St 1, Kamkor Village, Svay Por Commune. ***Tel*** *(053)-730-007.*
8–11am & 2–5pm Mon–Fri.

Phare Ponleu Selpak
NH5, Anhchanh Village, O'Char Commune. ***Tel*** *(053)-952-424.*
www.phareps.org

BATTAMBANG'S BAMBOO TRAINS

Noris (bamboo trains) are indigenous to Battambang province and seem to have developed in response to a lack of local public transport. A cheap and effective way for locals to travel, they were created from flatbed mine sweepers that were used in the Civil War of the 1980s. *Noris* are assembled on the track, which is often warped, and have no brakes. It is worth traveling by these trains for the experience.

A bamboo platform is *mounted on a steel frame with wheels a few inches from the track, making up the train's structure. Power is supplied from a motorcycle engine and belt drive housed at the rear axle.*

Running on a single track, *the bamboo trains are ideal for transporting produce and livestock. When trains heading in opposite directions meet, the one with the lighter load is removed to let the other pass.*

Killing Caves of Phnom Sampeau ❷

Road Map B6. 7 miles (11 km) SW of Battambang. *dawn to dusk daily.*

Halfway up Phnom Sampeau, a hill with several temples at its summit, and belying a peaceful rural scene, the Killing Caves of Phnom Sampeau tell yet another brutal tale of the atrocities perpetrated by the Khmer Rouge. The caves bore witness to the cruelty of the regime, during which victims were bludgeoned to death before being thrown from a skylight in the roof of the cave. There was one cave for male victims and another for women. The largest cavern is festooned with the victims' clothes. A glass memorial located in the cave displays the bones and skulls of the deceased. Next to it is a statue of a golden Reclining Buddha. Nowadays, local children hang around the base of Phnom Sampeau hoping to show visitors around the caves and summit for a small tip.

Reclining Buddha and glass memorial, Phnom Sampeau

Wat Ek Phnom ❸

Road Map C6. 7 miles (11 km) N of Battambang. *dawn to dusk daily.*

The journey to Wat Ek Phnom takes visitors through dense forest, lush rice fields, and bucolic villages dotted with houses where rice paper, used to wrap spring rolls, is made. After it is made, the circular paper is dried on mesh boards in the sun. Built in the 11th century, during the reign of King Suryavarman, this partially collapsed Angkorian temple comprises finely carved *prasats* (towers) mounted on a platform. The root-strangled ruins have been looted, although the lintel above the eastern entrance to the central tower has survived; it depicts the Churning of the Ocean of Milk by the gods and *asuras* (demons), a Hindu myth *(see p94)*.

Carving depicting the Churning of the Ocean of Milk, Wat Ek Phnom

Close to the temple is a small, peaceful pond that is covered with lily pads. There are several large, shady trees around the ruins, with a number of alfresco cafés that make for an excellent lunch venue. Opposite Wat Ek Phnom is a modern pagoda of the same name.

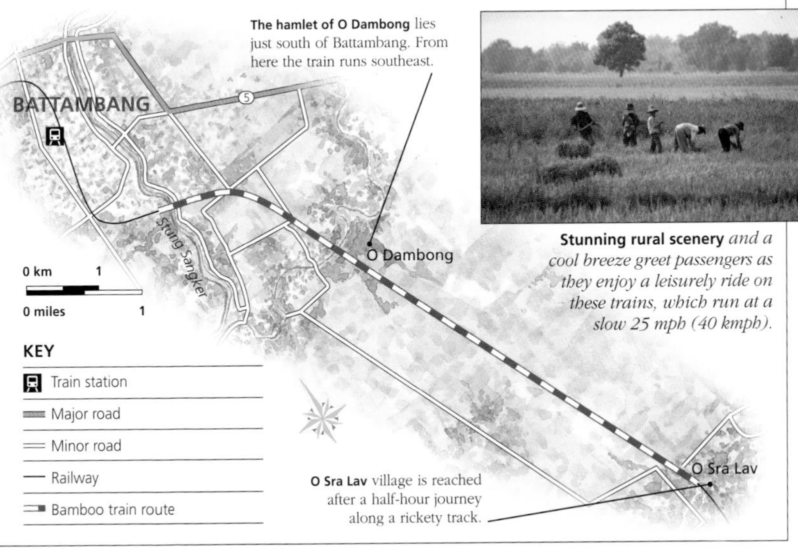

The hamlet of O Dambong lies just south of Battambang. From here the train runs southeast.

Stunning rural scenery *and a cool breeze greet passengers as they enjoy a leisurely ride on these trains, which run at a slow 25 mph (40 kmph).*

O Sra Lav village is reached after a half-hour journey along a rickety track.

Crumbling ruins of Wat Banan, resembling the layout of Angkor Wat

Wat Banan 4

Road Map C6. 17 miles (27 km) S of Battambang. *dawn to dusk daily.*

Reminiscent of Angkor Wat in terms of layout, this mountain-top temple on Phnom Banan is reached by a flight of 358 steps. Flanked by *naga* balustrades, the stone steps lead to five 11th-century *prasats*, which, despite having been looted in the past, are mostly upright. The views from the top are some of the best in the province, and visitors can buy drinks from vendors at the summit. Local children often trade hand fans in exchange for a tip.

From the temple, visitors can descend a narrow staircase to explore a group of three caves, with the help of local guides. Flashlights are essential since the caves are very dark. Visitors must be warned that one of the caves is still unmined and not safe to enter. The caves can also be quite a tight squeeze.

Kamping Poy 5

Road Map B6. 17 miles (27 km) W of Battambang. *dawn to dusk daily.*

Yet another poignant reminder of the brutal Khmer Rouge, Kamping Poy, also known as Killing Dam, stretches for some 5 miles (8 km) between two hills. Over 10,000 people, forced into slavery under the regime, lost their lives from malnutrition and execution, building what is now a largely worthless dam. It is believed that the dam was built in an attempt to re-create the irrigation system of ancient Angkor, although the scheme proved to be a failure. Today, there is nothing left of the sight except the sluice gates. The dam is now used by locals as a picnic spot. Visitors can take a boat, rowed by local boys, to the middle of the lake, but prices can often be exorbitant.

Azure waters ideal for a boat trip, Kamping Poy

Choob 6

Road Map C6. 55 miles (89 km) W of Siem Reap. *5,000.*

Stone carving, Choob

Located toward the northwest border with Thailand, the small village of Choob is worth a visit for its renowned sculptors, who sit by the roadside with their wares. Choob's sculptors are celebrated throughout the country for their craftsmanship and are often commissioned by temples to make huge, elaborate sandstone statues that can take months to complete. The village is a great place to buy magnificent souvenirs such as miniatures of *apsaras* or myriad statues of the Buddha.

Ang Trapeng Thmor Reserve 7

Road Map C6. 62 miles (100 km) NW of Siem Reap. **Tel** *(012)-520-828.* *dawn to dusk daily.* **www**.samveasna.org

Based around a water storage reservoir built in 1976 under the Khmer Rogue by slave labor, this wetland bird sanctuary occupies 19 sq miles (49 sq km). A mixture of grassland, dipterocarp, and paddy fields, the area was officially declared a Sarus Crane Reserve by royal decree in 2000. The sarus crane is an extremely rare and elegant bird depicted on bas-reliefs at the Bayon *(see pp74–5)*. Besides being a feeding ground for 300 sarus cranes, Ang Trapeng has more than 200 other species of birds, 18 of which have been classified as globally threatened. In addition to the birds, visitors may chance upon the large fruit bats that inhabit semi-submerged trees on the edge of the reservoir. The very fortunate may also sight the rare eld's deer.

It is possible to tour the preserve on a boat, but visitors must register at the Wildlife Conservation Society Office in the adjacent village first. While most people visit the preserve on a day trip from Siem Reap, overnight stays can also be organized through the Sam Veasna Center in Siem Reap.

LANDMINE ALERT

Landmine danger sign

Along with neighboring Laos, Cambodia is one of the most heavily mined places in the world. According to some estimates, the country has between 4 and 10 million mines. Unexploded Ordnance (UXO) from aerial bombs dropped by the US during the late 1960s and early 70s poses further danger. With China's burgeoning demand for scrap metal, impoverished and uneducated Khmers often take unnecessary risks to earn a few extra dollars by excavating these "sleeping" bombs. As a result, some 40,000 Khmers, many of them children, live as amputees today. However, only certain areas of the country are affected, with 70 percent of accidents occurring in the northwest (the last refuge of the Khmer Rouge forces). Since 1999, after the last fires of Khmer Rouge resistance were extinguished, no more mines have been laid. That same year, Cambodia ratified the Mine Ban Treaty.

Delicate stone carving on a wall, Banteay Chhmer

Banteay Chhmer 8

Road Map C5. 80 miles (130 km) N of Battambang. *dawn to dusk daily.*

Across a causeway, through a tumbledown gate, lies one of the largest and most mysterious complexes of the Angkor period. Banteay Chhmer, along with its satellite shrines and vast *baray* (reservoir) was constructed in the late 12th century during the reign of Jayavarman VII. Like the Buddhist-influenced Bayon, it features the enigmatic faces of Avalokitesvara and is well-known for the intricacy of its carvings. However, unlike the Bayon, Banteay Chhmer is rarely overrun with visitors, giving those who do come here a very different temple experience. Often, except for a few families who live and farm around these overgrown ruins, there is no one else here.

The temple complex is surrounded by two moats, with the outer moat measuring 1 mile (2 km) on each side. These moats are now dry and have been converted into rice paddies by local farmers. The complex also has several ceremonial walkways, collapsed towers, and courtyards, typical of other Angkorian structures. Among the highlights are the vast bas-reliefs on the outer walls, depicting life 900 years ago – including processions of elephants and scenes of conflict with neighboring Champa. Visitors can arrange for homestays with the locals, which gives them a chance to admire the temple at sunrise and sunset.

Banteay Tuop 9

Road Map B5. 74 miles (121 km) N of Battambang. *dawn to dusk daily.*

Built in the 12th century, about the same time as Banteay Chhmer 6 miles (9 km) to the north, Banteay Tuop, or Army Fortress, is believed to have been a tribute to the army of King Jayavarman VII after it defeated the Cham. Originally adorned with five *prasats*, the complex now has only four as one collapsed after looting by petty thieves. The remaining towers, however, are in good condition, and some of them feature timber from the 12th century.

View of *prasats* rising above the paddy fields, Banteay Tuop

Transport to Banteay Tuop can be a problem as there are no local buses. Visitors coming from Banteay Chhmer can ask for a *moto* ride from the market; the round trip takes about two hours; hired taxis are also available for the trip. Banteay Tuop is best visited at dusk; sunsets here are particularly spectacular.

Prasat Preah Vihear ⓾

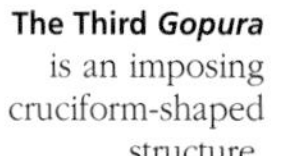

Naga balustrade

Set high on a cliff in the Dangkrek Mountains, close to the Cambodia-Thai border, Prasat Preah Vihear, or Sacred Shrine, enjoys the most spectacular setting of any ancient Khmer temple. Offering breathtaking views across the lush green plains below, this UNESCO World Heritage Site is believed to have been built on the site of a 9th-century sanctuary dedicated to Shiva, the Hindu God of Destruction. The greater part of the complex was constructed during the reigns of King Surayavarman I (r.1002–50) and Surayavarman II (r.1113–50), the great builder of Angkor Wat. The earliest surviving parts of the temple, however, date from the 10th century. Following the decline of Hindu worship in the Khmer Empire, the temple was dedicated to Buddhism.

Monumental Stairway
A steep stone staircase, the Monumental Stairway comprises 162 steps rising 394 ft (120 m) to the First causeway of Nagas.

The Third *Gopura* is an imposing cruciform-shaped structure.

To Second *Gopura*

Second causeway of Nagas

Bas-relief of Yama, the God of Death, riding a buffalo and resting on Kala, the Demon of Time.

UPPER LEVEL

This level comprises the impressive third and fourth *gopuras* and a causeway lined with *nagas* (serpents) leading to the Central Shrine, which is flanked by galleries offering superb views over the temple complex and the plains far below.

★ Churning of the Ocean of Milk
At the northern entrance to the third gopura *is a bas-relief that portrays the Hindu myth of creation, depicting Vishnu creating the Universe.*

STAR SIGHTS

- ★ Churning of the Ocean of Milk
- ★ Central Shrine and Prasat
- ★ Pei Ta Da Cliff

A QUESTION OF OWNERSHIP

Long claimed by both Thailand and Cambodia, Prasat Preah Vihear was finally declared Cambodian property by the International Court of Justice in 1962. Despite this, many Thais argue that the decision was unjustified and impractical – Preah Vihear was difficult to access from Cambodia, though now access from either side is via a smooth, surfaced highway. The dispute flared up again after UNESCO declared the temple a World Heritage Site in 2008. Gunfire in the recent past reportedly damaged more than 60 stones of the complex. Occasional skirmishes still occur. Investigate the current status before visiting, and be aware of the risks.

Cambodian soldiers guarding the complex

For hotels and restaurants in this region see pp214–15 and pp238–9

First Gopura
The lintels, crenellated stone eaves, and square pillars of the First Gopura *(gateway tower) are in relatively good shape. In the past, it was a resting place for pilgrims.*

VISITORS' CHECKLIST

Road Map C5. 162 miles (260 km) NW of Kompong Thom. *from Tbeng Meanchey, then moto.* 8am–4pm daily.

LIST OF SITES

Lower Level
Monumental Stairway ①
First causeway of Nagas ②
First Gopura ③

Middle Level
Second Gopura ④
Lion-headed pool ⑤

Upper Level
Third Gopura ⑥
Second causeway of Nagas ⑦
Fourth Gopura ⑧
Central Shrine and Prasat ⑨

0 meters 200
0 yards 200

Area illustrated

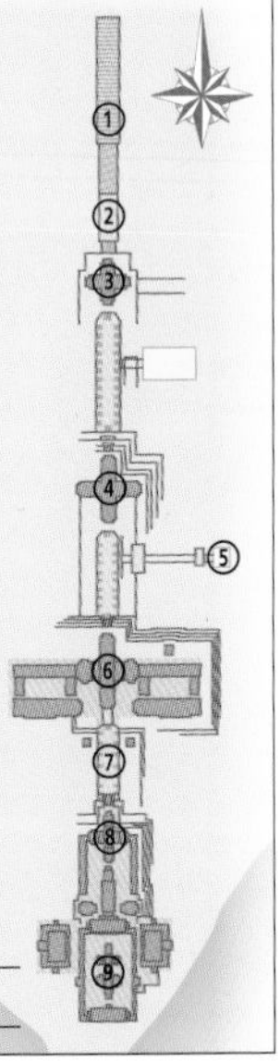

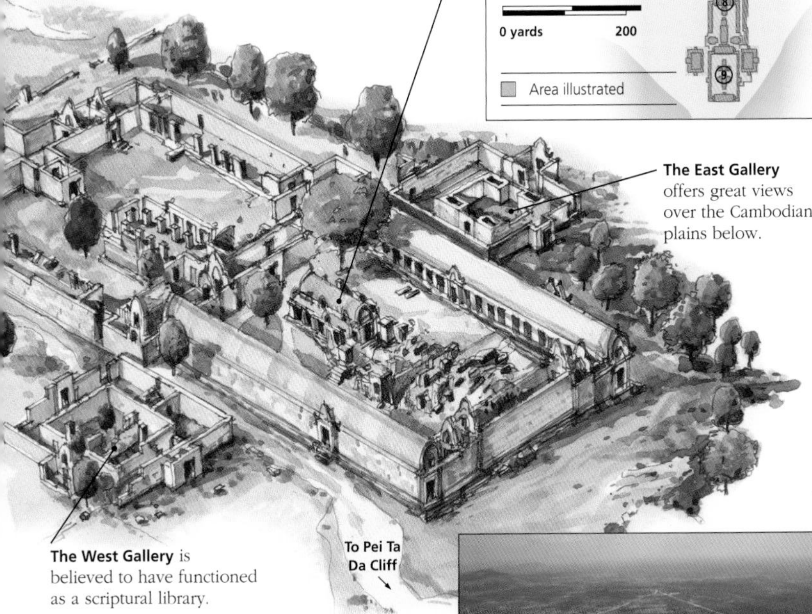

★ Central Shrine and Prasat
Located at the uppermost level of the complex, the Central Shrine and Prasat (religious hall) are completely dilapidated and await restoration. The shrine currently houses a Buddhist temple venerated by local Cambodian and Thai visitors.

The East Gallery offers great views over the Cambodian plains below.

The West Gallery is believed to have functioned as a scriptural library.

To Pei Ta Da Cliff

★ Pei Ta Da Cliff
Offering spectacular views of the surrounding plains 1,500 ft (500 m) below, the precipitous Pei Ta Da Cliff has a small cave beneath its edge, which is accessed by a narrow crevice that is blocked off at times for safety.

The stately ruins of the 10th-century temple Koh Ker ▷

Impressive seven-tiered pyramid of Prasat Thom rising out of a clearing in the jungle, Koh Ker

Koh Ker ⓫

Road Map C6. 81 miles (130 km) NE of Siem Reap. *dawn to dusk daily.*

Hidden in the forests of Preah Vihear province, enigmatic Koh Ker is finally on the visitor map thanks to improved roads and mine clearance. It was built during the reign of King Jayavarman IV (r.928–42), who had moved the capital of Angkor here for a brief period. Not long ago, it was one of the most inaccessible and heavily mined Angkorian temples. Today, visitors can safely reach and explore these ruins on a day trip from Siem Reap.

The complex has over 100 temples with 42 significant structures, the most impressive of which is Prasat Thom, a 131-ft (40-m) high, 180-ft (55-m) wide, seven-tiered sandstone pyramid. Complete with a steep central stairway, it offers dramatic views of the Kulen Mountain and the Dangkrek Mountains to the southwest and northwest respectively. A giant *garuda* (mythical beast, half-man, half-bird) statue sits atop the summit. To the southwest of Prasat Thom lies the huge Rahal Baray, into which the Stung Sen had been diverted to irrigate Koh Ker. Prasat Krahom, the second largest temple in the complex, is notable for its graceful lintel carvings, and its *naga*-flanked causeway. Also of interest are the temples Prasat Thneng and Prasat Leung, both of which lay claim to the largest Shiva *lingas* (phallic symbols) in Cambodia. Visitors can hire a car to go around the complex, but it is best visited as part of an organized tour from Siem Reap. The site is patrolled and maintained by the Apsara Authority's Community Heritage Patrol.

Kompong Thom ⓬

Road Map D6. 93 miles (150 km) SE of Siem Reap. *66,000.* *Prachea Thepatay St.* *daily.*

Situated at the heart of Cambodia along the banks of the Stung Sen, this busy artery town enjoys trade from the traffic en route to Siem Reap or Phnom Penh. Its original name was Kompong Pos Thom, derived from *posthom* meaning two snakes who, according to legend, lived in a cave here and were worshiped by the local Buddhist population. The cave's location has since been forgotten; however, relics of the recent past, namely the pre-Angkorian temple monuments of Sambor Prei Kuk, are increasingly drawing more visitors to this town, as is the quirky mountain temple of Phnom Santuk. The countryside surrounding Kompong Thom is picturesque, with buffalo lazing in roadside pools, and villagers riding their livestock-drawn carts across their farmlands. Visitors should keep an eye out for the home-made effigies outside houses, which are believed to ward off evil spirits.

Sambor Prei Kuk ⓭

Road Map D6. 19 miles (31 km) NE of Kompong Thom. *from Kompong Thom.* *limited access.*

Located east of the Tonlé Sap Lake in Kompong Thom province, this 7th-century

Ancient ruins of Preah Yeay Poun, Sambor Prei Kuk

For hotels and restaurants in this region see pp214–15 and pp238–9

complex of temples was constructed during the reign of King Isanavarman I in the Chenla period *(see p37)*. Spread over a large area of semi-cleared jungle, the ruins are all that remain of the ancient capital of Isanapura. There are three main complexes here – Preah Sambor (North Group), Preah Tor (Central Group), and Preah Yeay Poun (South Group). The sun-dappled, rectangular-shaped Lion Temple, guarded by a lion at its entrance, is one of the highlights of these ruins.

Unique to Sambor Prei Kuk are its many octagon-shaped *prasats* (towers). Despite being choked by the roots of strangler fig trees, some of these towers are in excellent conditions with lintels, columns, and pilasters displaying intricate carvings. Large bas-reliefs rendered in brick also represent some of the earliest attempts in this style – amazingly, Sambor Prei Kuk was pioneering new forms of artistry 150 years before the mighty Angkor. Visitors can hire trained guides, who can be found near the café, to show them around the ruins for a fee, while school children will try and tag along to practice their English. A cursory walk through the ruins will take about an hour. Given the low volume of foot traffic, and the welcome shade provided by the forest, these are rewarding and atmospheric ruins to visit, and can easily be covered in a day trip from Siem Reap.

Woman spinning raw silk into thread, Santuk Silk Farm

Phnom Santuk ⓮

Road Map D6. 11 miles (18 km) E of Kompong Thom. *from Kompong Thom.* *dawn to dusk daily.*

Rising to a height of 679 ft (207 m) above lush paddy fields, Phnom Santuk is the most sacred mountain in Kompong Thom province. It is approached via a stone pathway of 809 steps, flanked by gaudily rendered statues, and a number of fairly insistent beggars. Alternatively, visitors can drive up a steep road that snakes through thick jungle and past a resident colony of macaques. The complex at the summit has a gilded, white-walled central temple. A number of Buddha statues have been carved into the rock face, including a few Reclining Buddhas, all of which are over 33 ft (10 m) in length. Various interconnecting cement bridges between small shrines, statues of horses and deities, and a sculpture workshop add to the appeal of the place. There is also an active monastery whose friendly monks like to chat with visitors.

Lion guardian, Sambor Prei Kuk

The views from the summit are stupendous and are a welcome change from the infinite flatness of the lush rice plains. It is recommended that visitors take regular breaks and carry plenty of water should they decide to walk up the road.

Santuk Silk Farm ⓯

Road Map D6. Hwy 6. 11 miles (18 km) SE of Kompong Thom. ***Tel*** *(012)-906-604.* *7–11am & 1–5pm Mon–Sat.*

Just outside the village of Kakaoh, and opposite the start of the road that leads to Phnom Santuk, is the Santuk Silk Farm run by ex-Vietnam War veteran Bud Gibbons, and his wife. Visitors can view the various life stages of the silkworm – from egg to caterpillar to cocoon. Cocoons provide the base for the thread, which is then spun and woven into attractive *kramas* (scarves) by 15 local girls housed in a cooperative on-site. The *kramas* can be bought from a shop on the farm. Several mulberry trees dot the farm, the leaves of which are fed to the silkworms. Lunch can be provided, but the organizers need to be informed in advance.

Reclining Buddha carved out of rock, Phnom Santuk

Sandstone and laterite ruins of Wat Nokor, Kompong Cham

Kompong Cham ⓰

Road Map D7. 75 miles (120 km) NE of Phnom Penh. *1,915,000.* *from Phnom Penh.* *from Phnom Penh.* *daily.*

Sitting on the west bank of the Mekong River, the city of Kampong Cham takes its name from the exiled Cham people who, pursued by the Vietnamese, settled here in the 17th century. Although it is Cambodia's third largest city, capital of its most populous province, and something of a transport hub for the rest of the northeast, Kompong Cham retains a small-town appeal. The city has a number of run-down French Colonial buildings and the design of the city's grid system has a Gallic feel, with wide boulevards, statue-dotted squares, and a pleasant riverside promenade. By night, the city's streets glow with ornate lampposts and illuminated fountains. The 12th-century Wat Nokor, 1 mile (2 km) west of the city center is an interesting site.

Environs

Located 12 miles (19 km) north of town, the 6th-century **Han Chey** temple is a remnant of Angkorian architecture.

Kratie ⓱

Road Map D6. 43 miles (70 km) NE of Kompong Cham. *79,000.* *daily.*

Once an isolated backwater and only navigable by boat, Kratie now enjoys decent road links with the Lao border, Kompong Cham, Stung Treng, and Phnom Penh, making it a major crossroad both for foreigners and local trade. However, this Mekong-bordered town, formerly administered by the French, is still a sleepy place with a thriving local *psar* (market), a handful of dilapidated Indochinese villas that were spared US bombing, and an easy riverine atmosphere. Once a Khmer Rouge stronghold, it is now renowned for its beautiful sunsets and sightings of the endangered Irrawaddy dolphin some 9 miles (15 km) north near the village of **Kampie**. An estimated 70–85 of the bulb-nosed, small-finned dolphins live in the clay-brown stretch of the Mekong between Kampie and Laos. This village can be reached on a hired tuk-tuk or *moto*; the route follows a beautiful riverside stretch, past houses on stilts inhabited by rural families. From here, it is possible to hire a boat to go out on to the river. Sightings, though not guaranteed, are more than likely.

Just across the water from Kratie is **Koh Trong**, a sandbar island in the middle of the Mekong. Here, visitors will come across a floating village and an old stupa. The fortunate ones may also spot the rare Mekong mud turtle. Also worth a visit is the beautiful 19th-century temple Wat Roka Kandal, 1 mile (2 km) south of town. Wicker handicrafts, which are made by local women, are available here.

Wooden dolphin souvenir, Kampie

Stung Treng ⓲

Road Map D6. 87 miles (140 km) N of Kratie. *25,000.* *daily.*

Once a Lao-French administered outpost, the town of Stung Treng is now on the tourist map thanks to a new bridge and a cross-country road. Ironically, these make it easy to pass through the town without breaking the journey. Much of Stung Treng province's traffic still moves by water; the province is criss-crossed by several rivers including Tonlé Kong, Tonlé Sepok, Tonlé San, and the mighty Mekong River, which passes some 6 miles (10 km) east of Stung Treng town. The town and surrounding countryside have much to offer visitors, with a number of riverine sunset trips operating at inflated prices, and the Chenla period ruins of Prasat Preah Ko, a short distance away. Homestay and trekking options are also developing.

Ban Lung ⓳

Road Map E6. 93 miles (150 km) NE of Stung Treng. *25,000.* *Highland Tour (088)-988-8098.* *daily.* **www.** tourismcambodia.com

The country's northernmost region, Ratanakiri province is often referred to as the Wild East, of which Ban Lung is the provincial capital. The town's nickname, *dey*

Striking view of the Mekong River from the town of Kratie

For hotels and restaurants in this region see pp214–15 and pp238–9

krakhorm, meaning red earth, derives from the red dust that settles on everything from people's faces to the leaves of trees, giving the place a surreal autumnal feel. Ban Lung is best visited between November and February when the rains have stopped and the dust has not yet become a nuisance. During the wet season, from July to September, the town's roads become quite impassable.

Ban Lung is little more than a transportation and accommodations hub for the many riches that lie on its fringes; these include waterfalls, bottle-green crater lakes, minority villages, and ethnic animist cemeteries. Two-day treks in the **Virachey National Park**, 31 miles (50 km) to the north of Ban Lung, are recommended. A number of eco-trekking organizations are starting to take shape here. Elephant rides to local waterfalls, of which Ka Tieng is the most impressive, can be organized by most guesthouses.

Yaek Lom Lake ⓴

Road Map E6. 3 miles (5 km) E of Ban Lung.

Believed to have been formed some 700,000 years ago, this volcanic, bottle-green crater lake is the main attraction around Ban Lung. The lake is ringed by thick green jungle and when viewed aerially, it forms a near perfect circle. The area is peaceful and a visit here makes for a memorable day with morning swims and wooden jetties to sunbathe on. The visitors' center can provide information on Ratanakiri's ethnic minorities, a number of whom live near Ban Lung. Many of these tribes believe the lake to be an especially sacred place and according to their legends, monsters inhabit its clear waters. An easily navigable path runs around the lake and can be walked in an hour. Admission to the lake is administered by the local Tompuon tribe, with the money being used toward improving the condition of their villages. Visitors can reach the lake either on foot or by tuk-tuk from Ban Lung.

Visitors enjoying the beautiful scenery and cool waters, Yaek Lom Lake

Sen Monorom ㉑

Road Map E6. 230 miles (370 km) NE of Phnom Penh. *7,000.* *from Phnom Penh.* *Phnom Penh.* *daily.*

Capital of Mondulkiri, the largest of Cambodia's provinces, Sen Monorom is a picturesque little place often referred to as "the Switzerland of Cambodia" for its grassy landscape, rolling hills, and two large lakes. Covering a very small area, this sparsely populated town has a marketplace and a few guesthouses. The area is rich in river valleys, waterfalls, and teal-green deciduous forests, and is also home to tigers, bears, and a number of smaller endangered animals. However, illegal logging in the past 15 years and an increase in plantations have decimated the forests, driving these animals farther inland, much to the dismay of wildlife conservationists.

A house in an ethnic Phnong village, Sen Monorom

Among the other attractions around Sen Monorom are one- and two-day treks in and around the ethnic Phnong villages, famous for their elephants. Visitors can learn the art of elephant training here, with the help of the Elephant Valley project. Motorcycles are available for hire in Sen Monorom, but visitors should bear in mind that the roads are undeveloped and there are very few road signs.

Bonsraa Waterfalls ㉒

Road Map E6. 22 miles (35 km) E of Sen Monorom. *from Sen Monorom.* *dawn to dusk daily.*

Accessed via a toll road from Sen Monorom, the Bonsraa Waterfalls are now easy to reach and lie 22 miles (35 km) west of the Vietnamese border. This double-tiered waterfall, plunging some 115 ft (35 m) into dense jungle, is the country's most famous and dramatic cascade. The upper tier of the waterfall is 33 ft (10 m) in width and although the thundering water is very powerful, the lower, narrower tier with an 82-ft (25-m) drop, is much more spectacular. To see it from the bottom of the falls, visitors can cross the river and follow a crooked path weaving down a precipitous stairway. *Motos* can be hired from Sen Monorom to travel to the falls and back.

SOUTHERN CAMBODIA

The most relaxed, lush part of the country, Southern Cambodia is blessed with dazzling white-sand beaches and richly forested national parks. Faded Colonial architecture, lively beach bars, and beautiful virgin islands are on offer in this sparsely populated region. Visitors can engage in a variety of activities, from jungle treks and boat trips to snorkeling and diving.

Stretching from the Thai border in the southwest to Vietnam's Mekong Delta frontier in the southeast, Southern Cambodia is a region of myriad attractions. In the north are the relatively inaccessible Cardamom Mountains, a supremely biologically diverse range. Until the late 1980s these mountains were one of the last strongholds of the Khmer Rouge, whose presence, coupled with the difficult terrain, deterred loggers. The amazing variety of wildlife in the Cardamom Mountains includes elephants, sun bears, tigers, pangolins, Siamese crocodiles, and primates.

The biggest draws of the area are its pristine beaches and virgin islands. Sihanoukville, with its mix of ramshackle buildings and fancy hotels, continues to draw visitors despite its lack of urban planning. The town's fine-sand beaches and turquoise waters are a haven for watersports enthusiasts. A number of tour operators and diving companies, which can assist travelers with planning activities, operate in the town. Several uninhabited and sparsely populated islands lie just off the coast of Sihanoukville and make for excellent day-trip options. Apart from tourism, the main sources of income in the coastal areas remain agriculture, fishing, and salt production.

The region is also home to several wildlife preserves. Ream National Park envelops a vast swath of coastland, with mangrove forests and coral reefs, in contrast to the expansive pine forests of Kirirom National Park. The rain forest preserve of Botum Sakor National Park is home to elephants and hornbills, while Bokor National Park's old French hill station has been renovated with a hotel complex. Other attractions include the tiny town of Kep, with its crumbling Modernist buildings, and the captivating temple ruins of Phnom Da in Takeo province.

Brightly colored fishing boats and houses on stilts lining the wharf, Kampot

◁ **Popular beach with huts and sun loungers, Sihanoukville**

Exploring Southern Cambodia

A heady combination of beaches, islands, and national parks makes Southern Cambodia a delight to explore. Koh Kong, near the Thai border, is beginning to establish itself as an ecotourism center, with picturesque waterfalls, forests, and mangrove preserves. In the south, bustling Sihanoukville has some of Southeast Asia's most gorgeous beaches and pristine offshore islands. Kampot, which lies to the east of Sihanoukville, is an important town with a delightful river setting and an atmospheric French quarter, and serves as an ideal base for trips to Bokor National Park. Tiny Kep, a former French resort, still retains a quiet rustic feel, while Takeo province is home to the ancient temple of Phnom Da, which is accessible only by boat from Angkor Borei.

Lush mangrove forests, Botum Sakor National Park

SIGHTS AT A GLANCE

Towns and Cities

Kampot 11
Kep 16
Koh Kong 5
Neak Luong 21
Sihanoukville pp106–7 1
Svay Rieng 22
Takeo 19

Places of Worship

Phnom Chhnork 14
Phnom Sorsia 15

Historical Sites

Angkor Borei 20

Islands and Beaches

Koh Kong Island 8
Koh Tonsay 18

National Parks and Preserves

Bokor National Park 13
Botum Sakor National Park 10
Cardamom Mountains 9
Kep National Park 17
Kirirom National Park 4
Peam Krasaop Nature Reserve 7
Ream National Park 2

Areas of Natural Beauty

Kbal Chhay Cascades 3
Tatai Waterfalls 6
Tek Chhouu Falls 12

For additional map symbols *see back flap*

GETTING AROUND

The road system in Southern Cambodia has improved greatly. All the main routes are well paved and generally in good condition, although all are single-lane highways. The bus network is reasonably efficient and since distances are not great, journeys are not too tiring. Shared taxis supplement buses, particularly on the Sihanoukville – Kampot route. These usually stop to allow travelers to take pictures en route. Car-rental agencies are common in Sihanoukville and motorcycle rental companies operate in most towns. Boats are available to offshore islands and riverside towns, and to explore parks and temple ruins such as Phnom Da.

A busy street in the provincial town of Svay Rieng

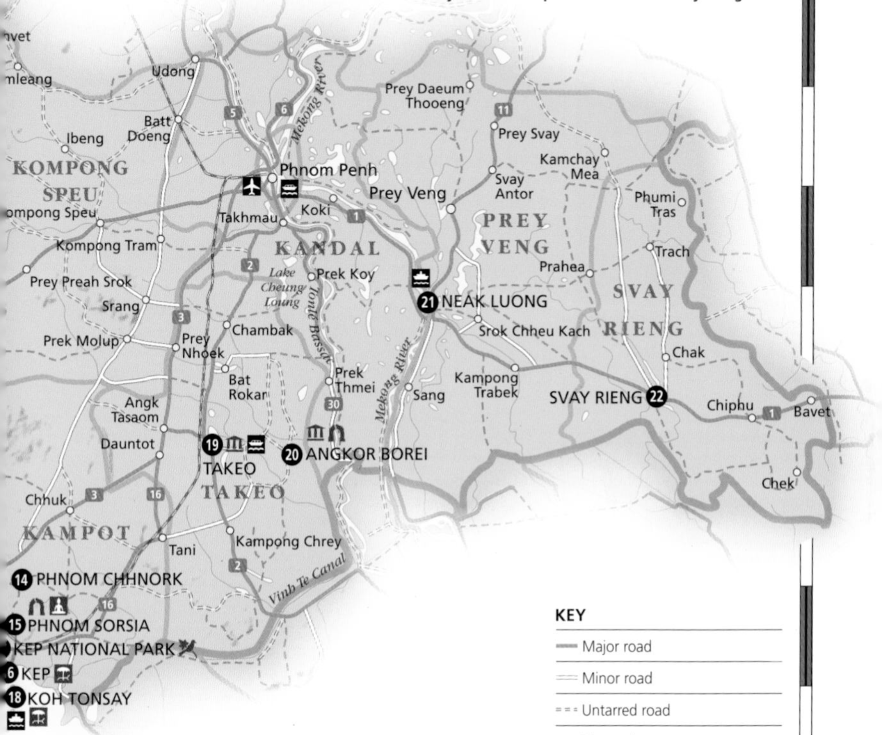

KEY

- Major road
- Minor road
- Untarred road
- Dirt track
- Railway line
- International border
- Provincial border
- Peak

SEE ALSO

• ***Where to Stay*** pp216–17

• ***Where to Eat*** pp239–41

Verdant forests surrounding the rocky ledges of Tatai Waterfalls

Sihanoukville ❶

Golden Lion statue at a traffic circle

With its stunning white-sand beaches and azure waters, Sihanoukville is Cambodia's principal beach resort. Spread across three districts, the town encompasses a large port zone and was named after the former king, Sihanouk. Locals, however, still refer to it by its old name, Kompong Som. Although the town is of no real architectural interest, it is now the focus of large-scale international investment and visitors will find excellent facilities including banks, restaurants, bars, Internet cafés, and upscale hotels. The town's international airport resumed flights in 2011.

Entrance to the Airport Club, Victory Beach

Victory Beach

2 miles (3 km) NW of town center.

The pretty, white-sand bay of Victory Beach is located directly below Victory Hill. Its southern end is also known as Lamherkay Beach. Victory Beach is about 984 ft (300 m) long, and its western orientation means that it is perfectly aligned to view sunsets. The Airport Club located here has a DJ and dancing at night, and it also serves drinks and meals. Located about 1 mile (2 km) offshore is Koh Pos, or Snake Island, which is easily accessible by boat.

Independence Beach

2 miles (3 km) SW of town center.

Another lovely tropical bay, Independence Beach gets its name from the renovated Independence Hotel on the hilltop directly north of this stretch of coastline. It is a privately owned space, with fine, pale sand and some wonderful swimming. Visitors can either buy a drink or two from the hotel's beach café to avoid paying an entrance fee, or head straight to the southern section of the beach, a small part of which is open to all. However, the beach here is crowded with street vendors selling trinkets and fruits.

Sokha Beach

1 mile (2 km) SW of town center.

With shimmering white sand and the sea a surreal shade of turquoise, Sokha Beach is

Poolside at the Independence Hotel, Independence Beach

certainly worth a visit. The crescent-shaped stretch of sand runs for about 1 mile (2 km) between two small wooded bluffs. Directly behind the beach is the sprawling Sokha Beach Resort (*see p217*), which officially owns this stretch. Visitors who want to linger have to pay an entrance fee, which includes use of the resort's pool. The beach has deck chairs and snack stalls operated by the resort.

Occheuteal Beach

1 mile (2 km) S of town center.

This beach is the main tourist hot spot in Sihanoukville, and is the closest to the hotel strip. The beach's northern end is heavily built up. The small rocky cove here, known as Serendipity Beach, is the most pleasant part of Occheuteal Beach despite there being no sand. It is home to upscale bungalows as well as some of the town's best-known bars and restaurants. In contrast, the southern end is far less developed.

This casuarina-lined beach plays host to sunbathers and watersports enthusiasts who

Numerous beach bars and cafés lining the shore, Occheuteal Beach

For hotels and restaurants in this region see pp216–17 and pp239–41

can rent tubes, banana boats, and jet skis to enjoy the warm water. A strip of shack-like bar-restaurants along the beach also offer cheap beer deals and seafood specials.

Unfortunately, the beach suffers from erosion, which is a serious problem here as most buildings have been built too close to the water. Visitors may come across some unpleasant sights, such as sand bags, owing to the rapid development taking place. However, half way down the beach, there is a nice stretch of white sand and shallow water.

Prek Treng Beach

4 miles (6 km) NW of town center.

Located north of the port, Prek Treng Beach is a fairly deserted, long, thin crescent of sand with shallow blue water. Visitors are advised to bring their own drinks and snacks as there are no facilities available here. At high tide, this beach is quite narrow and the shoreline is rocky in places.

Otres Beach

4 mile (6 km) SE of town center.

Immediately south of Occheuteal, behind a small headland, Otres Beach is a wonderful golden stretch of sand, lined with graceful casuarina trees. The beach itself is narrow, but about 2 miles (3 km) long and dotted with sun loungers, which visitors can use in exchange for a drink or a snack. Although a lot of the land here has been bought by developers, for the time being the place is still pristine.

There are a number of small-scale bungalow operations, which offer inexpensive accommodations right on the beachfront with very little traffic to disturb the peace. The beach is not served by public transport but can be reached by rented cars or tuk-tuks from the town center, or on foot from Occheuteal Beach.

VISITORS' CHECKLIST

Road Map C7. 112 miles (180 km) SW of Phnom Penh. *62,000.* *corner of Sopheakmongkol & 109 Sts, (034)-933-894.* *daily.* *Wave Music Festival (late Oct–early Nov).*

Peaceful stretch of sand and water, Prek Treng Beach

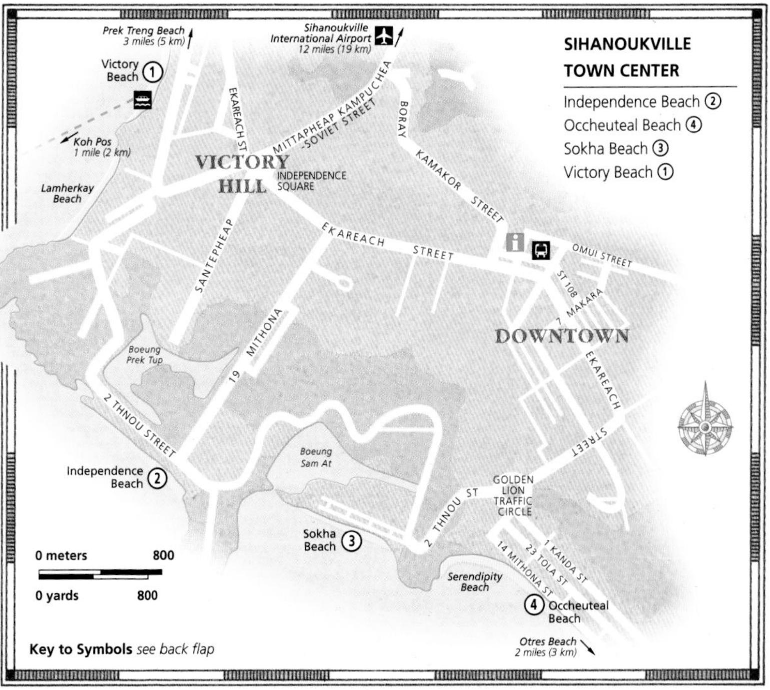
Prek Treng Beach 3 miles (5 km)
Sihanoukville International Airport 12 miles (19 km)
Victory Beach ①
Koh Pos 1 mile (2 km)
Lamherkay Beach
VICTORY HILL
INDEPENDENCE SQUARE
EKAREACH ST
MITTAPHEAP KAMPUCHEA-SOVIET STREET
BORAY
KAMAKOR STREET
SANTEPHEAP
EKAREACH STREET
OMUI STREET
ST 108
7 MAKARA
DOWNTOWN
EKAREACH STREET
19 MITHONA
Boeung Prek Tup
2 THNOU STREET
Boeung Sam At
Independence Beach ②
2 THNOU ST
GOLDEN LION TRAFFIC CIRCLE
Sokha Beach ③
1 KANDA ST
23 TOLA ST
14 MITHONA ST
Serendipity Beach
④ Occheuteal Beach
Otres Beach 2 miles (3 km)
0 meters 800
0 yards 800
Key to Symbols see back flap
SIHANOUKVILLE TOWN CENTER
Independence Beach ②
Occheuteal Beach ④
Sokha Beach ③
Victory Beach ①

Ream National Park ❷

Road Map C7.12 miles (19 km) SE of Sihanoukville.
Park HQ (016)-767-686.
7am–5pm daily.

Encompassing 82 sq miles (212 sq km) of coastal land, the varied landscape of Ream National Park includes white-sand beaches, mangrove forests, and the Prek Toeuk Sap Estuary. The park's marine section comprises the islands of Koh Thmei and Koh Seh, as well as some offshore coral reefs. Thmor Thom, a fishing community consisting of 200 inhabitants, is also located inside the park.

Ream National Park is particularly rich in birdlife with a recorded list of over 150 species that includes the Indian pied hornbill, sea eagle, grey-headed fish eagle, and storks. Its forests are home to sun bears, deer, snakes such as pythons and the king cobra, macaques, silver langurs, and pangolins. Closer to the Prek Toeuk Sap river, visitors may chance upon monkeys and several kinds of kingfisher skimming the water. In the rainy season, it is also possible to catch sight of the endangered Irrawaddy dolphin.

Most visitors explore the national park on a boat trip along the river, which passes through lush mangroves and forests on its way to the sea. Boat trips are an excellent way to view wildlife on the riverbanks. The river also offers good opportunities for swimming close to its beaches. Jungle hikes can be organized with national park rangers who speak English, as it is not possible for visitors to hike on their own.

Colorful coral reefs in the waters off Ream National Park

Sihanoukville's Islands

Located offshore from the beaches of Sihanoukville *(see pp106–7)*, this group of 20 or so idyllic palm-fringed islands are a good day-trip option from the mainland. Basic accommodations are also available on some of the islands. While a few are completely uninhabited, tiny communities inhabit others, surviving on fishing and farming.

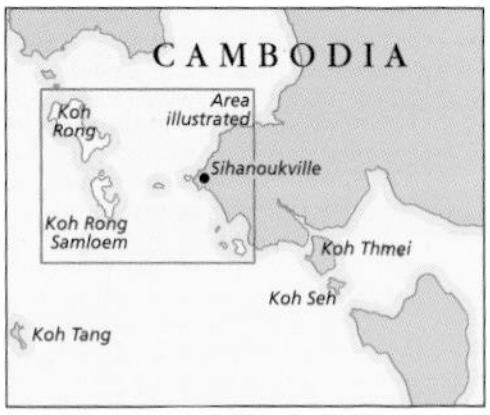

CAMBODIA
Area illustrated
Koh Rong
Sihanoukville
Koh Rong Samloem
Koh Thmei
Koh Seh
Koh Tang

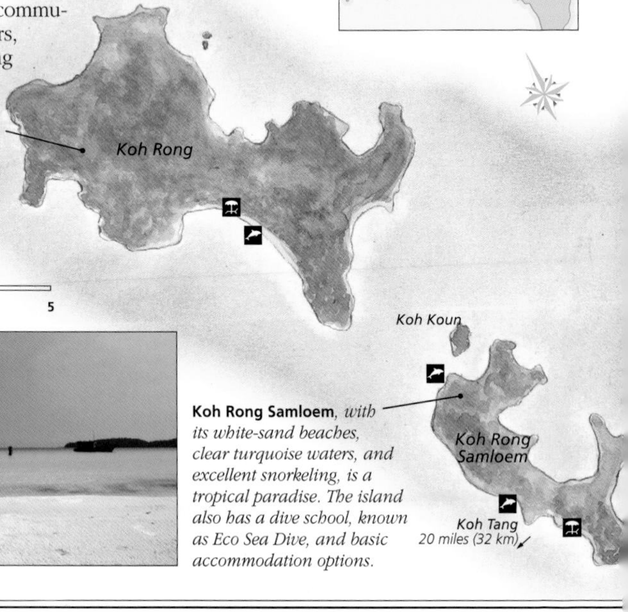

Koh Rong, the largest island in the group, has beautiful unspoiled beaches, perfect for strolls. Its calm waters are home to a variety of marine life.

Koh Rong

0 km 5
0 miles 5

Koh Koun

Koh Rong Samloem, *with its white-sand beaches, clear turquoise waters, and excellent snorkeling, is a tropical paradise. The island also has a dive school, known as Eco Sea Dive, and basic accommodation options.*

Koh Rong Samloem

Koh Tang
20 miles (32 km)

Kbal Chhay Cascades ❸

Road Map C7.11 miles (18 km) N of Sihanoukville. *Sihanoukville (034)-933-894.*

A popular spot with domestic tourists as it was featured in the Cambodian movie *Chao Pos Keng Kong* (The Giant Snake), the Kbal Chhay Cascades offer the chance of a refreshing dip. Upstream there are rocky ledges and sandy coves for sunbathing. However, the water flow reduces toward the end of the rainy season and the swimming is not so good.

On Sundays, the place is packed and litter is a real problem. Facilities here include snack and souvenir stalls, picnic platforms, and changing booths. Visitors can also get to the falls by *motos* and motorcycles.

Water gushing over rocky ledges, Kbal Chhay Cascades

Kirirom National Park ❹

Road Map C7. 68 miles (110 km) NE of Sihanoukville. *7am–5pm daily.*

This intriguing national park occupies a remote plateau about a two-hour ride inland from Sihanoukville. It lies at an elevation of about 2,296 ft (700 m), making the climate here far less oppressive than on the coast, and Kirirom's extensive pine forests reflect the temperate altitude. Visitors can avail themselves of ranger-guided walks to **Phnom Dat Chivit**, or End of the World Mountain, from where the view of the Elephant and Cardamom mountain ranges to the west is spellbinding. Ox-cart rides and gentle hikes to pretty waterfalls are also popular and there is a good web of forest trails. Wildlife here includes elephant, tiger, pileated gibbon, banteng, gaur, and sun bear, although sightings are rare.

The park has a basic guesthouse with a restaurant, offering fine views over the forest, particularly at sunset. There is also an upscale resort with manicured lawns that is popular with weekenders from Phnom Penh.

Diving *off the coasts of Koh Rong Samloem, Koh Tas, and Koh Tang offers great views of coral reefs, home to marine life such as lionfish, seahorses, and whale sharks.*

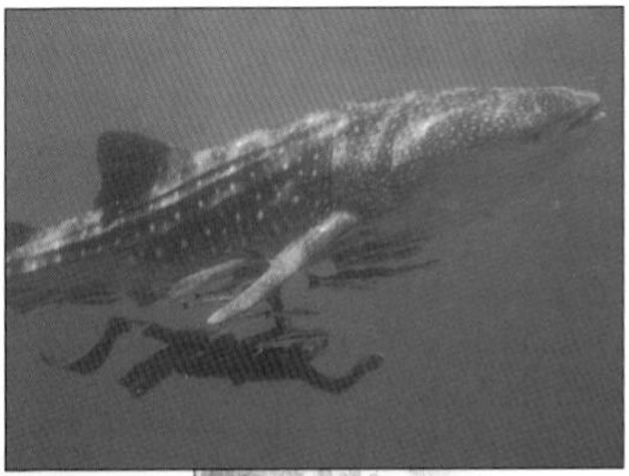

VISITORS' CHECKLIST

Koh Pos is 1 mile (2 km) W of Sihanoukville. *available for trips to and between the islands.* *tours to the islands can be arranged by tour operators and guesthouses in Sihanoukville.*

KEY

Beach

Dive site

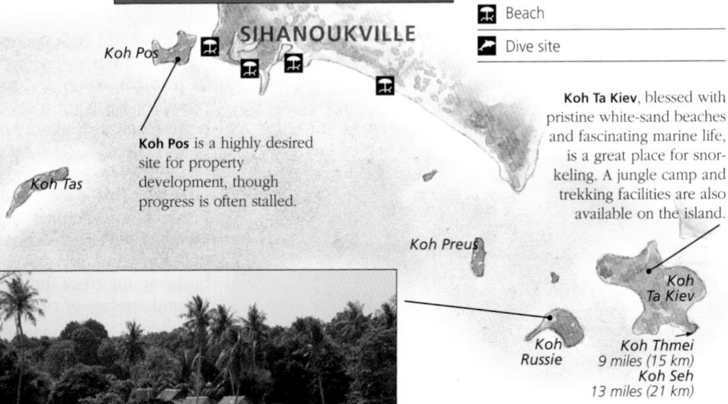

SIHANOUKVILLE

Koh Pos

Koh Tas

Koh Preus

Koh Ta Kiev

Koh Russie

Koh Thmei 9 miles (15 km)

Koh Seh 13 miles (21 km)

Koh Pos is a highly desired site for property development, though progress is often stalled.

Koh Ta Kiev, blessed with pristine white-sand beaches and fascinating marine life, is a great place for snorkeling. A jungle camp and trekking facilities are also available on the island.

Koh Russie, *or Bamboo Island, has a lovely fine-sand beach on its west coast. The east coast, although not as inviting as the west, is frequented by day-trippers.*

Charred remains of a once splendid Colonial villa, Kep

Kep ⓰

Road Map C7. 109 miles (175 km) S of Phnom Penh. *4,500.*

Once known as Kep-sur-Mer, the town of Kep was an upscale resort for the rich and influential of French Indochina in the 1930s. Today, it is little more than an overgrown village in a scenic location, surrounded by a lofty forested headland, and the sea on three sides. A profusion of greenery and thick tree cover add to the easy appeal of the town. In recent years it has become Cambodia's most successful micro-resort, with a new range of ecolodges and guesthouses mushrooming across town.

The town was overrun by the Khmer Rouge in 1975, who torched most symbols of Colonial prosperity, leaving behind blackened shells of the once sprawling buildings and villas. Despite their devastation, Kep's Modernist concrete villas remain the town's best-known attractions. Although dishevelled and ruined, these structures are charred reminders of a more prosperous time and are certainly worth a visit.

Visitors will also find the town's beaches a pleasant distraction. **Kep Beach**, located on the edge of the Kep peninsula, is about 1 mile (2 km) long and strewn with pebbles. The dark grey sand is quite unlike the Caribbean vision of paradise, and is dotted with sun loungers. The bay's waters are extremely shallow and quite safe for children, although adults may have to wade a long way out for a decent swim. **Coconut Beach**, a short distance east of Kep Beach, is popular with locals.

The region's most renowned dish, the delicious and spicy Kep pepper crab *(see p229)*, is served in every restaurant on the strip known as Crab Market, north of town, and is definitely worth a try. There are several pepper farms nearby where visitors can see the vine-like plant and also buy the famous and pungent Kep peppercorn.

The hill behind Kep offers fine views. Those keen to hike can follow a track through the jungle, accessed from behind the Veranda Natural Resort.

Kep National Park ⓱

Road Map C7. 1 mile (2 km) NW of Kep. *from Kep.*

One of the smallest protected preserves in Cambodia, Kep National Park occupies the hilltop directly behind Kep town. A 5-mile (8-km) long trail loops around the hillside, passing through an evergreen forest, and takes about 3 hours to hike. En route, visitors will come across views of Kampot and Angkoul Beach, and a pagoda, before arriving at Sunset Rock, which offers fine vistas over the sea to Koh Tonsay. Unfortunately, farmers have encroached on the park's lower reaches and wildlife sightings are rare. The park is reached by a 4WD vehicle from the bottom of the hill.

Restaurants on stilts lining the waterfront in Crab Market, Kep

Visitors lazing around on a busy beach, Koh Tonsay

Koh Tonsay ⓲

Road Map C7. 4 miles (6 km) S of Kep. *from Kep.*

A beautiful wooded island just offshore from Kep, Koh Tonsay, or Rabbit Island, is so called because its profile is said to resemble that of a rabbit. The island is inhabited by around 200 people who make a living by fishing and harvesting coconuts and seaweed (for Chinese cosmetics). It is possible to walk around the entire island in just a couple of hours.

The main attraction here is a lovely sheltered beach with a narrow strip of golden sand and great swimming. There are about half a dozen bungalow operations in Koh Tonsay, all offering similar, simple wood-and-thatch huts, most without en suite facilities. Several of them have restaurants with well-stocked bars. Visitors can also make trips to the islands of Koh Pos and Koh Svai nearby.

Flora and Fauna of Coastal National Parks

Cambodia's coastal parks are incredibly diverse, comprising a wide variety of flora and fauna. In the Cardamom Mountains, the rain forests stretch right down to the sea and some of the best-preserved mangrove estuaries in Asia are also on this coastline. Shallower waters contain rich seagrass beds, the diet of dugongs and green turtles. Many of Cambodia's 77 offshore islands have reefs, which are home to hundreds of varieties of coral and fish. These ecosystems, however, are under severe threat and many species are endangered because of loss of habitat and deforestation, illegal wildlife trading, destructive fishing, and poaching. Farming and forestry concessions, even inside national parks, have led to the removal of wildlife territory and land being cleared for wood chip production.

White-bellied sea eagle

Coconut palms provide vital income and sustenance for coastal communities who use almost every part of the tree.

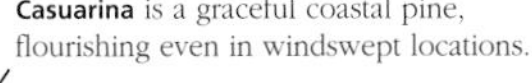

Casuarina is a graceful coastal pine, flourishing even in windswept locations.

FLORA

Coastal Cambodia contains some of the richest forest environments in Southeast Asia. At lower altitudes, the dense tropical rain forests can soar to a height of almost 164 ft (50 m) or so.

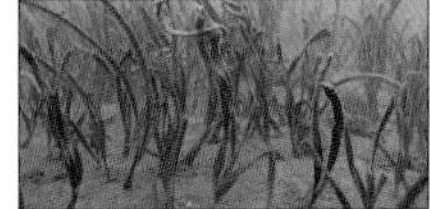

Marine seagrass *forms an essential part of the diet of green turtles and dugongs.*

Hawksbill turtles *are found in shallow waters along the coast where sponges, which are their main diet, are also common.*

FAUNA

The coastal waters of Cambodia are quite shallow, not more than 199 ft (60 m) deep. The extensive reefs are rich in variety, consisting of hard and soft corals, and teem with marine life such as crabs, fish, and turtles – a haven for scuba divers.

Seahorses *are a unique variety of fish. They flourish in the shallow waters off Sihanoukville.*

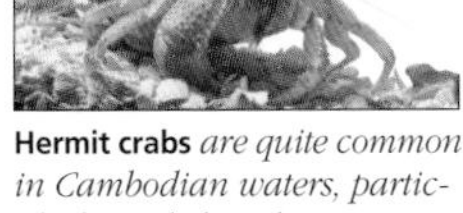

Hermit crabs *are quite common in Cambodian waters, particularly in sheltered areas around the mangrove forests.*

Whip coral *are characterized by long brush-like strands in a variety of colors. Growing in reefs, they provide a habitat for several species of fish.*

The white-tip reef shark *is a shark that grows up to about 5 ft (1.5 m) in length. It is seldom aggressive unless provoked.*

Picturesque lakefront promenade bordered by coconut palms, Takeo

Takeo 19

Road Map D7. 48 miles (77 km) S of Phnom Penh. *42,000.* *St 4, Takeo (032)-931-323.*

A provincial capital, Takeo is located on the fringe of a vast flood plain that forms a vital wetland area. Although not on the tourist map, Takeo's broad streets are visited by those en route to the impressive early Khmer temple of Phnom Da, not far from town. As a result, the town has several facilities, including modest hotels, Internet cafés, and a couple of banks with ATMs. There are not many impressive sights here, although the lakeside promenade has a certain charm, including a dilapidated pier. The Provincial Museum, a short distance from the lakefront promenade, is also worth a visit for its local archaeological exhibits. Visitors could also try the town's culinary specialty, *bong khorng* (giant prawns) fried with garlic and lemon juice, served in several restaurants and street stalls.

Angkor Borei 20

Road Map D7. 13 miles (21 km) E of Takeo. *14,000.* *from Takeo.*

A highly enjoyable boat ride from Takeo takes visitors to the small riverside settlement of Angkor Borei, one of the oldest pre-Angkorian sites in Cambodia. This scruffy, isolated town was earlier known as Vyadapura, capital city of the ancient Hindu kingdom of Funan, which rose to prominence between the 1st and 6th centuries AD. The town's unpaved streets and general air of poverty provide little evidence of its illustrious past; it was once a key center of Hindu civilization and culture. Many of its residents are ethnic Vietnamese – the border with Vietnam is just a few miles to the east – and visitors will be able to catch a glimpse of fishermen wearing conical hats, typical of Vietnam's rural folk.

Seventh-century statue from Phnom Da

The **Takeo Archaeological Museum**, located on the canal bank, is a reminder of the area's former glory. This interesting museum has a small, eclectic collection of artifacts from the region, including Funan-style ceramics that date back 2,000 years, *lingas* (phallic symbols), a 6th-century Standing Buddha, a 12th-century sandstone statue of Lakshmi, Hindu Goddess of Wealth, and ancient images of the Hindu gods Shiva and Vishnu.

Environs

Situated 2 miles (3 km) south of Angkor Borei, **Phnom Da** is an exquisite, partly ruined temple. Standing on the summit of an isolated hill, it has exceptional views over lush, green paddy fields stretching deep into Vietnam 5 miles (8 km) away, and across the wetlands to Takeo.

Phnom Da's ruins, rising to a height of 59 ft (18 m), are approached by 142 steps leading up the hill, and visitors are usually guided by barefooted local children. The temple's red-brick foundation dates from AD 514 and its

Façade of Takeo Archeological Museum, Angkor Borei

For hotels and restaurants in this region see pp216–17 and pp239–41

intricate carvings have been weathered by centuries of rainfall, while the walls are cracked and penetrated by plants. Despite its dilapidated condition, there still remains much to admire – carved pillars, bas-reliefs of *nagas*, and an imposing stone doorway. However, most of the carvings have been taken away to museums in Phnom Penh and Angkor Borei. Below the temple are several cave shrines that are still used for religious offerings and prayers of good fortune.

Takeo Archaeological Museum
Riverbank, Angkor Borei. ***Tel*** *(012)-201-638.* *7:30am–4pm daily.*

Phnom Da
from Angkor Borei.

Stone steps leading to the temple ruins of Phnom Da, Angkor Borei

Neak Luong ㉑

Road Map D7. 39 miles (63 km) SE of Phnom Penh. *24,000.* *from Phnom Penh.*

Located on the east bank of the Mekong, Neak Luong is a busy transit town with a devastating history. During the Vietnam War, the town was bombed by a US B-52, which dropped a 20-ton (18 tonne) load on the town center, resulting in the deaths of almost 150 people. This incident is depicted in the opening sequence of the 1984 British film, *The Killing Fields*.

Today, travelers along Highway 1 on their way to the Vietnamese border and Ho Chi Minh City regularly pass through Neak Luong.

Ferry chartering visitors and cargo across the Mekong, Neak Luong

Car ferries also shuttle people and transport across the Mekong River, which can result in long waits during busy times. Japan has agreed to fund the construction of a 121-ft (37-m) high bridge here, but the project has been fraught with delays.

The town also has a huge, bustling market where locals peddle fruit and a variety of fried snacks such as crickets. Other than this, there is little reason for visitors to stay in Neak Luong.

Svay Rieng ㉒

Road Map D7. 70 miles (113 km) SE of Phnom Penh. *23,000.* *from Phnom Penh.*

A provincial capital roughly half way between Phnom Penh and Ho Chi Minh City in Vietnam, the town of Svay Rieng is bypassed by most travelers, except those desperately in need of a meal or a drink. The Vietnamese border at Bavet is a short journey from here.

BOMBING OF NEAK LUONG

On August 6, 1973, American B-52s accidentally destroyed Neak Luong in an attempt to arrest the advance of the Khmer Rouge to Phnom Penh. The 20-ton (18 tonne) load dropped on the town led to the deaths of almost 150 civilians. This incident was immortalized in the film *The Killing Fields* (1984), where US journalist Schanberg, played by Sam Waterstone, and his Cambodian fixer Dith Pran, arrive in Neak Luong after reports of the bombing. They find a devastating scene – a smoldering town and bloodied survivors who beg Schanberg to photograph their misery. Days later, the US Congress called a halt to the bombardment known as Arclight. Journalists, including John Pilger, argue that this bombing campaign was a key factor in driving people to support the Khmer Rouge.

A moving scene from the 1984 film *The Killing Fields*

LAOS AREA BY AREA

A PORTRAIT OF LAOS

A land of rich social and ethnic diversity, Laos displays French, Vietnamese, Thai, and Chinese influences in its distinct cultural potpourri. Its great geographical variety also harbors a wealth of native flora and fauna. This natural beauty, coupled with splendid Buddhist architecture and pleasantly agreeable people, makes a trip to Laos a memorable experience.

LAND AND ECOLOGY

Laos touches the temperate northern perimeter of Southeast Asia and extends deep into the heart of the tropical Mekong River valley. The rich lands in between are home to a range of flora, from tall, pale hardwoods and montane evergreen forests to shrub and bamboo undergrowth. Its fauna includes such endangered species as the Laotian black gibbon and the Asiatic tiger. The network of rivers that feed into the great Mekong provide fish, water for crops, and transport for people and goods. However, many of these resources are under threat from activities such as logging. The government has addressed this issue by establishing 20 National Protected Areas, covering 10 percent of the land area. Laos has also recently established itself as an ecotourism destination with trekking and rafting as ideal ways to economically benefit local populations while conserving the environment.

Sprawling urban landscape, Pakse

Monks offering prayers in front of Buddha statues

POLITICS AND THE ECONOMY

Ruled by a monarch until 1975, Laos became a Communist state when the Lao People's Democratic Republic (Lao PDR) came to power. The new government chose to isolate the country from the rest of the world with the exception of its Socialist neighbor Vietnam and the Soviet Bloc. However, since 1989, the policy of Jintanakan Mai (New Thinking) has reduced the role of the government in the economy and allowed free enterprise to re-emerge. Today, the economic prospects of the country are improving and economic growth averages 7 percent annually. A rising urban middle class, with no ties to the Communist elite, are now buying mobile phones, motorcycles, and cars. At the same time, many young Lao are leaving their villages for work in the cities and sending money home. There is also increased foreign investment with hydroelectric power projects, mining, and tourism leading the economic advances in the country.

◁ Riverside cafés at the foot of majestic karst cliffs, Luang Prabang province

SOCIETY AND RELIGION

The effects of modernization have not been far reaching, with a majority of the population still continuing an agrarian existence based on the land, the seasons, and the family. Within the family, the culture is both patriarchal and hierarchal, with senior members owing support and protection to the juniors, who reciprocate with obeisance and loyalty. At the same time, women are considered secondary to men in traditional Lao society. Even though women constitute a majority of the workforce, fewer girls are sent to school, although such norms are now beginning to change.

The impact of the Communist Revolution notwithstanding, Lao society remains rooted in the traditions of Theravada Buddhism, whose tenets remind its followers of the impermanence of their existence and the pitfalls of desire and acquisition. Even those residents of Laos who follow other faiths, such as the largely Christian Vietnamese, the Muslim South Asians, and animist minorities, are subtly enjoined to follow the culture, if not the religion, based on Buddhist beliefs. Religion therefore, forms an essential part of society, reflected in the daily almsgiving ceremony to Buddhist monks.

Man playing Lao *lanat*

Weaver in Ban Xang Hai village, near Luang Prabang

Flooded rice fields in Vang Vieng

CULTURE AND THE ARTS

As in the case of religion, Lao traditional culture and art has proved resilient in the face of Communist assault. Many manifestations of the country's culture, music, dance, architecture, and literature have their roots in Buddhism. Lao music and dance is inevitably similar to that of neighboring Thailand, and to a lesser extent, Cambodia. The hypnotic flute called *khuy* is accompanied by a reed-driven pan pipe known as the *khene*, with a back beat provided by drums and *lanats* (xylophones). Music usually accompanies dances, such as performances of *Phra Lak Phra Lam*, the Lao version of the Hindu epic, *Ramayana*. This didactic tale is portrayed in temple art, both in murals and the bas-relief panels usually found on the doors and windows. Laos's expertly handwoven textiles, in both cotton and silk, are uniquely designed, with each highland minority creating its own style of textile. The country is also well known for its silversmiths, who are adept at creating exquisite jewelry, notably the intricate belts that accompany the handwoven *phaa sinh* skirt of traditional Lao women's attire.

LAOS THROUGH THE YEAR

The Lao word for festival, *boun,* refers to the Buddhist act of merit-making *(see pp22–3).* Indeed many festivals in Laos are related to the Buddhist religion, although some celebrate specific rural events such as the harvest, planting, or the onset of the rains. Laos officially uses the Gregorian calendar, but several festivals are celebrated according to the traditional Lao calendar, based on solar and lunar calculations. However, events often fall on different days in different parts of the country. In addition to these, Lao people also celebrate festivals that are specific to a locality, such as Boun Wat Phu Champasak, which is celebrated at Wat Phu near the town of Champasak, and Boun That Luang, which is celebrated in Vientiane. Most temples also hold an annual fair, although the date varies from temple to temple.

Rice farmer with harvested crop

Revelers celebrating Boun Pi Mai, the Lao New Year, Vientiane

HOT SEASON

Probably the most difficult time of the year, the hot season is often dusty or humid, although places at higher altitudes such as the Xieng Khuang plateau are cooler. This is followed by the rice harvest season and the Lao people await the coming of the rains, marking the beginning of the agricultural cycle.

MARCH

Lao Women's Day *(Mar 8),* nationwide. Public holiday and day off for all female employees.

Boun Pha Vet *(end Mar/early Apr),* nationwide. Celebrations include performances of the Buddhist *Jataka* tales accompanied by traditional music in village temples, general merrymaking, and sermons delivered by the temple's abbot. An auspicious time for Lao men to enter monkhood.

APRIL

Lao New Year *(Apr 14–16),* nationwide. Known as Boun Pi Mai in Lao, the impressive New Year celebrations last for up to four days and are celebrated with an abundance of water.

The first day of the festival is celebrated by building stupas of sand along river banks or in temples, commemorating an act of piety by an Indian king who was an early follower of the Buddha. On the second day, in Luang Prabang, three red-faced figures representing the guardian spirits of the city, Phu Noe, Na Noe, and Sing Keaw Sing Kham, parade through the streets, make offerings at the river, and are ritually fed by the locals. Traditional beauty pageants are held in the evening. The third day is celebrated with more water throwing and *baci sukhuan* ceremonies at home. Devotees in Luang Prabang climb up Mt Phou Si to make merit at the That Chomsi stupa. On the fourth

THE BACI SUKHUAN CEREMONY

This ceremony is central to Lao culture. *Baci sukhuan* (pronounced basee sookuan) refers to a calling of the spirits. It involves tying strings to the wrists of the person to whom it is dedicated. The ceremony is held at birth, marriage, before or after a trip, when a new job starts, or any other significant event in a person's life. Its aim is to concentrate the spiritual forces, which is believed to help the person face the next part of their life with vigor.

A man getting *baci* strings tied to his wrist, *baci sukhuan* ceremony

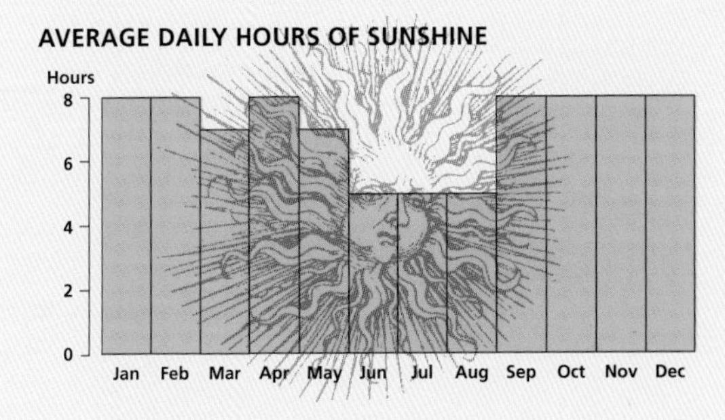

Sunshine Chart
Even during the rainy season, most days have some sunshine. The tropical sun can be very fierce, and adequate precautions against sunburn and sunstroke should be taken. A sun hat, sunscreen, and sunglasses are highly recommended items. Drinking plenty of water is essential.

day, the sacred Phabang statue is carried in a solemn procession from the National Museum to Wat Mai, where it is ritually cleansed. The festival ends with a performance of *Phra Lak Phra Lam*, the Lao version of the *Ramayana*, in the National Museum Complex.

MAY–JUNE

International Labor Day *(May 1)*, nationwide. Parades are organized by socialist groups and sports competitions are held in Vientiane.
Boun Visakha Busaa *(May full moon)*, nationwide. This Buddhist festival commemorates the Buddha's birth, death, and enlightenment. It is celebrated at *wats* with sermons and chanting during the day and candle-lit processions during the evening.
Boun Bang Fai *(mid May)*, nationwide. Better known as the Rocket Festival, this pre-Buddhist fertility event occurs at the height of the hot season and implores the gods to send the rains by launching homemade rockets skyward. Elaborately decorated bamboo rockets are built by villagers who carry them in a procession before launching them. The celebrations continue for two entire days.

Rockets being fired on the occasion of Boun Bang Fai

RAINY SEASON

Culturally, this is a time of repose and reflection, with a lull in agricultural activity. During this season, all Buddhist monks are required to remain in their temples and concentrate on spiritual development. It is also the traditional time for Lao men to make merit by temporarily entering into monkhood.

JULY

Boun Khao Pansa/Khao Watsa *(early Jul)*, nationwide. This festival marks the beginning of the Buddhist Rains Retreat, often referred to as the Buddhist Lent. During this time, devout Buddhists strictly observe the precepts of their faith. Locals visit temples to give alms and listen to chanting and sermons.

AUGUST–SEPTEMBER

Boun Haw Khao Padap Din *(Aug full moon)*, nationwide. During this somber festival dedicated to the deceased, prayers are offered for the spirits of dead family members. People present rice cakes to monks who are believed to act as intermediaries, transferring merit to the departed. This is also an occasion for traditional boat races in Khammuan province and Luang Prabang. Races take place on the Nam Khan in Luang Prabang.

Boat crews in elaborately carved boats racing each other, Suang Heua

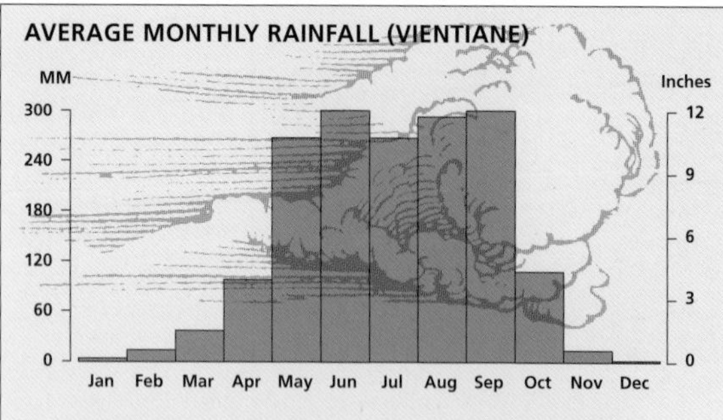

Rainfall Chart
Rainfall is not evenly distributed. Places in the north, such as Xieng Khuang, Phongsali and parts of Luang Nam Tha province, and the Bolaven Plateau in the southeast get over 120 inches (3,000 mm) annually, but Vientiane and Luang Prabang get only 67 inches (1,700 mm).

Locals carrying a prize-winning boat to the Mekong during Lai Heua Fai

COOL SEASON

Perhaps the best time of the year in Laos, when there is a welcome coolness in the air and a substantial drop in temperature. The northern areas of the country, however, are much colder, almost brutally so for the locals. A period of agricultural transition, numerous festivals occur during this time of the year, often in celebration of the harvested crop, or in preparation for the next agricultural cycle.

OCTOBER–NOVEMBER

Boun Ok Pansa/Ok Watsa *(early Nov)*, nationwide. Held three full moons after Boun Khao Pansa, this festival marks the end of the monastic Rains Retreat and the beginning of the cool season. Monks are presented with new robes and other supplies. Candle-lit processions are held in all *wats* in the evening.
Boun Fai Payanak *(Nov full moon)*, Pak Ngum district. Held at the end of the Rains Retreat, this event occurs once at this full moon and then again in May. Red, round fireballs, said to represent *naga* spirits, emerge from the Mekong River, moving upward. Locals gather along the riverfront to watch this fascinating phenomenon.
Boun That Luang *(Nov full moon)*, Vientiane. The celebrations actually begin at Wat Si Muang, where the city pillar is located. Here, respects are paid to Sao Si, the guardian goddess of Vientiane. The crowds then move to That Luang, where offerings are made to gathered monks, and a procession with representatives of all the country's various ethnic groups gathers around the stupa. There are candle-lit processions and spectacular firework displays. An international trade fair set up nearby also draws local shoppers.
Lai Heua Fai/Boun Nam *(variable)*, nationwide. Also known as the Boats of Light Festival, this event resembles Loy Krathong in Thailand and Diwali in India. Candle-lit processions are followed by participants proceeding to a nearby river to mount their candles on small bamboo-leaf boats laden with flowers, which are then set adrift.

In every *wat* in Luang Prabang, a large boat is constructed from bamboo strips and decorated with hundreds of small lanterns. These boats are taken to Wat Xieng Thong and after a winner is declared, they are set adrift in the mighty Mekong River.
Suang Heua *(variable)*, nationwide. Boats are carried to a nearby river and raced. The boats are believed to lure the *naga* river spirits back into rivers from the rice fields.

DECEMBER

Lao National Day *(Dec 2)*, Vientiane. Military parades and political speeches to commemorate the victory of the Communist government in 1975.

Ethnic Lao participating in a parade at That Luang, Vientiane

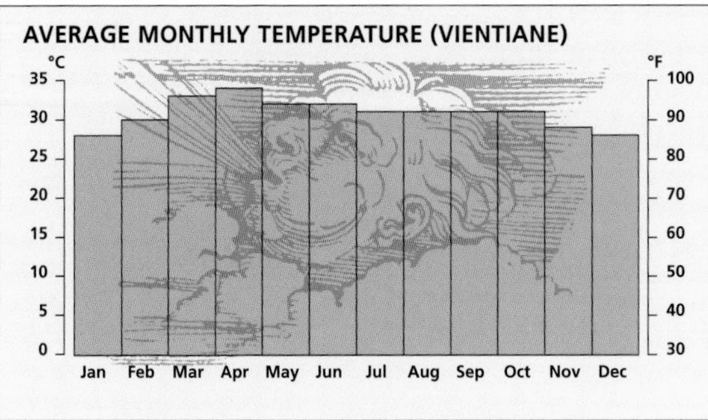

Temperature Chart
With the exception of the cool season from November to January, most parts of Laos are hot. During the rainy season, from May to September, humidity adds to the discomfort. During all periods except the hot season, elevated regions are cool and temperatures can fall to below freezing at night.

That In Hang Festival *(early Dec)*, Savannakhet. An important Buddhist worship site, That In Hang hosts a major temple fair attended by devotees from across the country. The door to the inner sanctum of the stupa is only opened at this time, and male devotees make merit with offerings. A trade fair, musical and dance performances, and sports competitions are held.
International New Year's Day *(Dec 31)*, nationwide. The event is celebrated with *baci sukhuan* ceremonies at home, and large parties, including New Year's Eve countdowns among the urban elite in the capital, Vientiane.
Hmong New Year *(variable)*, Xieng Khuang province. The Hmong ethnic minority also celebrate their New Year with grand feasts. Women dress in their traditional finery and teenagers engage in an unusual courting ritual, which involves tossing a ball between various rows of enthusiastic boys and girls.

Hmong girl in traditional dress

JANUARY

Boun Khun Khao *(end Jan/ early Feb)*, nationwide. This rural festival is particularly important to rice farmers since it celebrates the successful harvest of their crop. At the local temple, unhusked rice is piled into pyramid-shaped mounds and blessed by the gathered monks. This ceremony is followed by a lavish feast and traditional music.

FEBRUARY

Vietnamese Tet/Chinese New Year *(end Jan/early Feb)*, Savannakhet and Vientiane. Colorful dragon dance troupes pass through the streets to the accompaniment of firecrackers, drums, and gongs. All businesses close for three days.
Lao Elephant Festival *(mid Feb)*, Sainyabuli. This festival is held to raise awareness of the need to conserve the environment of the Asian elephant. There are processions, demonstrations, and opportunities to learn more about this great mammal.
Boun Makha Busaa *(Feb full moon)*, nationwide. An important religious event culminating on a full moon night. These are candle-lit processions where the faithful circumambulate the temple compounds. Boun Khao Chi, also known as Rice Cake Festival, commemorating the harvest, is also celebrated.
Boun Wat Phu Champasak *(Feb full moon)*, Wat Phu Champasak, Champasak province. This temple fair attracts visitors from across the country. Pilgrims make offerings at holy sites in the *wat*. Kickboxing and cockfighting take place on the last day.
Boun That Sikhot *(Feb full moon)*, south of Thakhek, Khammuan province. A popular fair by the riverside, attracting visitors from all over Khammuan province.

Elephant procession during the Lao Elephant Festival

PUBLIC HOLIDAYS

New Year's day (Jan 1)
Pathet Lao Day (Jan 6)
Army Day (Jan 20)
Lao Women's Day (Mar 8)
Lao People's Party Day (Mar 22)
Lao New Year (Apr 14–16)
International Labor Day (May 1)
Children's Day (Jun 1)
Boun Khao Pansa (early Jul)
Lao Issara Day (Aug 13)
Liberation Day (Aug 23)
Freedom from France Day (Oct 12)
Boun Ok Pansa (early Nov)
Lao National Day (Dec 2)

THE HISTORY OF LAOS

The borders of present-day Laos date from the 20th century, but the region has been populated for thousands of years. Its Tai-Lao-speaking people, although relatively recent arrivals, have an expansive and distinguished history. The stage of many wars and empire builders, Laos has been politically stable since 1975, and is now attracting thousands of visitors.

Evidence of human settlement in the Laos area reaches as far back as 500 BC, when a megalithic culture flourished in Northern Laos, around a site called the Plain of Jars. Southern Laos was ruled for a time from Champa, a coastal kingdom in what is now Vietnam, until the Cambodia-based Angkorian Empire took control of this territory. Angkorian influence eventually extended as far north as present-day Vientiane, and more tentatively, to Luang Prabang.

Statue of Fa Ngum, Vientiane

Laos was initially populated by Austro-Asiatic groups such as the Mon-Khmer-speaking people. The Lao themselves began arriving in the first millennium AD. These immigrants belonged to the Lao-Tai linguistic group, who originated in mountainous southern China and came seeking richer soil, a warmer climate, and escape from the expanding Han Chinese. Over the centuries, those who stayed in the mountains largely retained their animistic beliefs and tribal organization, and those who ventured into the lowlands came into contact with Mon-Khmer people, accepting the latter's methods of agriculture, statecraft, religion, and writing, while keeping some of their own languages and elements of social organization. In the late 13th century, the Khmer Empire weakened, and a number of Tai-speaking, Theravada Buddhist kingdoms sprang up along the Mekong River.

THE LAN XANG KINGDOM

In the 14th century, the Lao kingdom Lan Xang (Million Elephants), centered on Luang Prabang, came into being. Its founder, the semi-legendary Fa Ngum, was an ethnic Lao who spent much of his life as an exile in the Angkorian court. In the 1340s, he was sent north with a 10,000-man army to negotiate with vassal cities and keep them from falling under Ayutthayan control. Instead, Fa Ngum broke away from Angkor in a series of campaigns and, in 1353, founded Lan Xang. Over the next few years, he gained the allegiance of principalities around the Mekong, and extended his kingdom into what is now northeastern Thailand.

Fa Ngum was deposed by his son, Un Heuan, for obscure reasons. His successor then set about consolidating his power through army recruitment and by marrying into the royal families of Ayutthaya and Chiang Mai.

TIMELINE

500 BC Modern-day Champasak (Southern Laos) ruled by Champa kingdom; megalithic culture in the Plain of Jars, Northern Laos

AD 900–1300 Most of Laos is subordinate to the Khmer Empire at Angkor

1431 Ayutthayan armies sack Angkor, causing the demise of the Khmer Empire

500 BC | AD 1 | 500 | 1000 | 1500

Stone jars excavated at the Plain of Jars

1353 Fa Ngum founds Theravada Buddhist Lao kingdom of Lan Xang

1374 Un Heuan replaces Fa Ngum as ruler of Lan Xang

◁ **Gold relief at Wat Mai Suwannaphumaham, built in the 14th century during the Lan Xang Kingdom**

The 16th and 17th centuries were a golden age for Lan Xang. The first Westerners in Laos, visiting in the 1640s, left accounts of a peaceful and prosperous kingdom, a hospitable population, and a capital richly ornamented with religious buildings. A Dutch merchant noted that Buddhist monks in Vientiane were "more numerous than the armies of the German Emperor." However, by 1700, the kingdom had broken into four semi-independent principalities, forced to pay tribute to Ayutthaya.

Siamese troops with artillery on elephant back advancing into Laos to combat French expansion

SIAM AND VIETNAM

In the latter half of the 18th century, Luang Prabang was sacked by the Burmese army, and Vientiane by the Siamese army. Siam was a kingdom based in Thonburi, across the river from Bangkok. It soon became the paramount state in the region, and Lan Xang effectively disappeared. For most of the 19th century, the lowland areas were dependent on Siam, and Vietnam controlled much of the mountainous north. The key figure in this period of Lao history was Chao Anou, a nobleman who became the king of Vientiane under Siamese protection in 1804. Fifteen years later, after he gained control over the southern principality of Champasak, Anou mounted a military campaign against Bangkok in an effort to establish an independent Lao kingdom. The campaign was a disaster: the Siamese army burned down Vientiane and moved its population into Siam. Anou was captured and taken to Bangkok, where he died. For the remainder of the century, the Siamese court maintained tight control over Lao populations on both sides of the Mekong, while the newly empowered Nguyen dynasty in Vietnam took over much of what is now Northern Laos.

Wat doors depicting 17th-century Dutch merchants

FRENCH RULE

In the late 1850s, France expressed imperial interests in Indochina by taking possession first of southern Vietnam and then of Cambodia. By 1885, the French had annexed central and northern Vietnam. Eight years later, after threatening Siam with full-scale war, they were able to peaceably acquire the territory east of the Mekong, that is, most of present-day Laos. Thus, in 1907, Laos was formally united for the first time since 1700, under French rule. Three of its four principalities were ruled directly, without princes, and the fourth (Luang Prabang), by a powerless and cooperative monarch.

A pioneer in developing Franco-Lao relations was the adventurous geographer Auguste Pavie, who had

TIMELINE

Crest of the Dutch East India Company

1637–49 Reign of King Surinyavongsā, considered the Golden Age of Lan Xang

1700 Lan Xang broken into four semi-independent principalities that pay tribute to the Kingdom of Ayutthaya

1600 | 1650 | 1700 | 1750

1563 Vientiane made capital of Lan Xang in an effort to escape Burmese threats

1641 Gerritt van Wuysthoff, a representative of the Dutch East India Company, is among the first Europeans to arrive in Laos

Buddha at Wat Si Saket, built by Chao Anou

convinced the Lao upper class that being protected by France would be preferable to submitting to open-ended Siamese control. As a result, France's Colonial burden, such as it was, was lightened by a friendly elite and the mildness of French economic intervention. During this period, Laos contained only seven percent of Indochina's people, generated one percent of its foreign trade, and in the 1930s, employed fewer than 500 French administrators. Throughout the Colonial period, the kingdom was overwhelmingly rural – less than two percent of the population lived in provincial towns. Vietnamese immigrants dominated the civil service as well as the small commercial sector.

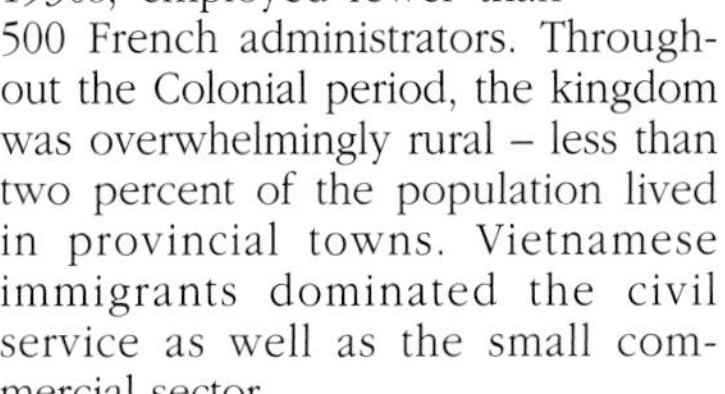

King Sisavang Vong (1885–1959)

EARLY 20TH CENTURY

The idea of independence for Indochina did not arise until World War II, when parts of the region had openly gone into revolt. When France fell to Germany in 1940, the French and Lao were defenseless against the irredentist claims of the pro-Japanese regime in Bangkok. After a brief war aimed primarily at regaining provinces lost in 1907, Thailand (as Siam had renamed itself in 1939) took over those parts of Laos that lay west of the Mekong. Stung by the territorial loss, and fearful of further claims, the French proclaimed Laos to be a unified protectorate in 1941. However, in March 1945, the Japanese military imprisoned French civil servants and soldiers throughout Indochina and made local rulers declare independence. The Lao king, Sisavang Vong, the most loyal ruler in the region, refused to do so for a month.

Japan's surrender at the end of World War II created a power vacuum in Indochina. In Laos, this gave rise to three conflicting camps – a pro-French royalist faction led by the king; the Lao nationalists, who as the Lao Issara (Free Lao) formed a government in exile in 1945; and Vietnamese Communists recruited from the Vietnamese population and supported by quasi-independent northern Vietnam. These groups maneuvered against each other in what they hoped would soon be an independent kingdom. Their dispute revealed deep fissures within the different parts of Laos, between Communists and non-Communists and within the Lao elite.

French steamer on a Mekong tributary in Southern Laos, late 19th century

1771 Burmese armies sack Luang Prabang

1782 Siam seizes power in Vientiane

1828 The Siamese army burns down Vientiane

1885 French annex central and northern Vietnam

1941 Thailand annexes Lao territory west of the Mekong after the Franco-Thai war

1893 French seize Lao territories east of Mekong

1800 | **1850** | **1900**

1804 Chao Anou becomes king of Vientiane

Postcard from French-Colonial Laos

1907 Franco-Siamese treaty establishes current borders of Laos

1945 Encouraged by the Japanese, the Lao king reluctantly declares independence

STRUGGLE FOR INDEPENDENCE

Foreign and domestic nation builders in Laos were thwarted in their efforts to unify the country by embedded habits of regionalism, rivalries among the Lao elite, poor communications, and by the devastation of the First Indochina War and the Vietnam War. When Laos was drawn into the First Indochina War, few of its people had strong political ideas. Those who did were either members of the Vietnamese-dominated Indochina Communist Party (ICP) or were associated with the nationalist movement called Lao Issara. Supported by the Francophobic authorities in Thailand, Lao Issara had formed an interim government.

In 1946, the French returned in force, establishing a new Kingdom of Laos with Sisavang Vong as its ruler. They hoped that the gesture would unify their protectorate and set it on the road to eventual independence. In 1950, they awarded Laos partial independence, keeping control over the nation's defense and foreign affairs. Four years later, following the Geneva Conference, Laos obtained full independence.

Prince Souvanna Phouma (1901–84)

In this postwar era, two Lao princes played important political roles. Prince Souvanna Phouma worked for Lao Issara until 1949, when he returned to Laos, and was often prime minister of Laos in later years. His half-brother, Prince Souphanouvong, broke with Lao Issara in 1949 and joined the Vietnamese-led resistance movement known as Pathet Lao.

Pro-Communist demonstrators marching against US Imperialism in the streets of Vientiane

THE VIETNAM WAR

The Geneva Conference stipulated that Pathet Lao troops would be stationed in two provinces of Northern Laos bordering Vietnam, pending a demobilization which never occurred. Fissures soon developed between these Communist enclaves and successive pro-Western, or neutralist, governments in Laos. In 1960, a fight broke out between the Pathet Lao and the poorly trained Lao army. In an effort to establish stability in the kingdom, a second Geneva Conference was held in 1961–2, where the warring parties pledged to support a neutral Laos. However, the agreement was soon subverted by both the US and North Vietnam. From 1964 onward, eastern Laos was subjected to intensive aerial bombardment – a largely unsuccessful US effort to disrupt the extensive North Vietnamese supply lines known as the Ho Chi Minh Trail. In Northern Laos, surrogate forces paid by the US fought Pathet Lao forces backed by North

TIMELINE

1950 France grants Laos partial independence

1954 Following the first Geneva Conference, Laos gains full independence

1964 US begins bombing Communist targets in Laos

Carrying supplies along the Ho Chi Minh Trail in Laos

1955 | 1965 | 1975

1946–54 First Indochina War

1954–75 Vietnam War

1961–2 Second Geneva Conference supports a neutral government in Laos

1973 Cease-fire between the US and North Vietnam

1975 Lao King Sisavang Vatthana abdicates; the LPRP takes over peacefully in Vientiane

US artillery and Lao refugees crossing the border into South Vietnam, 1971

Vietnam. Efforts to establish a neutral government in Vientiane came to nothing. After a cease-fire between the US and North Vietnam in 1973, fighting subsided in Laos.

COMMUNISM AND STABILITY

Once Vietnam was unified under the Communists and Cambodia had fallen to the Khmer Rouge *(see p40)*, a Communist Lao state was only a matter of time. The last king of Laos, Sisavang Vatthana, abdicated in December 1975, and on the following day the Lao People's Democratic Republic (LPDR) was formally established. The Lao People's Revolutionary Party (LPRP), an offshoot of the Indochinese Communist Party (ICP), led the new state.

The Communists who took power in 1975 have never been seriously challenged, but the early years of the new regime were hard for people unsympathetic to Marxism-Leninism. Many were herded into "re-education" camps and many more sought refuge in Thailand. Over the years, the LPRP displayed extraordinary survival skills and rarely resorted to popular repression. Vietnamese guidance was welcomed, especially from 1975 to 1990. In the late 1980s, as the Cold War ended, Vietnam withdrew most of its forces and the LPRP relaxed its top-down economic policies. Market forces re-emerged, Buddhist practices revived, tourism picked up, and relations warmed with Thailand. Symbolically, a bridge across the Mekong, the first in Lao history, was completed in 1994. Laos joined the Association of Southeast Asian Nations (ASEAN) in 1997.

In the 21st century, Laos exchanged the patronage of Vietnam for the corporate protection of ASEAN and the benefits, such as they are, of globalization, which include massive investment in the country and the assurance of a less impoverished future.

The Thai-Lao Friendship Bridge across the Mekong

1988 Vietnamese troops officially withdraw from Laos as the Cold War draws to a close

1997 Laos joins the Association of Southeast Asian Nations (ASEAN)

Choummaly Sayasone, President of the Lao People's Democratic Republic

1985 | 1995 | 2005 | 2015

1994 Inauguration of the first bridge spanning the Mekong River

Flag of Laos, officially, the Lao People's Democratic Republic

2006 Choummaly Sayasone elected General Secretary of the Lao People's Revolutionary Party

Laos at a Glance

Owing to its geographical expanse, Laos encompasses amazingly diverse terrains. Much of the country is covered by steep, verdant mountain ranges, which gradually give way to plateaus and mixed deciduous forests. The mighty Mekong River dominates the topography of the land and runs through nearly its entire length. Vientiane, the capital city, has many beautiful Buddhist temples while the ancient royal capital of Luang Prabang is home to the Phabang, the country's most sacred Buddha image. The south is renowned for a magnificent inland archipelago, a counterpoint to the remote mountainous regions of the north.

Wat Xieng Thong (see pp160–61), *located at the tip of the Luang Prabang peninsula at the confluence of the Mekong River and the Nam Khan, is an exquisite Buddhist temple. It has great historical significance as the coronation venue of Lao kings.*

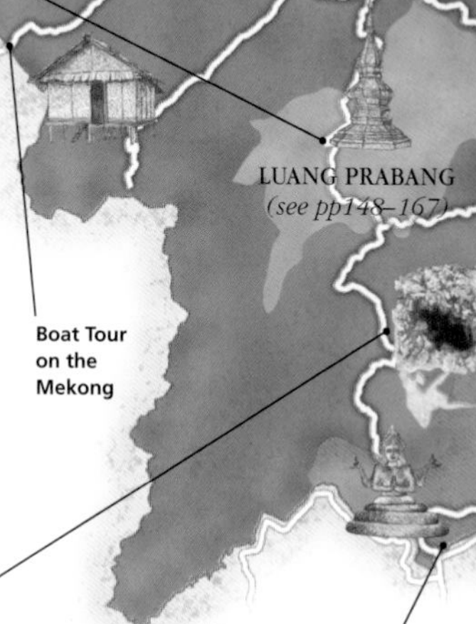

Vang Vieng (see pp172–3) *draws numerous visitors due to its signature activity of tubing on the Nam Song. Surrounded by stunning mountain scenery, the limestone karst cliffs are perfect for spelunking. Other attractions include rock climbing and kayaking.*

Xieng Khuan (see p146), *also known as Buddha Park, is home to a collection of enigmatic statuary made by a Lao holy man, Luang Phu Bounleua Soulilat. Sculptures range from Hindu gods to mermaids and a giant Reclining Buddha.*

A Boat Tour on the Mekong (see pp184–5) *offers splendid views of the region's striking karst limestone mountain slopes, pastoral life, and herds of wild elephants. Boat tours beginning at Huay Xai, the last border town before Thailand, are an ideal way to explore the area.*

Plain of Jars (see p175), *named for the hundreds of giant stone urns left behind by an ancient megalithic culture, remains an archaeological enigma. The area witnessed intense bombing during the Vietnam War* (1954–75).

Savannakhet *(see pp192–3)* is a charming riverside town that is connected to Thailand by the Thai-Lao Friendship Bridge.

Wat Phu Champasak (see pp196–7), *the largest archaeological site in the country, offers superb examples of Khmer architecture. The Buddhist Lao, who revere the site, have added their own religious iconography to the temple.*

The Bolaven Plateau (see p198) *is home to several ethnic minorities such as the Katu, who cultivate rice and other temperate crops such as coffee.*

Si Phan Don *(see pp202–3)* is an inland archipelago on the Mekong River just north of the Cambodian border.

VIENTIANE

The capital of Laos, Vientiane is also Asia's smallest capital. The city's plan of intersecting streets and boulevards dates from the early 20th century; these are lined with fine examples of Buddhist and Colonial-era architecture. Once a sleepy backwater, today Vientiane is in the midst of a revival and the city's chic restaurants and boutiques have begun to attract local and international visitors.

Located on a bend in the wide Mekong River, the capital city of Laos has survived numerous changes over the centuries. Over 1,000 years ago it was a Khmer trading post. In the 16th century it became the capital of the Lao kingdom, but was ultimately destroyed by the Siamese in 1828. The French Colonialists appropriated the country as part of their Indochinese empire in the late 19th century and Vientiane was chosen to be their administrative capital. During the Cold War (1945–91), it was flooded with refugees as the rest of the country witnessed intense bombing and the city suffered through its time as a Soviet-era Socialist backwater.

Vientiane has undergone rapid changes over the last couple of decades. The strict Communist stance of the country was relaxed after the collapse of the Soviet Union in 1991 and new business ventures sprung up around the city. Many Lao exiles also returned to reclaim properties they had abandoned as they fled the Communist regime and are now re-establishing homes and businesses here.

The religious architecture of Vientiane is splendid and its numerous *wats* are positively vibrant with worshipers. The Lao National Museum has world-class exhibits covering Lao history from prehistoric times till the more recent Communist Revolution of 1975, and the Buddhist art on display at Haw Pha Kaew is the best in the country. The city's restaurants and hotels offer Lao and Western cuisine, at reasonable prices, and are often located in restored French Colonial buildings. While the riverfront along Fa Ngum Road is being redeveloped, which will result in a riverside park, visitors looking for peace and quiet can head upstream, west of Khun Bulom Road, where they can enjoy a sundown drink by the Mekong.

A French-style restaurant with alfresco dining near Nam Phu Square, Vientiane

◁ **Beautifully molded bronze statues of the Buddha on the terrace of Haw Pha Kaew, Vientiane**

Exploring Vientiane

A few of the most interesting places in Vientiane, such as the Haw Pha Kaew, Wat Si Saket, and Wat Ong Teu Mahawihan, lie between Samsenthai Road and the Mekong River. The lively Talat Sao, where visitors can buy an array of items, is located near Lan Xang Avenue, which leads to the French-inspired Patuxai monument, while Setthathirat Road has numerous cafés, boutiques, and restaurants. Closer to the river border with Thailand is the Xieng Khuan (Buddha Park), with its huge collection of statues. Visitors keen on the outdoors can head to Phu Khao Khuay NPA, where they can enjoy hikes and nature walks.

A sandstone sculpture at Xieng Khuan

SIGHTS AT A GLANCE

Places of Worship
Pha That Luang 9
Wat Ong Teu Mahawihan 4
Wat Si Muang 1
Wat Si Saket 3
Wat Sok Pa Luang 8

Museums
Haw Pha Kaew 2
Kaysone Phomvihane Memorial Museum 10
Lao National Museum 5

Sites of Interest
Beerlao Brewery 11
Patuxai 7

Market
Talat Sao 6

Areas of Natural Beauty
Phu Khao Khuay National Protected Area 13
Xieng Khuan 12

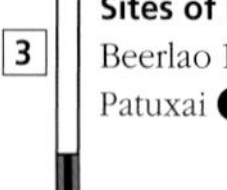

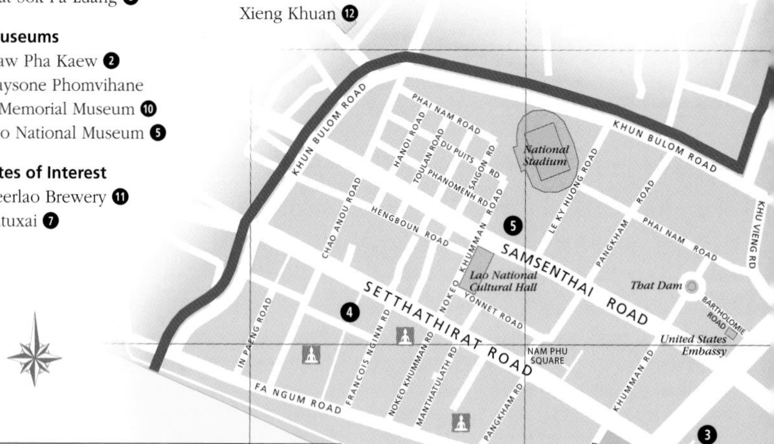

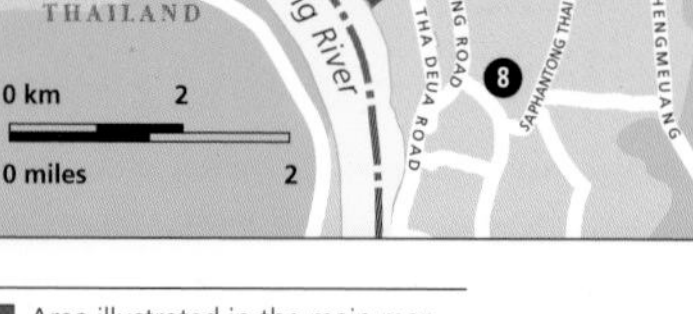

Area illustrated in the main map

SEE ALSO

- ***Where to Stay*** pp218–20
- ***Where to Eat*** pp242–4

GETTING AROUND

Most of the main sites in Vientiane are within comfortable walking distance of each other, but bicycles are available for rent from a number of guesthouses and rental shops across the city. This is a good option for those who want to avoid walking in the tropical heat. Motorcycles are another way of getting around the city and can be rented for a few dollars per day. Tuk-tuks can be found outside tourist spots and hotels or flagged down on roads. For journeys to areas around Vientiane, taxis or buses are better options.

VISITORS' CHECKLIST

Road Map B3. *300,00.*
Wattay International Airport.
Lao National Tourism Administration, Lan Xang Ave, (021)-212-248. *daily.*
Boat Racing Festival (Oct), Boun That Luang (Nov).
www.tourismlaos.org

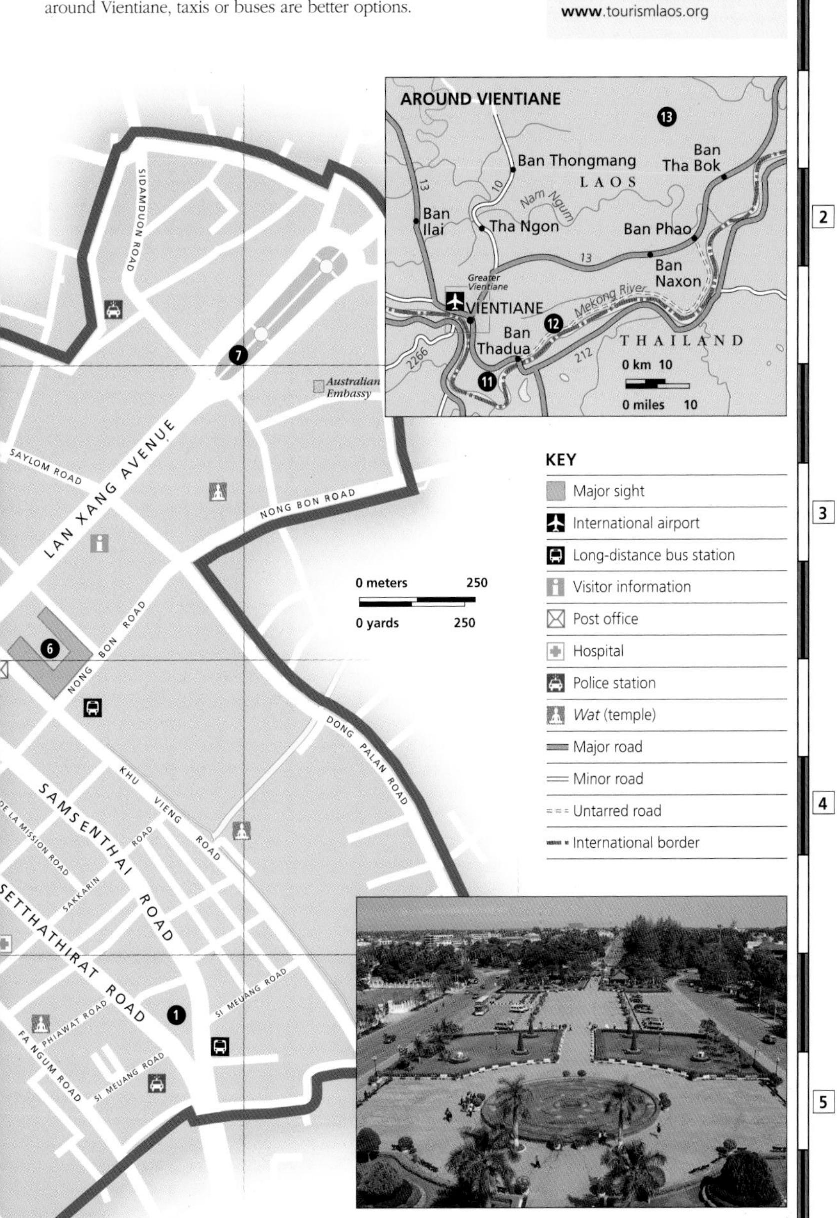

A view of the city from the top of the Patuxai

Wat Si Muang ❶

Convergence of Setthathirat & Samsenthai Rds. **City Map** D5. 🚗 ◻ *8am–3pm daily.* 🎫

One of the best-known temples in Vientiane, Wat Si Muang houses the *lak muang*, or city pillar, which was installed here by King Setthathirat in 1563 after he moved the Lao capital from Luang Prabang to Vientiane. The temple was razed by the Siamese when they sacked the city in 1827 and later rebuilt.

Today, the temple is a vibrant place of worship and considered particularly auspicious by devotees who come here to perform a variety of rituals. The current *sim* (ordination hall) dates from 1915 and is divided into two chambers. Inside the front chamber, devotees are blessed by a monk with lustral water and a *baci* string *(see p124)* is tied to the wrist. After this, supplicants with a particular wish prostrate themselves before what was once a Buddha image, but is now only a melted lump having been damaged when the Siamese set the temple on fire. The ritual involves lifting the image three times above the head while expressing the wish. The inner sanctum of the temple houses the city pillar, now gilded and wrapped with a sacred cloth. Incense is burned here and candles are lit as offerings to the city spirit. The blackened ceiling of this chamber is testament to the number of offerings made here.

Devotees offering prayers in the main *sim*, Wat Si Muang

Manicured gardens leading up to the main entrance, Haw Pha Kaew

Behind the temple are the laterite remains of an ancient Khmer religious site, next to which a statue of Vientiane's godmother, Sao Si, is located. Legend has it that when the city pillar was installed, Sao Si jumped beneath it to appease malevolent spirits and bring good fortune to the city. Today, worshipers make fervent offerings to commemorate her sacrifice. East of the temple compound stands a statue of King Sisavang Vong (r.1904–59), holding a copy of the country's first legal code. The statue, a gift from the Soviet Union, was installed here in 1974. Although the royal family perished in prison camps in the northeast, the statue was spared.

An offering, Wat Si Muang

Haw Pha Kaew ❷

Setthathirat Rd. **City Map** C4. 🚗 ◻ *8am–noon & 1–4pm daily.* 🎫

The original structure of this temple-turned-museum was destroyed by the Siamese in 1827. It was reconstructed under the supervision of the Lao prince Souvanna Phouma, a French-trained engineer and later prime minister of the country during the French Colonial period. Once the exclusive temple of Lao kings, Haw Pha Kaew is no longer a functioning Buddhist temple, but a national museum of splendid Buddhist art.

Ironically, it is named for a precious piece of religious art, the Pha Kaew (Emerald Buddha), which is no longer here. Made of jade, it is as important an icon as the Phabang *(see p153)* in Luang Prabang. However, it was seized by the Siamese in 1779, and has remained in Wat Phra Kaew in Bangkok ever since. A signboard, both in Lao and English, expresses the Lao peoples' indignation at this act. However, this well-traveled talisman actually originated in India and spent much time in Thailand until King Setthathirat took it from Chiang Mai when the Lao kingdom of Lan Xang ruled northern Thailand.

Today, the main attraction of this impressive museum is the magnificent collection of bronze Buddha images on a terrace surrounding the building. These have been collected from various temples in the country. Artifacts inside the building include smaller Buddha images, Khmer stelae, bronze frog drums, and a large Seated Buddha image. The beautifully landscaped gardens of the museum offer a verdant respite from the heat of central Vientiane.

Wat Si Saket ❸

Setthathirat Rd. **City Map** C4.
8am–noon & 1–4pm daily.

The oldest *wat* in Vientiane, Wat Si Saket was spared the destruction wrought by the Siamese when they burned the rest of the temples in the city. Wat Si Saket was built in 1818 for King Anouvong, popularly known as Chao Anou, and it was here that Lao nobility swore loyalty to him. Anouvong turned against his original allies, the Siamese, and lost his capital, and his life, for this decision.

The architectural feature that makes this temple unique is the cloister, or covered gallery, surrounding the central *sim*. The inner walls of the cloister are filled with over 2,000 Buddha images arranged in symmetrical niches facing the *sim*. The *sim* itself has an exquisite five-tiered roof, which was restored by the French twice, resulting in a ceiling with a rather European finish. A carved wooden *hao thian* (candle holder) lies near the altar. One of the highlights of this enchanting ancient collection of Buddhist art is a *háang song nam pha*, a *naga*-headed trough. It is kept in the covered gallery and used for pouring lustral water over the Buddha images during the Lao New Year *(see p124)*.

Covered cloister with niches containing Buddha images, Wat Si Saket

Exhibits of historical significance on display, Lao National Museum

Wat Ong Teu Mahawihan ❹

Setthathirat Rd. **City Map** B3.
8am–5pm daily.

The *wat's* name, meaning Temple of the Heavy Buddha, derives from the 19-ft (6-m) tall bronze Buddha statue, dating from the 16th century, which is kept within the *sim*. The site is significant as it is believed to have been used for religious purposes since the 3rd century. A few Khmer stelae are housed in a *sala* (open-sided hall) within the complex. Monks from all over Laos come to study in the school that is housed in the *wat*. Visitors can strike up an enlightening conversation with these erudite young men. The school is directed by the Hawng Sangkhalat (Deputy Patriarch) of the Lao monastic order.

Intricate detail of façade, Wat Ong Teu Mahawihan

Lao National Museum ❺

Samsenthai Rd. **City Map** B3.
8am–noon & 1–4pm daily.

Once known as the Lao Revolutionary Museum and derided by foreigners for its Socialist Realism and overt propagandizing, the Lao National Museum is gradually being revamped. It now offers fascinating exhibits, well displayed and illuminated, with informative captions in English. The museum traces the history of the country from prehistoric times to the present. The displays, showcasing artifacts from both the Lao Pako archaeological site and the Plain of Jars *(see p175)*, as well as Khmer- and Buddhist-era exhibits, are excellent. The Buddhist-era room features a rare Thai Lue Buddha image, which resembles an animist icon. The life-sized re-creations of the Khmer lintels of Wat Phu Champasak *(see pp196–7)* are impressive, as are the original Hindu artifacts from the temple, including Shiva and Ganesha statues. The modern-era exhibits mainly comprise photographs of revolutionary heroes, which are interesting relics of those times, while the displays of cluster bombs dropped by the Americans are chilling. The second floor has a display on minority cultures.

A shop with numerous brightly colored souvenirs on sale, Talat Sao

Talat Sao 6

Corner of Lan Xang Ave & Khu Vieng Rd. **City Map** D3. *8am–6pm daily.*

Clearly referring to a bygone era when it functioned as a wet market for the housewives of Vientiane, Talat Sao, meaning Morning Market, has long since been transformed into an interesting complex of shops. A large portion of the structure dates from the 1960s, and has shops selling electronic goods such as refrigerators as well as other home appliances, catering mainly to local needs. Visitors will also find shops selling handicrafts, antiques, jewelry, and 24-karat gold ornaments. Other items of interest include textiles, particularly the beautiful handwoven silk and cotton *pha sins* (sarongs) worn by Lao women, which make attractive souvenirs. Accompanying the *pha sins* are magnificent hand-worked silver belts and silver ornaments such as bracelets and earrings. Bargaining is *de riguer* for anything bought here, and antiques and gemstones are best left to those with sound knowledge of such items, since fakes abound. However, some of the reproduction antiques, generally from Vietnam, are quite attractive. These items are usually priced and sold as reproductions, though visitors should be wary of buying overpriced pieces. There is a small air-conditioned mall on the southwestern side of the market, and a major hotel and retail construction project has transformed the market's structure, although the goods on offer have remained the same.

The food court on the third floor of the mall, where delicious local cuisine is available, is an ideal stop for weary shoppers. Visitors eager to experience an authentic Lao market selling fresh local produce such as vegetables, flowers, meat, and tobacco can stop by Khua Din, which lies to the east of Talat Sao, just past the bus station.

Patuxai 7

Lan Xang Ave. **City Map** D2. *8am–5pm daily.* *for tower only.*

At first sight, the Patuxai, which means Victory Gate, brings to mind the Arc de Triomphe in Paris. The monument was constructed in 1964 to commemorate the lives lost during the course of the Lao Civil War, fought between 1953 and 1975. It is made of concrete, which is rumored to have been donated by the Americans for the construction of a new airport. The arch is adorned with the typically Lao mixture of Buddhist and Hindu iconography along with bas-reliefs of *apsaras* facing fierce demons from the Hindu epic, *Ramayana*.

A spiral staircase leads to the top of the monument. En route visitors will pass dozens of souvenir shops that specialize in T-shirts. Once at the top, visitors are rewarded with excellent views across Lan Xang Avenue toward the Mekong River. The Patuxai is best visited early in the morning in order to avoid the heat, and the crowds brought by tour buses.

Vibrant reliefs adorning the ceiling of the Patuxai

TYPES OF TUK-TUK

Colorful jumbo tuk-tuk

Three types of tuk-tuk ply the streets of Vientiane. The first is the tourist tuk-tuk, which visitors will usually find waiting in queues outside tourist hot-spots. Although hiring one of these should not be expensive, drivers generally quote very high prices and also produce laminated fare tables to prove the legitimacy of their demands. The second is the wandering tuk-tuk, which can be hailed from anywhere, although it is best not to do so from near a queue of the tourist tuk-tuks. Prices are negotiable and cheaper than those demanded by tourist tuk-tuk drivers. Lastly, there is the jumbo, which charges a set price and follows a fixed route. These are the cheapest and can be boarded from tuk-tuk stations. It is worth traveling by one of these vehicles for an interesting local experience.

A wandering tuk-tuk plying the streets of Vientiane

Gilded structure of the Lao national monument, Pha That Luang

Wat Sok Pa Luang ❽

Off Khu Vieng Rd. **City Map** A5. *8am–3pm daily.*

A visit to this simple *wat*, located in a quiet outer suburb, presents an interesting alternative to visiting the grand temples that line the streets of Vientiane. The compound of the *wat*, whose name means Forest Temple, is filled with shady trees. Just outside the entrance to the *wat* is a house offering traditional massages as well as herbal saunas that are available in the afternoons, every day of the week. The temple also offers courses in Vipassana, which is a type of Buddhist meditation.

Carving at Wat Sok Pa Luang

Pha That Luang ❾

That Luang Rd. **City Map** B4. *8am–noon & 1–4pm daily.* *Boun That Luang (Nov).*

This important religious monument, whose name means The Great Stupa, is also the symbol of Lao nationhood. Its image appears on the currency as well as the national seal. Excavations have indicated the existence of a Khmer site here dating from around the 12th century, long before the Pha That Luang was erected in its present form. King Setthathirat ordered its construction when he moved the Lao capital from Luang Prabang to Vientiane in the mid-16th century. After the Siamese razed the city in 1827, the site was abandoned, and bandits seeking gold and jewels later destroyed the edifice. The French rebuilt it in the 1930s with the aid of drawings made by French explorers who had visited the abandoned site in 1867.

Today, the That Luang lies in a large compound behind a statue of King Setthathirat, and is flanked by two Buddhist temples. The main stupa reaches 148 ft (45 m) above ground level, and is surrounded by three platforms of decreasing size, each of which is surrounded by rows of smaller stupas and lotus petal-shaped crenulations. A cloister on the outermost wall contains both Lao and Khmer Buddha images. Boun That Luang, held here in November *(see p126)*, is among the most important festivals in Vientiane and lasts for several days.

Kaysone Phomvihane Memorial Museum ❿

NH13, Ban Sivilay, Muang Saythani. **City Map** B4. *8am–noon & 1–4pm daily.*

Located on the main road south out of Vientiane, this museum is divided into two parts. The first is a grandiose memorial to the late president and founding father of Communist Laos, Kaysone Phomvihane, and the second is the actual house in which he lived after the Communists seized power in 1975. The memorial is a huge, well-kept hall that includes a scale model of the late president's childhood home in Savannakhet *(see p192)* and various revolutionary memorabilia. More interesting, however, is his home, which is located on what was once a US military and CIA base, which the Pathet Lao occupied after its former occupants were ousted. It is a modest, single-story bungalow and has been kept exactly as it was when Kaysone Phomvihane resided here, with his library, work table, and other personal items on display. The house is a short distance from the memorial hall, but staff are happy to guide visitors there.

Bronze statue of Kaysone Phomvihane in front of his memorial

One of the four archways of the Patuxai monument, Vientiane ▷

ພັກປະຊາຊົນປະຕິວັດລາວທີ່ມີກຽດສະ
TAIPAN HOTEL

Giant Reclining Buddha amid several smaller statues, Xieng Khuan

Beerlao Brewery ⓫

Thadeua Rd, 8 miles (13 km) SE of Vientiane. **Tel** *(021)-812-001.*
9–11:30am & 1–4pm daily.
www.beerlao.la

Winner of many international awards, Beerlao is Laos's bestselling brand of beer and is exported to 13 countries worldwide. Originally established by the French, this brewery was nationalized in 1975. Since 2002, however, it has been a joint venture with the Danish brewing giant, Carlsberg. The company produces a variety of beers such as light, dark, and draft, and has a huge production capacity of 55 million gallons (210 million litres) of beer per annum. Located on the outskirts of Vientiane, the brewery welcomes visitors, who are given a free guided tour that includes a walk through the brewing and bottling areas, and a video detailing the company's history. There is plenty of free beer to be had at the end of the tour. Although individuals are tended to, it is the larger groups that get more attention.

Official Beerlao logo

Xieng Khuan ⓬

Thadeua Rd, 16 miles (26 km) SE of Vientiane. *from Vientiane.*
8am–5pm daily.

Also known as Buddha Park, Xieng Khuan is located in a pleasant meadow next to the Mekong and surrounded by shady trees. This collection of ferro-concrete statuary far exceeds the standard Hindu-Buddhist syncretism that can be seen in most Lao temples. The sculptures are products of the vivid imagination of the Lao guru Luang Phu Bounleua Soulilat. Inspired by the teachings of a Hindu holy man whom he met in a cave in Vietnam, Luang Phu proceeded to create this collection based on his own visions. Luang Phu was not popular with the Communists, and in 1975 he left Laos to create a similar collection of statuary in a park directly across the river in Nong Khai, Thailand, the main stupa of which is visible from here.

Made by amateur artists under Soulilat's direction, this eclectic collection ranges from an enormous Reclining Buddha to statues of Hindu gods, holy men battling with crocodiles, enormous insects, and vestal virgins dancing on giant cobras. Particularly interesting is the large spherical structure at the front of the park, which can be entered through the gaping mouth of a 10-ft (3-m) tall demon head. Inside are staircases leading to three different levels said to represent hell, earth, and heaven. They finally emerge at the top of the structure which overlooks the park. Nearby is a riverside café, which provides a cool and relaxing stop for visitors.

Beer bottles ready to be transferred into crates, Beerlao Brewery

For hotels and restaurants in this region see pp218–20 and pp242–4

Phu Khao Khuay National Protected Area ⓭

30 miles (48 km) NE of Vientiane. *from southern bus terminal to Ban Tha Bok.* *National Tourism Administration, Vientiane, (021)-212-251.* **www.** trekkingcentrallaos.com

Covering an area of over 770 sq miles (2,000 sq km), Phu Khao Khuay, meaning Buffalo Horn Mountain, is the closest National Protected Area to Vientiane and is excellent for visitors who do not have the time or opportunity to see nature preserves farther afield. The area's wildlife includes the tiger, Asiatic black bear, sun bear, clouded leopard, elephant, and a plethora of smaller mammals and bird species. Many wild orchids and other flora are also found here. Trekking, boat trips, swimming, nature walks, and village home-stays are some of the activities and experiences on offer. It is also possible to observe wild elephants.

The entrance to Phu Khao Khuay NPA is off Route 13 going north from Vientiane at kilometer 92, just before the village of Ban Tha Bok. Here, a turnoff on the left signposted to Long Xane leads to the NPA. Although visitors can explore the area independently using a rented motorcycle or car, it is best to hire local guides as their knowledge of the area will make the trip much more interesting. Independent guides are available in Ban Hat Khai, but language remains a challenge. Green Discovery *(see p287)* in Vientiane offers tours to the elephant observation tower near the village of Ban Na, and other parts of Phu Khao Khuay. Vientiane Orchidées *(see p261)* organizes treks that combine boat travel and nature walks, focusing on the many species of wild orchids that flourish in the NPA. Both companies offer one-day and several-day trips from Vientiane.

Boating down a river, Phu Khao Khuay National Protected Area

Ban Hat Khai

5 miles (8 km) N of Ban Tha Bok.

The village of Ban Hat Khai is an ideal place from which to take boat tours and trekking trips deep into Phu Khao Khuay, particularly to the spectacular 328-ft (100-m) high cliff of Pha Luang. Some 3 miles (5 km) north of Ban Hat Khai lies the beautiful Tat Xai waterfall, which is a popular picnic spot for residents of Vientiane. Although not as impressive, the Tat Leuk waterfall, located 3 miles (5 km) west of Ban Hat Khai, has a natural pool at its foot that is excellent for swimming. The visitors' center here can arrange treks and provide information on the conditions of all the trails and rivers in the area, which change with the seasons. Visitors can also rent tents and other basic camping equipment from the visitors' center for a small fee.

Bright yellow orchid

Ban Na

4 miles (6 km) SW of Ban Tha Bok.

A typical Lao village with lush paddy fields, Ban Na is a great stop for visitors keen to observe wild elephants. The elephant observation tower at Pung Xai, 4 miles (6 km) from here, is located next to a salt lick and is favored by these majestic beasts. Those lucky enough may get a chance to view the herd in its natural environment should their visit coincide with the herd's.

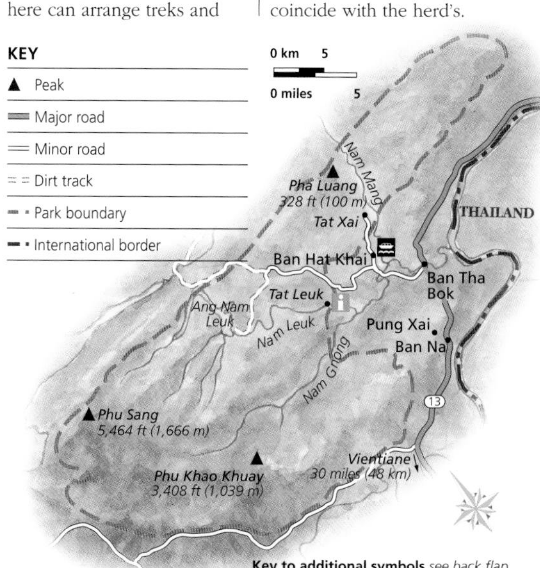

Key to additional symbols *see back flap*

LUANG PRABANG

Nestled amid verdant mountains on the banks of the Mekong, Luang Prabang is as enticing for its natural beauty as for the resplendent golden façades of its many wats. *This is a city of amazing contrasts, where solemn Buddhist monks appear perfectly at home among stylish hotels and restaurants. The city's Colonial heritage, reflected in its architecture and cuisine, adds to its charm.*

Located on a compact peninsula formed by the confluence of the Mekong and its tributary, the Nam Khan, Luang Prabang is the former royal capital of Laos. In 1353, Fa Ngum, a Lao prince who had been exiled to the Khmer capital of Angkor, returned and established the first Lao kingdom here, which he named Lan Xang Hom Khao, meaning Kingdom of a Million Elephants and the White Parasol, aptly reflecting the kingdom's military power and royal status. Shortly thereafter, Fa Ngum's Khmer benefactors sent the sacred Phabang, a golden Buddha image, from Sri Lanka. It is from the Phabang that the city has taken its current name. Although the country's administrative capital was moved to Vientiane in 1545, Lao royalty continued to reside here until the Communist takeover in 1975. Over the next decade and more, the city plunged into desolation as thousands of people, including businessmen, academics, and royalty, left it to escape the Communist regime. Luang Prabang finally reopened to the world after the fall of the Soviet Bloc in the 1990s.

In 1995, the city was designated a UNESCO World Heritage site, and today it remains the uncontested cultural capital of Laos. Its university attracts hundreds of students from the ethnically diverse northern provinces, and numerous hotels, restaurants, and shops have been established to cater to the steady influx of tourists. The locals, however, continue a traditional lifestyle with farming and small-scale trading being two of the primary methods of making a living.

Luang Prabang's main attractions include its many *wats*, which are best explored on foot. Beyond the urban center, in the surrounding countryside, lie several rustic village temples, caves, and waterfalls. Boat tours are also a great way to explore the undiminished beauty of the area.

Robed Buddha images lining a gold stencilled wall in the Chariot Hall, Wat Xieng Thong

◁ The Nam Khan riverside with the beautiful Wat Mai Suwannaphumaham in the foreground

Exploring Luang Prabang

The heart of Luang Prabang, also known as the Old Town, lies on a peninsula between the Mekong and the Nam Khan. All sights of interest, most hotels, and restaurants are located on this promontory or immediately to its south. At the center of this area lies the landmark Mt Phou Si, site of the much-revered stupa, That Chomsi. Close to the city's commercial hub is the National Museum Complex, the former home of Lao royalty. The enchanting Night Market, a great place to pick up exquisite handicrafts made by ethnic minorities, is also close by. The northeastern end of the peninsula is dominated by beautiful and ancient *wats* with the magnificent Wat Xieng Thong situated at its tip. The refreshing Tat Sae and Tat Kuang Si Waterfalls are a short distance away from the city.

A pleasant outdoor café, frequented by travelers

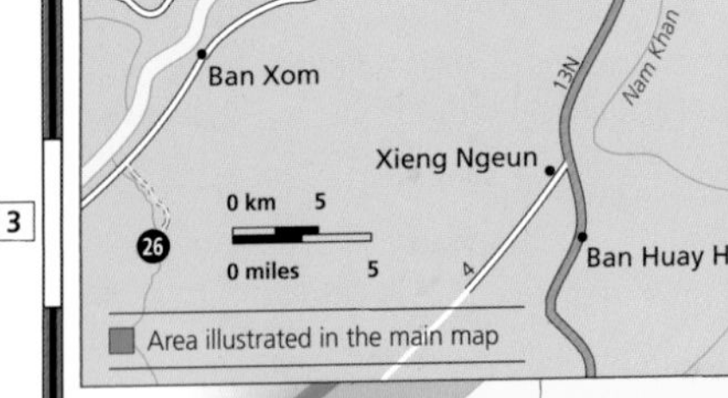
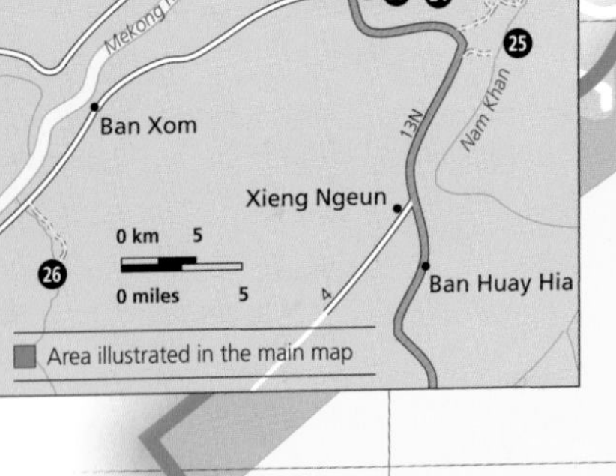

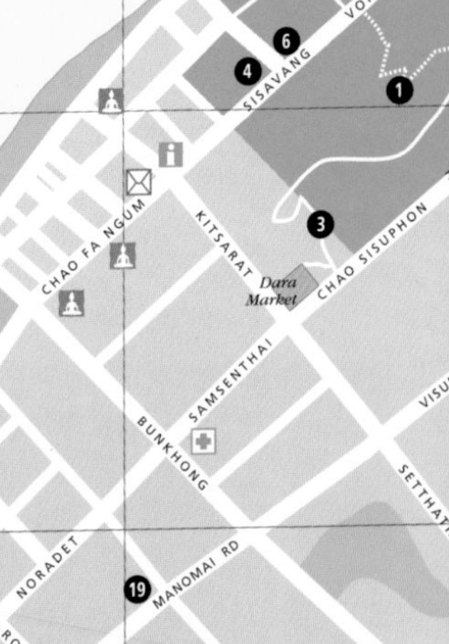

Intricate gilded façade of the *sim*, Wat Pa Phai

KEY

- Street-by-Street map *see pp152–3*
- International airport
- Ferry port
- Visitor information
- Post office
- Hospital
- *Wat* (temple)
- Major road
- Minor road
- Untarred road
- Ferry route

VISITORS' CHECKLIST

Road Map B2. 90,000. *Luang Prabang International Airport. Sisavang Vong Rd. daily. Lao New Year (mid-Apr), Lai Heua Fai (Nov), Suang Heua (Nov).*

Tree of Life mosaic on the rear wall of the *sim*, Wat Xieng Thong

GETTING AROUND

The Luang Prabang peninsula has four streets that run parallel to each other. These streets are intersected by numerous small lanes running perpendicular to the two rivers. Street names can get a little confusing since the same road is sometimes referred to by different names. However, street names are often irrelevant as directions are given by the nearest landmark or the neighborhood. Fortunately, all sights are located close to each other and can easily be covered on foot. Tuk-tuks ply the regular routes in Luang Prabang and can be hired for sightseeing within the city as well as for sights around it.

SIGHTS AT A GLANCE

Towns and Villages

Ban Phanom and Mouhot's Tomb 23
Ban Xang Khong 24

Places of Worship

Mt Phou Si and That Chomsi 1
Santi Chedi 22
Wat Aham 17
Wat Choum Khong 8
Wat Khili 14
Wat Mai Suwannaphumaham 4
Wat Manolom 19
Wat Nong Sikhunmuang 11
Wats on the West Bank 21
Wat Pa Phai 9
Wat Sene 12
Wat Si Boun Huang 13
Wat Siphoutabath 2
Wat That Luang 20
Wat Visounarat 18
Wat Xieng Mouan 7
Wat Xieng Thong pp160–61 16

Museums

National Museum Complex 5
School of Fine Arts 10
Traditional Arts and Ethnology Centre 3

Historical Site

UNESCO Maison du Patrimoine 15

Market

Night Market 6

Areas of Natural Beauty

Tat Kuang Si Waterfalls 26
Tat Sae Waterfalls 25

SEE ALSO

• ***Where to Stay*** pp220–22
• ***Where to Eat*** pp244–5

Street-by-Street: Old Town

Monk with an umbrella

The southern end of the Luang Prabang peninsula has several attractions: the Mekong and Khan rivers, a vibrant morning market, and religious and secular architecture. The National Museum Complex, which lies between the Mekong and Mt Phou Si, was constructed by the French between 1904 and 1909 as a residence for King Sisavang Vong. It can be reached by a staircase lined with frangipani trees. The *wats* here range from the rustic Wat Siphoutabath to the splendid Wat Mai Suwannaphumaham. This area also has an assortment of shops, boutique hotels, art galleries, cafés, and restaurants.

MEKONG RIVER
SUVANBANLANG
SOTIKA KUM
SISAVANG VONG ROAD

Wat Choum Khong
Two Chinese gods guard the entrance to this temple, which was completed in 1856. The temple is surrounded by a verdant garden, ideal for relaxing. The sim *is encircled by sculptures of the Buddha in various poses* 8

★ National Museum
A unique blend of French and Lao architectural styles, this building houses the sacred Phabang statue. Of equal interest is the throne room with its glass mosaics, as well as the royal artifacts on display 5

Wat Mai Suwannaphumaham
Elaborate gilded bas-reliefs, which depict scenes from the Phra Lak Phra Lam, *the Lao version of the* Ramayana, *adorn the front veranda of this* wat 4

STAR SIGHTS

- ★ National Museum
- ★ Mt Phou Si and That Chomsi

Wat Xieng Mouan has a UNESCO-sponsored school on its premises that teaches young monks the arts associated with temple decoration, such as stenciling and lacquerwork ❼

Wat Pa Phai

Located in a tree-filled compound, this simple temple is noted for its ornate decoration. The front doors and the surrounding area are not only gilded, but also covered with multicolored glass mosaic tiles ❾

KEY

– – – Suggested route

Shophouse Cafés

Several Colonial-era shophouses line Sisavang Vong Road. These now serve as cafés and restaurants, and are ideal places to relax and observe local street life.

★ Mt Phou Si and That Chomsi

A flight of 328 steps leads to the top of Phou Si, which means Sacred Mountain in Lao. The simple Buddhist stupa at its summit, That Chomsi, is visible across Luang Prabang and also provides great vistas of the city ❶

THE PHABANG

Devotees carrying the Phabang statue

This 32-inch (83-cm) tall golden Buddha image stands with raised palms in a pose symbolizing protection. The Phabang has bestowed its name on the city. It is also believed to confer spiritual protection on the Lao nation, and Buddhist legitimacy on the country's rulers. A Cambodian king presented it to King Fa Ngum, the founder of the Lan Xang Kingdom. The statue was stolen and, later, returned twice by Siamese kings. It now rests within the National Museum *(see p156)*.

Mt Phou Si and That Chomsi ❶

Sisavang Vong Rd. **City Map** C3. *8am–6pm daily.*

Meaning Sacred Mountain in Lao, Mt Phou Si is perhaps the best-known landmark in Luang Prabang. The hill, and the 79-ft (24-m) high **That Chomsi** (a four-sided stupa), on its summit, are visited by locals on the first day of the Lao New Year *(see p124)*.

There are three sets of stairs leading to the summit – one from the National Museum *(see p156)*, where the entry fee is collected, another from the Nam Khan's side, and a third that winds up from behind Wat Siphoutabath. Visitors will find a couple of old temples on the lower slopes of the hill as they make their way up the 328 steps leading to That Chomsi. The stupa, dating from 1804, is more impressive when seen from afar; the adjacent *sim* is rather basic. There are resting places en route but the stunning views of the city from the top certainly make the climb worthwhile.

Elegant Thai-style architecture of Wat Siphoutabath

Wat Siphoutabath ❷

Phou Si Rd. **City Map** D3. *8am–3pm daily.*

This Thai-style temple, constructed in 1851, takes its name from the stylized Buddha footprint located above the temple on the path to Mt Phou Si. In the same compound as Wat Siphoutabath is another temple, Wat Pa Khe, whose name is sometimes used to refer to the whole complex. Of particular interest are the bas-relief carvings of Dutch merchants on the doors and window shutters of the two temples. Well executed and in typical Lao style, they are depicted wearing tricorn hats with feathers, tall boots, and with a parrot on each shoulder. The window shutters show a long-haired Westerner with a dog at his feet.

Ethnic crafts on display, Traditional Arts and Ethnology Centre

Traditional Arts and Ethnology Centre ❸

Between Dara Market and Mt Phou Si. **City Map** C4. ***Tel*** *(071)-253-364.* *9am–6pm Tue–Sun.* *by prior arrangement.* **www**.taeclaos.org

This privately run museum, housed in the restored home of a French judge, at the base of Mt Phou Si, offers an excellent insight into the ethnic cultures of Laos. The museum focuses on the preservation and interpretation of traditional arts, crafts, lifestyles, and culture. Its permanent collection displays over 200 objects from 17 minority groups. These include clothing, religious artifacts, and household objects as well as jewelry.

The museum's fair-trade shop sells handicrafts made by local artisans at competitive prices. There is also an excellent café serving food and drinks, with great views of the distant mountains.

Wat Mai Suwannaphumaham ❹

Sisavang Vong Rd. **City Map** C3. *8am–3pm daily.*

Among the most important *wats* in Luang Prabang, Wat Mai Suwannaphumaham has an opulent exterior covered in red, black, and gold stencil. Inaugurated in 1788, the *wat's* construction took almost 70 years. While restorations have taken place several times, it is one of the few temples in Luang Prabang to have survived in its original form. The *wat* is revered because it was, for decades, the home of the Pha Sangkharat, the most senior monk in Laos. It is also important because the sacred Phabang statue *(see p153)*, the guardian talisman of Luang Prabang, was kept here between 1894 and 1947.

The structure of the *wat* is influenced by both the Luang Prabang style and vernacular architecture. Its *sim* has an impressive five-tiered roof with gilded bas-reliefs on the front veranda. Vivid scenes from the epic *Phra Lak Phra Lam* cover some panels along with scenes of Lao village life.

Detailed gold stenciling, Wat Mai Suwannaphumaham

Lao Temple Architecture

A *wat* complex usually consists of several buildings in addition to the main ordination hall or *sim*. The *sims* in Lao *wats* differ from place to place and are constructed with variations in the style and design of the roof. While the *sims* of Luang Prabang-style *wats* are noted for their multi-tiered roofs, which almost reach the ground, the Vientiane style features tall and narrow roofs. The Xieng Khuan style, on the other hand, is known for low, single-tiered roofs. The primary decorative color of Lao *wats* is gold, symbolizing the light of the sun. Stencils, bas-reliefs, mosaics of colored glass or tiles, and painted murals are all used both to create geometric patterns and to depict religious teachings. Syncretism, or the mixing of various faiths and cultural beliefs, abounds in these places, and elements of both Hinduism and animism are easy to find.

***Naga* balustrade**

WAT COMPLEX

The layout of a *wat* complex reflects its diverse functions, which are not limited to worship. It is common to find schools, community centers, and health clinics here. All *wats* are surrounded by an exterior wall and all buildings, except the library, are built on the ground, not on stilts.

Hor kang *houses the* wat's *ceremonial drums. These drums are usually sounded to awaken the monks at dawn, and call them for morning and evening prayers.*

DECORATIVE ELEMENTS

A variety of murals, carved wooden panels, stencils, gilded statuary, and glass mosaics tiles are used to adorn *wats*.

Murals *are usually hand painted or stenciled. They depict popular tales from the* Jataka *and the* Phra Lak Phra Lam, *the Lao version of the epic* Ramayana.

Dok heuang pheung *is the triangular gable area above the front door of the* sim.

Dok so faa *are metallic roof decorations, often depicting parasols or pagodas.*

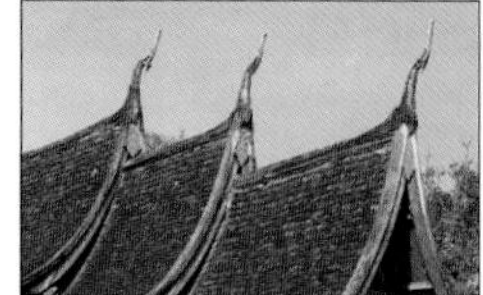

So faa *are roof finials that point upward, often in the shape of a* naga *(serpent).*

National Museum Complex ❺

Sisavang Vong Rd. **City Map** C3.
8:30am–11:30am & 1:30pm–3:30pm Wed–Mon.
inside the museum.

The former home of Lao royalty, the National Museum Complex lies between the Mekong River and Mt Phou Si. Designed by French architects, the palace in the complex was constructed for King Sisavang Vong (r.1904–59), who had then recently ascended the throne. When the monarchy was overthrown in 1975, the country's Communist rulers converted the palace into the National Museum.

The attractive double cruxiform-shaped single-story building is a mixture of Lao and European styles. The walkway is lined with Cuban royal palms that frame a gable above the main entrance. This gable is decorated with a bas-relief of a three-headed elephant protected by a parasol, surrounded by intertwined *nagas* (serpents) – the symbol of the Lan Xang Hom Khao Kingdom. In the background, a graceful spire resembling a Buddhist stupa points skyward. The most sacred of Luang Prabang's religious icons, the Phabang, is currently housed in a room in the front wing of the palace. However, its final resting place, **Wat Ho Pha Bang**, near the main gate, is in the process of being re-constructed.

Cuban royal palms bordering the path to the National Museum

Statue of King Sisavang Vong

Upon entering the National Museum visitors will pass through the former king's reception room, which houses murals painted by French artist Alex De Fautereau in the 1930s. These are idyllic representations of life in old Luang Prabang. The impressive throne room is painted red and covered with mosaics depicting Lao rural life, similar to those in the Red Chapel at Wat Xieng Thong (*see pp160–61*). The effect is even more dazzling in this massive but enclosed chamber. Behind the throne room lie the private quarters of the royal family, where many of their personal belongings, such as a collection of records and a wind-up phonograph player, are displayed. The furniture in both the king's and queen's bedchambers has been left intact. The atmosphere is familial and far from grandiose. The final stop inside the palace is a hall reserved for diplomatic gifts, notably some moon rocks and a plaque from US President Richard Nixon. This hall also contains two large portraits of King Sisavang Vatthana and Queen Kampoui, painted by a Soviet artist.

A large statue of King Sisavang Vong stands to the left of the main gate and the Royal Ballet Theatre behind. Here evening dance performances of the *Phra Lak Phra Lam* epic are performed three times a week at 6pm.

NATIONAL MUSEUM COMPLEX

LIST OF SITES

- King Sisavang Vong Statue ④
- Lotus Pond ⑥
- Main Gate ①
- Royal Ballet Theatre ⑤
- Royal Barge Shelter ⑦
- National Museum ②
- Wat Ho Pha Bang ③

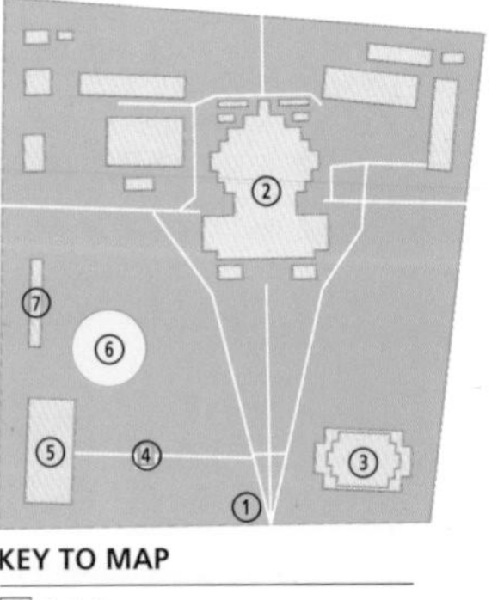

0 meters 100
0 yards 100

KEY TO MAP

- Buildings
- Lawns

Night Market ❻

Sisavang Vong Rd. **City Map** C3.
6pm–10pm daily.

Every evening, Sisavang Vong Road, the main commercial street of peninsular Luang Prabang, closes to traffic and becomes an open-air market offering a wide variety of colorful local handicrafts among other things. Textiles predominate, especially the intricately woven Lao silk and cotton. Particularly popular is the interesting geometric appliqué work – fashioned into everything from bedspreads to bedroom slippers – which the

Hmong minority have made famous. Silverware, imitation antiques, ceramics, hand-woven baskets, and mulberry paper products are all on offer. Lao beer T-shirts and Lao rice whiskey, as well as scorpions and snakes suspended in bottles make for an intriguing browse. The goods are not of the quality found in upscale boutiques, but the prices reflect this fact and good-natured bargaining is expected. At the southern end of the market, superb baguette sandwiches await hungry shoppers.

Vendors selling a variety of textile products, Night Market

Wat Xieng Mouan ❼

Sotika Kuman Rd. **City Map** C3.
8am–3pm daily.

The construction of this temple was ordered by King Chantarath (r.1851–72) in 1853 to house some particularly melodious temple drums which he had acquired. Consequently, the original name of the temple meant Monastery of the Melodious Sounds. For reasons lost in time, the name has changed to mean Monastery of the Amusing City. A school on the premises of the temple, inaugurated by UNESCO with a grant from the Norwegian government, aims to preserve traditional art forms in Laos. Novice monks produce various forms of traditional arts and crafts, such as stenciling, woodcarving, lacquerwork, and cement sculpture. These products are on display in a small exhibition hall within the premises. The *sim* of the temple features a veranda encircling the entire building with impressive columns in the front. The drums that inspired the temple's construction are kept in a temple of their own in the front left corner of the compound.

Wat Choum Khong ❽

Sotika Kuman Rd. **City Map** C3.
8am–3pm daily.

Located next to Wat Xieng Mouan, Wat Choum Khong is accessible by a passage that connects the two compounds. It was originally constructed in 1843, though the temple has been restored several times since, most recently with the help of students from the school in Wat Xieng Mouan. According to legend the *wat* takes its name from an image of the Buddha, which was cast here from a bronze *khong* (gong). A variety of modern but attractively styled Buddha images depicting the various *mudras* (hand positions) used in classical Buddhist statuary have been placed among the rows of shrubs and trees within the garden of this temple, which is particularly verdant and well kept. The ordination hall of the *wat* is in classic Luang Prabang style, with a heavily gilded lintel above the center of three elaborate front doors, eaves with curved brackets, and recessed windows.

Ornate peacock motif on the door to the *sim*, Wat Pa Phai

Wat Pa Phai ❾

Off Sisavang Vattana Rd.
City Map C3. *8am–3pm daily.*

The name of this *wat* means Bamboo Forest Monastery, but the origin of this appellation is unclear. The original date of its construction is also debatable, placed either at 1645 or 1815. There is a Siamese influence on the architectural style of the *wat*, apparent from the narrow base and high, steep roof lines. The main feature is the ornate pediment surrounding the doorway to the *sim*. It resembles those seen in temples in Chiang Mai, Thailand, in that it is decorated with a protruding peacock motif festooned with colored glass mosaic tiles. This archway rises in three successive levels and *nagas* mingle with birds in flight. The door panels depict a leaping figure of Rama holding a staff, trouncing the head of a lion. Around this doorway are murals depicting scenes of village life in a simple, artistic style.

Elaborately decorated exterior of the main *sim*, Wat Xieng Mouan

Carved *naga* balustrades adorning the staircase, Wat Nong Sikhunmuang

School of Fine Arts ⓾

Sotika Kuman Rd. **City Map** D3. ***Tel*** *(071)-212-047.* *8am–4pm daily.*

Signposted in French as the École des Beaux Arts, this charming single-story building in a tree-filled compound dates from the 1920s and is an excellent example of the Colonial architecture of the period. With an aim to promote traditional Lao art, the School of Fine Arts offers a four-year certificate program for students who have completed their secondary education. Specialized courses include painting, sculpture, graphic art, ceramics, metalwork, traditional drawing, and lacquerware. There is also provision for an 18-month internship post-graduation in a student's hometown. The school plays a major role in ensuring the continuation of traditional art and craft in Laos. There is also an exhibition center in the complex that displays and sells beautiful paintings, carvings, and sculptures made by the students.

Wat Nong Sikhunmuang ⓫

Sotika Kuman Rd. **City Map** D3. *8am–3pm daily.*

Originally constructed with wood in 1729, during the reign of King Inta Som, Wat Nong Sikhunmuang was completely destroyed by a fire in 1774. The only surviving piece of the original temple is a bronze statue of the Buddha known as Pha Sao Ong Sanesakid. The statue was originally brought here by a local merchant whose raft grounded mysteriously near the temple after a harrowing journey downriver from Thailand.

The current structure, restored by Thai artisans in the 19th century, is rather contemporary, and painted in bright colors. Of architectural interest is the elaborate roof referred to as *dok so faa* *(see p155)*; its 15 parasols suggest a royal connection since parasols are symbolic of royalty in Laos. Staircases on either side of the temple are adorned with *naga* balustrades. This temple attracts many Buddhist visitors, particularly during festivals, because of the Pha Sao Ong Sanesakid. Now housed in the *wat's sim*, this sacred statue is said to be endowed with special powers to grant the wishes of supplicants.

Wat Sene ⓬

Sakkarin Rd. **City Map** D2. *8am–3pm daily.*

This Thai-style temple's name refers to an initial donation of a 100,000 *kip* (*sene* in Lao) to start the construction work. It was built in 1714, and restored in 1957 to commemorate the 2,500th year of the Buddhist era. Located prominently on Sakkarin Road, the central road of Luang Prabang, this is the first in a series of temples that line the street for about 656 ft (200 m). With a stunningly beautiful exterior of bright red and gold, the *wat* is noted as the storage space for two of the largest and most attractive boats used in the annual Suang Heua boat racing festival *(see p126)*. The *sim* is similarly painted a brilliant red and covered with stencils depicting a menagerie of mythical animals; the interior of the *wat* is also intricately decorated. A smaller chapel at the front of the *wat* houses a Standing Buddha image and an immense drum and gong used to signal the *wan sin* (holy days) of Buddhism. An adjacent upright carved stone tablet portrays a stylized footprint of the Buddha.

Stenciled figures, Wat Sene

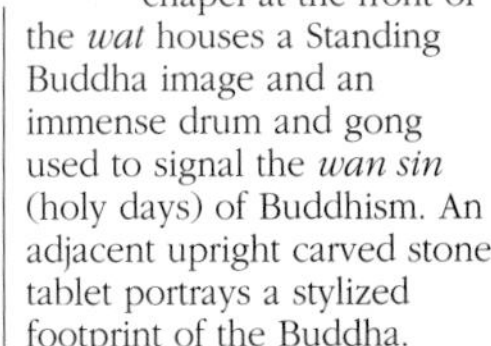

The Thai-style red and gold façade of Wat Sene

The impressive UNESCO Maison du Patrimoine, an excellent example of Laos's Colonial heritage

Wat Si Boun Huang ⓭

Sakkarin Rd. **City Map** D2.
8am–3pm daily.

Located just up the street from Wat Sene, after passing Wat Sop, this temple has a tree-lined lawn that is more inviting than the cemented floors of most of the present-day temple compounds in Luang Prabang. Multi-hued bougainvillea, frangipani, and palm trees provide not only shade, but also add a splash of color to the leafy compound.

This temple is said to have been constructed during the reign of King Sotika Kuman (r.1749–68). The four columns in front of the veranda of the relatively small *sim* carry lotus petal capitals. Notable here is the gable above the superbly decorated doors depicting a Buddhist symbol known as the *Dharmachakra*, or the Wheel of Law, which symbolizes rebirth. The roof of the *wat*, typical of the Luang Prabang style, has only two tiers, but its edge is lined with elegant and understated replicas of classical temple roof finials known as *so faa*.

Wat Khili ⓮

Sakkarin Rd. **City Map** D2.
8am–3pm daily. *Lai Heua Fai (early Nov).*

This *wat* is a rare example of the ornate style of temples built in the mountainous Xieng Khuang province. Its full name, Wat Souvanna Khili, can be translated to mean Monastery of the Golden Mountain. It was built in 1779 by Prince Chao Kham Sattha, who hailed from that region. Its construction is said to have established a good relationship between the two rival principalities of Xieng Khuang and Luang Prabang.

The Xieng Khuang style of *sim* is characterized by a wide and low profile. The front wall of Wat Khili's *sim* is decorated with six beautiful Tree of Life mosaics – smaller versions of the now famous mosaic on the back of Wat Xieng Thong's *sim* *(see pp160–61)*. The *wat's* window shutters are ornately carved with human-like forms believed to be that of Prince Siddhartha, later known as the Buddha, while the gables above are alive with bas-reliefs of zoomorphic phantasmagoria. Near the front of the *wat*, a somewhat incongruous two-story building blending Colonial and traditional Buddhist styles of architecture, is an interesting addition to the complex.

Elaborately carved door with gold stencil, Wat Si Boun Huang

UNESCO Maison du Patrimoine ⓯

Sakkarin Rd. **City Map** E2.

Located at the far northern end of the Luang Prabang peninsula, the UNESCO Maison du Patrimoine is an imposing but graceful structure that provides a contrast to the Buddhist temples and simple residences that characterize the neighborhood. This two-story building, dating from 1932, was once the Customs House of the ruling French Colonial government. From here, duties were levied on all Lao exports, the most lucrative of which was opium. This attractive building now belongs to the Lao government, and is the headquarters of UNESCO consultants who advise local authorities on urban conservation and the administration of the World Heritage Site status that was bestowed on Luang Prabang in 1995. Now referred to as La Maison du Patrimoine, or Heritage House, the large windows and high ceilings of the building present an excellent example of Colonial-era architecture. Although the place is not open to the public, visitors are welcome to take a leisurely stroll through the large and well-kept garden surrounding the building.

Wat Xieng Thong ⓰

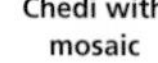

Chedi with mosaic

Considered by the locals to be the most important symbol of their country's religious heritage, Wat Xieng Thong, meaning Gold City Monastery, is notable for the brilliant colored-glass mosaics that adorn the exterior of several of the main buildings within the temple complex. These mosaics depict standard Buddhist iconography, such as lotus blossoms, as well as scenes from Buddhist scriptures and the daily lives of the Lao people. The *sim* was built in 1560 by King Setthathirat and the temple enjoyed royal patronage until 1975. It has served as a coronation venue for several Lao kings.

Mosaics depicting fishermen and Buddhist monks, Red Chapel

Tripitaka Library
Holy texts and the Phaman, *a Buddha image believed to have the power of invoking floods, are housed in the library.*

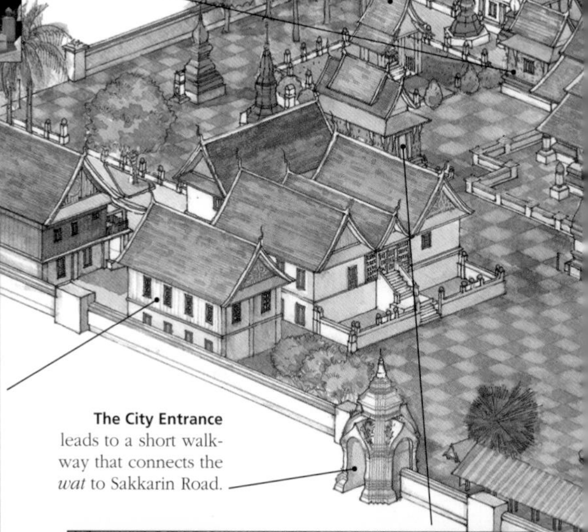

Sitting Buddha Pavilion

Meditation Hall

Monks Quarters
Monks and young novices, who have been ordained in this wat, *live in the monks' quarters within the complex.*

The City Entrance leads to a short walkway that connects the *wat* to Sakkarin Road.

STAR SIGHTS

★ Red Chapel

★ Sim (Ordination Hall)

★ Royal Funerary Carriage House

★ Red Chapel
Christened La Chapelle Rouge by the French, the Red Chapel has red exterior walls with glass inlay work depicting religious and rural scenes. It also houses an expertly sculpted bronze Reclining Buddha.

For hotels and restaurants in this region see pp220–22 and pp244–5

★ Sim (Ordination Hall)
Apart from its sweeping roof lines, the sim *has a carved, gilded Wheel of Life bas-relief with green mosaic lotus buds atop newel posts framing the entrance. The side walls have a rich gold and black motif with stencils depicting* apsaras *and lions, while the back wall has a stunning Tree of Life mosaic.*

VISITORS' CHECKLIST

City Map D2. Between Sakkarin Road and the Mekong River.
8am–4pm daily.

Drum Pavilion
The massive drum inside this pavilion is sounded on special prayer days and at festivities such as the boat races.

Boat Shelter

The elephant head fountain spouts lustral water that is collected by devotees to wash Buddha images in their homes.

Riverside Entrance

Chedis (stupas), which usually contain Buddhist relics, dot the enclosure.

★ Royal Funerary Carriage House
An elaborately carved and gilded structure, the Royal Funerary Carriage House contains the impressive 39-ft (12-m) high gilded chariot that transported the remains of King Sisavang Vong to his cremation.

Boat Shelter
The boats built here have led many boat crews to success in the annual boat races held during the Lao New Year and Suang Heua (see p126).

Panoramic view of Luang Prabang from the top of Mt Phou Si ▷

Elegantly sculpted stupas in front of the entrance to Wat Aham

Wat Aham 17

Phommathat Rd. **City Map** C4.
8am–3pm daily.

This *wat* is situated outside the main peninsular grid of the Old Town, across the street from a charming residential neighborhood of winding lanes. There are two huge banyan trees located in the temple grounds, said to house the spirits of the guardian deities of the city, Phu Noe and Na Noe. The shaggy-haired and red-faced effigies representing these spirits are kept in the grounds of the temple and are carried at the head of a procession during Lao New Year. The green compound also houses an attractive *sim* with statues from the *Phra Lak Phra Lam* epic guarding its front doors. The Corinthian-style columns of the *sim* are artistically decorated with lotus buds, while the gable on the back of the *sim* carries murals depicting the Buddha addressing his followers.

Mythical guardian, Wat Aham

Wat Visounarat 18

Phommathat Rd. **City Map** C4.
8am–3pm daily.

Originally constructed in 1512, this temple was named after King Visounarat, during whose reign it was built, making it the oldest extant Buddhist place of worship in the city. Located adjacent to Wat Aham, and connected to it by an arched passageway, the temple is also known as Wat Visoun. The door panels on the *sim* depict Hindu deities, and a gilded screen inside portrays a battle from the Hindu epic, *Ramayana*. In front of the temple's *sim* lies one of Luang Prabang's most famous landmarks, *that makmo*, meaning watermelon stupa. Officially, however, it is referred to as *that phatum*, meaning lotus stupa, named for its bulbous, hemispherical shape. The original stupa was razed by Chinese Black Flag Haw marauders in 1887 and was rebuilt in 1898 under the patronage of King Sakkarin Kamuk. In 1914, it was struck by lightning and revealed a cache of gold, bronze, and crystal Buddha images that the marauders had missed. These treasures are now on display at the National Museum Complex (*see p156*).

Wat Manolom 19

Manomai Rd. **City Map** C5.
8am–3pm daily.

Located on the site of an earlier temple raised by King Fa Ngum, the founder of the Lan Xang Dynasty, Wat Manolom is situated in a quiet residential area 1 mile (2 km) west of the center of the Old Town area of Luang Prabang. It was the first home of the sacred Phabang statue for almost 11 years. The current *sim* was built in 1972 and has an intricately engraved door

Monks walking past the watermelon stupa, Wat Visounarat

at the northern entrance flanked by a pair of lions. A revered statue of the Buddha, made of bronze, 20 ft (6 m) high and weighing 2 tons (2000 kg), which had been badly damaged by Chinese Black Flag Haw marauders in 1887, is now housed inside the *sim*. This long-eared statue is distinctly Thai-Sukhothai in style. Inside the *wat* compound are a group of gold stupas resembling the famous Pha That Luang (*see p143*) in Vientiane.

Wat That Luang ⓴

Wat That Luang Rd, Near Phu Vao Rd. **City Map** B5. *8am–3pm daily.*

Built in 1818, this temple is one of the most important in Luang Prabang, and is located fairly close to Wat Manolom. The *wat* houses the ashes of King Sisavang Vong (r.1904–59), whose funeral chariot is kept in Wat Xieng Thong (*see pp160–61*). That Luang means royal stupa and the *dok so faa* ornamentation with the 15 parasols on the roof of the *sim* denotes the temple's royal status. The *sim* is noteworthy for its gold and silver-lacquered door panels depicting various divinities. An elegant stupa, now weathered black, adjoins the *sim*. The members of Luang Prabang's royalty gather here on October 29 each year to commemorate King Sisavang Vong.

Wats on the West Bank ㉑

West Bank of the Mekong River. **City Map** D2. *from Wat Xieng Thong or behind the National Museum Complex.* *8am–3pm daily.*

As spectacular as the temples of the Old Town of Luang Prabang are, it is worthwhile to deviate from the usual routine by visiting the relaxing and informal rural *wats* on the West Bank of the Mekong River. Most are within walking distance of each other across the Mekong from Wat Xieng Thong. It is easy to negotiate a round trip with a boatman on the steps leading to the river outside the temple.

Murals at the front entrance, Wat Long Khun

The first of the *wats*, **Wat Long Khun**, meaning the Monastery of the Happy or Blessed Song, was where prospective kings of Laos would meditate for three days before their coronation at Wat Xieng Thong. The front of its *sim* is decorated with interesting but fading murals depicting Chinese gentlemen in elaborate costumes. The interior of the *sim*, with its somewhat garish linoleum flooring, exudes a welcoming simplicity missing in some other temples in Luang Prabang. The tree-filled *wat* complex is a great place to relax and absorb the rural atmosphere.

Carved peacock, Wat Xieng Men

A short distance upstream from Wat Long Khun lies the small, abandoned cave-shrine called **Wat Tham Xieng Maen**. Local boys volunteer as guides to and around the inside of the small cave. A path downstream along the river from Wat Long Khun will, after a short distance, lead to the bottom of a hill from where a steep flight of steps lead up to **Wat Chom Phet**. This *wat* is more renowned for its spectacular views of the surrounding area than being of any real architectural or cultural interest.

The last stop, **Wat Xieng Men**, is about 2 miles (3 km) downstream from this group of temples. Although it can be reached on foot, it is easier to go by boat. Built in the second half of the 16th century, the *wat's* small but well-proportioned *sim* has an elaborate three-tiered roof with separate eaves covering the front veranda. The portico above the front door is of an intricate designs as are both the exterior and interior columns. The current *sim* was constructed in the 1920s but artifacts from an earlier building on this site have been preserved, including an embroidered cloth believed to be over 300 years old.

The exquisite three-tiered roof of Wat Xieng Men on the Mekong's West Bank

Devotees offering prayers in front of Buddha statues, Santi Chedi

Santi Chedi 22

3 miles (5 km) E of Luang Prabang. *8am–5pm daily.*

Built in 1988 with donations from affluent Lao living abroad, Wat Phra Pone Phao, popularly known as Santi Chedi (Peace Pagoda), is a forest meditation retreat. A particular favorite with most visitors to Luang Prabang, this golden, bell-shaped stupa is visible from various spots in the city, although Mt Phou Si *(see p154)* offers the best views. Located on a hilltop along the banks of the Nam Khan, the *chedi* also offers excellent views of the city, particularly from the upper story of the outer terrace, which is definitely worth climbing. En route to the terrace, visitors will pass walls decorated with brightly colored murals, painted in natural colors. These murals, in addition to the standard *Jataka* tales which recount the lives and deeds of the Buddha, portray in intricate detail the punishments awaiting sinners in hell.

Ban Phanom and Mouhot's Tomb 23

4 miles (6 km) E of Luang Prabang. *from Luang Prabang.* *9am–5pm daily.*

Settled during the reign of King Sisavang Vong, Ban Phanom is populated by people of the Thai Lue ethnic group, who traditionally inhabit the areas around Luang Nam Tha and Muang Sing. The Thai Lue were required to serve the palace as weavers and dancers, since their women are famous for both these skills. Although the dance traditions eventually disappeared, the weaving of both cotton and silk continues today. The women sell their goods either from their homes or at the village crafts' center. The prices and quality of goods are at par with those sold in Luang Prabang's Night Market *(see pp156–7)*, although visitors are advised to bargain a little before buying anything.

About 3 miles (5 km) beyond Ban Phanom, along the Nam Khan, and approached by an unpaved but well-marked road, lies the tomb of the French explorer Henri Mouhot. The first Westerner to visit Luang Prabang, Mouhot is often referred to as the "discoverer" of Angkor Wat, as it was his vivid description (published in English after the French showed little interest in his journals) that spread the word about the glories of Angkor in Europe. Mouhot later traveled to Luang Prabang from Thailand and spent three months here, before contracting malaria and dying in 1861, at the young age of 35. His tomb was discovered in 1990 and restored by representatives from his hometown in France. The simple, whitewashed tomb, which is surrounded by large trees, has a small statue of the explorer erected nearby and is a must-see for any visitor to Luang Prabang.

Displaying a selection of locally woven cloth, Ban Phanom

ALEXANDRE-HENRI MOUHOT (1826–61)

An enterprising adventure-seeker, Henri Mouhot began his career teaching in Russia; experimented with the early photographic techniques of Louis Daguerre; studied botany; and finally set off in search of exotic destinations in Asia. After his visits to Angkor, he traveled to Luang Prabang, which, like many other foreigners, he found extremely pleasing, describing it as "a little paradise." Mouhot also described the Mekong River as possessing "almost an excess of grandeur," and noted that it appeared navigable – this inspired the early French Colonialists in Indochina to search for an ultimately unsuccessful river route to China.

Henri Mouhot

Ban Xang Khong 24

3 miles (5 km) E of Luang Prabang. *9am–5pm daily.*

A picturesque village nestled on the banks of the Mekong River, Ban Xang Khong is a haven of traditional Lao art and craft. The village was originally known for its intricate weaving of textiles by artisans who live and work in houses scattered along the dirt road running parallel to the river. Today, however, local artisans have also taken to producing attractive *sa* paper, which is made from the bark of the mulberry or *sa* tree. The bark of the tree grows back, making it a renewable resource. Visitors can not only watch local men and women at work, but also take advantage of great shopping opportunities – products can be bought directly from the workers. Prices here are not necessarily cheaper than in the Night Market, but the environment is more relaxed and the lighting better for viewing the intricately woven pieces of cloth and paper.

Ban Xang Khong can also be reached by crossing one of the seasonal bamboo bridges running across the river from Luang Prabang, or the permanent old bridge, on foot or on a two-wheeler.

Tat Sae Waterfalls ㉕

11 miles (18 km) SE of Luang Prabang. **Tel** *(020)-429-0848 (for tour bookings). tuk-tuk from Luang Prabang. from Ban En. 9am–5pm daily.*

Located on a tributary of the Nam Khan, the beautiful Tat Sae Waterfalls are often compared to the more spectacular Tat Kuang Si Waterfalls a little farther away. The falls' milky waters rush over natural limestone formations, falling into clear turquoise-colored pools that are ideal for swimming and bathing. However, the falls are less powerful than Tat Kuang Si, and in the dry season are reduced to a mere trickle. Nevertheless, it continues to be a popular spot for visitors and locals alike.

Picnickers enjoying the beauty of the spectacular Tat Kuang Si Waterfalls

The area is usually quite busy on weekends, although there are not too many people here on weekdays. There are several other attractions in the vicinity, which include a zip line tour that takes adventure-seekers above the forest canopy and falls, as well as an exciting elephant trek in the surrounding hills and dense forest.

The Tat Sae Waterfalls can easily be reached by taking the road to the village of Ban En, 10 miles (16 km) south of Luang Prabang, followed by a short boat ride down the charming Nam Khan.

Tat Kuang Si Waterfalls ㉖

20 miles (32 km) SW of Luang Prabang. *from Luang Prabang. from Luang Prabang, then tuk-tuk. 9am–5pm daily.*

The multitiered Tat Kuang Si Waterfalls are a pleasant alternative for visitors looking for something more than the numerous *wats* that Luang Prabang has to offer. The water gushes over limestone formations collecting in azure pools at the base of the falls.

The lower levels of the falls are great for a picnic, with food vendors hawking the usual grilled fish or chicken. A trail ascending to the left of the falls leads to a much quieter set of pools above the 197-ft (60-m) high main falls. A second trail leads to more pools and a cave. Visitors are advised to be careful while climbing, since the mist from the falls not only keeps the area green, but also slippery.

Tat Kuang Si is accessible either by road or by boat along the Mekong followed by a short tuk-tuk ride. The falls are ideal for a day trip from Luang Prabang, although organized tours often propose half-day excursions, usually in the afternoon, when it is warmer and very pleasant.

Lower levels of the picturesque Tat Sae Waterfalls enclosed within green, leafy environs

NORTHERN LAOS

Spectacular mountain scenery, remote riverside settlements, a broad mosaic of minority cultures, places of historical significance, and the opportunity to trek off the beaten path – Northern Laos offers all this and more to the discerning traveler. From the sobering wartime sites on the Plain of Jars and Vieng Xai to tubing and rock climbing in Vang Vieng, a visitor is often spoiled for choice.

Northern Laos may seem isolated, but in fact it lies at a political and geographical crossroad, sharing borders with Thailand, Myanmar, Vietnam, and China. This strategic geographic location has resulted in periods of turbulence in its history. While the region benefited from regular cross-border trade with the Thais and the Vietnamese, it also had to endure hostility not only from its trading partners, but also the Burmese who periodically invaded Laos during the 16th century. Westerners, such as the French and the Dutch, have coveted the resources and river routes of Northern Laos, and its location as a strategic buffer zone cost it dearly during the 19th century.

Lying at an average altitude of over 3,000 ft (1,000 m), Northern Laos is noticeably cooler than the rest of the country and offers a diverse topography. The rivers, which were the main means of transport through the rugged mountains of the region, also provide livelihoods through fishing. The region is inhabited by over two dozen ethnic minorities, including the Hmong, Mien, and Akha, who make a living by cultivating crops such as corn and rice, and making handicrafts such as hand-woven textiles and silver jewelry.

Today, the region's many wonders, from its charming towns to thickly forested hills and mountains, are slowly opening up to tourism and visitors will find an enchanting array of places and activities to choose from. National Protected Areas (NPAs) such as the Nam Ha NPA and the Bokeo Nature Reserve are home to an amazing variety of animals, and a haven for wildlife enthusiasts. Adventure sport enthusiasts will find Vang Vieng an exciting town, with plenty of activities such as spelunking, kayaking, and rock climbing on offer. The mysterious Plain of Jars site is also well worth a visit.

A local fruit and vegetable market selling fresh produce, Muang Sing

◁ Retired Buddha statues of various sizes at the Pak Ou Caves, Luang Prabang province

Exploring Northern Laos

A trip to Northern Laos can be a delightful experience with a wide variety of activities to indulge in – from adventure sports to visits to beautiful Buddhist temples. While the capital, Vientiane, is well known for its *wats* and memorials, Vang Vieng, with a range of outdoor activities, is Northern Laos's adventure capital. Phonsavan and the Plain of Jars to the east are also popular attractions. Another exciting option is a boat or road tour from Huay Xai to the former royal capital Luang Prabang, which can be an interesting excursion. In fact, boat tours either on the Mekong between Huay Xai and Luang Prabang, or on the beautiful stretch of the Nam Ou between Luang Prabang and Phongsali are defining moments of any visit to Northern Laos.

A monk at prayer in the ornamented *sim* of Wat Nam Kaew Luang, Muang Sing

SIGHTS AT A GLANCE

Towns and villages

Ban Nam Di 11
Luang Nam Tha 10
Muang Khua 8
Muang Ngoi 7
Muang Sing pp182–3 13
Nong Khiaw 6
Phongsali 9
Phonsavan 2
Sam Neua 3
Vang Vieng 1

Historical Sites

Plain of Jars p175 5
Vieng Xai 4

National Parks and Preserves

Bokeo Nature Reserve 14
Nam Ha National Protected Area 12

Tours

A Boat Tour on the Mekong pp184–5 15

SEE ALSO

• ***Where to Stay*** pp222–4

• ***Where to Eat*** pp246–7

For additional map symbols *see back flap*

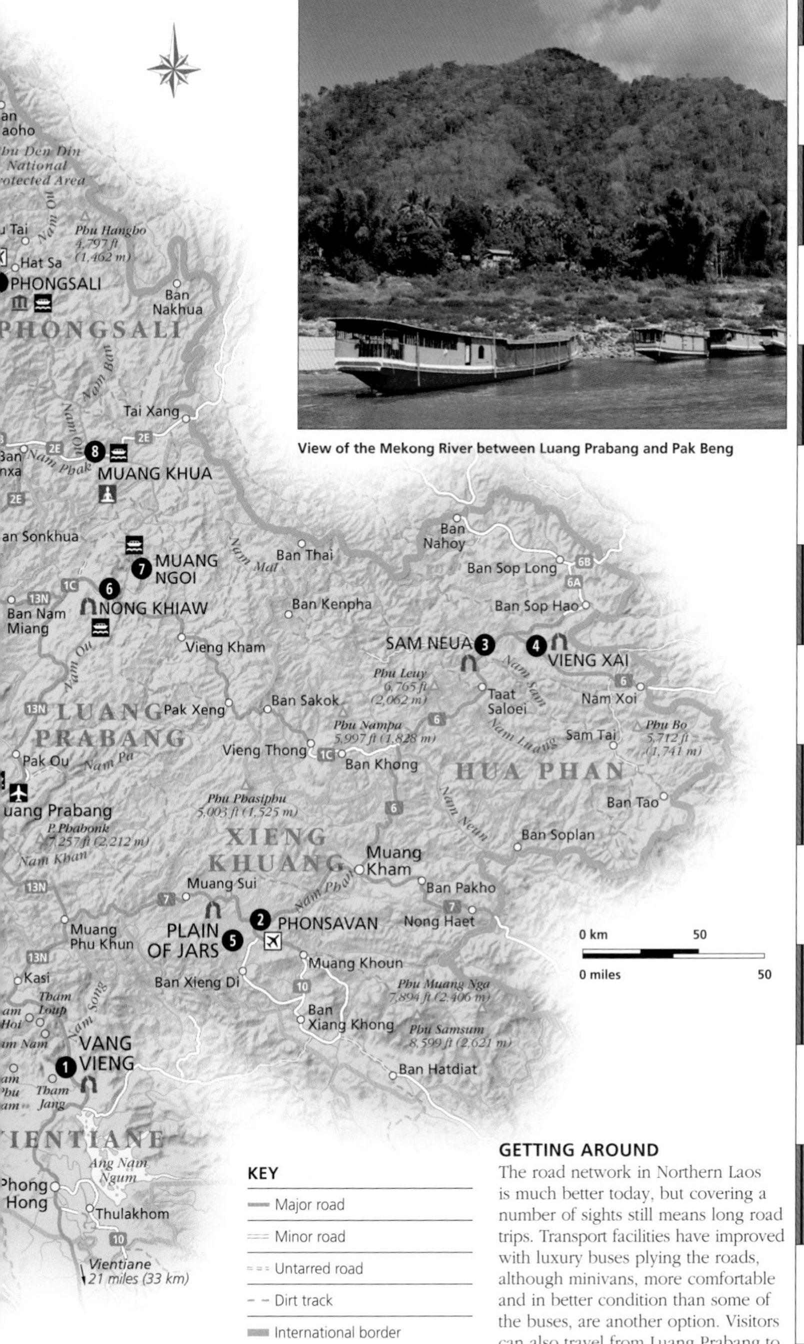

View of the Mekong River between Luang Prabang and Pak Beng

KEY

- Major road
- Minor road
- Untarred road
- Dirt track
- International border
- Provincial border
- Peak

GETTING AROUND

The road network in Northern Laos is much better today, but covering a number of sights still means long road trips. Transport facilities have improved with luxury buses plying the roads, although minivans, more comfortable and in better condition than some of the buses, are another option. Visitors can also travel from Luang Prabang to Phongsali by boat; the Mekong cruise from Huay Xai to Luang Prabang is also a good choice.

Backpackers strolling through the main street, Vang Vieng

Vang Vieng ❶

Road Map B2. 90 miles (150 km) N of Vientiane. *40,000.*

Located on the banks of the Nam Song and surrounded by majestic limestone karst peaks, the town of Vang Vieng has always been a magnet for visitors to Laos. Initially a quiet place visited by a handful of visitors keen to enjoy the natural beauty of the area, Vang Vieng today is a bustling town that serves as the jumping-off point for various adventure sports in the vicinity. However, indiscriminate development in tourist infrastructure has robbed the town of its quaint feel, and its streets are now lined with concrete guesthouses and busy bars.

Nevertheless, the town draws visitors keen to go rock climbing, abseiling, and spelunking in the karst mountains, which are a honeycomb of caves, some with rivers running through them. Tubing is another option although mud volleyball, rope swings, and an endless supply of *lao lao,* a distilled rice spirit, offered by the riverside bars, are popular. Note that Vang Vieng has a growing reputation for safety issues and crime. Any adventure activities undertaken should be done with careful consideration.

Environs

Located close to the Nam Song, just across from the Vang Vieng Resort, **Tham Jang**, also known as Tham Chang, is one of the most easily accessible caves in Vang Vieng. Used as a bunker in the early 19th century, the cave is approached by a flight of stairs leading to its mouth. Visitors can follow the well-marked path within and emerge at a second, higher entrance, which offers a fantastic view over the valley. It is also possible to swim in the spring at the mouth of the cave, and follow it for about 164 ft (50 m) inside.

Located some 5 miles (8 km) west of Vang Vieng, **Tham Phu Kham** is another interesting stop. Also known as Blue Lagoon, for the azure stream running in front of the cave, it is great for a refreshing dip.

Entrance to the fascinating Tham Hoi, Tham Sang Triangle

The cave is considered sacred by locals and houses several bronze images of the Buddha. The journey to Tham Phu Kham, passing stunning and majestic karst landscapes, can be done on foot, by bicycle, or even in a hired tuk-tuk.

The **Tham Sang Triangle**, a group of four caves, all within walking distance of each other, is located 8 miles (13 km) north of Vang Vieng and is a popular destination for daytrippers. The first of these caves, Tham Sang, gets its name from the elephant-shaped stalactite formations within. A clearly marked path from here leads through rice fields for less than a mile to the entrances of Tham Hoi and Tham Loup. Tham Hoi is a sacred cave with a large Buddha image at the entrance, while Tham Loup, the more attractive of the two, has impressive stalactite formations. The final stop is Tham Nam, meaning water cave, which is located 1,321 ft (400 m) south of Tham Hoi. Depending on the season, it is possible to wade into the cave or rent a tube to go in. Visitors can complete the return journey to Vang Vieng on hired kayaks or tubes.

Elephant-shaped stalactite, Tham Sang

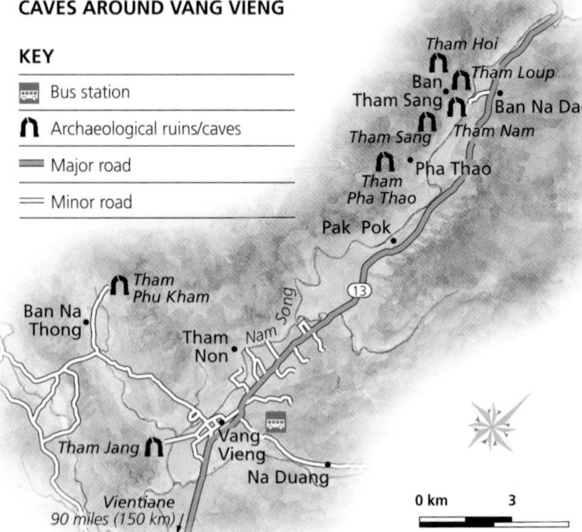

Tham Jang
8–11:30am & 1–4:30pm.

Tham Phu Kham
8:30am–4:30pm.

Tham Sang Triangle
8:30am–4:30pm. *including tubing or kayaking.*

For hotels and restaurants in this region see pp222–4 and pp246–7

Activities around Vang Vieng

A varied landscape comprising steep mountains, limestone caves, and the robust Nam Song make Vang Vieng an ideal venue for those seeking adventure sports. While the ever-popular ride on a mountain bike is a great way to appreciate the scenery and provide a good workout, spelunking, or cave exploration, and navigating steep trails and water channels deep inside these caves has its own charms. Some visitors also seek the additional thrill of rock climbing. Floating down the Nam Song on a giant tube has also become inextricably linked to the Vang Vieng experience. Tubing, and related activities such as zip lining, giant swings, and mud volleyball, especially appeal to young travelers. However, those seeking less energetic activities can always go on long, relaxing, kayaking trips down the Nam Song.

Cyclist in Vang Vieng

Tubing, *Vang Vieng's signature activity, is done on hired inflatable tractor tyre tubes down the Nam Song. The starting point lies 3 miles (5 km) north of town and the entire route is lined with noisy beer bars. Those not planning to stop at the bars can start farther upstream at the bridge to Ban Tham Sang.*

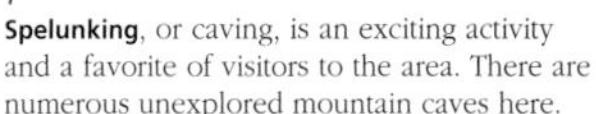

Spelunking, or caving, is an exciting activity and a favorite of visitors to the area. There are numerous unexplored mountain caves here.

Rock climbing and rappelling *can be undertaken near Tham Non, 2 miles (3 km) north of town. Here, routes for varying skill levels have been bolted and basic courses for novices are also available.*

Mountainbiking *is a great way to explore Vang Vieng. Cycling along Route 13 is easier since it is paved, but the trails on the west side of the Nam Song are idyllic, although demanding.*

Zip lines *usually start from one of the many riverside bars and include a hand grip attached to a pulley that slides down an inclined cable. Zip-liners cling on to the grip and let go at the other end to fall into the water.*

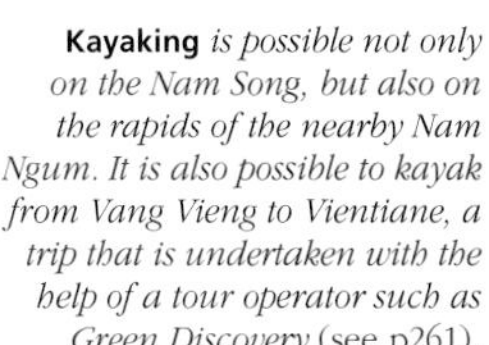

Kayaking *is possible not only on the Nam Song, but also on the rapids of the nearby Nam Ngum. It is also possible to kayak from Vang Vieng to Vientiane, a trip that is undertaken with the help of a tour operator such as Green Discovery* (see p261).

Defused UXO, Mines Advisory Group's Visitor Information Centre, Phonsavan

Phonsavan ❷

Road Map C2. 132 miles (220 km) SE of Luang Prabang. *50,000.* *from Vientiane or Luang Prabang.* *(061)-312-217.*

Capital of Xieng Khuang province, Phonsavan was built after the Vietnam War ended in 1975. The former capital, Muang Khoun, like most of the province, was completely destroyed by heavy fighting. Chosen simply because of its proximity to an airport, today Phonsavan is mainly of interest as a jumping-off point for the Plain of Jars. However, there are a variety of other intriguing sights in town, which can be of interest to a visitor. The **Mines Advisory Group's UXO Visitor Information Centre**, located in the center of town, is an enlightening place. Although the war memorabilia on display can be disturbing, there is a wealth of information including a video documentary on the devastation wrought by cluster bombs and other ammunition. Visitors will also find the Mulberries Silk Farm, on Route 7 just past the bus station, an absorbing stop. A fair-trade company dedicated to enabling local villagers to revive the art of high-quality silk production, Mulberries Silk Farm not only grows mulberry bushes, but also spins its own silk, which is then made into stylish garments and accessories.

The surrounding hilltops provide magnificent views of the town, hills, and plains. The two hilltop war memorials – the Lao War Memorial and the Vietnamese War Memorial – a short distance south of town, are certainly worth a visit. Tired travelers can, on their way back from the hills, stop at the atmospheric Auberge de Plaine des Jarrres *(see p223)*, at the top of Phu Padaeng, for a refreshing drink on the pleasant open-air terrace.

Sam Neua ❸

Road Map C2. 132 miles (220 km) NE of Phonsavan. *35,000.* *from Phonsavan.* *(064)-312-567.*

The capital of the northeast province of Hua Phan, Sam Neua lies nestled in a small valley that is often shrouded in fog. On clear days, however, the sparkling Nam Sam, which flows through this quiet town, is a pleasure to behold. The town usually plays host to visitors on their way to the nearby Vieng Xai caves, or to those heading to the Vietnamese border crossing 48 miles (80 km) to the east at Nam Xoi.

Sam Neua is famous for the intricacy of the handwoven textiles produced here. These can be found in the market close to the river, or at the homes of the weavers themselves. Visitors can be directed to the weavers' homes by the town's excellent local tourist information office, located on the main street.

Visitors entering a cave, Vieng Xai

Vieng Xai ❹

Road Map C2. 20 miles (32 km) E of Sam Neua. *from Sam Neua.* *from Sam Neua.* *Kaysone Phomvihane Memorial Cave Tour Office, (064)-314-321.* *9am–4pm daily.* *tours leave at 9am & 1pm.*

Tucked away among the karst mountains of the Annamite Mountain Range near the Vietnamese border, this isolated valley initially served as the shelter and hiding place for Pathet Lao leaders, including Kaysone Phomvihane and Prince Souphhanu Vong, during the Vietnam War (1954–75). The caves in the valley were used not just as their homes, but as communication centers, hospitals, and small factories. Also used as a secret military area, it was the location of prison camps where key members of the former regime, notably the royal family, were incarcerated. These caves are now open to visitors. It is also possible to visit another huge cave nearby where mass political rallies and musical and theatrical performances from friendly Socialist countries were held.

The caves are best visited as a day trip from Sam Neua on the obligatory guided tour, which includes excellent oral histories delivered via audio headsets. Visitors with enough time, however, can stay overnight in any one of the local guesthouses and explore the quiet back roads of this spectacular and pristine valley on rented bicycles.

Plain of Jars ❺

Tuk-tuks from Phonsavan

Scattered across over 50 separate sites, the curious stone jars that give the area its name, have puzzled archaeologists since the 1930s. Hewn from several types of local stone, they range in height from 18 in to 9 ft (50 cm to 3 m). Research here discovered human remains and burial offerings, which date the jars back to about 2,500 years. These give credence to the theory that the jars were in fact funerary urns, although other theories posit that they were used for grain or wine storage. Seven of these sites, now cleared of UXO (Unexploded Ordnance), are open to the public.

VISITORS' CHECKLIST

Road Map C2. 6 miles (10 km) SW of Phonsavan. ✈ 🚗 *from Phonsavan.* ℹ *Phonsavan (061)-312-217.* ◯ *8am–4pm daily.* **Note:** *visitors must pay heed to warning signs and stay on the marked paths.*

Site 25 · LAOS · Muang Kham · Site 23 · Phakeo · Site 1 · Phonsavan · Site 2 · Site 3 · Site 16 · Muang Khoun · 0 km 20 · 0 miles 20

LOCATOR KEY

- Sites open to the public
- Area illustrated

An old Russian tank, damaged by extensive bombing during the war, can also be visited during a tour of these sites.

KEY

- Domestic airport
- Area of natural beauty
- *Wat*
- Viewpoint
- Major road
- Minor road
- Dirt track

Site 1 (Thong Hai Hin)
Containing 331 jars, this site is spread across a hillside. It also has the largest discovered jar, which local legend describes as the wine cup of the mythical king Khun Cheum, who is said to have freed locals from oppression.

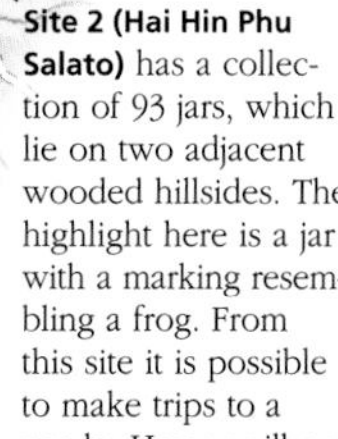

Site 2 (Hai Hin Phu Salato) has a collection of 93 jars, which lie on two adjacent wooded hillsides. The highlight here is a jar with a marking resembling a frog. From this site it is possible to make trips to a nearby Hmong village.

Site 1 · Phonsavan 2 miles (3 km) · 10 · Site 2 · Tat Lang · Site 3 · Ban Xieng Di · 0 km 1 · 0 miles 1

Site 3 (Hai Hin Lat Khai)
An attractive site located at the top of a hill offering scenic views, Site 3 lies on the outskirts of Ban Xieng Di, inhabited by the Phuan ethnic group. Nearby is a Buddhist temple and a stupa damaged during the war.

Bomb Craters
Some sites, such as Site 1, are located near spots where heavy fighting took place during the Vietnam War, and large bomb craters are still visible here.

The enigmatic stone jars scattered across a plain, Plain of Jars, Phonsavan ▷

Chinese-built concrete bridge spanning the Nam Ou, Nong Khiaw

Nong Khiaw 6

Road Map B1. 78 miles (126 km) NE of Luang Prabang. *6,000.* *from Luang Prabang.* *from Luang Prabang or Muang Ngoi.*

The town of Nong Khiaw straddles the Nam Ou, split by an impressively tall bridge built by Chinese engineers in 1976. Most travelers arrive here from Luang Prabang by boat or road – the new, well-surfaced Route 13 runs parallel to the river most of the way and offers picturesque views.

The Tham Pha Tok caves, located 2 miles (3 km) east of the town, where villagers hid from B-52 bombers during the Vietnam War (1954–75) draw many visitors. The village of the Khamu ethnic group, a short distance east along the same route, is also a popular destination among visitors. Another wonderful option for those who want to relax is to sit on the balcony of a riverside guesthouse and admire the mountain scenery. On longer stays, adventure seekers can also opt for trekking and mountain-bike excursions. The staff at guesthouses can arrange such activities for their patrons.

Muang Ngoi 7

Road Map B1. 20 miles (32 km) NE of Nong Khiaw. *2,000.* *from Nong Khiaw or Muang Khua.*

A sleepy village, Muang Ngoi nestles on the east bank of the Nam Ou. Owing to its location on a small plain, it is suited for growing rice in an otherwise mountainous area. Inaccessible by road, it has no electricity, and no cars; factors that contribute to its charm. Local attractions, apart from the calm and the scenery, are a few caves in a forested area that can be reached by fording a mountain stream about 3 miles (5 km) east of the village. The caves are best explored in the company of a local guide.

Boats docked by the riverside, Muang Khua

Muang Khua 8

Road Map B1. 67 miles (107 km) N of Muang Ngoi. *20,000.* *from Luang Prabang.* *from Nong Khiaw or Hat Sa.*

Farther upstream on the Nam Ou lies the bustling riverside town of Muang Khua. With precipitous mountains on either side of the river, Muang Khua resembles Nong Khiaw, but the atmosphere is much less placid – a steady stream of goods-laden trucks from Vietnam pour into the town, which is a busy commercial center. To escape the hustle and bustle, visitors can take a quick walk across the wooden suspension bridge spanning the Nam Phak, a tributary of the Nam Ou, to visit the local temple, Wat Srikkhounmoung. This interesting temple has *Ramayana*-based bas-reliefs and statues reflecting the syncretic nature of Lao Buddhism. It also has a temple bell that has been fashioned from an American cluster bomb casing.

From Muang Khua, a road leads 40 miles (60 km) east to the border post at Tai Xang, which is an international crossing, allowing all nationalities to enter and leave Laos from here. Across the border lies Dien Bien Phu, where the 1954 battle that ended the

For hotels and restaurants in this region see pp222–4 and pp246–7

French presence in Southeast Asia was fought. However, it is impossible for visitors to cross the border into Vietnam from here without obtaining a visa in advance.

Environs

A sparsely populated riverside village in Phongsali province, **Hat Sa** seems to be perpetually shrouded in mist. There are no real sights here and still no regular supply of electricity, although limited accommodation options are available. It is from here that buses leave for Phongsali after the trip up the Nam Ou. The adventurous can continue farther north by boat to the remote village of Ou Tai, where the mountain scenery is said to be the most striking in the area.

Hat Sa
56 miles (90 km) N of Muang Khua.
from Muang Khua.

Rice fields near the village of Ou Tai, north of Hat Sa

Locals selling fresh produce at the morning market, Phongsali

Phongsali 9

Road Map B1. 240 miles (386 km) N of Luang Prabang. *10,000.* *from Udomxai.* *from Nong Khiaw.*

At 4,290 ft (1,430 m), the town of Phongsali is the highest provincial capital in Laos, giving it an agreeable climate in summer but making it less than comfortable during the misty winter. Reached only via a rough 10-hour drive from Udomxai, or a two-day boat trip from Nong Khiaw, the town is off the tourist track. The province is home to 22 ethnic minorities, the largest being a Sino-Tibetan group called the Phunoy. The **Phongsali Provincial Museum of Ethnic Minority Cultures** in the heart of the town documents these groups. Visitors could also take a stroll through the cobblestone roads crisscrossing the Phunoy village to the nearby morning market, which is great for people-watching. On the northeast edge of the town, **Phou Fa**, or Sky Mountain, has a stupa at the top reached by 400 steps.

Environs

Located 9 miles (4 km) southeast of town on the road to Udomxai is **Ban Komaen**, where a 400-year-old tea tree stands in the midst of a modern plantation and local teas are also available for tasting. Farther afield, to the northeast of the province, trekking in the **Phu Den Din National Protected Area (NPA)**, which covers 506 sq miles (1,310 sq km), is spectacular.

Phongsali Provincial Museum of Ethnic Minority Cultures
Ban Sansary, Muang Phongsali, Khoueng Phongsali.
7:30–11:30am & 1:30–4:30pm Mon–Fri. *Sat–Sun.*

Phou Fa
NE of town center.

THE CHINESE CONNECTION

Phongsali could easily be confused with a town in China – the people, language, and even street signs have more in common with China than Laos. Indeed, Phongsali is much easier to reach by road from China than Laos, and the border, now open to Lao and Chinese nationals only, is a mere 42 miles (70 km) away. The Chinese influence here began during the Vietnam War when the Chinese established a consulate in Pathet Lao-liberated territory, which still survives as the Phou Fa Restaurant (*see p247*). Today, however, the influence is strictly commercial; Laos imports Chinese goods such as toys, clothing, and manufactured food products, and many Chinese have established tea gardens here. In fact, the species of tea that grows in the wild here has its origins in the neighboring Chinese province of Yunnan. It is used to produce compressed blocks of the fermented Pu-erh tea that improves, and increases in value, with age.

A woman of the Phunoy tribe picking tea leaves

Luang Nam Tha ⑩

Road Map B1. 124 miles (200 km) NW of Luang Prabang. *35,000.* *from Vientiane.* *from Huay Xai, Muang Sing, or Luang Prabang.* *Provincial Tourism Office, (086)-211-534.* **Note:** *boat tours on the Nam Tha between Huay Xai and Luang Nam Tha (Jun–Feb).* **www**.luangnamtha-tourism.org

This provincial capital was the scene of fierce fighting during the civil war and the current town is actually the result of recent construction – the original town, a few miles south, was razed to the ground by bombing. Happier times reign today, and Luang Nam Tha has emerged as an important center of ecotourism.The town is located within the boundaries of the Nam Ha National Protected Area and attracts adventure seekers for activities such as trekking, boating, and cycling. The town itself, often shrouded in mist until afternoon, is pleasant, with good restaurants, a small night market, as well as the **Luang Nam Tha Museum**, which houses various local artifacts, including ethnic clothing and ceramics.

Environs

For a taste of semirural village life, visitors can head to the prosperous villages on the opposite bank of the Nam Tha, reached by crossing a bamboo footbridge over the river. Another interesting destination is **That Phum Phuk**, a gilded stupa which sits atop a hill overlooking the valley. The original stupa was destroyed by aerial bombing.

Extensive terrace farming, Nam Ha National Protected Area

Luang Nam Tha Museum
Behind Kaysone Monument.
Mon–Thu 8:30am–11:30am, Fri 1:30pm–3:30pm.

That Phum Phuk
4 miles (6 km) SE of Luang Nam Tha.

Ban Nam Di ⑪

Road Map B1. 4 miles (6 km) E of Luang Nam Tha. *500.*

Located just off Route 1 on the road to Luang Prabang, the village of Ban Nam Di is known for the unique paper made by the Lanten people. This paper is not only used to render their Taoist religious texts, but has also become a source of income as a handicraft item. Visitors can also stop at an attractive waterfall, a short distance from the village.

Nam Ha National Protected Area ⑫

Road Map A1. 10 miles (16 km) W of Luang Nam Tha. **www**.ecotourismlaos.com

One of the 20 National Protected Areas (NPA) established by the Lao National Tourism Authority with assistance from UNESCO, this protected area covers 859 sq miles (2,224 sq km) and extends all the way to the Chinese border. The project aims to protect the environment by using sustainable ecotourism as a means to supplement villagers' incomes and deter them from taking part in activities that can harm the environment.

The forest cover here is largely first growth and the area is a watershed for four rivers, notably the Nam Ha, which gives the NPA its name. The Nam Ha NPA is rich in both flora and fauna. A large variety of animals, such as clouded leopard, tiger, gaur, a muntjac species, Asian elephant, as well as 228 bird species, are found here. Tour agencies in Luang Nam Tha are active participants in the project and a couple of them offer a variety of tours in the NPA, ranging from one-day trips to several-day excursions, which can be undertaken on foot, by kayak, or bicycle.

A busy fresh goods market, Luang Nam Tha

Minorities of Northern Laos

Northern Laos, mainly home to the Lao Sung, or Highland Lao, has the highest percentage of ethnic minorities in the country. These communities include the Hmong, Akha, and Mien. However, the Thai Lue, a Lowland Lao people, also live here. Each of these groups is easily distinguished by their unique, brightly colored attire, elaborate jewelry, and distinct language. Proud upholders of their cultures, the Lao Sung have complex religious beliefs and cultural practices, which include stories passed from one generation to the next, systems of kinship dictating norms of marriage, and a confounding system of taboos. The Highland Lao are as culturally different from each other as they are from the Lowland Lao. The best place to meet members of these minorities is usually the local market, where they come to sell their produce, particularly medicinal and edible plants collected in the jungle.

Local Mien craft for sale

Hmong embroidery is unique, with tribal histories often woven into the cloth.

Hmong *are a group of Sino-Tibetan people found across Southeast Asia. They assisted the Americans during the Lao Civil War and their relationship with the Communist authorities is strained.*

A Hmong village *consists of a cluster of about 20 huts. The huts, with dirt floors, thatched roofs, and no windows, are usually located adjacent to main roads.*

Akha *are easily distinguished by the elaborate silver headdress worn by their women. Their religious beliefs are a mix of animism and ancestor worship and they speak a Tibeto-Burmese language.*

Akha women *are skilled weavers and also do needlework. They can often be spotted walking the streets of Luang Nam Tha and Muang Sing, hawking their handicrafts to passersby.*

Thai Lue *are considered a Lowland Lao people. They are Buddhists, and known for their unique style of temple architecture characterized by elaborate wooden or alloy fretwork. Thai Lue women are said to be very beautiful.*

Clothing of the Mien includes a maroon boa-like collar extending downward.

Mien *are also known as the Yao. They practice Taoism and use a form of Chinese characters to write their religious texts. Mien women are distinguished by their black turbans.*

Lanten *are a sub-group of the Mien. A Chinese term, Lanten refers to their use of indigo dyes. They are best known for their paper-making skills.*

Muang Sing ⓭

Located on a broad river-fed plain northwest of Luang Nam Tha, Muang Sing was an important Thai Lue principality until the late 1800s. It was later occupied by the French but slipped into obscurity after their departure. Today, however, the town is witnessing a revival in its fortunes. The recent opening of the border with China, only 5 miles (8 km) to the north, has helped invigorate the local economy, and garlic is now a major cash crop. There are few transport facilities, although tuk-tuks ply the road and a new bus terminal has been set up.

Thongs **adorning the inside of Wat Luang Ban Xieng Jai**

Muang Sing Exhibition Museum

Northern left corner of Route 17.
9am–4pm Mon–Fri.

Housed in the former home of a local prince, the well-proportioned wooden structure of Muang Sing Exhibition Museum is as impressive as the exhibits within. The museum focuses on the ethnic minorities of the area, such as the Hmong, Lolo, and Akha, with displays of clothing, musical instruments, religious artifacts, and tools used in their daily lives. Upstairs, there are panels explaining the history of Muang Sing and the work of archaeologists who uncovered the original dimensions of this once walled city. The staff, when available, usually runs a video program, which shows in vivid detail the town's intriguing past.

Elegant wood-carved façade of Muang Sing Exhibition Museum

Wat Luang Ban Xieng Jai

Off Route 17, behind the Muang Sing Exhibition Museum.
8am–3pm daily.

Located just behind the museum, this *wat* is among the most popular religious sights in town. It attracts hordes of worshipers,

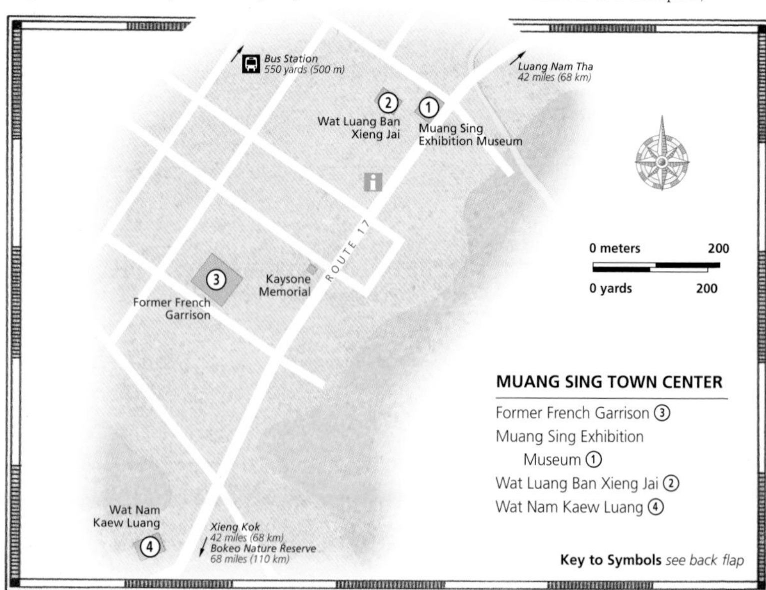

especially early in the morning, when it is quite lively. The *wat's* architectural style is typically Thai Lue, with silver-painted filigree fretwork on the edges of the *sim's* exterior, and colorful *thongs* (long prayer flags) hanging inside.

Former French Garrison

Off Route 17, W of Kaysone Memorial.

Once an important military base for Moroccan and Senegalese troops, this garrison is among the last few remnants of the French Colonial era in Muang Sing. Now converted into a Lao Army base, its crumbling brick ramparts are all that remain of what was once a strategic point where the spheres of French, English, and Chinese influence met. There may be other remnants of French presence within the walls of the garrison, but its premises are off limits for visitors. In fact, visitors who linger too long are hurried along by soldiers, and photography is strictly prohibited.

VISITORS' CHECKLIST

Road Map A1. 42 miles (68 km) NW of Luang Nam Tha. *9,000.* *Off Route 17 (020)-239-3534.* *Boun That Xieng Tung (Nov).*

Wat Nam Kaew Luang

Off Route 17, near the beginning of the road to Xieng Kok.

8am–3pm daily.

Situated on the southern edge of town, this Buddhist temple sits in a tree-filled compound and houses two beautiful *sims.* The *wat's* monks' quarters, built in the Thai Lue style, were formerly a *wihan* (assembly hall).

Naga-headed eaves decorating the columns at Wat Nam Kaew Luang

OPIUM

Northern Laos lies within the infamous Golden Triangle and opium *(Papaver somniferum)* has a long history here. The Hmong and other Highland Lao people had traditionally used the drug as a medicine, but soon learned its value as a cash crop, encouraged by the French who taxed the drug and controlled its export throughout Indochina. Muang Sing was a major collection point for the drug, with large quantities of it changing hands openly in the market. During the Vietnam War (1954–75), the Americans moved in to fill the void left by the French, allowing their Hmong allies free reign to transport the cargo on military aircrafts; Royalist Lao generals too filled their pockets by refining raw opium into heroin. Following its reputation as a drug tourism destination, the government cracked down on the racket, but even today, small patches of opium are tended in the remote mountain areas.

Hmong woman harvesting opium, Muang Sing

Multistory tree house with a zip line at The Gibbon Experience

Bokeo Nature Reserve ⓮

Road Map A1. 68 miles (110 km) SW of Muang Sing. ***Tel*** *(084)-212-021.* **www**.gibbonexperience.org

Covering 475 sq miles (1,230 sq km) of mixed deciduous forests, Bokeo Nature Reserve is home to endangered animals such as the black crested gibbon, migrating populations of wild buffalo, elephants, and several species of birds.

The only way to visit the preserve is through **The Gibbon Experience**, which offers a unique adventure travel opportunity. As part of two- or three-day tours, visitors stay in the Bokeo Nature Reserve in multistory tree houses that serve as the base camp. These are reached by an exhilarating zip line. The elusive black gibbon, and a wide variety of flora and fauna, can be observed on day treks before returning to the base camp for the night. The site lies deep within the jungle and is accessed by a three-hour drive from Huay Xai, followed by a one-hour trek, which can be demanding. Visitors are advised to carry water and insect repellent.

A shy black crested gibbon, Bokeo Nature Reserve

A Boat Tour on the Mekong ⓯

An ideal way to soak up the beauty of Northern Laos is on a boat trip along the Mekong River. The tour offers stunning views of the surrounding landscape, including wooded mountains bordering the river, huge boulders jutting out from below the rapids, and unhurried views of bucolic country life – the tending of vegetable gardens, fishing, weaving, and even wild elephants stopping by for a drink. Although chartered speedboats are available along the tour route, these are usually not safe. Instead, visitors can take the comfortable cruise offered by Luang Say Mekong Cruises. The cruise makes an overnight stop at Pak Beng.

Huay Xai ⑧
The last town in Laos before the border crossing to Thailand, Huay Xai is usually the starting point for boat tours entering Laos from Thailand. The town, with shops selling precious and semiprecious gemstones, is the gateway for The Gibbon Experience *(see p183)*.

KEY

- Visitor information
- Major road
- Minor road
- Untarred road
- International border

Ban Huay Sanei ⑦
The French once established a gold-mining operation in this village. Even today, villagers can be seen panning for gold here.

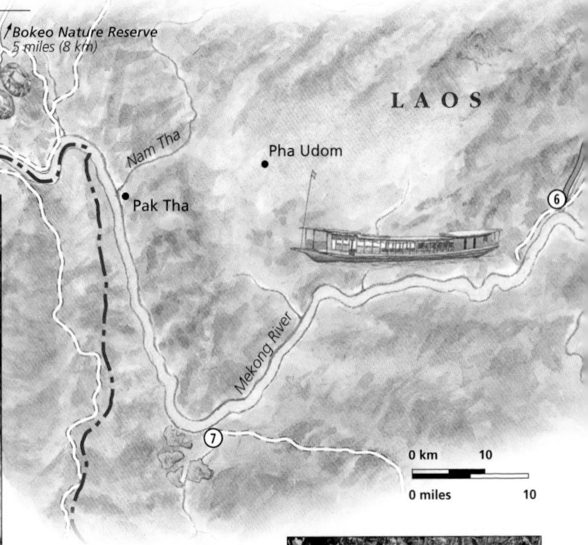

Bokeo Nature Reserve 5 miles (8 km)
Chiang Khong
⑧
LAOS
Nam Tha
Pha Udom
THAILAND
Pak Tha
⑥
Mekong River
⑦
0 km 10
0 miles 10

Pak Beng ⑥
A small town located on a steep hillside, Pak Beng is the midway resting point between Huay Xai and Luang Prabang. Popular sights in town include the pleasant Wat Sim Jong Jaeng, with a simple but refined *sim*. There is also an interesting morning market at the top of the hill.

Hong Sa ⑤
An isolated town, Hong Sa is the elephant capital of Laos. Primarily used for logging, the elephants are also available for safaris, lasting one or several days, through the surrounding jungle. The nearby Thai Lue village of Vieng Kaew offers excellent textiles and other handicrafts.

Pak Ou Caves ②
Located at the base of a towering limestone cliff, the Pak Ou Caves have been venerated, since pre-Buddhist times, as the home of river spirits. It became customary to "retire" Buddhist images here, when new offerings to various *wats* left no space for older or damaged images.

TIPS FOR TOURISTS

Starting point: *Luang Prabang*
Duration: *2 days*
Visitor Information: *Luang Say Mekong Cruises, 50/4 Sakkarin Rd, Ban Wat Sene, Luang Prabang;* ***Tel*** *(071)-252-553*
www.luangsay.com

Had Tur ③
A picturesque Thai Lue village built on stilts, Had Tur is well known for its woven silk fabrics and is an ideal stopover for visitors keen to purchase local handicrafts.

Ban Xang Hai and Ban Thin Hong Villages ①
Nestled along the Mekong River, the villages of Ban Xang Hai and Ban Thin Hong are famous for *lao lao (see p231)*, the home-made spirit produced from sticky rice. They are also referred to as the "whiskey villages."

LAO ELEPHANT FESTIVAL

Once known as the Kingdom of a Million Elephants and the White Parasol, Laos is among the few Asian countries where this mammal is still found in large numbers. Nevertheless, elephants continue to be endangered and the Lao Elephant Festival is aimed at increasing awareness of the need to protect this noble beast. This two-day festival usually includes traditional *baci sukhuan* ceremonies *(see p124)*, prayers by monks, elephant shows, as well as lectures on conservation. The event is organized by the NGO Elefantasia.

Monks and spectators at the Lao Elephant Festival

Ban Baw ④
Settled over 600 years ago by members of three different ethnic tribes – Lao Lum, Thai Lue, and Shan – Ban Baw is also renowned for the brewing of *lao lao*. The village women are skilled weavers of cotton and silk textiles and sell their handiwork at reasonable prices.

CENTRAL AND SOUTHERN LAOS

Lying between the Mekong and the Annamite Mountain Range, Central and Southern Laos appeals for its rich culture, history, and natural beauty. While "Mekong towns" such as Pakse and Thakhek, and the Khmer-built Wat Phu Champasak highlight the region's architectural brilliance, the temperate Bolaven Plateau and the pristine Si Phan Don are still isolated and relatively unexplored.

Central and Southern Laos has not only been molded by a number of civilizations and cultures that have settled here from time to time, but also by its geography. The transport and food sources afforded by the mighty Mekong encouraged many civilizations, notably the Champa, Chenla, and Khmer empires, to flourish along its banks from the 5th century AD onward. The French settled the three major towns of Thakhek, Pakse, and Savannakhet during the early 20th century, leaving behind a distinct cultural imprint. At the same time, the Vietnamese entered the country from the east across the narrow band of land between the South China Sea and the Mekong. They put down roots here, intermingling with the local population and contributing to the cultural melting pot that is Southern Laos.

The Mekong River has provided an efficient means of transport and trade with neighboring countries such as Thailand and Vietnam. Despite this, much of the region, except the three main towns along its banks, was off most tourist itineraries due to poor infrastructure. With the construction of the Friendship Bridge in December 2006, however, there has been an increase in visitors and today the region is slowly opening its treasures to the world.

Among the other attractions of the region are the mountainous Dong Natad and Dong Phu Vieng National Protected Areas, and the wetlands of the Xe Pian. The Bolaven Plateau, with its French-era coffee plantations, and the World Heritage Site of Wat Phu Champasak are also gaining popularity. The Si Phan Don, or Four Thousand Islands, is another interesting diversion.

An idyllic view of the sun setting over the Mekong near Si Phan Don

◁ **Majestic karst limestone formations overlooking lush paddy fields near Thakhek**

Exploring Central and Southern Laos

The main attractions of the region lie in the south, and the riverside towns of Thakhek, Savannakhet, and Pakse serve as ideal starting points for exploring these sites. The cave networks of Tham Kong Lo and Mahaxai, best visited from Thakhek, are a great draw for adventure seekers. But it is the ancient Khmer ruins of Wat Phu Champasak that remain the highlight of the region. The Si Phan Don archipelago is also becoming a popular destination. The southeast is dominated by the beguiling Bolaven Plateau with its refreshing waterfalls and a host of ethnic minority villages. The National Protected Areas (NPAs) of Dong Natad and Dong Phu Vieng present a great opportunity to interact with Laos's ethnic minorities.

Typical market selling fresh fruit and vegetables, Pakse

KEY

- Major road
- Minor road
- Untarred road
- Dirt track
- International border
- Provincial border
- Peak

SIGHTS AT A GLANCE

Towns and Cities
Champasak ⓫
Pakse ❿
Savannakhet pp192–3 ❻
Thakhek ❶

Places of Worship
That Ing Hang ❼
That Sikhot ❷

Museums and Galleries
Wat Phu Champasak Museum ⓭

Historical Sites
Ho Nang Sida and Hong Tha Tao ⓮
Wat Phu Champasak pp196–7 ⓬
Wat Tomo ⓰

Islands and Beaches
Don Daeng ⓯
Si Phan Don pp202–3 ⓳

National Parks and Preserves
Dong Natad National Protected Area ❽
Dong Phu Vieng National Protected Area ❾
Xe Pian National Protected Area ⓲

Areas of Natural Beauty
Bolaven Plateau ⓱
Kong Leng Lake ❹
Mahaxai Caves ❸
Tham Kong Lo ❺

Crossing the Mekong River on a boat near Champasak

For additional map symbols *see back flap*

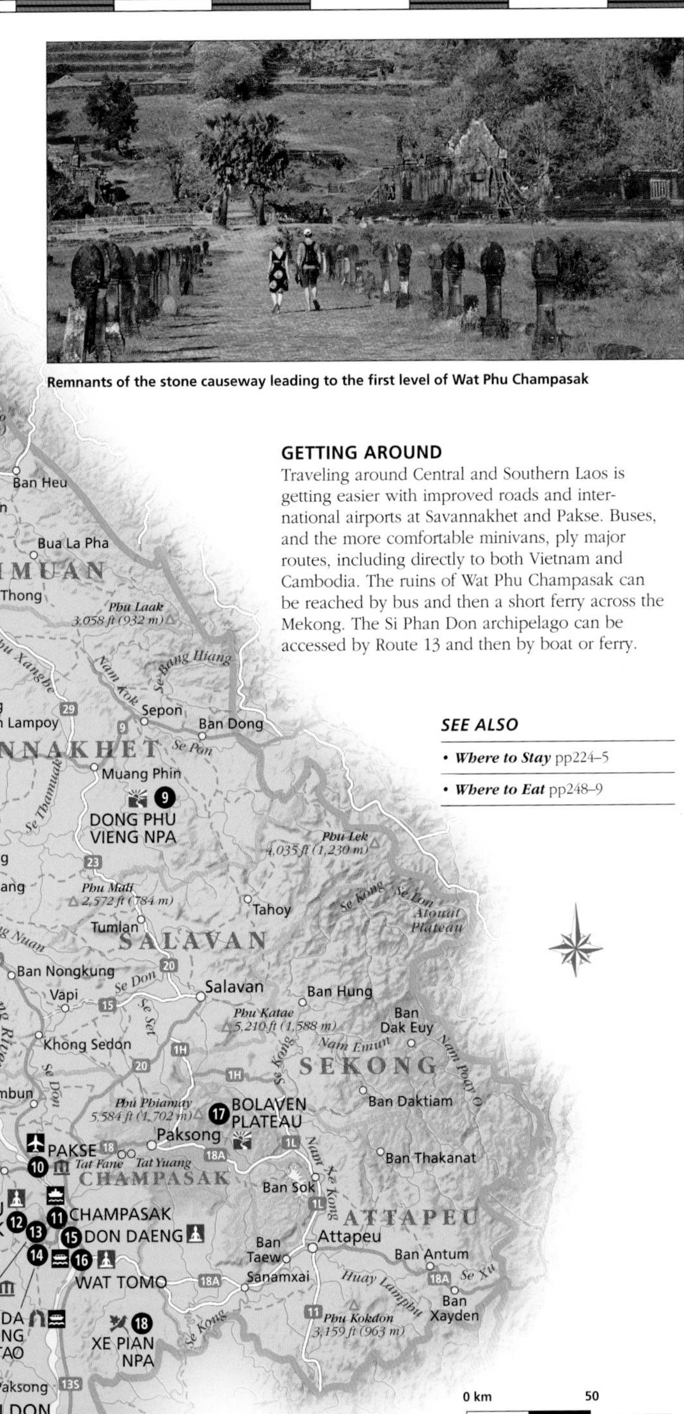

Remnants of the stone causeway leading to the first level of Wat Phu Champasak

GETTING AROUND

Traveling around Central and Southern Laos is getting easier with improved roads and international airports at Savannakhet and Pakse. Buses, and the more comfortable minivans, ply major routes, including directly to both Vietnam and Cambodia. The ruins of Wat Phu Champasak can be reached by bus and then a short ferry across the Mekong. The Si Phan Don archipelago can be accessed by Route 13 and then by boat or ferry.

SEE ALSO

- ***Where to Stay*** pp224–5
- ***Where to Eat*** pp248–9

Colonial-style fountain in the central town square, Thakhek

Thakhek ❶

Road Map D3. 220 miles (350 km) S of Vientiane. *70,000.* *Vientiane Rd (051)-212-512.* *Boun That Sikhot (Feb).*

Capital of Khammuan province, Thakhek was settled by the French in the 1920s. Although there are no major tourist attractions here, it remains a pretty settlement surrounded by majestic karst mountains and the meandering Mekong River. Inevitably, Colonial influence on the town is still visible in its buildings, the central town square and fountain, and wide avenues. An attractive tree-lined esplanade along the river is ideal for enjoying the cool breeze. Thakhek is an excellent resting point for visitors traveling by land to various places in Southern Laos. It is also a cross-over point for travelers to and from the neighboring countries of Thailand and Vietnam.

Thakhek is a convenient base from which to organize trips to the fascinating caves, waterfalls, and soaring limestone mountains of the **Phu Hin Pun National Protected Area**. This spectacularly beautiful preserve, covering an area of 610 sq miles (1,580 sq km), was established in 1993 and is home to a number of endangered species, such as the Douc langur, Francois's langur, Assamese macaque, 43 species of bat, sooty babbler, and limestone leaf warbler. Visitors can also take advantange of the exciting adventure and ecotourism facilities in Thakhek, which include trekking and kayaking. These trips can be organized by visitors on their own or through tour operators such as Green Discovery whose office is located in the Inthira Hotel Sikotabong *(see p225)* on Chao Anou Road; the local tourism office is also helpful. The NPA can be reached by tuk-tuk.

Kayakers on the Mekong

Phu Hin Pun National Protected Area
3 miles (5 km) N of Thakhek.
www.ecotourismlaos.com

That Sikhot ❷

Road Map D3. 4 miles (6 km) S of Thakhek. *8am–6pm daily.* *Boun That Sikhotabong (Feb).*

Formally known as Pha That Sikhotabong, this stupa and the adjacent *wat* (temple) are located on a site that dates from the Khmer principality of Sri Khotabhura. They ruled this area from the 6th to the 10th centuries AD. The site was restored and reconsecrated by the famous Lao King Setthathirat in the 16th century. The unique lotus bud-shaped stupa is of considerable religious significance to the Lao people and pilgrims visit it from across the country to attend the annual fair, Boun That Sikhot, which is held in February. The stupa's riverside location makes it a pleasant place for people to visit at sunset.

Sprawling grounds housing the lotus bud-shaped stupa of That Sikhot and its adjoining *wat*

Footbridge leading to the Buddha Cave, Mahaxai Caves

Mahaxai Caves ❸

Road Map D3. Off Route 12, 5 miles (8 km) E of Thakhek. *8:30am–4:30pm daily.*

A few miles east of Thakhek, the landscape along Route 12 begins to change with sheer karst formations looming on both sides of the road. These cliffs are riddled with caves, several of which are quite impressive, and all a cool respite from the heat of the day. The first of these, 5 miles (8 km) east of Thakhek, is **Buddha Cave**, known locally as Tham Pa Fa. This cave is popular with locals who come to venerate the 229 Buddha statues here, some of them 500 years old. Another 4 miles (6 km) ahead, to the right of Route 12, lies **Tham Xiang Liab**. This cave is about 656 ft (200 m) long and emerges in an isolated valley with pools ideal for swimming. Among the last of the caves, **Tham Nong Aen** lies farther ahead and is famous for the constant flow of cool air from its depths. The caves can be reached by tuk-tuk from Thakhek.

Kong Leng Lake ❹

Road Map D3. 30 miles (48 km) N of Thakhek. *8:30am–4:30pm daily.*

This isolated lake, over 21 ft (70 m) deep in the center, lies in the foothills of the Phu Hin Pun NPA. Depending on the weather, the lake is either an emerald green or deep blue in color. Sacred to locals, the lake is believed to be inhabited by spirits capable of ringing a gong on full moon nights, thus giving the lake its name, which means "evening gong." Fishing is not allowed here and swimming has been restricted to certain areas.

The best way to visit the lake is as part of an organized trek from Thakhek, which also includes visits to local villages and other caves.

THE HO CHI MINH TRAIL

Named by the Americans, the Ho Chi Minh Trail is a vast system of parallel trails, roads, bridges, and a diesel pipeline, which was used by the North Vietnamese Army to transport troops and material to its forces during the Vietnam War (1954–75). A major point of entry into Laos was the Mu Gia pass, via which Route 12 now enters Vietnam. Tours are available from Lak Sao, 126 miles (202 km) north of Thakhek. Visitors can see war debris, including the remains of Russian surface-to-air missiles used to defend the trail from bombing. However, be aware that UXO still remains a problem here.

Aerial view of the Ho Chi Minh Trail through Laos

Tham Kong Lo ❺

Road Map C3. Off Route 8, 80 miles (130 km) N of Thakhek. *8:30am–4:30pm daily.*

A visit to the Tham Kong Lo, a magnificent creation of nature, is the highlight of any trip into the karst highlands of Central Laos. This dramatic cave is entered on a motorboat, from the downstream end of the Nam Hin Boun, which runs for 4 miles (6 km) through the cave. The ride into the cave includes a stop at a hidden valley located on the upstream end and the entire trip takes about 2 hours. Once back, visitors can enjoy a swim at any one of the large pools located close to the entrance or buy some great picnic food from vendors stationed here.

Tham Kong Lo has become popular, especially with locals, since the construction of the 24-mile (40-km) long paved road from the junction with Route 8. Decent guesthouses in the area also make this an excellent overnight trip from nearby Thakhek.

Visitors at the deep awning of the magnificent Tham Kong Lo

Savannakhet 6

A small, bustling town, Savannakhet's rarely used official name, Muang Kaysone Phomvihane, refers to its status as the birthplace of Laos's Communist patriarch, Kaysone Phomvihane, whose childhood home is located in the town center. Much of the activity in the town is due to the new bridge from neighboring Thailand and the road connecting it to the Vietnamese border. Fortunately, the town's expansion has not affected its old Colonial charm. The downtown area is dotted with several historic buildings, a Taoist temple, and St. Theresa's Catholic Church, all of which are best visited on a rented bicycle.

Statue of St. Theresa

Buddha images being made in the factory at Wat Sainyaphum

Chao Mahesak Shrine

Tha Hae Rd. *8am–5pm daily.*

Built under the shade of a huge bodhi tree on the riverside, the Chao Mahesak Shrine is a highly revered religious landmark. Locals come here to pay respects to a diverse pantheon of deities and spirits, including Chao Mahesak, who is mythically linked to the town's founding. A statue of the deity can be found in front of this elevated shrine. Inside, elaborate statues depict Chao Mae Kuan Yim, the Chinese Goddess of Mercy, as well as some Taoist deities. Fortune-tellers offering their services to locals are a common sight here and the smell of burning incense is all pervasive.

Colonial buildings overlooking the main square, Savannakhet

Wat Sainyaphum

Tha Hae Rd. *8am–5pm daily.*

Lying across the street from the Chao Mahesak Shrine and occupying a full block is Wat Sainyaphum, the largest Buddhist temple in town. It is a pleasant complex constructed in a wide variety of architectural styles showing European as well as Chinese influences. Several parts of the building are adorned with bas-reliefs of mythical animals.

VISITORS' CHECKLIST

Road Map C4. 80 miles (130 km) S of Thakhek. 150,000. *Chaleun Muang Rd, (041)-212-755.* *That Ing Hang Festival (Feb full moon).*

A small factory toward the riverside entrance of the temple, where cement images of the Buddha are cast, painted, and consecrated, is an interesting stop. Visitors can also explore the large school close by, where monks are taught the precepts of Buddhism.

Savannakhet Dinosaur Museum
Khanthabuli Rd. *8am–noon & 1pm–4pm daily.*
Another interesting stop, the Savannakhet Dinosaur Museum displays fossilized remains of a large brontosaurus and other specimens discovered in the province. Visitors can take guided tours of the museum accompanied by curators who were present at the digs where the fossils were found. They not only explain the importance of these specimens, but also provide information on other paleontological sites in the Savannakhet area.

Wat Rattanalangsi
Chao Kim Rd. *8am–5pm daily.*
Situated in a pleasant tree-filled complex, Wat Rattanalangsi was built in 1951. The temple exhibits several examples of the syncretic inclusion of Hindu icons that characterize Lao Buddhist temples, such as a statue of Brahma, the God of Creation. The three-level gilded drum-and-gong-tower at the back of the compound is striking, as is the 45-ft (15-m) long Reclining Buddha.

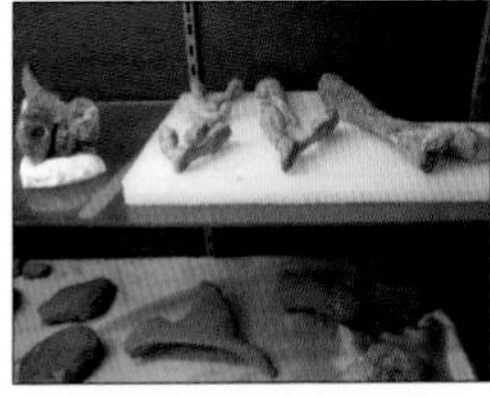

Exhibits on display at the Savannakhet Dinosaur Museum

Devotees kneeling outside the stupa, That Ing Hang

That Ing Hang ❼

Road Map D4. 10 miles (16 km) NE of Savannakhet. *7am–6pm daily.* *That Ing Hang Festival (Feb full moon).*

Of great religious significance to the Lao people, That Ing Hang is related to both the 10th-century Khmer empire of Sri Khotabura and King Chao Fa Ngum's return from Cambodia in the 14th century. The stupa was rebuilt several times and in its present form is an attractive four-tiered edifice with a lotus bud-shaped pinnacle. The complex is surrounded by a covered gallery containing 329 identical images of the Buddha. Women are not permitted into the inner sanctum surrounding the stupa. That Ing Hang can be reached by tuk-tuk from Savannakhet.

Dong Natad National Protected Area ❽

Road Map D4. 10 miles (16 km) NE of Savannakhet. *Savannakhet Eco-Guide Unit, Ratsaphanith Rd, (041)-214-203.* **www.** savannahkhet-trekking.com

Among Laos's smallest NPAs, Dong Natad is easily accessed from Savannakhet. One of the highlights of any visit to this NPA, besides the verdant forest and several pristine lakes, is the opportunity to interact with locals who have inhabited this area for hundreds of years. Living in harmony with the environment, they earn their livelihood from non-timber forest products such as wild honey, edible insects, rattan, medicinal plants, and *nang* oil from dipterocarps, which is used as fuel.

It is possible to visit the area in a tuk-tuk on a day trip from Savannakhet or, alternatively, arrange a homestay in one of the villages in the forest. Cycling and trekking are both options and visitors can either explore the area on their own, or engage the services of a guide from the Savannakhet Eco-Guide Unit.

Dong Phu Vieng National Protected Area ❾

Road Map D4. 110 miles (180 km) E of Savannakhet. *Savannakhet Eco-Guide Unit, Ratsaphanith Rd, (041)-214-203.* **www.** savannahkhet-trekking.com

This remote NPA is home to a small Mon-Khmer ethnic minority called the Katang, who even today remain unaffected by modernization, steeped as they are in their own distinct culture and belief systems. It is possible to visit this area as part of a tour organized by the Savannakhet Eco-Guide Unit, which has established treks in close cooperation with the local people. The demanding trek begins at Muang Phin on Route 9 heading toward Vietnam. Visitors spend a couple of nights in the Katang villages, and the journey culminates with a boat trip on the Se Bang Hieng River.

Trekkers walking the forest trail through the Dong Natad NPA

Finely carved stone lintel at the Champasak Provincial Museum, Pakse

Pakse ⓾

Road Map D5. 140 miles (230 km) S of Savannakhet. 90,000. *Provincial Tourism Office, near the bus station on the Se Don, (031)-212-021.*

Located at the confluence of the Don and Mekong rivers, Pakse, capital of Champasak province, was founded by the French in 1905. The Colonial Art Deco-style architecture of Pakse's downtown area, with several high-rise buildings, makes it more urban than the other towns along the Mekong. The town has become particularly busy after the completion of a Japanese bridge across the Mekong just south of town, which has enabled brisker trade with Thailand.

Although Pakse serves as a jumping-off point for sights such as Wat Phu Champasak and Si Phan Don *(see pp202–3)*, the town has several attractions of its own. The Dao Heuang Market, situated close to the bridge, is a huge complex rivaling Vientiane's Talat Sao *(see p142)*, where local textiles and produce, such as coffee from the Bolaven Plateau *(see p198)*, are on offer. Another interesting sight is the Champasak Palace Hotel *(see p225)*, built as a palace for Chao Boun Oum Na Champasak, a prince who held ceremonial sway in the area until the Communists seized power in 1975. Although the prince never really lived here, the former palace remains a popular attraction. The most interesting stop, however, is the **Champasak Provincial Museum**, which has some excellent Khmer lintels taken from sites throughout the province. Visitors will also find walking along the riverfront esplanades a pleasurable experience.

Champasak Provincial Museum
Route 13. *8–11:30am & 2–4pm Mon–Fri.*

Champasak ⓫

Road Map D5. 21 miles (34 km) SW of Pakse. *3,000.* *from Pakse.* *from Ban Muang.* *from Pakse.* *Champasak Visitor Information Center, (020)-220-6215.*

A small town on the west bank of the Mekong River, Champasak was once the royal capital of the Na Champasak principality, which ruled much of Southern Laos. Popular due to its proximity to the majestic Wat Phu Champasak ruins to the south and as a jumping-off point for Don Daeng, Champasak today is a sleepy town with the only remnants of royalty being two Colonial-style royal residences located just south of the fountain in the center of town. Due west of these buildings lies Wat Thong, the temple where the town's sovereigns performed religious rites, and where their cremated ashes now lie. The town is a pleasant place to relax after a tiring day at Wat Phu. It also has a variety of accommodation options that range from guesthouses to the upscale Inthira Hotel Champanakone *(see p224)*.

Wat Phu Champasak ⓬

See pp196–7.

Wat Phu Champasak Museum ⓭

Road Map D5. 5 miles (8 km) S of Champasak. *from Champasak.* *8:30am–4:30pm daily.* **www**.vatphou-champassak.com

Housed in a modern building situated close to the entrance of the Wat Phu complex, this museum has excellent exhibits telling the story of this ancient temple as well as those of the other Khmer sites in the area. The museum is well lit and all the exhibits are

A sprawling Colonial villa en route to Champasak

captioned in English. The statuary on display includes a stone figure of Nandi, the sacred bull and the mount of Shiva; an elaborate and well-preserved statue of Vishnu, the Protector of Creation, one of the gods in the Hindu pantheon; a Garuda, the eagle mount of Vishnu, and Ganesha, the elephant god. Amid this impressive display of Hindu iconography also stands an elegant 8th-century Dvaravati image of the Buddha, since the pre-Angkorian Khmers were followers of both Hinduism and Buddhism. The museum also contains an excellent collection of sandstone lintels, with intricate stone carvings, recovered from the private collection of Prince Boun Oum, and brought here for safekeeping. Another interesting piece is the carved stone water spout *(see p197)* that originally carried holy water to the central Shiva *lingam* (phallic symbol) in the uppermost temple of Wat Phu. Pride of place in this museum, however, is given to the artistically unimpressive, but historically significant, 5th-century Sanskrit inscription that was found at Wat Luang Gau, near the town of Champasak. This stone inscription contains a clear mention of the original founder of the stunning Wat Phu Champasak – a Cham king named Devanika – thus laying to rest any doubts about the origins of the temple.

A statue at Wat Phu Champasak Museum

Ho Nang Sida and Hong Tha Tao ⓮

Road Map D5. 1 mile (2 km) S of Wat Phu Champasak. *from Champasak.*

Although not as magnificent or significant as the Wat Phu complex, the two Khmer sites of Ho Nang Sida and Hong Tha Tao are an interesting side trip to any visit to Wat Phu. Located south of Wat Phu, they are accessed by turning left just before the two main galleries on the first level of the complex. The first, Ho Nang Sida, dates to the 10th century and is venerated by locals. A tree growing through the center of this crumbling shrine is festooned with Buddhist prayer flags put up by devotees who come here to pray. A mile farther south lies the site of Hong Tha Tao, which was once a rest house for travelers venturing to and from the ancient capital of Angkor. Although neither of these sites are of much architectural interest, they are quite atmospheric and certainly worth a visit.

Don Daeng ⓯

Road Map D5. 0.5 miles (1 km) E of Champasak. *from Pakse.* *from Ban Muang.*

An island located in the middle of the Mekong River, across from Champasak, Don Daeng has recently emerged as a popular destination for visitors keen to experience life along the Mekong. The island is ringed by eight separate

Riverboats anchored at a pier on Don Daeng

villages, which are connected by an unpaved track. Sights around the island include the beautiful Wat Ban Boung Kham, situated on the south-west coast. The *wat* was built over a former Khmer shrine, indicating the island's history.

Visitors will find adequate accommodation facilities at the community guesthouse in the village of Ban Hua Daeng, located on the northern edge of Don Daeng. There is also the luxurious La Folie Lodge *(see p224)*, a mile south, on the west coast. Don Daeng provides easy access to the forested precincts of Wat Tomo *(see p198)* nearby.

Ancient, crumbling ruins of the atmospheric Ho Nang Sida

Wat Phu Champasak ⓬

Champa flower

Named a World Heritage Site by UNESCO in 2001, Wat Phu, meaning Mountain Temple, is located in the foothills of the Lingaparvata Mountain, now known as Phu Phasak. Sacred to at least three different cultures, the temple is believed to have been revered by the Champa Empire during the 5th–8th centuries. Most of the present edifices, however, are pre-Angkorian, built around the beginning of the 9th century. In more recent times, the Lao Buddhist kingdom of Lan Xang converted the Hindu temples into structures honoring their own faith.

Crocodile Stone
The crocodile was a divine being for the ancient Khmers and this stylized carving on a flat stone clearly dates from that period. The stone's function remains unclear.

Main Temple Lintels
Intricately carved lintels above the 12 entrances to the main temple depict Hindu and Buddhist deities.

Carving of Holy Trinity
Behind the main temple sanctuary is a bas-relief in stone depicting the Hindu holy trinity.

MAIN TEMPLE
The uppermost part of the complex, the main temple houses the altar where the Shiva *lingam* once stood.

★ Shiva Lingam Sanctuary
Located in the innermost part of the main temple, the Shiva lingam *sanctuary now houses a large Buddha statue and several smaller icons. It is regularly visited by devotees with offerings.*

STAR SIGHTS

★ Shiva Lingam Sanctuary

★ Nandi Pavilion

★ Worship Pavilions

For hotels and restaurants in this region see pp224–5 and pp248–9

Holy Spring
This underground spring once fed a channel that delivered holy water to the Shiva lingam *via a stone spout. The spout is now on display in the Wat Phu Champasak Museum.*

VISITORS' CHECKLIST

Road Map D5. 5 miles (8 km) S of Champasak. *(020)-576-8280.* *8am–5pm daily; open late during full moon.* *Boun Wat Phu Champasak (Feb). Tuk-tuks are available from Champasak. Sound and light shows at every full moon.*

Champa-lined stairs
The steep staircase leading to the upper levels is lined with pretty champa trees. These trees bear the dok champa *blossoms, the national flower of Laos.*

Khmer Dvarapala
A stone statue, clad in Buddhist robes, stands guard over the inner sanctum of the temple. According to local lore it portrays the legendary founder of Wat Phu.

★ Nandi Pavilion
This smaller pavilion, dedicated to the sacred bull Nandi, the mount of Shiva, stands close to the worship pavilion. The statue of Nandi, however, is now in the museum.

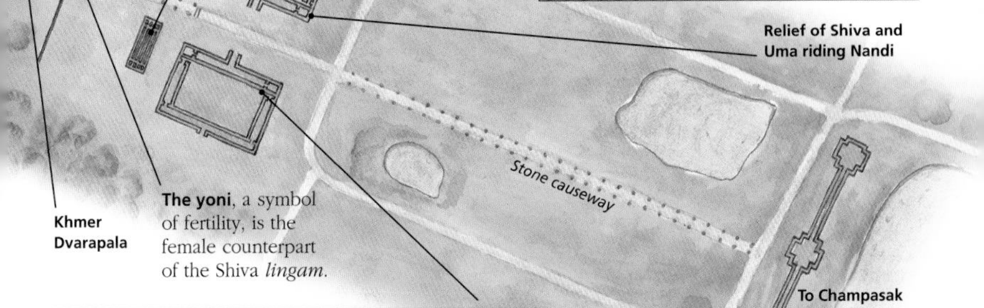

Half-buried statues

Relief of Shiva and Uma riding Nandi

Stone causeway

Khmer Dvarapala

The yoni, a symbol of fertility, is the female counterpart of the Shiva *lingam.*

To Champasak *5 miles (8 km)*
To Wat Phu Champasak Museum *see pp194–5*

0 meters 50
0 yards 50

★ Worship Pavilions
Two impressive pavilions, notable for their detailed bas-reliefs, are in the process of being restored. Experts believe that they served as separate worship facilities for men and women.

Visitors on a coffee plantation tour in the town of Paksong

Wat Tomo 16

Road Map D5. 30 miles (48 km) S of Pakse. *from Champasak or Don Daeng.* *8am–5pm daily.*

Lying on the east bank of the Mekong River, a short distance south of Wat Phu Champasak *(see pp196–7)*, the Khmer ruins of Wat Tomo, also known as Ou Muang, date from the 9th century. This *wat* was built in honor of Rudrani, the wife of Shiva, the God of Destruction. The temple is constructed of laterite, and while the best lintels are now in the Champasak Provincial Museum *(see p194)*, some artifacts still remain, including a unique *mukhalinga*, which is an ornately carved *lingam* (phallic symbol). Situated in a shady forest of tall trees, the *wat* makes for an excellent day trip from the town of Champasak or Don Daeng. It is also accessible by land from the east side of the Mekong River. In fact, when the water level is high, boats can come within 100 ft (30 m) of the temple, otherwise it is a 15-minute walk from the river in the dry season.

Bolaven Plateau 17

Road Map E5. 47 miles (78 km) E of Pakse. *from Pakse.* *8:30am–4:30pm daily.*

The French Colonialists found the temperate climate and rich soil of the Bolaven Plateau particularly suitable for habitation and cultivation. They planted the area with coffee, cardamom, and vegetables. This region can be explored from the town of Paksong – local coffee can be tasted here – which lies 14 miles (23 km) south of the plateau. Bolaven literally means Home of the Laven, which is the largest ethnic group that lives here. Besides the Laven, this region is home to many ethnic minorities such as the Alak and the Katu. The plateau was the site of intense battles during the Vietnam War (1954–75) and some areas, especially the Attapeu province, remain uncleared of UXO (Unexploded Ordinance). Today, the area is renowned for its waterfalls. Among the more popular are Tat Fane, a 360-ft (120-m) high cascade, and the 120-ft (40-m) high Tat Yuang, which is great for swimming. Visitors who wish to explore the area further can stay at the Tadlo Lodge Hotel *(see p224)*, which is close to a couple of waterfalls. Treks to minority villages can be arranged from here as well.

Traditionally dressed Laven

Lush greenery surrounding a viewpoint, Bolaven Plateau

Xe Pian National Protected Area 18

Road Map D5. 30 miles (48 km) S of Pakse. *from Pakse.* *Visitor Information Center (031)-212-177.*

Beginning roughly at Wat Tomo and continuing south to the Cambodian border, Xe Pian National Protected Area covers an area of 1,000 sq miles (2,600 sq km). It sustains a variety of wildlife, including the tiger, Asiatic black bear, banteng, wild ox, gibbon, hornbill, and crane. The area is best explored from the Kingfisher Ecolodge *(see p225)*, located near the village of Kiet Ngong at the northeastern corner of the NPA. It is possible to arrange treks deeper into the NPA from here. Elephant treks to Phu Asa, an interesting flat-topped mountain nearby, can also be arranged.

Charming Kingfisher Ecolodge, Xe Pian National Protected Area

Wildlife of Southern Laos

The geographical features of Southern Laos make it a particularly rich area in terms of wildlife. The Bolaven Plateau, with its sparse human habitation and cool climate, sustains a variety of wildlife, while the steep cliffs and caves in the limestone karst formations found throughout Southern Laos attract several kinds of animals. They provide secure habitats for birds as well as smaller mammals. Indeed, it is in this part of the country that several species, once thought extinct, have been rediscovered. Notable among them are the Laotian rock rat and the spindlehorn. Even larger mammals such as bears, tigers, elephants, and a variety of primates, often victims of poachers, have relatively large populations here.

Poster for Elephant Village

The Indochinese tiger, *a magnificent feline, has been relentlessly hunted for its skin and bones, driving it to the brink of extinction. It is believed to number less than 100 in the wild in Laos.*

MAMMALS

The region is home to a plethora of mammalian species ranging in size from the Asian elephant to the humble squirrel. Several species, such as the lesser panda and the pygmy slow loris, are unique to Laos.

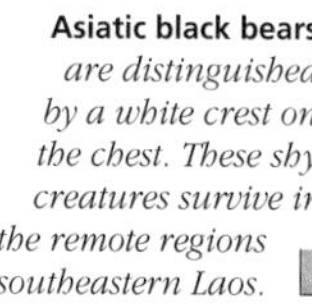

Asiatic black bears *are distinguished by a white crest on the chest. These shy creatures survive in the remote regions of southeastern Laos.*

The spindlehorn *sports long, curving horns. A forest-dwelling bovine, it resembles an antelope and was identified in 1992 in Vietnam.*

Golden fur distinguishes the female.

Yellow-cheeked crested gibbons *engage in elaborate mating songs and live over 50 years in the wild. Adult males are black with golden cheeks, while females are golden.*

BIRDS

Over 700 species of birds are found in Laos including such magnificent creatures as the Sarus crane. While indiscriminate hunting has put a few species on the endangered list, many are prolific breeders and their populations are, in fact, increasing.

Hornbills *are characterized by a large and often colorful beak. Over 50 species of hornbill have been discovered. These birds prefer to nest in small caves in the limestone karst.*

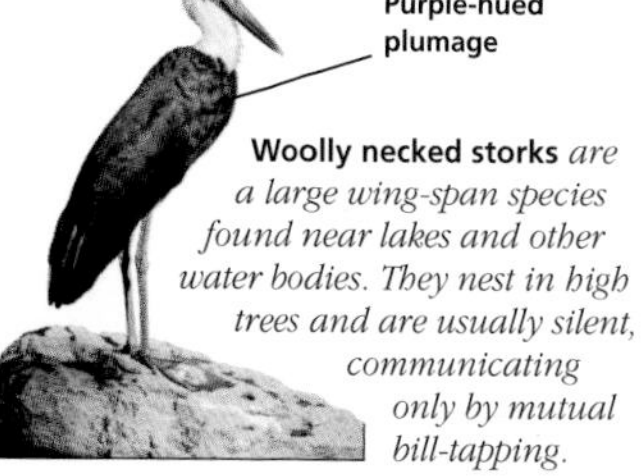

Purple-hued plumage

Woolly necked storks *are a large wing-span species found near lakes and other water bodies. They nest in high trees and are usually silent, communicating only by mutual bill-tapping.*

The Sarus crane, *at a height of 6 ft (2 m), is the world's tallest non-migratory flying bird. It is distinguished by the red plumage on its head and has a wing span of 8 ft (2.4 m).*

Verdant hillsides encompassing the scenic Tat Yuang, Bolaven Plateau ▷

Si Phan Don ⓳

Visitors enjoying a boat ride

Located between Champasak and the Cambodian border, Si Phan Don, or Four Thousand Islands, is an inland archipelago comprising thousands of islands, islets, and sand bars. The entire area covers a distance of some 30 miles (50 km) along the Mekong River from the northern tip of the largest island, Don Khong, to the massive Khon Phapeng Waterfalls in the south. These islands are inhabited by villagers who continue to lead a self-sufficient lifestyle, fishing and growing their own rice and other crops. However, the area's isolation from the outside world has changed, with tourism bringing in more visitors and three of the main islands already on the electricity grid. A few of the islands have accommodation facilities and better roads have improved connectivity to Pakse.

Ban Hua Khong
Mekong River
Don Hinyai
Don Khong
Tham Phu Khiaw
Muang Saen Nua
Kampong Sralau
LAOS
Ban Thaphao
Ban Loppadi Cho

The residence of Khamtay Siphandone, former president of the Lao PDR, is located near the village of Ban Hua Khong, at the northern end of Don Khong. The house is usually unoccupied and visitors are free to explore the grounds.

★ Don Khong

Lush green fields and hills dot the landscape of Don Khong. The best way to explore the island is on a bicycle or motorcycle since the roads are in good condition. This island has several good hotels centered around Muang Khong.

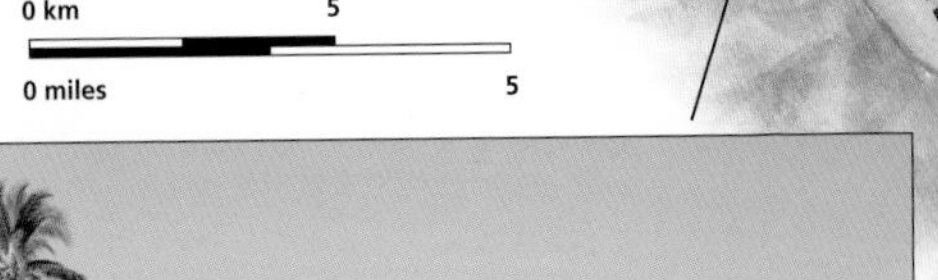

Muang Khong

The main town on Don Khong, Muang Khong serves as a ferry port for boats arriving from the mainland. Local attractions include Wat Muang Khong, which has impressive naga *statuary and the interesting Tham Phu Khiaw.*

STAR SIGHTS

- ★ Don Khong
- ★ Khon Phapeng Waterfalls
- ★ French Railway

For hotels and restaurants in this region see pp224–5 and pp248–9

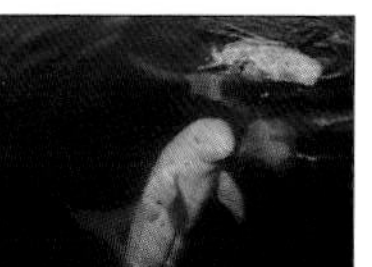

Distinct box-shaped snout of the Irrawaddy dolphin

IRRAWADDY DOLPHINS

Found in the waters of the Mekong River between Don Khon and the Cambodian border, the Irrawaddy dolphin *(Orcaella brevirostris)* is considered sacred by the Lao people. They never intentionally fish or trap this species, although destructive fishing techniques, such as gill netting, have reduced their numbers drastically. Trips to see the dolphins are organized from Don Khon.

VISITORS' CHECKLIST

Road Map D5. 81 miles (135 km) S of Pakse. *from Pakse to Don Khong and Ban Nakasang. between islands. between Don Khong & Don Det and Don Det & Don Khon; not available during the dry season. Khon Phapeng Waterfalls.*

KEY

- Ferry port
- Riverboat pier
- Cave
- Major road
- Minor road
- Ferry route
- International border

Pakse 81 miles (135 km)
Champasak 47 miles (75 km)
Ban Khinak
Don Som
Ban Nakasong
Ban Sat Tai
Don Det
Ban Thakho
Ban Khon
Li Phi Waterfalls
Don Khon
Anlung Chheuteal
CAMBODIA
Preah Angkoal
Mekong River
135

Kayaking
With a number of waterways criss-crossing the region, kayaking is the perfect way to get between the smaller islets while enjoying the scenery along the river. Kayaks are available for rent on Don Khong.

★ Khon Phapeng Waterfalls
These thunderous waterfalls, the largest on the Mekong and counted among the biggest in Southeast Asia, make up in volume what they lack in height, particularly in the rainy season. The falls are a popular tourist spot, with hundreds of visitors arriving regularly.

★ French Railway
Built by the French in the early 20th century, this 7-mile (12-km) long railway helped cargo ships circumvent the two mighty waterfalls blocking their passage upstream on the Mekong River. Remnants of this project can still be seen today.

Don Det can be reached either by a scenic two-hour boat ride from Don Khong or a quick trip from the mainland village of Ban Nakasong. The island's inexpensive accommodation facilities, coupled with its easy-going pace, attract many visitors.

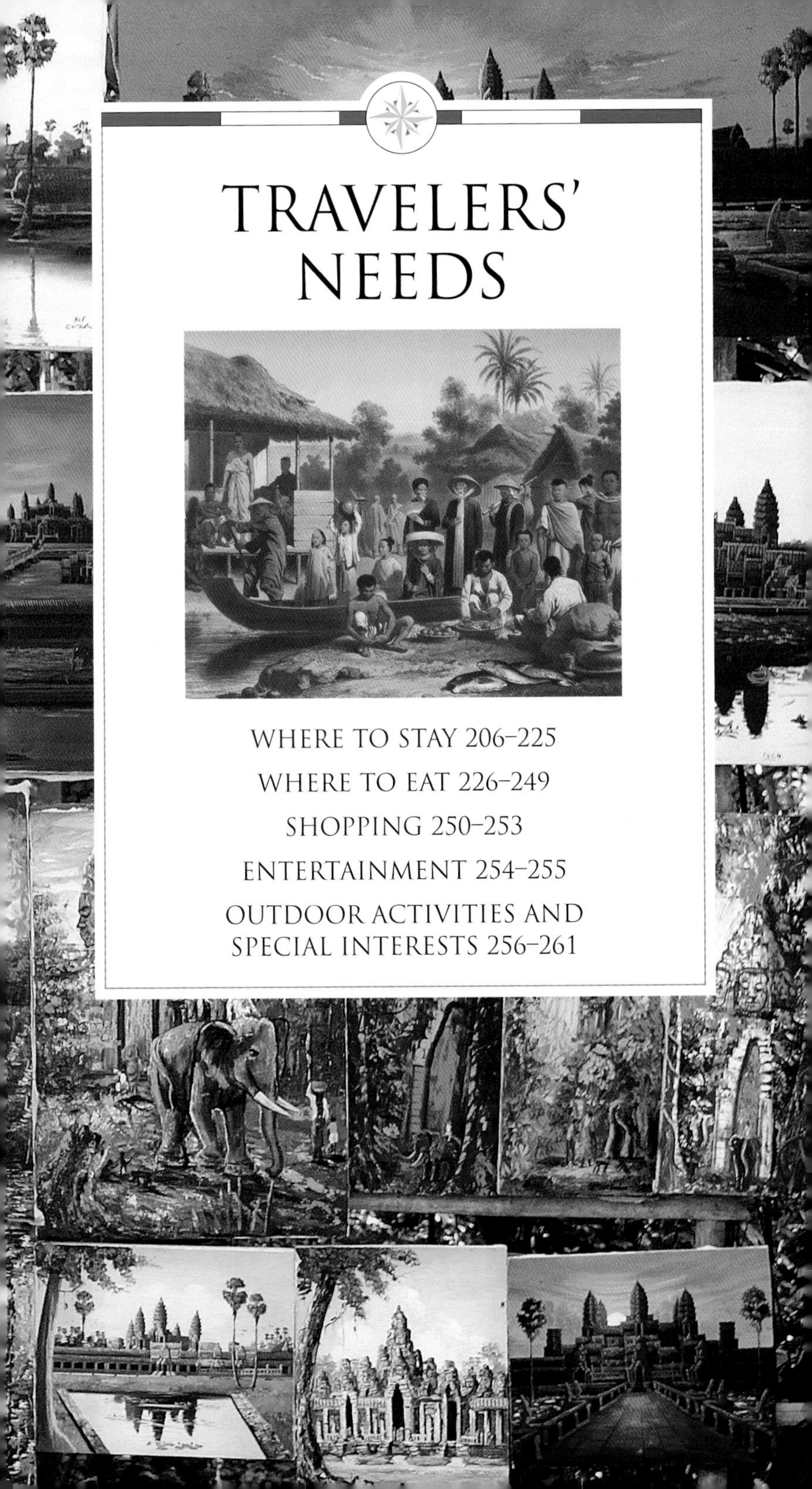

TRAVELERS' NEEDS

WHERE TO STAY

Accommodations in both Cambodia and Laos vary widely, from basic guesthouses to restored Colonial villas serving as boutique hotels. Luxury international chains, however, are mostly confined to larger towns and cities such as Siem Reap, Phnom Penh, and Sihanoukville in Cambodia, and Luang Prabang and Vientiane in Laos. A wide variety of midrange accommodation options are also available, and are often great value for money. These establishments offer both air-conditioned and non-airconditioned rooms, with the former being more expensive. Homestays are another option and are becoming increasingly popular, especially in Laos. They not only present an opportunity to contribute directly to the community, but are also an excellent way to experience authentic rural life.

Flower arrangement at a boutique hotel

The tastefully decorated lobby of the Raffles Hotel in Phnom Penh, Cambodia

HOTEL GRADING

There is no official grading system for hotels in Laos and Cambodia. Price and the facilities offered are usually the best indicators of what to expect. Typically, establishments charging more than US$100 will fall into the upscale category for the US and Europe. Most upscale hotels offer a variety of options, from private suites to less expensive rooms. Guesthouses, on the other hand, are very different from luxury hotels, not only in terms of the facilities on offer, but also in the absence of room service, concierge services and other amenities.

LUXURY HOTELS

Several international hotel chains, such as Raffles *(see p212)* and Amansara *(see p214)*, have representation in major cities such as Phnom Penh and Siem Reap, and offer the same quality of facilities and service they provide in other parts of the world. While Luang Prabang and Vientiane also have their fair share of international hotels, in addition, these cities have a wide variety of boutique hotels, such as Auberge Le Calao *(see p220)* in Luang Prabang.

These international hotels, in several cases, offer menus and interiors designed by people of global repute. Most hotels also have a busy events calendar with performances, such as traditional dance, during the evening and other events during the day.

Boutique hotels, on the other hand, offer a more specialized service with accommodations often in atmospheric, lovingly restored French villas. They are smaller in size, with fewer rooms, but will pay more attention to detail. Siem Reap, in particular, is experiencing a growth in this sector, although the term "boutique" is often loosely applied. Fortunately for visitors, due to increasing competition, such establishments may reduce their prices and there are some really beautiful rooms in good boutique hotels that can be had for a reasonable rate.

RESORT HOTELS

Several resort hotel chains have been quick to establish themselves in Cambodia, given its extraordinary archaeological treasures and pristine coastline. The coastal town of Sihanoukville *(see pp106–7)*,

External façade of a popular boutique hotel in Luang Prabang, Laos

◁ Brightly colored local art on sale, Angkor

The tranquil gardens of the Knai Bang Chatt Hotel in Kep, Cambodia

in particular, is home to a number of resort hotels, as is Siem Reap, where visitors often combine a luxury trip with an exploration of the ancient temples. The Victoria Angkor Resort and Spa *(see p214)* in Siem Reap is a typically lavish 1930s building, which gives its guests the chance to relax in a spa, sample world-class cuisine, and also enjoy organized trips to the majestic temples of Angkor.

Resort hotels are not very common in Laos yet, but with several multinational investors keen to tap into the untouched beauty of the country, many more of these places are likely to appear in the near future.

GUESTHOUSES AND MID-RANGE HOTELS

Guesthouses are usually family-run in both countries and offer good value for the budget traveler. With basic amenities such as a fan and an en suite or shared bathroom, these often house-proud establishments are thoughtfully furnished, with flowers in the rooms and friendly service at reception. They are also great places to meet other travelers and exchange tips. Indeed, they may be the only option available for travelers in certain remote areas.

Mid-range hotels, on the other hand, start at around US$15 and may go up to as much as US$50, with a huge difference in the kind of facilities and service on offer. While some mid-range hotels are tastefully designed and may offer a pool, excellent food, and service, the less expensive ones may barely justify the price. It is therefore best to look around before settling on one.

Laos usually offers better value, both in guesthouses and mid-range hotels. The quality of service provided, and the facilities on offer are on the whole much better than in Cambodia.

BUDGET HOTELS

Budget hotels are functional, inexpensive, and only slightly better than a guesthouse in terms of decor and furnishings. Unfortunately, service in these establishments can leave much to be desired and hygiene is often only an afterthought. Although these hotels usually have fairly large rooms (sometimes even with a balcony), as well as modern amenities such as cable TV, there is not much to recommend such places except the price. As a rule, rooms without any windows are cheaper. Budget hotels are usually patronized by Khmer businessmen on work trips, and visitors must always carefully scrutinize these establishments, as some of them double up as brothels.

A no-frills budget hotel on a quiet street in Vientiane, Laos

HOMESTAYS

The concept of staying with a friendly local family, usually a member of an ethnic minority group, to enjoy the opportunity to discover their lifestyle, is particularly popular in Laos. Homestays are also gaining ground in Cambodia. They are especially common in remote areas such as Ratanakiri and Mondulkiri provinces. Although such stays may not be as comfortable as staying in a hotel or resort, they are an enchanting way to experience authentic rural life. Board and lodging is generally shared with the host family and visitors may also get to participate in a few daily activities.

Laos, with its large number of ethnic minorities, offers a varied homestay experience. However, when staying with a local family, visitors should remember to follow certain rules of etiquette, which include always eating the food offered, never littering the surroundings, and also refraining from giving sweets or medicine to the children.

Elegant interior of a spacious bedroom in The Apsara, Luang Prabang

RENTAL APARTMENTS

Those who do not wish to stay in a hotel or resort and for whom homestays are not an option, can always rent their own apartment. The best place to look for rental apartments in Phnom Penh or the rest of Cambodia is in the local **Cambodia Yellow Pages**. This also has a website that lists apartments for rent, accompanied by a wealth of photos and making it easier for guests to choose. Visitors can also check the **Immo Laos** website in Laos, which offers properties for rent. Advertisements for rooms for rent often appear on bulletin boards, usually at restaurants, cafés, and bars, or in the classified section of local weekly newspapers, or at the back of popular publications. *Paisai? What's On?*, for instance, is a free and informative monthly magazine, widely available in Vientiane, which also lists properties for rent.

PRICES

Cambodia and Laos offer a wide range of accommodations, with varying prices. The least expensive among them are usually the budget hotels where a room with a fan and an en suite bathroom can be had for as little as US$4, with the better options costing up to US$20. Mid-range options cost anywhere between US$15 and US$50 with the higher-end range offering not only a good location, but also modern amenities such as a swimming pool, air conditioning, and cable TV. Breakfast is usually included in the room rate. The most exclusive boutique hotels, however, will cost well over US$100, although cheaper options are also available. Boutique hotels in Laos are considerably cheaper, even though they provide the same level of style and service. The most expensive and upscale hotels in Cambodia range from US$150 to US$300 per night, while in Laos, a stay at a posh hotel such as Settha Palace Hotel *(see p219)*, in Vientiane, will cost much less.

BOOKING

Travelers visiting popular areas during the peak season, between November and February, may find all places, especially high-end hotels and international resorts, completely booked. It is therefore recommended to book a room in advance, especially if staying in cities such as Siem Reap and Luang Prabang, to avoid any last-minute hassles.

All the major hotels in both countries have their own websites, as do several mid-range establishments. Guests can always contact these establishments online and several of them also have online booking options. The official **Tourism of Cambodia** website also offers assistance with in online booking and can help in finding the right hotel. **The Laos Hotel and Guesthouse Booking Service** is also well run and has a comprehensive website that can be used to make bookings.

CHECKING IN

Guests are generally asked for their passport when checking in, and certain hotels may even keep the passport for the duration of the stay. Most hotels, however, will only record a guest's details and

Visitors arriving at guesthouse on Serendipity Beach, Sihanoukville

return the passport. Smaller hotels only ask for them as a security measure.

TAXES

Most major hotels in Cambodia and Laos levy a 10 percent tax and an additional 5 per cent service charge, both of which are detailed in the bill. Booking through a tour operator, however, is a good way of ensuring a discount on rates and taxes. Mid-range hotels will usually include tax and service charge costs in the price.

BARGAINING

Asking for a discount is usually a good idea, especially for those who are staying for more than one night at a hotel. Rates will go down with every extra couple of nights. Bargaining is common in both these countries, and visitors need not shy away from asking for a reduction. It is polite to stop bargaining when a mutually agreeable price has been reached, especially when the other person has stopped dropping his figures.

Most guesthouses, on the other hand, have low prices to begin with and visitors should refrain from asking for any discount, although many guesthouse owners will be happy to offer a cheaper rate for a guest who is staying for a longer duration. As a rule, less desirable, smaller rooms, especially those with no windows, will be available for considerably lower rates.

An inexpensive hotel advertising its services, Sihanoukville

TIPPING

Gratuities are not usual in Cambodia or Laos, and tipping is not an essential part of their culture. So, unless someone has been particularly helpful, visitors should not feel in any way obliged to tip. That said, both Cambodia and Laos are economically developing countries and tips are often a good way of supplementing salaries, especially if a visitor is pleased with the service provided. US$1 is considered adequate, although the amount can be larger if staying at an expensive hotel.

DIRECTORY

BOOKING

The Laos Hotel and Guesthouse Booking Service
www.laos-hotel-link.com

Tourism of Cambodia
www.tourismcambodia.com

RENTAL APARTMENTS

Cambodia Yellow Pages
www.yellowpages-cambodia.com

Immo Laos
www.immo-laos.webs.com

FACILITIES FOR CHILDREN

Expensive, upscale hotels, equipped with with modern amenities such as swimming pools, tennis courts, and table tennis facilities, usually have a family room and other facilities to keep children occupied. Most other hotels, however, will not be able to provide any special facilities for families traveling with children.

Children under the age of 12 years are usually allowed to stay in a hotel free of charge. Cots and high chairs are available in upscale accommodations but not elsewhere, so traveling to these countries with children can be challenging, unless visitors make their own provisions.

A swimming pool in a luxury hotel with stunning views of the surrounding mountains, Vang Vieng

Choosing a Hotel in Cambodia

Most of the hotels in this guide have been selected across a wide price range for their good value, facilities, ambience, and location. Hotels are listed by area and arranged alphabetically within the same price category. For map references, see pp60–61 for Phnom Penh and the inside back cover for other locations.

PRICE CATEGORIES
These price ranges are for a standard double room per night, including taxes and service charges, during high season. When available, breakfast is included.

- $ Under $20
- $$ $20–$50
- $$$ $50–$100
- $$$$ $100–$150
- $$$$$ Over $150

PHNOM PENH

CENTRAL PHNOM PENH Coffee Korner $
174, St 155, next to Psar Tuol Tom Pong ***Tel*** *(023)-993-683* ***Rooms*** *10* **City Map** *C5*

As the name suggests, this establishment began as a coffee shop, but has now expanded into a good budget guesthouse along with a spa. The place is immaculate and free of the unsavory characters that sometimes frequent budget places in this city. All the rooms have free Wi-Fi.

CENTRAL PHNOM PENH Skypark Guest House $
78, St 111 ***Tel*** *(023)-992-718* ***Rooms*** *50* **City Map** *C2*

The perfect budget accommodations for those seeking a clean and safe place to sleep, Skypark Guest House offers good value for money. The staff speak English and Thai and are available around the clock. Bathrooms have hot and cold water. A few inexpensive Chinese restaurants are located nearby.

CENTRAL PHNOM PENH Amber Villa & Restaurant $$
1A, St 57 ***Tel*** *(023)-216-303* ***Rooms*** *7* **City Map** *D3*

A good mid-range choice due to its central location, Amber Villa & Restaurant has nice airy rooms with large windows, some of them overlooking a pleasant garden. The management is reliable and the staff is friendly and efficient. This place gets many return visitors and favorable reviews. **www.amber-kh.com**

CENTRAL PHNOM PENH Anise Hotel $$
2c, St 278 Off 57, Beoung Keng Kang 1 ***Tel*** *(023)-222-522* ***Fax*** *(023)-222-533* ***Rooms*** *18* **City Map** *D4*

Situated in the peaceful NGO area near Independence Monument, a 10-minute walk from the downtown area, this family-run, mid-range choice has large, high-ceilinged rooms with free Wi-Fi. Although the neighborhood does not offer interesting nightlife, there are many quality restaurants close by. **www.anisehotel.com.kh**

CENTRAL PHNOM PENH Billabong $$
5, St 158 ***Tel*** *(023)-223-703* ***Fax*** *(023)-998-472* ***Rooms*** *15* **City Map** *D2*

Set in an idyllic tropical garden with a large free-form salt-water swimming pool, Billabong is a 10-minute walk from the Mekong River and the Central Market. Rooms vary in size and price and include facilities such as cable TV and laundry services. This hotel is well maintained and the staff pleasant. **www.thebillabonghotel.com**

CENTRAL PHNOM PENH Blue Lime $$
42, St 19z (off St 19) ***Tel*** *(023)-222-260* ***Rooms*** *23* **City Map** *E2*

Located down a quiet street behind the National Museum *(see p50)*, this small hotel has a lovely salt-water swimming pool. The decor is artistically modern and minimalist, using concrete as a design element. The hotel's alfresco restaurant, located by the pool, serves well-prepared food. **www.bluelime.asia**

CENTRAL PHNOM PENH Bright Lotus Guesthouse 1 $$
22, St 178 ***Tel*** *(023)-990-446* ***Rooms*** *16* **City Map** *E2*

A good and inexpensive guesthouse in the riverfront area near the National Museum, Bright Lotus Guesthouse offers clean rooms, which are priced according to their size and the facilities offered. The airy restaurant on the first floor is reasonably priced and serves a variety of dishes. **www.thebrightlotus1.com**

CENTRAL PHNOM PENH Del Gusto Boddhi Tree $$
43, St 95 ***Tel*** *(023)-211-396* ***Rooms*** *9* **City Map** *D4*

A charmingly restored 1930s Colonial house in a quiet part of the city, this hotel offers a variety of rooms with a range of facilities such as free Wi-Fi and hot showers, depending on the price. All rooms have teakwood floors. The garden here is tranquil, and the food and service are outstanding. **www.boddhitree.com**

CENTRAL PHNOM PENH Frangipani Villa 90s $$
25, St 71 ***Tel*** *(012)-687-717* ***Rooms*** *15* **City Map** *D5*

Restored according to the 1960s style of Khmer Architecture, Frangipani Villa 90s has a lovely garden adjacent to the hotel's restaurant, which serves both Khmer and Western fare such as spicy fish *amok* and Caesar salad respectively. Bright and airy rooms come with free Wi-Fi and cable TV. **www.frangipanihotel.com**

Key to Symbols *see back cover flap*

CENTRAL PHNOM PENH Golden Gate Hotel $$

9, St 278, Beoung Keng Kang 1 ***Tel*** *(023)-427-618* ***Fax*** *(023)-427-712* ***Rooms*** *105* ***City Map*** *E3*

Located close to the Independence Monument, this hotel is clean and safe and offers good value for money. All rooms have cable TV and bathrooms come with bathtubs. Laundry service and breakfast are included in the rate. There are a number of bars and restaurants in the area. **www.goldengatehotels.com**

CENTRAL PHNOM PENH Hotel California 2 $$

79 Sisowath Quay ***Tel*** *(077)-503-144* ***Rooms*** *10* ***City Map*** *E1*

Located by the river, near the confluence of the Mekong and the Tonlé Sap, the Hotel California 2 offers clean rooms with cable TV for a fair price. The hotel can also make arrangements for those interested in motorcycle tours, kayaking, and exploring off-beat destinations. **www.cafecaliforniaphnompenh.com**

CENTRAL PHNOM PENH Hotel Scandinavia $$

4, St 282 ***Tel*** *(023)-214-498* ***Rooms*** *16* ***City Map*** *E4*

Noted for its artistic decor and attached art gallery, Hotel Scandinavia is conveniently located near the Independence Monument. Rooms are decorated with laquered Chinese-Khmer style furniture and have en suite bathrooms. Its restaurant and bar are popular with local expats.

CENTRAL PHNOM PENH Paragon $$

219 Sisowath Quay ***Tel*** *(023)-222-607* ***Rooms*** *40* ***City Map*** *E1*

An affordable choice, Paragon is located in the busy area on the riverfront, so those choosing to stay in this hotel should try for a room on a high floor, especially if they want a decent view of the river. The hotel also provides good travel information and services such as booking bus tickets.

CENTRAL PHNOM PENH Aram Boddhi Tree Boutique Hotel $$$

70, St 244 ***Tel*** *(023)-211-376* ***Rooms*** *8* ***City Map*** *E3*

Situated in the heart of old Phnom Penh near the Royal Palace *(see pp52–5)*, this building was originally constructed in 1950. Rooms are not huge but have high ceilings, large windows, and contemporary Asian decor. The garden is verdant and tranquil with views of the golden spires of the Royal Palace. **www.boddhitree.com**

CENTRAL PHNOM PENH Bougainvillier Hotel $$$

277 C Sisowath Quay ***Tel*** *(023)-220-528* ***Fax*** *(023)-220-529* ***Rooms*** *38* ***City Map*** *E2*

Located on the riverfront, Bougainvillier Hotel has a variety of rooms, some offering river views, although those facing the garden are quieter. Rooms have polished wood furniture. The restaurant serves excellent royal Khmer and classic French cuisines. The neighborhood abounds with bars and restaurants. **www.bougainvillierhotel.com**

CENTRAL PHNOM PENH Imperial Garden Villa & Hotel $$$

315 Sisowath Quay ***Tel*** *(023)-219-991* ***Fax*** *(023)-219-992* ***Rooms*** *122* ***City Map*** *F3*

Enjoying a central location, this modern, low-rise luxury hotel offers a choice of standard rooms or villas of up to four bedrooms. Both are good value for money compared to other similar accommodations in Phnom Penh. A quiet place, despite its proximity to the Royal Palace and Sisowath Quay. **www.imperialgarden-hotel.com**

CENTRAL PHNOM PENH Juliana Hotel $$$

16, St 152 ***Tel*** *(023)-880-530* ***Rooms*** *118* ***City Map*** *C2*

Popular with business travelers, Juliana Hotel, which is located near the Olympic Stadium, has tastefully decorated rooms surrounding a beautiful pool, and offers services such as a spa and traditional massage. The hotel's two restaurants offer superb lunch and dinner buffets as well as authentic Chinese cuisine. **www.julianahotels.com**

CENTRAL PHNOM PENH Kabiki $$$

22, St 264 ***Tel*** *(023)-222-290* ***Rooms*** *11* ***City Map*** *E3*

Under the same management as the Blue Lime, the Kabiki is child friendly with a shallow pool and bunk beds in some of the rooms. The decor uses a lot of wood, which adds to the cosy atmosphere. All rooms have air conditioning, cable TV, and en suite bathrooms with hot water. **www.thekabiki.com**

CENTRAL PHNOM PENH The Quay $$$

227, Sisowath Quay ***Tel*** *(023)-224-894* ***Fax*** *(023)-224-893* ***Rooms*** *16* ***City Map*** *E2*

Managed by the Foreign Corespondents' Club group, The Quay is a sleek new hotel that uses minimalist decor and eco-friendly practices to achieve what they call "intelligent indulgence and contemporary civility". The hotel's Chow restaurant serves good Asian fusion cuisine. **www.thequayhotel.com**

CENTRAL PHNOM PENH Villa Langka $$$

14, St 282 ***Tel*** *(023)-726-771* ***Rooms*** *43* ***City Map*** *E4*

Close to the Independence Monument, this is a secluded, tranquil, and clean boutique hotel with good views of the ancient spires of Wat Lanka. The pool is surrounded by trees and the rooms blend modern and traditional styles. The restaurant is popular with expats for lunch. Service is reliable. **www.villalangka.com**

CENTRAL PHNOM PENH Amanjaya Pancam $$$$

1 Sisowath Quay ***Tel*** *(023)-214-747* ***Fax*** *(023)-219-545* ***Rooms*** *21* ***City Map*** *E2*

This four-story building has a lovely Colonial atmosphere right by the river between the Royal Palace and Wat Phnom *(see pp50–51)*. All rooms are suites, and have been tastefully decorated with traditional Cambodian motifs. The K-West restaurant on the first floor is vibrant and has a varied menu. **www.amanjaya-pancam-hotel.com**

CENTRAL PHNOM PENH Raffles $$$$$

92 Rukhak Vithei Daun Penh, off Monivong Blvd **Tel** *(023)-981-888* **Fax** *(023)-981-168* **Rooms** *210* **City Map** *D1*

Originally opened in 1929, but refurbished and taken over by the Raffles Group in 1997, this opulent Art Deco-style building has several chic suites. The gardens are beautifully landscaped, the spa is excellent, and the staff is friendly and helpful. The hotel has several bars and restaurants. **www.raffles.com**

CENTRAL PHNOM PENH Sofitel Phnom Penh Prokeethra $$$$

26 Old August Site, Sothearos Blvd **Tel** *(023)-999-200* **Rooms** *201* **City Map** *F4*

Sofitel is Phnom Penh's most luxurious accommodation. Located on a southern stretch of the Mekong River, across from Diamond Island, the hotel features multiple swimming pools, spa, health club and four restaurants. Do Forni, its Italian restaurant, is the finest dining in the city. **www.sofitel.com**

CENTRAL PHNOM PENH The Pavilion $$$$

227, St 19 (behind Botum Pagoda) **Tel** *(023)-222-280* **Rooms** *20* **City Map** *E3*

Dating from the 1920s, The Pavilion is the restored home of King Sihanouk's mother. The architecture is an original combination of Khmer and French styles and some rooms have private pools or Jacuzzis, while others have balconies overlooking a shady garden. A bit hard to find so it is best to take a taxi there the first time. **www.thepavilion.asia**

ANGKOR

SIEM REAP Babel Guesthouse $

Wat Bo Rd **Tel** *(063)-965-474* **Rooms** *23* **Road Map** *C6*

This guesthouse is good value for money with spotless white rooms, large bathrooms, and full-sized baths. There are pleasant spots in the tropical gardens to relax in and the place, although basic, is welcoming. The staff is friendly and can speak both English and French.

SIEM REAP Earthwalkers $

Sala Kanseng Village, Sangkat No. 2 **Tel** *(012)-967-901* **Rooms** *20* **Road Map** *C6*

One of the original backpacker haunts, Earthwalkers now represents amazing value with a new block of rooms overlooking its swimming pool. It also has a dormitory. The food is fresh and varied and the crowd friendly. Staff can help with trips to the temples of Angkor. **www.earthwalkers.no**

SIEM REAP Ivy Guesthouse $

West of Pokambor Ave, near the river **Tel** *(012)-800-860* **Rooms** *17* **Road Map** *C6*

An intimate travelers' guesthouse with pretty gardens, hammocks, and pleasant rooms, some with air conditioning, Ivy Guesthouse offers great value for money and is only a five-minute walk from the center of town. The food is delicious and the staff friendly.

SIEM REAP Rosy's Guesthouse $

74, Phum Slor Kram **Tel** *(063)-965-059* **Rooms** *15* **Road Map** *C6*

This attractive old villa is run by a Western couple and offers great value, with Wi-Fi, TVs, and DVD players in all rooms (air conditioning is optional). Rosy's Guesthouse has plenty of hammocks to relax in in the lounging area. The staff is friendly and always ready to help guests. **www.rosyguesthouse.com**

SIEM REAP Smiley's Guesthouse $

West of Sivatha Rd **Tel** *(012)-686-060* **Rooms** *30* **Road Map** *C6*

A great place for those on a budget, Smiley's Guesthouse offers large rooms in a somewhat bland building. However, the food is decent and the staff friendly. Wi-Fi is free and air conditioning optional for an extra charge. Bicycles can also be rented for a small fee. **www.smileyguesthouse.com**

SIEM REAP Tanei Guesthouse $

Phumi Vihea Chen **Tel** *(012)-757-867* **Rooms** *32* **Road Map** *C6*

Located in a quiet lane in the heart of Siem Reap, Tanei Guesthouse offers immaculately clean, chic, mid-range accommodations with modern facilities. It also has a Khmer and International fusion restaurant, as well as a free pick-up service. Overall, great value for money. **www.taneiguesthouse.com**

SIEM REAP WatsUp Guesthouse $

Wat Damnak area **Tel** *(063)-966-091* **Rooms** *14* **Road Map** *C6*

A favorite among budget travelers, WatsUp is situated in a quiet area within easy walking distance of the Old Market and Pub Street and offers great value for money. All rooms have air conditioning and TV. Western breakfasts and Khmer lunches are also available.

SIEM REAP Dead Fish Tower Inn $$

Sivatha Blvd at Dead Fish Plaza **Tel** *(016)-330-821* **Rooms** *35* **Road Map** *C6*

This strangely named inn is a well established place with clean, comfortable rooms. Much of its charm comes from its quirkiness: there is a crocodile pool, and guests receive a free welcome head massage. The lively restaurant, offering Thai and Khmer dishes, hosts traditional Cambodian dance shows.

Key to Price Guide *see p210* **Key to Symbols** *see back cover flap*

SIEM REAP Eight Rooms $$

138/139 Streoung Thmey Village, Svydangkum Commune ***Tel*** *(063)-969-788* ***Rooms*** *8* ***Road Map*** *C6*

A gay-friendly, stylish flashpacker (read affluent) option, Eight Rooms offers clean rooms, a relaxing roof terrace, and free pick-up facility from the airport. Wi-Fi is available in the lobby and garden. The staff is friendly and helpful. **www.ei8htrooms.com**

SIEM REAP Rithyrine Angkor Hotel $$

No. 0509, Wat Bo Village ***Tel*** *(012)-543-475* ***Rooms*** *30* ***Road Map*** *C6*

Rithyrine is a pleasant mid-range hotel with large guest rooms and a courtyard restaurant and swimming pool. Much of the building is exquisitely decked out in solid wood furnishings and carvings. A basic breakfast and free Wi-Fi is included with the room. Most featured restaurants and shops are a 15-minute walk away.

SIEM REAP Shadow Of Angkor I $$

353, Pokambor Ave ***Tel*** *(063)-964-774* ***Fax*** *(063)-964-774* ***Rooms*** *15* ***Road Map*** *C6*

This river-view guesthouse is housed in an old French Colonial building and is very close to the Old Market. Its rooms are clean and simple with white walls. Facilities include free Wi-Fi in rooms, bicycle rental, and massage and laundry services. **www.shadowofangkor.com**

SIEM REAP Golden Banana B&B $$$

Near Wat Damnak ***Tel*** *(063)-761-259* ***Rooms*** *25* ***Road Map*** *C6*

This gay-friendly, quiet, stylish hotel with a centerpiece swimming pool, sits on the eastern side of the Stung Siem Reap, just a five-minute walk from the Old Market. All rooms are set within pagoda-style bungalows and Wi-Fi is available free of charge. **www.golden-banana.com**

SIEM REAP Hanuman Alaya $$$

5 Krom 2, Phoum Treang ***Tel*** *(063)-760-582* ***Fax*** *(063)-760-582* ***Rooms*** *13* ***Road Map*** *C6*

Tucked away from the hustle and bustle of Siem Reap, Hanuman Alaya is decorated with antiques and handicrafts indigenous to the area and has a lovely wood finishing. Rooms are large, cool, and immaculate. The staff is friendly, the restaurant superb, and there is a lovely pool to relax in. **www.hanumanalaya.com**

SIEM REAP Mysteres d'Angkor $$$

235 Phum Slorkram ***Tel*** *(063)-963-639* ***Rooms*** *23* ***Road Map*** *C6*

Situated in a traditional, wooden Khmer house, Mysteres d'Angkor is a tranquil French-run boutique hotel, which has tastefully decorated rooms and a lovely decked pool surrounded by lush gardens. The hotel has a friendly bar and restaurant, bicycles for rent, and provides a laundry service. **www.mysteres-angkor.com**

SIEM REAP Shinta Mani $$$

Junction of Oum Khum and 14th St ***Tel*** *(063)-761-998* ***Fax*** *(063)-761-999* ***Rooms*** *15* ***Road Map*** *C6*

Conveniently located in the heart of the French Quarter and set in a magnificently restored Colonial mansion, Shinta Mani is a wonderful hotel. Besides all the usual luxurious facilities, the hotel also holds art exhibitions, and provides vocational training to underprivileged youths. The hotel restaurant is a gourmet's delight. **www.shintamani.com**

SIEM REAP The River Garden $$$

11 Phoum Treang ***Tel*** *(063)-963-400* ***Rooms*** *18* ***Road Map*** *C6*

Traditional, luxurious Khmer accommodations are on offer at The River Garden, which is located on the road to the temples of Angkor. The rooms are tastefully finished and have balconies, large bathtubs, and great views of the hotel's tropical gardens. The hotel also runs cooking classes. **www.therivergarden.info**

SIEM REAP Viroth's Hotel $$$

St 23 ***Tel*** *(063)-761-720* ***Fax*** *(063)-760-774* ***Rooms*** *7* ***Road Map*** *C6*

A diminutive boutique hotel, Viroth's has contemporary-styled rooms finished in cream linen and the outdoor areas have anti-mosquito lamps. The salt-water pool is small but exquisite, as are the massages and rooftop Jacuzzi. Viroth's is the epitome of what a boutique hotel really should be. **www.viroth-hotel.com**

SIEM REAP Royal Bay Inn Angkor Resort $$$$

1 Oum Khun St, Svay Dangkum ***Tel*** *(063)-760-500* ***Fax*** *(063)-760-503* ***Rooms*** *62* ***Road Map*** *C6*

A hint of boutique intimacy surrounds this large hotel complex. Fashionable and well situated in the French Quarter, Royal Bay Inn Angkor Resort has a wealth of amenities including revitalizing massages on site and a handsome restaurant. **www.dayinnangkor.com**

SIEM REAP Tara Angkor Hotel $$$$

Charles de Gaulle Rd ***Tel*** *(063)-966-661* ***Rooms*** *206* ***Road Map*** *C6*

The Tara Angkor Hotel has a dizzying list of amenities including a choice of two restaurants, Wi-Fi, spa, concierge service, and a super-sized swimming pool. The rooms are tastefully finished and heavy on luxury. The hotel also has cooking classes for those eager to learn a few Thai and Khmer dishes. **www.taraangkorhotel.com**

SIEM REAP Sojourn Boutique Villas $$$$

Treak Village Rd, Treak Village ***Tel*** *(063)-923-437* ***Villas*** *10* ***Road Map*** *C6*

With boutique villas beautifully finished with a stylist's eye, and huddled around a perfect pool with a swim-up bar, Sojourn Boutique Villas is a perfect getaway for the weary traveler. This hotel takes great pride in its service and leaves no stone unturned to satisfy its guests. **www.sojournsiemreap.com**

SIEM REAP Amansara $$$$$

262 Krom 8, Phum Beong Don Pa **Tel** *(063)-760-333* **Fax** *(063)-760-335* **Rooms** *12* **Road Map** *C6*

This 1960s-style hotel is easily the most exclusive accommodations in the city. The Amansara has a small collection of rooms, each of which has its own hot tub and pool. An exquisite hotel, it is favored by A-list celebrities seeking low-key privacy. **www.amanresorts.com**

SIEM REAP Apsara Angkor $$$$$

Route 6, Airport Rd **Tel** *(063)-964-999* **Fax** *(063)-964-567* **Rooms** *168* **Road Map** *C6*

Just about everything is on offer at the Apsara Angkor. The rooms feature wooden floors and are exquisitely decorated with colorful Khmer silks. Facilities include poolside Internet access, a 24-hour on-call doctor, baby-sitting services, special facilities for the disabled, and free airport pick-up among others. **www.apsaraangkor.com**

SIEM REAP FCC Angkor $$$$$

Pokambor Ave **Tel** *(063)-760-280* **Fax** *(063)-760-281* **Rooms** *31* **Road Map** *C6*

A byword for style in Cambodia, the FCC fuses contemporary cool with elegant Indochinese decor, open-plan restaurants, and stylish bars. This is all coupled with an inviting pool and minimalist, fresh rooms. The FCC also enjoys a lovely riverfront location. **www.fcccambodia.com**

SIEM REAP La Résidence d'Angkor $$$$$

River Rd **Tel** *(063)-963-390* **Rooms** *62* **Road Map** *C6*

Set among lush manicured gardens, this hotel has stylish wood and laterite rooms, each with their own hot bath or Jacuzzi along with Wi-Fi. The hotel's spa is excellent. Staff can arrange tours to the temples, and bicycles are also available for rent. **www.residencedangkor.com**

SIEM REAP Park Hyatt Siem Reap $$$$$

Sivatha Blvd **Tel** *(063)-966-000* **Fax** *(063)-966-001* **Rooms** *107* **Road Map** *C6*

An architecturally modern and chic place, this Art Deco hotel has a centerpiece courtyard crowned by a banyan tree, which is surrounded by a bar and minimalist rooms finished in dark wood. The staff is courteous and the spa superb. The hotel also has a great New York-style deli that serves delicious snacks. **www.siemreap.park.hyatt.com**

SIEM REAP Raffles Grand Hotel d'Angkor $$$$$

1 Charles de Gaulle St, Khum Svay Dang Kum **Tel** *(063)-963-888* **Rooms** *120* **Road Map** *C6*

The epitome of Colonial style and contemporary service, also one of the most established, the Raffles Grand Hotel d'Angkor has hosted a number of illustrious guests including Charles De Gaulle, Charlie Chaplin, and Bill Clinton. The hotel also has several restaurants and an outstanding spa. **www.raffles.com**

SIEM REAP Victoria Angkor Resort and Spa $$$$$

Central Park, PO Box 93145 **Tel** *(063)-760-428* **Rooms** *130* **Road Map** *C6*

One of the best-loved hotels in Siem Reap, Victoria Angkor Resort and Spa is a beautiful old Colonial villa, favoring lavish Colonial interiors, with fine cuisine, old-world service, and a fantastic spa and swimming pool. A short distance from the temples of Angkor, it looks out on to the Royal Park. **www.victoriahotels.asia**

NORTHERN CAMBODIA

BAN LUNG Lakeside Chheng Lok Hotel $

Central Ban Lung **Tel** *(012)-957-422* **Rooms** *54* **Road Map** *E6*

While not a very attractive building, this large but humble hotel is pleasantly located on the lake at the edge of town. The staff is very helpful and friendly, and speak some English. Rooms have all the basics like air conditioning, cable TV, Wi-Fi and private showers.

BAN LUNG Treetop Guesthouse $

Phum No.1, Laban Seak Commune **Tel** *(012)-490-333* **Rooms** *18* **Road Map** *E6*

A cheap, yet comfortable option, Treetop Guesthouse is located in beautiful, rural countryside near the town. The part-alfresco restaurant dishes up great pizzas, burgers, and local curries. Rooms are wood walled and have mosquito nets, tasteful linen, and en suite bathrooms. **www.treetop-ecolodge.com**

BAN LUNG Sovann Kiri Hotel $$

Rd 78 **Tel** *(012)-654-373* **Rooms** *26* **Road Map** *E6*

This hotel is modern and spacious, and has a pleasant staff, but few visitors to do it justice. Finished in a Thai-Roman style, the rooms have wooden sleigh beds, tiled floors, and clean bathrooms with hot showers. Cable TV and air conditioning are also available.

BAN LUNG Terres Rouge Lodge $$$

Beside Boeng Kansaign Lake **Tel** *(075)-974-051* **Rooms** *17* **Road Map** *E6*

Run by a former French paratrooper, Terres Rouge Lodge is undoubtedly the best accommodations in town. Its boutique-style rooms are decorated with handicrafts made by ethnic minorities, while its alfresco restaurant and lounge are great to relax in. Lush grounds dotted with birds of paradise add to its appeal. **www.ratanakiri-lodge.com**

Key to Price Guide *see p210* **Key to Symbols** *see back cover flap*

BATTAMBANG Banan Hotel $$

NH 5, Prek Mohatep Village, Sangkat Svay Por ***Tel*** *(053)-953-242* ***Rooms*** *30* ***Road Map*** *C6*

Built in 2006, Banan Hotel is a clean, if somewhat nondescript, establishment. The hotel offers three-star comfort with fresh, modern rooms that come with wood finishing and tiles, and hot water in the bathrooms. Cable TV in the rooms and proximity to the ferry port add to its value. The staff is friendly and very helpful.

BATTAMBANG Rottanak Resort $$

Ko Rd, Rottanak Village ***Tel*** *(053)-953-255* ***Rooms*** *38* ***Road Map*** *C6*

This modern hotel features tastefully furnished cabanas huddled around an attractively decked pool. Its courtyard garden is peaceful, the staff friendly, and the Khmer food served in its bar and restaurant delicious. Facilities include Wi-Fi, laundry service, and motorcycles for rent. **www.rottanakresort.com**

BATTAMBANG Royal Hotel $$

West of Psar Nath ***Tel*** *(053)-952-522* ***Rooms*** *42* ***Road Map*** *C6*

An old favorite in Battambang, the Royal Hotel is clean, large, and centrally located, making it popular with tour groups and independent travelers alike. Rooms are spacious and come with TVs. A reasonably priced Internet facility is available in the lobby. The rooftop restaurant provides panoramic views.

BATTAMBANG La Villa $$$

185 Pom Romcheck 5 ***Tel*** *(053)-730-151* ***Rooms*** *26* ***Road Map*** *C6*

Housed in a 1930s French Colonial mansion, this guesthouse features a wealth of antiques and stays true to the period in which the house was built with linen furnishings and bamboo furniture. Dinner, served in the atrium, is a delightful experience. The rooms upstairs are larger with private reading areas. **www.lavilla-battambang.net**

KOMPONG CHAM Mekong Hotel $

56, Samdach Pann Rd ***Tel*** *(042)-941-536* ***Rooms*** *37* ***Road Map*** *C6*

The best of a limited bunch in Kompong Cham, Mekong Hotel represents good value, with cavernous bathrooms and comfortable, if sparse, bedrooms. The hotel offers cable TV, and a basic restaurant, and also rents bicycles to guests. The staff is friendly and helpful.

KRATIE Heng Heng II Guesthouse $

Rue Preah Surmarit ***Tel*** *(012)-929-943* ***Rooms*** *23* ***Road Map*** *D6*

This riverside guesthouse might be described as a flashpacker joint as it falls somewhere between a guesthouse and a hotel. The rooms facing the Mekong River are the best since they are large and airy with capacious bathrooms that have hot water, and a veranda in front.

KRATIE Heng Oudom $

South St, corner of Central Market ***Tel*** *(072)-971-629* ***Rooms*** *10* ***Road Map*** *D6*

This is a modest hotel with clean rooms right in the heart of the Central Market and close to the Mekong River. The building itself is redolent of the French Colonial era with lovely Art Deco touches to its exterior, and pleasantly finished rooms with balconies and basic amenities.

KRATIE Santeheap Hotel $

Preah Soramarith Rd ***Tel*** *(072)-971-537* ***Rooms*** *18* ***Road Map*** *D6*

Located a short distance from the Central Market, in a peaceful spot close to the river, Santeheap Hotel is a good base for dolphin sightings in Kampie. Rooms are spacious, clean, and considerably more lavish than anything else on offer in town, with a choice of fan or air conditioning.

KRATIE You Hong Guesthouse $

North side of the market ***Tel*** *(012)-957-003* ***Rooms*** *15* ***Road Map*** *D6*

Representing great value and a level of comfort and hygiene not usually available at these prices, house-proud You Hong Guesthouse requires guests to take their shoes off at the entrance. Its rooms are sparkling clean, and overlook the bustling market below. The staff is well informed and friendly.

SEN MONOROM Nature Lodge $

Comka Tai Village, Spean Meanchey Commune ***Tel*** *(012)-230-272* ***Cabins*** *21* ***Road Map*** *E6*

Certainly the most enchanting place to stay in town, Nature Lodge lives up to its moniker with blissfully peaceful surroundings, simple cabins, and friendly staff who believe in eco-friendly principles. Nightly bonfires, hammocks, and treehouses are among the other attractions of this place. **www.naturelodgecambodia.com**

STUNG TRENG Gold River Hotel $

Kandal Village ***Tel*** *(012)-980-678* ***Rooms*** *50* ***Road Map*** *D6*

Although the Gold River is no great architectural beauty, its spacious interiors, which have been lavishly decorated, more than make up for it. The rooms come equipped with plasma TVs, refrigerators, and big bathtubs in the bathrooms. This hotel also has lovely river views. **www.goldenriverhotel.com**

STUNG TRENG Sok Sambath Hotel $

St 2 ***Tel*** *(016)-746-666* ***Rooms*** *37* ***Road Map*** *D6*

A block away from the river, and certainly the best among a limited bunch in Stung Treng, Sok Sambath is clean and comfortable, with well-sized bedrooms with TVs and hot water in the bathrooms, and a friendly staff. The restaurant on the first floor sells standard Khmer food.

SOUTHERN CAMBODIA

KAMPOT Blissful Guesthouse $

Postbox 0727 ***Tel*** *(012)-513-024* ***Rooms*** *10* ***Road Map*** *C7*

As the most popular backpacker place in town, Blissful Guesthouse is always busy, so book well ahead. The rooms are scattered around a rambling old Colonial house, some with en suite bathrooms. There is a highly popular bar downstairs, with happy-hour specials and a leafy garden to relax in. **www.blissfulguesthouse.com**

KAMPOT Kampot Guesthouse $

River Rd ***Tel*** *(012)-512-931* ***Rooms*** *25* ***Road Map*** *C7*

A basic but friendly guesthouse away from the riverside, down a quiet street lined with backpacker hotels. Rooms are tidy and efficient with hot water, fan or air-conditioning, and cable TV. Free Wi-Fi is available in the small downstairs restaurant. Most of Kampot is within walking distance.

KAMPOT Mea Culpa $$

44 Sovansokar (behind Governor's Mansion) ***Tel*** *(012)-504-769* ***Rooms*** *17* ***Road Map*** *C7*

Located in the French Quarter, Mea Culpa is a superb Irish-run guesthouse set in a handsome villa. Excellent service provided by an accommodating team. The spotless rooms have TVs, DVDs, and private showers. The restaurant is good and serves great pizza. The garden is well maintained and beautiful.

KAMPOT Moliden Guesthouse $$

Across the old bridge, Riverside Rd ***Tel*** *(012)-820-779* ***Rooms*** *12* ***Road Map*** *C7*

Situated by the riverside close to the old bridge in the heart of Kampot, this small guesthouse has a great location. There is a choice of rooms, either with fan or air conditioning, all with en suite, hot-water bathrooms. The café-restaurant on the first floor has a large outdoor patio.

KAMPOT Riki Tiki Tavi $$

South end of Riverside Rd ***Tel*** *(012)-235-102* ***Rooms*** *6* ***Road Map*** *C7*

Located below the Riki Tiki Tavi restaurant *(see p240)*, these stylish rooms are very well presented, with attractive Oriental fittings, Modern art, and furniture. Facilities include cable TV, hot showers, and free Wi-Fi. With its riverfront location and attention to detail, it is easy to see why Riki Tiki Tavi is so popular. **www.rikitikitavi-kampot.com**

KEP Tree Top Bungalows $

St 33, Thmey Village, Prey Thom Commune ***Tel*** *(012)-515-151* ***Rooms*** *17* ***Road Map*** *C7*

One of the newer establishments in town, Tree Top Bungalows has a dozen quirky looking wood-and-thatch bungalows that have been built on high stilts so patrons can enjoy the sea view. It has a large grassy plot of land and the restaurant serves delicious Khmer food.

KEP Botanica $$

National Rd 33a ***Tel*** *(016)-562-775* ***Rooms*** *5* ***Road Map*** *C7*

One of the best backpacker joints in town, Botanica has a selection of rustic bungalows set in a jungle-like garden bursting with tropical plant life. The kitchen serves food from around the globe and the restaurant stocks excellent Belgian beer. Also on offer is Wi-Fi and free bicycles for guests. **www.kep-botanica.com**

KEP Jasmine Valley $$

Near Kep Market ***Tel*** *(077)-599-248* ***Rooms*** *6* ***Road Map*** *C7*

Just below the Kep National Park *(see p116)*, with a fine valley location and views of the sea and offshore islands, this new eco-resort is a great place to stay. It has six solar-powered bungalows constructed from mud, brick, bamboo, and thatch, as well as two treehouses. It also has a café-restaurant. **www.jasminevalley.com**

KEP Le Flamboyant $$$

Entrance to the town of Kep ***Tel*** *(016)-713-823* ***Rooms*** *6* ***Road Map*** *C7*

An upscale choice set in spacious grounds with a stunning swimming pool, Le Flamboyant has well-presented suites that boast air conditioning and private terraces. The restaurant is renowned for its inventive French and Khmer cooking. Wi-Fi is also available. **www.flamboyant-hotel.com**

KEP Knai Bang Chatt $$$$$

Phum Thmey, Sangkat Prey Thom, Khan Kep ***Tel*** *(012)-349-742* ***Rooms*** *11* ***Road Map*** *C7*

Unquestionably the most upscale and stylish address in Kep, this Belgian-run lifestyle resort has Modernist Le Corbusier-style villas set in lush grounds by the seashore. This resort has been very well executed. Facilities include an infinity pool, a first-class spa, and a sailing club. **www.knaibangchatt.com**

KOH KONG TOWN Asian Hotel $$

1 Village, Sangkat Smach MeanChay, Khemarak Phummen City ***Tel*** *(035)-936-667* ***Rooms*** *38* ***Road Map*** *B7*

Right on the harborfront, this large modern hotel has panoramic views. Rooms are large and well appointed, all with TVs and en suite bathrooms. Visitors can pay extra for a family room or a river view. The hotel also has a mini-mart, Internet access, a snack bar, and a rooftop restaurant. **www.asiankohkong.com**

Key to Price Guide *see p210* **Key to Symbols** *see back cover flap*

KOH KONG TOWN Oasis Resort $$

1 mile (2 km) N from the town center ***Tel*** *(092)-228-342* ***Rooms*** *5* ***Road Map*** *B7*

Located in a tranquil place with views over the countryside, the British-run Oasis Resort is a peaceful retreat. Five family-sized air-conditioned bungalows are grouped around a lovely infinity pool. The resort also offers a large DVD library, pool table, and excellent travel advice. **http://oasisresort.netkhmer.com/**

KOH KONG TOWN Koh Kong International Resort Club $$$

Phum Cham Yeam, Srok Mondoul Seyma ***Tel*** *(011)-555-706* ***Fax*** *(012)-456-507* ***Rooms*** *210* ***Road Map*** *B7*

A huge casino resort hotel close to the Thai border with rooms set in lavish grounds with a vast pool, Koh Kong International Resort Club mainly draws Thais on vacation. Facilities, which include a fitness center and spa, are excellent and the atmosphere is family-friendly.

KOH RONG Broken Heart Guest House $$

Koh Rong ***Tel*** *(011)-649-424* ***Rooms*** *13* ***Road Map*** *C7*

Beautiful Koh Rong is slated for huge tourism development, but visitors can still enjoy the untouched beauty of this island paradise. The Broken Heart Guest House offers a back-to-nature experience where travelers stay in simple bamboo bungalows and life revolves around swimming, snorkeling, sunsets, and sundowners. **www.bhgh.info**

KOH RONG SAMLOEM Lazy Beach $$

Koh Rong Samloem ***Tel*** *(016)-214-211* ***Rooms*** *14* ***Road Map*** *C7*

An ideal get-away-from-it-all, Lazy Beach offers simple, clean wooden huts with en suite showers, great food, sunsets, and inexpensive drinks. There are board games and beach volleyball and the owners do not permit boatloads of day-trippers to spoil the peace. **www.lazybeachcambodia.com**

SIHANOUKVILLE Monkey Republic $

Behind Serendipity Beach ***Tel*** *(012)-490-290* ***Rooms*** *12* ***Road Map*** *C7*

The efficiently run Monkey Republic is an ideal choice for those looking for lively accommodations. It has plenty of simple bungalows close to the beach; the newer ones come with private bathrooms. The restaurant-bar here is always packed with a fun-loving crowd.

SIHANOUKVILLE Small Hotel $

Off Ekareach St, behind Caltrex Petrol Station ***Tel*** *(034)-934-330* ***Rooms*** *11* ***Road Map*** *C7*

Owned by a Swedish-Cambodian couple who look after their guests very well, Small Hotel offers neat, spotless rooms, some with hot water, and all with air conditioning. The lounge area has a sociable atmosphere. Swedish specialties such as sausage with dill-stewed macaroni are not to be missed. **www.thesmallhotel.info**

SIHANOUKVILLE Cloud 9 $$

Serendipity Beach ***Tel*** *(012)-479-365* ***Rooms*** *9* ***Road Map*** *C7*

An extremely attractive place, Cloud 9 has wooden bungalows that cling to the hillside to make the most of the sweeping views over Occheuteal Beach *(see pp106–7)*. Local textiles add a splash of color to the bungalows. The area is quiet and the seafront restaurant here is a delightful place for a drink or meal. **www.cloud9bungalows.com**

SIHANOUKVILLE Otres Shack $$

Near Queens Hill, Otres Beach ***Tel*** *(097)-799-3580* ***Rooms*** *3* ***Road Map*** *C7*

The best accommodations option on Otres Beach *(see p107)*, the Otres Shack is actually a stylish British-run place with just three beachfront rooms, all finished to a very high standard with good quality mattresses and shabby-chic decor. Facilities include Wi-Fi and a great ocean-facing restaurant.

SIHANOUKVILLE Sihanoukville Villa Hotel $$$

Off Serendipity Beach ***Tel*** *(012)-1600-374* ***Rooms*** *15* ***Road Map*** *C7*

A stylish and comfortable place, Sihanoukville Villa Hotel offers clean rooms, all of which boast good attention to detail. The decor is attractive with original artwork and quality furniture. Facilities include en suite bathrooms, free Wi-Fi, and cable TV. The garden restaurant serves a fine range of cuisine.

SIHANOUKVILLE Independence Hotel $$$$

St 2 Thnou, Sangkat No.3, Khan Mittapheap ***Tel*** *(034)-934-300* ***Fax*** *(034)-933-660* ***Rooms*** *112* ***Road Map*** *C7*

In a class of its own, this graceful Art Deco-style landmark has reopened after a painstaking restoration. It boasts beautiful, verdant grounds, a large pool, and a fine private beach. Rooms are spacious and luxurious, although they do not boast Art Deco fittings. **www.independencehotel.net**

SIHANOUKVILLE Sokha Beach Resort $$$$

St 2 Thnou ***Tel*** *(034)-935-999* ***Fax*** *(034)-935-888* ***Rooms*** *176* ***Road Map*** *C7*

This huge hotel complex has rooms and suites along with a few villas on a wonderful private beach. The staff is very helpful and welcoming. The pool area is incredibly inviting and there is also a childrens' playground. Watersports and tennis are also on offer along with bicycle rentals. **www.sokhahotels.com**

TATAI RIVER Rainbow Lodge $$

Tatai Village, 12 miles (19 km) SE of Koh Kong Town ***Tel*** *(099)-744-321* ***Rooms*** *8* ***Road Map*** *C7*

This solar-powered eco-resort enjoys a sublime location on the banks of the Tatai River. Bungalows are simple, comfortable, and extremely pleasant. Terrific river trips, kayak excursions, and hikes are some of the facilities on offer. All meals are included in the price of the room and the cooking is excellent. **www.rainbowlodgecambodia.com**

Choosing a Hotel in Laos

These hotels have been selected across a wide price range for their good value, facilities, service, and ambience. Hotels are listed by area and arranged alphabetically within the same price category. For map references, see pp138–9 and pp150–51 for Vientiane and Luang Prabang respectively; check the inside back cover for other locations.

PRICE CATEGORIES

These price ranges are for a standard double room per night, including taxes and service charges, during high season. When available, breakfast is included.

- $ Under $20
- $$ $20–$50
- $$$ $50–$100
- $$$$ $100–$150
- $$$$$ Over $150

VIENTIANE

CENTRAL VIENTIANE Chaleunxay Hotel $

Khu Vieng Rd **Tel** *(021)-223-407* **Fax** *(021)-223-509* **Rooms** *50* **City Map** *C3*

Located just outside the main tourist area but a quick walk from the morning market and Samsenthai Road, Chaleunxay Hotel provides good value and clean rooms. The hotel is quite popular with visiting businessmen from Vietnam. Get a room facing away from the street for some peace and quiet.

CENTRAL VIENTIANE Saysouly Guest House $

Manthatulat Rd **Tel** *(021)-218-383* **Fax** *(021)-223-757* **Rooms** *16* **City Map** *B4*

A good budget choice in the middle of the action, this simple and clean guesthouse is located in an old two-story building. It offers shared and en suite baths, air conditioning, and cable TV. The staff is knowledgeable and helpful and the balcony upstairs is a good place to meet young travelers. **www.saysouly.com**

CENTRAL VIENTIANE Auberge Sala Inpeng $$

In Paeng St, Ban Wat Chan **Tel** *(021)-242-021* **Fax** *(021)-242-954* **Rooms** *9* **City Map** *B3*

Situated in a quiet lane between Wat In Paeng and the Mekong, in the temple district of downtown Vientiane, this collection of teakwood bungalows is set in a glorious garden. All the rooms have balconies and breakfast is served in the open-air reception area. Advance booking is advisable.

CENTRAL VIENTIANE Chanthapanya Hotel $$

138 Nokeo Khumman Rd, Ban Mixay **Tel** *(021)-244-284* **Fax** *(021)-244-283* **Rooms** *31* **City Map** *B3*

A step up in price and quality from other small hotels in downtown Vientiane, the rooms of Chanthapanya Hotel are particularly spacious and furnished with Lao handicrafts. All rooms have DVD players and cable TV. Centrally located, this hotel is popular with traveling businessmen.

CENTRAL VIENTIANE Family Hotel $$

Pangkham Rd **Tel** *(021)-260-448* **Fax** *(021)-260-447* **Rooms** *31* **City Map** *C3*

This modern-style hotel is built around a central courtyard, with airy rooms full of natural light. The location, just off Samsenthai Road, is both central and quiet. The efficient staff and the cleanliness of the place make up for its lack of ambience. Better than older guesthouses in the same price range. **www.familyhotellaos.com**

CENTRAL VIENTIANE Lane Xang Hotel $$

Fa Ngum Rd **Tel** *(021)-214-102* **Fax** *(021)-214-108* **Rooms** *70* **City Map** *B4*

Among the best hotels in Vientiane during the 1960s, Lane Xang took on a decidedly Stalinist feel after it was nationalized in 1975. Along with a fantastic location by the river, the hotel also offers large, high-ceilinged rooms, lively gardens, and a pool, as well as putting greens.

CENTRAL VIENTIANE Lani Guest House $$

Setthathirat Rd, Ban Haysok **Tel** *(021)-215-639* **Rooms** *12* **City Map** *B3*

Tucked away in a quiet part of the city, Lani Guest House is housed in an old converted villa. Its simple but pleasingly decorated rooms offer a perfect getaway, ensuring that its guests keep coming back. Breakfast is laid out on a lovely veranda. Booking in advance is advisable. **www.laniguesthouse.com**

CENTRAL VIENTIANE Villa Manoly $$

Phiawat Rd **Tel** *(021)-218-907* **Rooms** *25* **City Map** *D5*

Outside of the downtown area near Wat Si Muang *(see p140)*, Villa Manoly is an old Colonial villa, now converted into a guesthouse. Set in lovely, if somewhat unkempt gardens, the guesthouse offers large rooms, each different from the next. It is located in a quiet residential part of the city and also has a good swimming pool.

CENTRAL VIENTIANE Vongkhamsene Hotel $$

17/01 Manthatulat Rd **Tel** *(021)-219-922* **Fax** *(021)-219-923* **Rooms** *17* **City Map** *B4*

This centrally located four-story hotel lies between the Mekong River and Setthathirath Road. Fairly new and well-maintained, it represents better value than some of the other older hotels in the area. The rooms facing the street have nice balconies, but can be noisy. **www.vongkhamsenehotel.com**

Key to Symbols *see back cover flap*

CENTRAL VIENTIANE City Inn $$$

Pangkham Rd **Tel** *(021)-218-333* **Fax** *(021)-218-444* **Rooms** *40* **City Map** *C3*

Located just off Samsenthai Road next to the Lao Plaza Hotel, the City Inn is quiet, contemporary, and offers stylishly decorated rooms with nice balconies, although the views are not great. Popular with visiting NGO workers and businessmen, the hotel also has an excellent coffee shop. **www.cityinnvientiane.com**

CENTRAL VIENTIANE Don Chan Palace $$$

Unit 6, Piawat Village, Sisatanak District **Tel** *(021)-244-288* **Rooms** *239* **City Map** *D5*

This 14-story edifice built on an island in the Mekong is the tallest building in the country with rooms that offer spectacular views of the city. The hotel's Chinese restaurant gets good reviews. Although popular for government functions and conferences, the place has an impersonal feel. **www.donchanpalacelaopdr.com**

CENTRAL VIENTIANE Lao Orchid Hotel $$$

Chao Anou Rd **Tel** *(021)-264-134* **Fax** *(021)-264-138* **Rooms** *33* **City Map** *B4*

Consistently receiving good reviews, this five-story hotel just off Fa Ngum's riverside offers large, clean rooms and an excellent breakfast. The hotel staff is efficient and there is an interesting temple across the street. There are also some good restaurants in the neighborhood. **www.lao-orchid.com**

CENTRAL VIENTIANE Lao Plaza $$$

Samsenthai Rd **Tel** *(021)-218-800–1* **Fax** *(021)-218-808* **Rooms** *142* **City Map** *C3*

The first "five-star" hotel in the 1990s, Lao Plaza is a modern six-story building located in the heart of the city. Although not atmospheric, the hotel is efficient, clean, and offers good food. The swimming pool and spa are located on the hotel's second floor. Discounts are often available on request.

CENTRAL VIENTIANE Sabaidee $$$

Pangkham Rd **Tel** *(021)-265-141–2* **Fax** *(021)-265-143* **Rooms** *80* **City Map** *C3*

Among the larger hotels in the city with good rooms and standard service, the Sabaidee offers guests a comfortable stay. All rooms in this six-story building have Wi-Fi and are tastefully decorated. Its restaurant, called Champa Restaurant, is excellent and serves Thai and Western dishes. **www.sabaideeatlaohotel.com**

CENTRAL VIENTIANE Taipan Hotel $$$

Francois Nginn Rd **Tel** *(021)-216-906–9* **Fax** *(021)-216-223* **Rooms** *44* **City Map** *B4*

A mid-range option, Taipan Hotel is among the older upscale hotels in the city. The hotel offers excellent food and its bar is known for its wide collection of exotic vodkas and Scandinavian hors d'oeuvres. The hotel also has a small but clean swimming pool as well as a sauna.

CENTRAL VIENTIANE Green Park Hotel $$$$

Khu Vieng Rd **Tel** *(021)-264-098* **Fax** *(021)-236-064* **Rooms** *34* **City Map** *D4*

An attractive property, set amid verdant gardens, Green Park Hotel offers a contemporary take on traditional Lao architecture. The rooms have Lao-style pavilions with rich, wooden accents and fine furniture. The hotel also has an on-site spa as well as an hourly shuttle bus into the city. **www.greenparkvientiane.com**

CENTRAL VIENTIANE Salana Boutique Hotel $$$$

Chao Anou Rd, 112 Wat Chan Village **Tel** *(021)-254-254* **Fax** *(021)-254-250* **Rooms** *41* **City Map** *B3*

Located in the city center, Salana is elegantly furnished and decorated, making it one of the most stylish accommodations in downtown Vientiane. Rooms include Wi-Fi, a safety box, coffee and tea service and free breakfast. The on-site bar and café serves drinks and light meals. **www.salanaboutique.com**

GREATER VIENTIANE Auberge du Temple $$

Off Luang Prabang Rd, across from Wat Khunta **Tel** *(021)-214-844* **Rooms** *15* **City Map** *A5*

Owned by a Swiss-French family, Auberge du Temple offers well-decorated but simple rooms set in beautiful gardens, a short walk from the Mekong. A quiet, relaxed place, not far from the city center, the hotel also has an atmospheric sitting area, great for an evening drink.

GREATER VIENTIANE Mekong Sunshine Hotel $$

Sithanneau Village, Sithan Rd **Tel** *(021)-251-401* **Fax** *(021)-251-402* **Rooms** *44* **City Map** *A5*

Located in a quiet residential neighborhood between Luang Prabang Road and the river, the well-kept Mekong Sunshine is a relaxing place. Many of the rooms have river views and the en suite bathrooms also have bathtubs, a rarity among Lao guesthouses. It has a good restaurant and friendly, helpful staff. **www.mekong-sunshine-hotel.com**

GREATER VIENTIANE Nalinthone Guesthouse $$

Fa Ngum Rd, Ban Seetan Neua **Tel** *(021)-213-659* **Rooms** *12* **City Map** *A5*

Housed in a recently renovated family villa, on the unpaved upstream section of the Fa Ngum, Nalinthone Guesthouse is one of the best choices when it comes to budget hotels in Vientiane. Quiet and surrounded by tall, shady trees, some of its rooms overlook the river. The place is especially clean and the staff helpful.

GREATER VIENTIANE Beau Rivage Mekong $$$

Fa Ngum Rd, Ban Seetan Neua **Tel** *(021)-243-350* **Fax** *(021)-243-345* **Rooms** *16* **City Map** *A5*

This chic boutique hotel lies on the quiet, if unpaved, section of Fa Ngum that is free of traffic and shaded by trees. The decor is Euro-Modern, and some rooms have balconies overlooking the river. The adjacent Spirit House restaurant and Papaya Spa add to the attraction of staying here. **www.hbrm.com**

GREATER VIENTIANE Novotel Vientiane $$$

Unit 9, Ban Khountathong, Samsenthai Rd ***Tel*** *(021)-213-570* ***Fax*** *(021)-213-572* ***Rooms*** *172* **City Map** *A5*

One of the few international chain hotels operating in Laos, this modern low-rise building is decorated in the Art Deco style and offers excellent French food and efficient service. The hotel's pool and disco are popular with local expats. **www.novotel.com**

LUANG PRABANG

CENTRAL LUANG PRABANG Sivilay Guesthouse $

Ban Xieng Muan ***Tel*** *(071)-212-758* ***Rooms*** *16* **City Map** *C3*

A good choice for those on a budget, the Sivilay Guesthouse has an ideal location in a quiet area near the river and offers rooms with private baths. It consistently receives good reviews for its helpful staff and efficient service. Recommended for good value.

CENTRAL LUANG PRABANG Sok Dee Guesthouse $

Khem Khong Rd, Ban Wat Nong ***Tel*** *(071)-252-555* ***Rooms*** *12* **City Map** *D3*

A good choice for budget travelers, Sok Dee Guesthouse has a variety of rooms to suit different needs. The guesthouse makes up in efficiency and cleanliness for what it lacks in ambience. The manager is quite helpful with providing travel information.

CENTRAL LUANG PRABANG Vatthanaluck Guesthouse $

Across from Villa Santi annex ***Tel*** *(071)-212-838* ***Rooms*** *6* **City Map** *D3*

Situated in the heart of old Luang Prabang, this budget establishment is actually a shophouse run by a charming local family. Few travelers frequent the place, ensuring quiet and solitude for those who desire it. However, service is limited to room cleaning.

CENTRAL LUANG PRABANG Vilayvanh Guesthouse $

Ban Aphay ***Tel*** *(071)-252-757* ***Rooms*** *10* **City Map** *C4*

Located down a lane across the street from Wat Visounarat *(see p164)*, Vilayvanh Guesthouse is recommended for its clean, quiet rooms with hardwood floors in a largely residential area of the city, close to the Nam Khan. Besides providing cable TV in all rooms, the guesthouse offers traditional Lao massage to its patrons and also rents bicycles.

CENTRAL LUANG PRABANG Pack Luck Villa Guesthouse $$

Ban Wat Nong, opposite L'Elephant Restaurant ***Tel*** *(071)-253-373* ***Rooms*** *6* **City Map** *D3*

A stylish two-story place on a quiet side street in the heart of the city, this guesthouse has clean and comfortable rooms richly decorated with local wooden furniture, private baths, a minibar, and cable TV. A fitness center and spa are also among the facilities offered by this pleasant establishment. **www.packluck.com**

CENTRAL LUANG PRABANG Phousi Guesthouse $$

Choum Khong Rd ***Tel*** *(071)-212-973* ***Rooms*** *12* **City Map** *C3*

Located just north of the National Museum Complex *(see p156)*, this guesthouse has a modern façade but pleasing, traditional decor. A beautiful central courtyard with a refreshing artificial waterfall and tropical garden add to its appeal. The guesthouse offers efficient service and a good restaurant. **www.phousiguesthouse.com**

CENTRAL LUANG PRABANG Riverside Guesthouse $$

Kingkitsarat Rd, Ban Khili ***Tel*** *(071)-212-664* ***Rooms*** *8* **City Map** *D3*

With spectacular views of the Nam Khan from the balconies of its rooms, this family-run establishment is an intimate place with staff who are happy to help with travel information. Breakfast is served across the street from the hotel on a breezy terrace and is included in the room rate. **www.guesthouse-riverside.com**

CENTRAL LUANG PRABANG Sopha House $$

Kingkitsarat Rd, Ban Khili ***Tel*** *(020)-5554-5825* ***Rooms*** *5* **City Map** *D3*

A great location by the Nam Khan makes this wooden house a good choice for travelers. Run by a local whose warmth makes up for her limited knowledge of English, the establishment offers clean and comfortable rooms with small balconies overlooking the river. **www.sophahouse.com**

CENTRAL LUANG PRABANG Villa Chitdara $$

Khounxua Rd, Ban Wat Nong ***Tel*** *(071)-254-949* ***Rooms*** *15* **City Map** *D3*

Another intimate establishment with small, albeit well-decorated rooms, the Villa Chitdara is housed in a two-story building in a quiet part of the Old Town. Breakfast is served in an attractive central garden courtyard. The manager is well informed and speaks good English. **www.villachitdara.com**

CENTRAL LUANG PRABANG Auberge Le Calao $$$

Khem Khong Rd ***Tel*** *(071)-212-100* ***Rooms*** *6* **City Map** *D2*

An old favorite with visitors to Luang Prabang, Auberge Le Calao is a Colonial-style boutique hotel. All rooms are large and well furnished and some have nice balconies. The French restaurant in front of the hotel is excellent. Staff is friendly and knowledgeable, and enjoy practicing their English with guests.

Key to Price Guide *see p218* **Key to Symbols** *see back cover flap*

CENTRAL LUANG PRABANG Chang Heritage Hotel $$$

Kingkitsarat Rd, Ban Wat Sene ***Tel*** *(071)-253-553* ***Rooms*** *22* ***City Map*** *D3*

Located on the banks of the Nam Khan, Chang Heritage Hotel belongs to the group which also owns the Chang Inn. Its plush rooms are opulently decorated in traditional Chinese and Lao style. The garden is peaceful and the restaurant excellent, although there are plenty of other dining choices in this neighborhood. **www.the-chang.com**

CENTRAL LUANG PRABANG Le Bel Air $$$

1 Old Bridge Rd ***Tel*** *(071)-254-699* ***Fax*** *(071)-410-488* ***Rooms*** *21* ***City Map*** *D4*

Offering charming bungalows set in an expansive garden, as well as less expensive rooms in the main building, Le Bel Air is an excellent choice for visitors seeking a taste of traditional Lao hospitality. Efficient service is combined with several creature comforts including Wi-Fi and cable TV. **www.lebelairhotels.com**

CENTRAL LUANG PRABANG Lotus Villa Boutique Hotel $$$

Kounxoa Rd, Ban Phone Huang (near Wat Nong) ***Tel*** *(071)-255-050* ***Rooms*** *15* ***City Map*** *D3*

Housed in a traditional French-Lao style building in the heart of Luang Prabang, is Lotus Villa Boutique Hotel. The hotel's rooms and two suites have French windows opening on to a beautiful tropical garden. Facilities include complimentary Wi-Fi in all rooms. **www.lotusvillalaos.com**

CENTRAL LUANG PRABANG Sala Prabang Mekong Riverside Hotel $$$

Khem Khong Rd ***Tel*** *(071)-252-460* ***Rooms*** *49* ***City Map*** *C3*

One of the many hotels of the Sala Lao chain of ecotourist resorts, Sala Prabang's Colonial-era structure has been refurbished and expanded by architect Sinlasone Soumpholphakdy. With natural stone and lime-washed interiors, the rooms are fitted with hand-crafted wood furniture, air conditioning, and private baths. **www.salalao.com**

CENTRAL LUANG PRABANG The Apsara $$$

Kingkitsarat Rd, Ban Wat Sene ***Tel*** *(071)-254-670* ***Fax*** *(071)-254-252* ***Rooms*** *13* ***City Map*** *D3*

A tasteful hotel built in what was once a rice warehouse facing the Nam Khan, The Apsara has a classy appeal. The rooms are beautifully furnished and have large baths. Its restaurant is decorated with a collection of contemporary Asian art and offers appetizing food and great service. **www.theapsara.com**

CENTRAL LUANG PRABANG Villa Deux Rivieres $$$

Kingkitsarat Rd, Ban Khily ***Tel*** *(020)-7737-8575* ***Rooms*** *17* ***City Map*** *E2*

Spread over five low-rise villas along the Nam Khan, Villa Deux Rivieres offers a variety of well-decorated rooms, some facing the river, and others a tranquil garden. With consistently good reviews, the hotel offers guests a luxurious stay with facilities including Wi-Fi and traditional massage. **www.villadeuxrivieres.com**

CENTRAL LUANG PRABANG Ramayana Boutique Hotel and Spa $$$$

PO Box 123, Ban Pha Kham ***Tel*** *(071)-255-055* ***Rooms*** *26* ***City Map*** *C3*

Offering luxury accommodations, the Ramayana Boutique Hotel and Spa is housed in a grand Colonial-style wooden house next to the National Museum Complex. The rooms are tastefully decorated and quite comfortable. The emphasis here is on the spa treatments, although it is also known for its restaurant. **www.ramayana-laos.com**

CENTRAL LUANG PRABANG The Apsara Rive Droite $$$$

Ban Phan Luang ***Tel*** *(071)-254-670* ***Fax*** *(071)-254-252* ***Rooms*** *9* ***City Map*** *D3*

This hotel has large, opulent rooms with hardwood floors surrounding a swimming pool in a cool garden. Its unique location across the Nam Khan means that guests reach the hotel by boat. Guests, however, must be aware that the hotel does not allow children below the age of 12 years. **www.theapsara.com**

CENTRAL LUANG PRABANG Amantaka $$$$$

55/3 Kingkitsarat Rd, Ban Thongchaleun ***Tel*** *(071)-860-333* ***Fax*** *(071)-860-335* ***Rooms*** *24* ***City Map*** *D3*

This former French hospital has been converted into the epitome of understated luxury. Many of the rooms have attached pools and the spa is world-class. The hotel also has a boutique and art gallery featuring handicrafts made by local artists and hilltribe communities. **www.amanresorts.com**

CENTRAL LUANG PRABANG Mekong Riverview Hotel $$$$$

Mekong Riverside Rd, Xieng Thong Village ***Tel*** *(071)-254-900* ***Fax*** *(071)-254-890* ***Rooms*** *40* ***City Map*** *D2*

Located in the center of Luang Prabang's old town peninsula, all the temples, shops and restaurants are within walking distance. As the name suggests, a number of the lavishly furnished rooms have views of the Mekong River. Personal touches abound, most notably wine receptions hosted by the owner. **www.mekongriverviewhotel.com**

CENTRAL LUANG PRABANG Satri House $$$$$

057 Photisarat Rd, Ban That Luang ***Tel*** *(071)-253-491* ***Fax*** *(071)-253-418* ***Rooms*** *15* ***City Map*** *B4*

Located in a quiet residential area near Wat That Luang *(see p165)*, this classy place was once the home of a Lao prince. The rooms here are furnished with antiques, some belonging to the original owner. Includes large baths with big windows. The swimming pool and courtyard garden are a delight. **www.satrihouse.com**

CENTRAL LUANG PRABANG The Belle Rive Hotel $$$$$

Khem Khong ***Tel*** *(071)-260-733* ***Fax*** *(071)-253-063* ***Rooms*** *8* ***City Map*** *D2*

Located by the Mekong near Wat Nong Sikhunmuang, The Belle Rive is housed in two magnificent Colonial buildings dating from the 1920s. All rooms are unique and ornamented in a mixture of traditional Lao and contemporary styles. The views of the river are superb, as is the service. **www.thebellerive.com**

CENTRAL LUANG PRABANG Villa Santi $$$$$

Sakkarin Rd, Wat Sene ***Tel*** *(071)-252-157 Rooms 25* ***City Map*** *D3*

An upscale boutique hotel, Villa Santi is housed in a quaint, restored Colonial-era mansion that was once home to a Lao princess. Although the main villa only has five rooms, there are 20 less luxurious rooms in an annex around the corner. The second-floor balcony restaurant is quite atmospheric. **www.villasantihotel.com**

AROUND LUANG PRABANG La Residence Phou Vao $$$$$

3 PO Box 50 ***Tel*** *(071)-212-530* ***Fax*** *(071)-212-534* ***Rooms*** *32*

Dominating a hilltop on the south edge of the city, this hotel is an oasis of calm, with a great ambience, refreshing infinity pools, efficient service, and mouth-watering food. With great views of the city and mountains, the hotel has an intimate atmosphere that is very welcoming. **www.residencephouvao.com**

NORTHERN LAOS

HONG SA Jumbo Guesthouse $

Behind the Central Market ***Tel*** *(020)-5685-6488* ***Rooms*** *10* ***Road Map*** *B2*

Owned by a German expatriate and elephant lover, the Jumbo Guesthouse has a convivial atmosphere. Guests can not only enjoy the excellent food cooked by the owner, but also participate in a variety of outdoor activities organized by her, including elephant rides and several-day trekking trips. **www.lotuselephant.com**

HUAY XAI Sabai Dee $

Saykhong Rd ***Tel*** *(084)-211-405* ***Rooms*** *18* ***Road Map*** *A2*

An excellent choice for those on a budget, Sabai Dee offers two categories of rooms – with and without air conditioning. However, all rooms are clean and well ventilated with large bathrooms and pleasant open-air sitting areas with views of the river from each floor. The staff is polite and quite efficient.

HUAY XAI Arimid Resort $$

Saykhong Rd ***Tel*** *(084)-211-040* ***Rooms*** *24* ***Road Map*** *A2*

Located in the northern part of Huay Xai, near the Lao Red Cross sauna and massage service, the Arimid Resort offers a variety of independent bungalows set in a pleasant garden. The resort also arranges tours for those keen to explore the area.

LUANG NAM THA Dok Champa Hotel $

Route 3 ***Tel*** *(086)-260-003* ***Fax*** *(086)-211-075* ***Rooms*** *18* ***Road Map*** *B1*

Among the best small-scale establishments in Luang Nam Tha, Dok Champa Hotel is located in the town center and offers exceptionally clean rooms with fridges, a coffee-tea service, bathtubs, and cable TV. A great place to relax in after a rough and tiring trek in the mountains.

LUANG NAM THA Zuela $

Route 3, across the street from the Night Market ***Tel*** *(086)-312-183* ***Rooms*** *20* ***Road Map*** *B1*

The best choice for budget travelers, owing to its location in a quiet part of the town center, Zuela comprises two brick and wood buildings with relaxing sitting areas, friendly and helpful staff willing to offer travel tips, and well-maintained mountain bikes for rent. The restaurant is also quite good, serving both Lao and Western food.

LUANG NAM THA The Boat Landing $$

Ban Kone ***Tel*** *(086)-312-398* ***Fax*** *(086)-312-239* ***Rooms*** *12* ***Road Map*** *B1*

Located 4 miles (6 km) south of town, The Boat Landing was one of the first ecolodges in Laos. It lies on the banks of the Nam Tha and offers tastefully decorated wooden bungalows instead of rooms. The lodge also arranges boat trips and other tours for guests. **www.theboatlanding.laopdr.com**

MUANG KHUA Nam Ou Guest House $

Next to the boat landing ***Tel*** *(088)-210-844* ***Rooms*** *10* ***Road Map*** *B1*

A favorite with regulars to Muang Khua, despite an increase in the choice of accommodations now available, Nam Ou Guest House offers basic facilities. The adjoining restaurant serves good food. The staff is efficient and friendly and well-versed in English.

MUANG NGOI Lattanovongsa Guest House $

North of the boat landing ***Tel*** *(030)-514-0770* ***Rooms*** *12* ***Road Map*** *B1*

Built in a rather unusual style with cluster bomb casings making up its balustrades, Lattanovongsa Guest House offers comfortable, clean bungalows surrounding a pleasant garden. Meals are usually served in the large dining room, also made of old bomb shells.

MUANG SING Adima Guest House $

4 miles (7 km) north of Muang Sing ***Tel*** *(081)-212-372* ***Rooms*** *16* ***Road Map*** *A1*

Quite popular with trekkers and backpackers, Adima Guest House is conveniently located close to several Akha and Yao tribe villages, which can easily be approached from here. Although the accommodations are basic, the food is good and the surroundings amazing.

Key to Price Guide *see p218* **Key to Symbols** *see back cover flap*

MUANG SING Sing Charoen $

South of town center ***Tel*** *(081)-212-347* ***Rooms*** *22* ***Road Map*** *A1*

About a 10-minute walk from the town center, where the restaurants and ecotourism offices are located, Sing Charoen offers great value for money and is superior to most other establishments of its kind. The staff is efficient and friendly although their English is quite rudimentary.

MUANG SING Phou Lu Resort $$

South of town center ***Tel*** *(081)-212-348* ***Rooms*** *34* ***Road Map*** *A1*

One of the best choices in Muang Sing, Phou Lu Resort, down the lane from Sing Charoen, is decorated in the fascinating Thai Lue style. Set in a pleasant, spacious garden, the resort has clean and comfortable rooms that are equipped with private baths. Open verandas in front of each room ensure a lovely breeze at all times.

NONG KHIAW Seng Dao Guest House $

Ban Nong Khiaw ***Tel*** *(071)-810-001* ***Rooms*** *16* ***Road Map*** *B1*

Owned by a local policeman, Seng Dao Guest House is located on the northeastern side of the high bridge over the Nam Ou. The guesthouse provides good value bungalows set in a beautiful garden. The in-house restaurant offers great local food that is worth trying.

NONG KHIAW Nong Kiau Riverview $$

Ban Sop Huen ***Tel*** *(020)-570-5000* ***Rooms*** *15* ***Road Map*** *B1*

A step up in quality (and price) from the other lodgings in Nong Khiaw, Nong Kiau Riverview has large bungalows offering great views of the surrounding mountains. The establishment also arranges for a variety of outdoor activities including trekking, kayaking, mountainbiking, and rock climbing. **www.nongkiau.com**

PAK BENG Santisouk Guest House $

Next to boat pier ***Tel*** *(020)-5578-1797* ***Rooms*** *16* ***Road Map*** *A2*

Situated a short distance north of the pier, Santisouk Guest House has recently been refurbished. This establishment offers clean rooms, with private bathrooms and great views of the river. The guesthouse also has an attached restaurant that serves good local food.

PAK BENG Luang Say Lodge $$$

1 mile (2 km) North of Pak Beng Village ***Tel*** *(071)-252-553* ***Fax*** *(071)-252-307* ***Rooms*** *20* ***Road Map*** *A2*

This is where those taking the Luang Say Mekong cruise stay, but it is possible to book via the Luang Prabang office number given above. Fantastic bungalows with huge windows provide great views. Makes for a wonderful experience; well worth a two-day stay. Highly recommended. **www.mekong-cruises.com**

PHONGSALI Viphaphone Hotel $

Town center, next to the Post Office ***Tel*** *(088)-210-111* ***Rooms*** *10* ***Road Map*** *B1*

Clean and well furnished, the Viphaphone Hotel is easily recognized thanks to its striking yellow exterior. The rooms are large and clean with windows offering good views. Most of them also have a bath with a hot shower facility and a Western toilet. Although the staff does not know much English, it is efficient.

PHONSAVAN Anoulack Khen Lao Hotel $

Off Route 7, town center ***Tel*** *(061)-213-559* ***Fax*** *(061)-312-308* ***Rooms*** *70* ***Road Map*** *C2*

Most of the budget accommodations in Phonsavan are decidedly the worse for wear, but this seven-story hotel is located far enough off Route 7 to offer some peace and quiet. It is well decorated, with hardwood floors and immaculately clean rooms, and offers good value for money.

PHONSAVAN Auberge de Plaine des Jarres $$

Phu Pha Deng Hill ***Tel*** *(030)-517-0282* ***Fax*** *(030)-517-0011* ***Rooms*** *15* ***Road Map*** *C2*

Situated on top of a pine-covered hill outside Phonsavan, these well-decorated and tranquil cottages offer an excellent jungle retreat. The central lodge serves the best French food in the area. The lodge is owned by the son of French ecotourism pioneer, Claude Vincent, who is well-versed with the region and can offer helpful travel tips.

SAM NEUA That Muang Guest House $

Ban That Muang ***Tel*** *(064)-312-141* ***Rooms*** *10* ***Road Map*** *C2*

Located just up the hill from the gaudy tower-like edifice in the center of town, this new place has exceptionally clean, large rooms with windows and balconies offering great views over the paddy fields below. The owner speaks good English, and the restaurant across the street offers delicious food.

VANG VIENG The Elephant Crossing $$$

Ban Vieng Gaew ***Tel*** *(023)-511-232* ***Rooms*** *31* ***Road Map*** *B2*

Situated on the banks of the Nam Song, this modern three-story boutique hotel is a good choice for those who want to avoid the backpacker crowd and enjoy the area's natural beauty. The rooms have balconies with river and mountain views. Free Wi-Fi access. The riverside restaurant is great. **www.theelephantcrossinghotel.com**

VANG VIENG Riverside Boutique Resort $$$$

Ban Viengkeo ***Tel*** *(023)-511-726* ***Fax*** *(023)-511-729* ***Rooms*** *34* ***Road Map*** *B2*

Rooms here are luxuriously furnished with wooden furniture, fabrics and artifacts from the Tai Lue tribe. The restaurant offers indoor dining in air-conditioned comfort, as well as outdoor seating in the tropical garden, set against a magnificent backdrop of limestone mountains. **www.riversidevangvieng.com**

VIENG XAI Thavisay Hotel $

North end of town ***Tel*** *(020)-5571-2392* ***Rooms*** *18* ***Road Map*** *C2*

Located outside of the dusty village of Vieng Xai, this recently refurbished building is the best place for visitors wishing to stay overnight. Although the place is too remote to offer any luxury to its guests, it is clean and comfortable. There is a good restaurant next to a lake adjacent to the hotel and the caves are within walking distance.

CENTRAL & SOUTHERN LAOS

BOLAVEN PLATEAU Tadlo Lodge Hotel $$

Ban Tanglea, Route 20, Lao Ngam District ***Tel*** *(034)-211-089* ***Rooms*** *25* ***Road Map*** *E5*

Located 52 miles (86 km) NE of Pakse, on the route to Salavan, this is a great place to enjoy the temperate Bolaven Plateau. Bungalows lie on both sides of the Se Set, in a lovely forest close to the Tat Lo and Tat Hang waterfalls. Guests can not only enjoy good food, but also trek and go for elephant rides.

CHAMPASAK Souchitra Guesthouse $

Ban Wat Amard ***Tel*** *(031)-920-059* ***Rooms*** *22* ***Road Map*** *D5*

A good budget choice by the Mekong, across the street from the former royal residences, Souchitra Guesthouse has clean rooms with river views, a nice garden, and a convivial atmosphere to share travel tips. The restaurant is good and bicycles and motorcycles can be rented here for touring Wat Phu Champasak *(see pp196–7)*.

CHAMPASAK Inthira Hotel Champanakone $$$

Ban Wat Amard ***Tel*** *(031)-214-059* ***Fax*** *(031)-214-059* ***Rooms*** *8* ***Road Map*** *D5*

By far the best choice for those staying overnight in Champasak, the Inthira Hotel Champanakone has artistically designed free-standing bungalows built around an attractive central courtyard. The restaurant and bar in front is a beautifully restored old Chinese shophouse with a pleasant balcony. **www.inthira.com**

DON DAENG La Folie Lodge $$$$

NW coast of Don Daeng ***Tel*** *(020)-5553-2004* ***Rooms*** *24* ***Road Map*** *D5*

This luxurious resort on remote and pristine Don Daeng, across the river from Champasak and Wat Phu, has 12 duplex bungalows. The food is excellent and the swimming pool stunning. The resort can also arrange for tours to Wat Phu and Wat Tomo *(see p196–8)*, as well as organize exploration trips around the island. **www.lafolie-laos.com**

DON DET Mama Leuah Guesthouse & Restaurant $

Don Det ***Tel*** *(020)-5907-8792* ***Rooms*** *6* ***Road Map*** *D5*

Mama Leuah's is a quiet backpacker haven with only six rustic wooden bungalows. Accommodation is basic, with mosquito nets, fans and a shared or private shower. The restaurant provides home-style cooking (Laotian and Western favorites). A pleasant location on the water with an exclusive beach. **www.mamaleuah-dondet.com**

DON KHON Sala Don Khone $$

W of the bridge from Don Det ***Tel*** *(030)-525-6390* ***Rooms*** *17* ***Road Map*** *D5*

A resort by the excellent Sala Lao chain, the Sala Don Khone is built in and around what was once the French hospital on the island. Its expansive grounds are well maintained and the rooms are clean and tasteful. The service and food are exemplary for such a remote location. **www.salalao.com**

DON KHON Sala Phae $$

E of the bridge from Don Det ***Tel*** *(020)-5540-4233* ***Rooms*** *8* ***Road Map*** *D5*

Located close to the Sala Don Khone, Sala Phae, as its name suggests (*phae* means raft in Lao), is a floating hotel with two bungalows built on each raft. These luxurious accommodations offer picturesque views of the Mekong River and an exciting, fascinating stay. Breakfast can be taken at Sala Don Khone. **www.salalao.com**

DON KHONG Pon Guesthouse $

Ban Khang Khong ***Tel*** *(020)-227-0037* ***Rooms*** *16* ***Road Map*** *D5*

A long-standing favorite with budget travelers, Pon Guesthouse lies in the heart of Muang Khong village. It offers decent accommodations at reasonable prices and the food served at the riverside restaurant is also quite good. The staff is friendly and well-versed with the area and can arrange for boat trips in the vicinity.

DON KHONG Villa Muong Khong Hotel $$

Ban Khang Khong ***Tel*** *(020)-5551-5993* ***Fax*** *(031)-252-051* ***Rooms*** *42* ***Road Map*** *D5*

Located a short distance south of Muang Khong, this hotel offers good mid-range accommodations with a pleasant terrace overlooking the river. The restaurant and service are good, but the travel services on offer here are the real attraction – the staff knows the area better than anyone and can arrange great tours.

DON KHONG Senesothxuen $$$

Ban Khang Khong ***Tel*** *(030)-526-0577* ***Fax*** *(031)-251-459* ***Rooms*** *22* ***Road Map*** *D5*

The most luxurious place on the island, Senesothxuen is owned by Lao repatriates who strive to run things to an international standard. The location by the Mekong ensures great views from the rooms and the place is kept scrupulously clean. Wi-Fi is available at reasonable rates. **www.ssxhotel.com**

Key to Price Guide *see p218* **Key to Symbols** *see back cover flap*

PAKSE Champasak Palace Hotel $$

Corner of Route 13 and Rd 1 ***Tel*** *(031)-212-777–80* ***Fax*** *(031)-212-781* ***Rooms*** *60* **Road Map** *D5*

Built as a palace for a Lao prince who unfortunately never stayed here, the Champasak Palace Hotel building has been beautifully restored with wide balconies and a great view over the Se Don. The hotel's restaurant offers authentic Lao, Thai, and Vietnamese cuisines. The quality of service, however, may vary.

PAKSE Mekong Paradise Resort $$

Ban Nongsawang, S of the Japanese bridge ***Tel*** *(031)-254-120* ***Fax*** *(031)-252-864* ***Rooms*** *30* **Road Map** *D5*

Just downstream from the luxurious Champasak Grand, Mekong Paradise Resort is a charming resort located on the Mekong. With great views and a rustic atmosphere, it is an ideal place for those wanting to be close to Pakse. There are spacious balconies opening on to the river and pleasant gardens.

PAKSE Pakse Hotel $$

St 5, Ban Wat Luang ***Tel*** *(031)-212-131* ***Fax*** *(031)-212-719* ***Rooms*** *63* **Road Map** *D5*

This six-story Art Deco-style building in the center of downtown Pakse is managed by a friendly and knowledgeable Frenchman and his Lao wife. It offers a wide choice of accommodations, a rooftop restaurant with a panoramic view, and a good travel service. **www.paksehotel.com**

PAKSE Champasak Grand Hotel $$$

Mekong Riverside Rd ***Tel*** *(031)-255-111–8* ***Fax*** *(031)-255-119* ***Rooms*** *225* **Road Map** *D5*

The Champasak Grand Hotel is a 12-story building on the Mekong, next to the Lao Nippon bridge. With over 200 large, comfortable, and contemporary rooms with great views, the hotel also offers a pool and restaurant by the river. There is an interesting local market across the street. **www.champasakgrand.com**

SAVANNAKHET Xayamoungkhoun Guest House $

Ban Xayamoungkhoun, Ladsavongseuk Rd ***Tel*** *(041)-212-426* ***Rooms*** *15* **Road Map** *C4*

The best budget choice in Savannakhet, Xayamoungkhoun Guest House is an old Colonial-style house operated by a pleasant local family; the manager teaches English and can share good travel information. The place is clean and well kept and although it does not have a restaurant, there are enough eateries close by.

SAVANNAKHET Hoongthip Hotel $$

Ban Thameung, Phetsarath Rd ***Tel*** *(041)-212-262* ***Rooms*** *36* **Road Map** *C4*

A good mid-range choice in the center of town, Hoongthip Hotel is housed in a modern three-story building. Although the place lacks ambience, it is favored by businessmen en route to and from Vietnam, since it is clean and efficient and has a good restaurant. The hotel also offers car rental facilities and can provide good travel information.

SAVANNAKHET Daosavanh Resort & Spa $$$

Ban Thahea, S of downtown Savannakhet ***Tel*** *(041)-252-188* ***Fax*** *(041)-213-199* ***Rooms*** *83* **Road Map** *C4*

Located just south of Savannakhet, this beautiful riverside property is by far the best hotel in town. The huge swimming pool receives a cool breeze from the Mekong River. The rooms are equally refreshing and come equipped with cable TV as well as Wi-Fi facilities. **www.daosavanhhtl.com**

THAKHEK Thakhek Travel Lodge $

Route 13, between Km 2 and Km 3 ***Tel*** *(020)-5530-0145* ***Rooms*** *16* **Road Map** *D3*

Catering to a wide variety of travelers with accommodations varying from dormitory beds to airy rooms with attached baths, Thakhek Travel Lodge is one of the best places to stay for those planning trips to destinations in and around the province. The lodge also rents motorcycles and can provide visitors with the latest travel information.

THAKHEK Inthira Hotel Sikotabong $$

Chao Anou Rd ***Tel*** *(051)-251-237* ***Fax*** *(051)-251-237* ***Rooms*** *8* **Road Map** *D3*

Part of a small chain of hotels run by the Green Discovery tour company, the Inthira Hotel Sikotabong offers artistically designed rooms, although there are also some smaller ones that are no more than windowless cubicles. There is also a good restaurant and, of course, a travel agency. **www.inthirahotels.com**

THAKHEK Hotel Riveria $$$

Sethathirat Rd, Nabo Village ***Tel*** *(051)-250-000* ***Fax*** *(051)-251-188* ***Rooms*** *56* **Road Map** *D3*

One of Thakhek's fanciest hotels, this four-story building on the waterfront offers international standard accommodations with all rooms opening on to balconies and great views, and also equipped with Wi-Fi. The place is scrupulously clean and the staff is well trained. **www.hotelriveriathakhek.com**

THAM KONG LO Sala Kong Lor Lodge $$

4 miles (7 km) SE of Tham Kong Lo ***Tel*** *(020)-7776-1846* ***Rooms*** *15* **Road Map** *C3*

Part of a well-known chain of Lao ecolodges, these riverside bungalows are a great place to relax amid thick forests and lush green surroundings. The management can provide boats for those interested in visiting the caves. The river close by is great for swimming. **www.salalao.com**

XE PIAN NPA Kingfisher Ecolodge $$$

Ban Khiet Ngong ***Tel*** *(020)-5572-6315* ***Rooms*** *10* **Road Map** *D5*

On the periphery of the Xe Pian NPA, near the Phu Asa mountain, this lodge provides deluxe accommodations in bungalows on stilts as well as budget rooms. Owned by an Italian, it has a well-informed staff who know about the flora and fauna of the area. They also arrange elephant rides and treks into the NPA. **www.kingfisherecolodge.com**

WHERE TO EAT

The cuisines of Cambodia and Laos share many similarities with those of their neighboring countries, especially Thailand. At the same time, both countries have dishes that are distinctly Cambodian or Lao such as *amok* (fish cooked in coconut milk) and *laap* (meat salad) respectively. French Colonialists contributed to the cuisines of these two nations, evident from the roadside stalls and bakeries that sell baguettes and croissants. Parisian-style cafés are also common in urban centers. A variety of international cuisines are served at upscale restaurants in major cities such as Phnom Penh, Siem Reap, Vientiane, and Luang Prabang. From street vendors and barbecues on the beach to swanky cafés and restaurants in posh hotels, the food choices in Cambodia and Laos are varied, as are the prices.

Breakfast menu, The Chang Inn

Plush dining area of the Hotel De La Paix, Siem Reap

RESTAURANTS

The service at restaurants in upscale hotels in Phnom Penh, Siem Reap, Vientiane, and Luang Prabang is as flawless as diners might find in the West, and may even be better in some cases. In contrast, the average Khmer and Lao restaurant is an informal affair offering a balance of rice, vegetables, and meat. But visitors will also find Chinese, Vietnamese, and Indian influences in spring rolls, spare ribs, and curry, thanks to Cambodia's mid-way location between the three countries. Fish features heavily in Cambodian food, no doubt due to the presence of the Tonlé Sap, which is teeming with fish. *Prahoc*, a fermented fish paste, which is also found in Laos, is used to flavor many dishes. The average Lao and Khmer meal might consist of a soup, followed by a fish or meat dish, and salad. Rice is eaten with everything and often on its own; it can be found in rice noodle soup, rice porridge, and as an accompaniment to almost every dish. Sticky rice is one of the main staples of Lao food, and it is often sold in bamboo tubes by the roadside. Both countries have plenty of Gallic food on offer due to their French Colonial past, the most common items being the baguette and paté. There are also many French cafés and restaurants in all the major cities, where the steaks are tender, the tarts delicious, and the wines first class. Western fast-food chains and cuisine have also become popular with the increasing numbers of Western visitors; pizza is as likely to feature on the menu as local *amok*. In Laos, however, fast-food chains have only just arrived.

STREET FOOD

Eating a quick snack from a street vendor is a wonderfully Khmer and Lao thing to do, and the snacks are usually delicious. From fried crab, snake, frog, tarantula, beetle, cricket, *amok*, noodles, and meat to sugarcane, jackfruit, melon, rambutan, coconut, mangosteen, and crêpes, there is a wide variety of food available on street corners, both in the provinces and in the cities. Bear in mind that the best time to visit a vendor for breakfast is early in the morning between 6:00–8:30am when the food is freshly cooked. It is best to go to a stall that seems busy, attracting people from every strata of society; a crowded stall is a sure sign that the food is good. Another promising sign to look out for is more than one family member working the stall, since that means it is popular and generates enough work for the other members of the family. It is best to avoid consuming fruit smoothies with ice even if they look delicious. In most cases

Variety of street food on offer in Battambang

Various tropical fruit for sale in the local market, Luang Prabang

unpurified water will have been used to make the ice, and consuming it may cause or lead to stomach ailments.

VEGETARIAN OPTIONS

Both countries have an abundance of fruit, which is available on every street corner. Stir-fries and rice dishes with vegetables are very common, although it is likely that they will have been prepared in pans that have been used to cook meat. In more upscale restaurants in the cities, however, this might not be the case. However, in the provinces avoiding meat gets harder as the average Lao and Khmer does not understand the concept of vegetarianism. They believe that meat and fish are vital for strength and if travelers can afford them, then they should eat them. In Phnom Penh, Siem Reap, Vientiane, and Luang Prabang strict vegetarians can head to one of the many Indian restaurants where the hosts will be more sympathetic to the idea of a pure vegetarian meal. Luang Prabang offers the best vegetarian cuisine of all four cities and the most discerning menus. Several Western-run restaurants are more than likely to provide authentic vegetarian dishes and are usually careful about the way they should be cooked. Those vegetarians who are not overly strict about their dietary habits and can tolerate fish sauce will have no problem finding a satisfying meal.

BEER

The most popular Cambodian beverage is Angkor Beer, which is produced in Sihanoukville. In Laos there is Beerlao, which is particularly delicious and even cheaper than Angkor Beer. There are many other competitors on their heels, from Heineken to Tiger. Visitors will probably be approached by a "beer girl" at some stage in their travels in Cambodia, whose job is to promote a particular brand. Capturing a customer's loyalty is big business in both countries and beer companies go all out to procure patrons for their brands.

EATING CUSTOMS

Unlike in the West, meals in Cambodia and Laos are not served in a succession of dishes; if visitors order three separate dishes they will arrive all at the same time, or as and when they are cooked. Meals are a social event in both countries and a chance for families and friends to catch up. Individual bowls are arranged around a central platter of dishes and everyone shares each other's dish.

In the average earthy restaurant, be it in the market or off the street, visitors can expect to use chopsticks or cutlery. Visitors must use the communal spoon to serve food into their bowls, not their own implements. The common practice is to hold one's bowl to the mouth and spoon the food in with the chopsticks in the other hand. When using chopsticks, do not leave them together in the bowl pointing upward as this is a symbol of death. It is normal for a host to offer a guest more food than he would to his own family members; this must not be turned down. It is also good etiquette not to finish everything on the plate. Finally, the host should always be the first to sit down and taste the food.

A popular brand of beer in Laos

PRICES

Fast food from street vendors accompanied by a fruit shake will cost no more than a few dollars. Cambodian, Lao, and Western restaurant prices are usually reasonable unless visitors choose one of the upscale restaurants in the urban centers. Although budget travelers may find Cambodia a little more expensive than Laos, if they avoid beer and wine and stick to street stalls and cheap restaurants serving basic dishes, they can get by for as little as US$10 per day on an average.

TIPPING

Although tipping is not expected in the same way as it is in the West, it is significantly appreciated. Besides, a small tip of US$1 is almost equivalent to half a day's wages for some and can go a long way in supplementing their salary. Service, when it is good, should be rewarded, although visitors should not feel compelled to leave a gratuity if this is not the case.

Outdoor cafés surrounding Nam Phu Square, Vientiane

The Flavors of Cambodia

Cambodian food draws heavily on influences from Thailand, Vietnam, and China, while maintaining its own culinary tradition. Khmer meals are deliciously spicy and fragrant, with a characteristic sweetness derived from palm sugar, and sourness introduced by lime juice and tamarind. Fresh herbs and spices, including coriander, sweet basil, lemongrass, and fresh ginger are used judiciously. French influence is evident everywhere, typified by the ubiquitous roadside snack stalls selling crusty baguettes smeared with delicious pâté.

Sweet basil, lemongrass, and coriander

Skewers of barbecued frog at a food stall in Psar Nath, Battambang

SEAFOOD AND FISH

Fish is a key part of the Cambodian diet, including many freshwater species caught in the bountiful Tonlé Sap Lake, the wetlands around Takeo, and in the country's many rivers. Everything from huge catfish steaks to tiny tiddlers are available on Cambodian menus. On the coast, snapper and shellfish are popular, but perhaps Cambodia's most famous seafood dish is *K'damm mrek Kep*, or pepper crab, a specialty of the Kep region.

CURRIES AND SOUPS

Khmer curries are delicately spiced although unlike their Indian and Thai equivalents, they have the consistency of soup. The classic Cambodian curry is *amok*, usually made with fish and featuring lots of turmeric. Almost every meal includes a *samlor* (soup) dish, which is often quite sweet and flavored with coconut and spices.

SALADS

There are dozens of types of fresh salads available, with ingredients such as carrots, cucumber, green papaya, and unripe mango, often

Selection of Cambodia's luscious tropical fruits

CAMBODIAN DISHES AND SPECIALTIES

Palm sugar

Cambodian food has aroma, piquancy, and a zesty freshness that is addictive. Pungent and exotic, there is barely a dish (except, of course, desserts) that does not feature a seasoning of *prahoc* (fish paste) or *trey* (fish sauce). Rice is the main staple, and most meals are served with a bowl of steaming white or sticky rice, or noodles made from rice or wheat. Snacks include *num pang ang chia mui sach ko*, which is rounds of French bread baked with a spicy ground beef topping. You will also find *poat dot* (corn on the cob) and spring rolls (both vegetarian and with ground meat). Fast-food chains are everywhere in Phnom Penh and making their way to other cities as well. However, the toppings on a Cambodian "happy" pizza may include herbs you would not expect, so be careful.

Amok, *Cambodia's most famous dish, is a mild, piquant coconut milk curry traditionally made with fish.*

Vendors of meat, fruit, and vegetables at Psar Nath market

shredded or chopped. Thin strips of meat, fresh or dried shrimp, and plenty of fresh herbs may be added, and the dish laced with chopped peanuts. A popular dressing is *tirk trey chu p'em*, a sweet fish sauce with lime juice, a little chili, and garlic.

FRUITS AND SWEETS

Tropical fruits are abundant. Mangoes and bananas (including small, red-skinned "fingers") are everywhere, with many unusual varieties not found in the West. The small, purple-skinned *meangkhout* (mangosteen) with its subtle, sweet, and slightly sherbety flavor is a revelation. The hairy skin of the *sao meo* (rambutan) may be off-putting, but its fruit is succulent and reminiscent of a lychee; and the *salacca* (snake fruit) is sweet and slightly acidic in taste. The "king" of Cambodian fruits is, however, the *thouren*, the infamously smelly durian.

Cambodia's sweet desserts are an acquired taste, but rice pudding flavored with coconut and lime is delicious, as are bananas barbecued in their leaves and usually served with coconut sauce.

Freshly caught fish for sale at a market in Phnom Penh

DRINKS

It is vital to stick to bottled water, but ice is usually safe in cities. Cafés in tourist areas may have espresso machines, but visitors will usually be offered a strong, local coffee. Khmers, however, like theirs with ice and condensed milk. Beer is inexpensive, with lager-style Angkor being the most popular brand. Palm or rice wine is cheap but fierce.

AN EXOTIC MENU

Beetles *(kan te)* Fried dark green *kan te long* and *kan te touk* beetles (which look like cockroaches) are a popular Cambodian treat. Locals first remove the head and wings before devouring the bug.

Crickets *(jong-reut)* Demand for crickets grew in the Khmer Rouge years. They are usually deep-fried and enjoyed as an inexpensive, crunchy snack.

Eggs *(pong tea khon)* Boiled, fertilized duck and chicken eggs are served complete with the developed embryo.

Snakes *(bpoo-ah)* Small snakes are marinated and barbecued on bamboo sticks, *satay*-style.

Spiders *(a'ping)* Huge, deep-fried tarantula spiders are a specialty of Skuon, but eaten everywhere in Cambodia.

Cha kny'ey *is a delicious, fragrant dish of chicken stir-fried with lots of ginger, black pepper, and a little chili.*

K'damm mrek Kep, *or Kep pepper crab, is soft-shelled crab and green peppercorns in a garlic-flavored sauce.*

Bok L'hong *salad mixes grated, raw papaya, basil, and peanuts. Dried shrimp and tomato are often added.*

The Flavors of Laos

Green papaya, water buffalo skin, river moss, fish stewed in lime juice – at first reading, the culinary delights of Laos might seem a little daunting. It is, however, a case of a bite being worth a thousand words. While similar to the cuisine of neighboring Thailand, Lao food draws from its unique local ingredients and culinary traditions to offer flavors that are almost always spicy, though not necessarily fiery. Lemongrass, coriander, Kaffir lime, galangal, and chili peppers provide the base for a range of thrilling culinary experiences.

Fish sauce

Vegetables, spices, and fruit on sale in a market, Luang Prabang

RICE AND NOODLES

The mountainous geography of Laos dictates that sticky rice, which requires less irrigation than other varieties, is a staple here. Rolled into small balls and eaten with the fingers, it is the perfect accompaniment to many Lao dishes that are served as dips, or as a side dish with barbecued meat or fish.

Sticky rice, which comes in black, white, or purple varieties, is commonly ground by the Lao people into a flour from which a variety of noodles and crispy cakes are made. It is also distilled into various types of alcoholic beverages. Standard paddy rice is also eaten on special occasions, and the French Colonialists introduced wheat, which is used to make both baguettes and Chinese-style wheat noodles.

MEAT AND FISH

Laos is a land that is criss-crossed by rivers, all of which are teeming with fish. Grilled, minced, eaten raw, or made into various dips and sauces, freshwater fish are a major protein source for the Lao. Poultry (the French imported turkey, which is popular) and pigs are domesticated, but the Lao also have a real taste for wild game. Boar and deer

Selection of typical Lao herbs, spices, and flavorings

LAO DISHES AND SPECIALTIES

Luang Prabang is the home of Lao haute cuisine, and many esoteric specialties await the adventurous diner there. Vientiane has many dishes of French origin. Elsewhere, one can easily be content with standard Lao favorites. The most well known is *laap* (meat salad), which can be made from any sort of meat or fish, either steamed, stir-fried, or simply "cooked" by being marinated, seviche-style, in spices. The green papaya salad *tam mak hung* is pounded in a mortar and pestle, mixing the piquant flavor of unripe papaya with spicy condiments. The Lao love to barbecue, and fresh chicken, pork, and fish skewers are readily available. The condiment of choice is *paa daek*, a fermented fish sauce, a richer cousin of the ubiquitous sauce found throughout Southeast Asia.

Rice noodles

Pho *is a rich broth with rice noodles, vegetables, and meat. Originally Vietnamese, it is a favorite light Lao meal.*

are commonly served, but the menu extends to smaller creatures such as squirrels and field rats. Insects, including larvae, ant eggs, and bamboo worms, are very popular and a good source of protein Needless to say all, parts of the animals are used – buffalo skin is a favourite condiment and snack, and offal is considered preferable to meat, with market prices reflecting this.

Meats being grilled at a food stall beside the Mekong River

VEGETABLES AND FRUIT

Laos has a natural bounty of vegetables and fruits. From the rivers come an algae that is dried into sheets to form a delicious crispy snack called *kai paen*, which is eaten with a spicy chili dip called *jeow bong*. Papaya is used in the staple salad *tam mak hung*, and other tropical fruits are also plentiful. Wild mushrooms abound in the forests, while bamboo groves provide succulent shoots. The jungle is the source of the all-important sakan *(piper boehmeriaefolium,)* an aromatic vine used as a spice. Small riverside gardens cultivate delicate herbs.

Enticing array of cooked dishes being served in a Lao street market

DRINKS

Unsweetened Chinese tea, usually served at room temperature, accompanies most meals. From France comes strong coffee, served Vietnamese-style with a steel filter over the cup. Lao beer is cheap and excellent, while stronger spirits include *lao lao*, a distilled rice spirit similar to schnapps in flavor and potency. Luang Prabang has its own rice wine, made from purple rice, called *lao gaam*, which is sweet and strong.

ON THE MENU

Baguette Sandwich Fillings can include meat, cheese, vegetables, or the local pâté.

Barbecue Chicken, pork, beef, or even buffalo, always well marinated, are served on a bamboo skewer.

Kai Paen This river algae, fried and served as a snack, is delicious with beer.

Khao Lam Sticky rice with coconut cream, steamed and sold in a bamboo tube, makes a good, filling snack.

Spring Rolls These are a popular Vietnamese import, served with a piquant dipping sauce. Try the uncooked variety for a change.

Yum Salad Watercress, lettuce, tomato, and boiled egg are served in a light mayonnaise sauce with peanuts. A mild, not spicy, dish.

Mok Pa *uses pounded white fish blended with spices. The mixture is then wrapped in banana leaves and steamed.*

Laap, *the Lao national dish, is minced meat, poultry, or fish flavored with lime juice, onion, garlic, and mint.*

Or Lam *is a Luang Prabang specialty. Dried buffalo meat and skin are stewed with eggplant and spices.*

Choosing a Restaurant in Cambodia

The restaurants in this guide have been selected for their excellent food, location, and ambience. The listings highlight some of the factors that may influence choice, such as outdoor seating or live music. Entries are listed alphabetically by region. For map references, see pp60–61 for Phnom Penh; see the inside back cover for other locations.

PRICE CATEGORIES
The following price ranges are for a meal for two, made up of a range of dishes, including service tax, but no alcohol.

Ⓢ Under $5
ⓈⓈ $5–$10
ⓈⓈⓈ $10–$20
ⓈⓈⓈⓈ $20–$30
ⓈⓈⓈⓈⓈ Over $30

PHNOM PENH

CENTRAL PHNOM PENH Blue Pumpkin Ⓢ

245 Sisowath Quay ***Tel*** *(023)-998-153* **City Map** *E1*

A bright and cheerful all-white interior with tables and couches gives the Blue Pumpkin a light, airy and relaxed feel, overlooking the river. Here you'll find an extensive selection of home-made gelato, and the best baked goods in Cambodia. There's also a full menu of coffee, fruit shakes, sandwiches and pasta. Free Wi-Fi.

CENTRAL PHNOM PENH Coffee Korner Ⓢ

172/174, corner of sts 155 & 454, Psar Tuol Tom Pong ***Tel*** *(012)-867-667* **City Map** *C5*

The elegant Coffee Korner is the place to relax in after a shopping trip to the nearby Russian Market. Great selection of light meals featuring Western and Khmer cuisine. Dishes such as *amok* (minced fish in banana leaves) are fresh and not overly spiced. Refreshing cool drinks include iced coffees, cocktails, and fresh juices.

CENTRAL PHNOM PENH Little Noodle Shop Ⓢ

1, St 114 ***Tel*** *(023)-555-0511* **City Map** *E2*

A small but popular eatery located near the riverfront, Little Noodle serves fresh, Chinese-style pulled noodles and dumplings, made in view of diners. All noodle dishes are available boiled, steamed or fried. Beef, chicken, shrimp and vegetarian options available.

CENTRAL PHNOM PENH Seven Bright Restaurant Ⓢ

St 13 ***Tel*** *(012)-833-555* **City Map** *E1*

Featured in the Matt Dillon film *City of Ghosts*, Seven Bright is renowned for being clean and lively. A traditional Khmer restaurant, it is popular for its breakfast of noodle soup and delicious local coffee. The restaurant is celebrated for its Khmer food, live music, and great location.

CENTRAL PHNOM PENH The Shop Ⓢ

39, St 240 ***Tel*** *(023)-986-964* **City Map** *E3*

The most delicious bakery-cum-deli in town, this delightful little eatery serves a range of tasty Western fare and snacks, with mouthwatering salads, fresh sandwiches, and refreshing fruit smoothies, as well as plenty of pastries. Look out for the bakery's daily specials written in chalk on the blackboard.

CENTRAL PHNOM PENH USA Donut Ⓢ

Corner of St 51 & St 302 ***Tel*** *(023)-630-6040* **City Map** *E4*

On a quiet side street south of the Independence Monument and across from the popular Brown Coffee, USA Donut serves – you guessed it – delicious American-style donuts. Other stars-and-stripes favorites on the menu are the cheeseburger and the hot dog.

CENTRAL PHNOM PENH Boddhi Tree Umma ⓈⓈ

50, St 113 ***Tel*** *(023)-211-397* **City Map** *C4*

Located opposite Tuol Sleng Genocide Museum *(see p51)*, this small boutique establishment has a great kitchen turning out Asian fusion dishes, salads, and fruit shakes. The lush gardens are in contrast to the horrors of the museum across the road. The courtyard can get hot during the day, so guests may want to lunch in the shaded area.

CENTRAL PHNOM PENH Café Fresco ⓈⓈ

361 Sisowath Quay ***Tel*** *(023)-217-041* **City Map** *E1*

An air-conditioned heaven for visitors who wish to escape the heat, but a cosy patio with seating is also available. Café Fresco does an excellent impression of a New York deli with great subs and a range of coffees to choose from. Discounts are available on all pastries between 5pm and 8pm. Wi-Fi available.

CENTRAL PHNOM PENH Chiang Mai Riverside ⓈⓈ

227 Sisowath Quay ***Tel*** *(011)-811-456* **City Map** *E1*

The name says it all – the Chiang Mai serves Thai dishes at a scenic riverside location. The cuisine is more central Thai than northern, but no one quibbles since it is delicious and well presented at moderate prices. A photo menu helps those unfamiliar with the food. A long-standing favorite with locals.

Key to Symbols *see back cover flap*

CENTRAL PHNOM PENH Dosa Corner $$
5E, St 51, near Wat Lanka ***Tel*** *(012)-673-276* **City Map** *E3*

For those unfamiliar with Indian food, *dosas* are rice-based crêpes stuffed with meat and vegetables, and served with spicy sauces such as mango chutney. The Dosa Corner does over 15 varieties of these, and serves them with *lassi*, the Indian yoghurt drink. There are many other Indian favorites on the menu.

CENTRAL PHNOM PENH Irina Russian House $$
15, St 352 ***Tel*** *(012)-833-524* **City Map** *E4*

Step back in time to when the Russians were in Cambodia with this redolently Muscovite restaurant. It is all goulash and potatoes, *seliodka* (marinated herring) and homegrown vodka shots. Atmospheric and good fun, Irina Russian House makes for a pleasant change from Khmer and Western cuisine.

CENTRAL PHNOM PENH Kandal House $$
239 Sisowath Quay ***Tel*** *(012)-525-612* **City Map** *E1*

The great home-made pasta and wood-fired pizzas compete with the city's longest happy hour (3–8 pm), which is the biggest draw at Kandal House. All the standard Western favorites are on offer and some Asian dishes as well. Nice views of the river from the terrace. A favorite meeting place with travelers.

CENTRAL PHNOM PENH Khmer Surin $$
9, St 57, Boeung Keng Kang ***Tel*** *(023)-363-050* **City Map** *D3*

Located just south of the Independence Monument, this well-run, casual eatery is popular with NGO workers and locals for its hearty lunches. The interior has an Angkorian decor with lots of plants. Western dishes are available, but try Khmer favorites such as *lok lak* – slices of beef stir-fried with oyster sauce and green peppercorns.

CENTRAL PHNOM PENH K'nyay $$
25K, Boulevard Suramrarit CCN ***Tel*** *(023)-225-225* **City Map** *E3*

This totally vegan restaurant serves standard Cambodian dishes, with soy protein, taro root, and sweet potatoes replacing meat. The banana and jackfruit curries are excellent. Good dessert menu and plenty of juices and herbal infusions. Not only healthy, but settles much more lightly on the system than meat-based Khmer food.

CENTRAL PHNOM PENH Le Jardin $$
16, St 360 ***Tel*** *(011)-723-399* **City Map** *E4*

A real family café, Le Jardin lives up to its moniker with peaceful gardens, including a sandpit and treehouse for children to play in. There are plenty of shaded areas in which to enjoy the delicious breakfasts, crêpes, sandwiches, and coffees. However, Le Jardin's tasty ice creams are best eaten inside!

CENTRAL PHNOM PENH Le Rit's $$
71, St 240 ***Tel*** *(023)-213-160* **City Map** *E3*

This NGO-run café is operated by the charity NYEMO, which protects women and supports abandoned children. Le Rit's serves tasty European and Asian cuisine in pleasant indoor and outdoor settings. The menu features a variety of salads, and fish and meat dishes. Thai and Cambodian options are also available. Friendly staff.

CENTRAL PHNOM PENH Riverside Bistro $$
Corner of Sisowath Quay and St 148 ***Tel*** *(023)-213-898* **City Map** *E1*

Set in an old Colonial building, this corner joint offers outdoor dining in comfortable wicker chairs and views of the Tonlé Sap River. Inside, there are two pool tables and the eatery doubles as a bar later in the evening. The fresh food served here includes a range of Khmer and Western dishes. Friendly staff.

CENTRAL PHNOM PENH Saffron $$
17B, St 278 ***Tel*** *(012)-247-832* **City Map** *D3*

The best Pakistani cuisine in the city served in a relaxed contemporary ambience. The chicken masala is superb, and the rice preparations reveal Southeast Asian influences with a hint of lemongrass. Other typical fare includes crisp, hot samosas with light crusts. There is also an excellent wine list. Good value for money.

CENTRAL PHNOM PENH Sam Doo $$
56, Kampuchea Krom Blvd ***Tel*** *(023)-218-773* **City Map** *D2*

Phnom Penh's most popular Chinese restaurant, Sam Doo offers a wide variety of cuisine from Cantonese dim sum to spicy Sichuanese dishes, and a classic Beijing duck. The seafood in particular is fresh and delicious. As with the food, the atmosphere is authentically Chinese.

CENTRAL PHNOM PENH The Lazy Gecko Café $$
1D, St 258 ***Tel*** *(023)-500-1176*

Supporting a local orphanage, the Lazy Gecko Café serves tasty international fare and inspires with its cheerful atmosphere. Cambodian dishes are also available. There is a quiz night on Thursdays; on Saturdays it is possible to have dinner at the orphanage followed by a show put on by the children.

CENTRAL PHNOM PENH The Riverhouse Restaurant and Lounge $$
110, corner of Sisowath Quay ***Tel*** *(023)-212-302* **City Map** *E1*

This kerbside restaurant, overlooking the Tonlé Sap River, is famed for its imported Australian steaks and Asian fusion, French, and Khmer cuisines. Dishes such as tamarind prawns and Thai fishcakes are popular, while the cocktails are creative. The nightclub upstairs is always lively on weekends.

CENTRAL PHNOM PENH Tom Yum Kung $$
10, St 278 ***Tel** (023)-359-293* **City Map** *D4*

Some of the best Khmer and Thai dishes in the city are served at Tom Yum Kung. This is a small thatch-roofed place with simple decor. Diners find that the *tom kha gai* (chicken in coconut sauce with galangal) goes very well with the Thai beer on offer, and that the Khmer food is authentically prepared using quality ingredients.

CENTRAL PHNOM PENH La Volpaia $$$
Corner of sts 102 & 13 ***Tel** (023)-992-739* **City Map** *E1*

The atmospheric La Volpaia is an Italian restaurant with terra-cotta floors and a view of the Colonial-era Post Office Square. A great place for wood-fired pizzas, tasty pasta, and a wide array of imported steaks, as well as a rich wine selection. The setting is convivial, the owner charming, and the service smart.

CENTRAL PHNOM PENH Le Duo $$$
17, St 228 ***Tel** (023)-991-906* **City Map** *D3*

Located in a quiet garden villa, Le Duo excels with wood-fired pizzas and pasta dishes, as well as more Sicilian cuisine. The centerpiece oven where the pizzas are cooked makes for a pleasant focal point in the pleasant, air-conditioned interior. Good wine list. Open daily from 11:45am–2:15pm and 6:15–10:15pm.

CENTRAL PHNOM PENH Pop Café $$$
371 Sisowath Quay ***Tel** (012)-562-892* **City Map** *E2*

Owned and run by an Italian expat, this excellent restaurant lays claim to being the best of its kind in the city; it is certainly the most popular. Lasagna, salads, pastas, all dished up fresh and with an atmosphere to match. Air-conditioned interior. Good value for money.

CENTRAL PHNOM PENH Bai Thong $$$
100–102 Sothearos Blvd ***Tel** (023)-211-054* **City Map** *F3*

There is a bit of everything on offer at Bai Thong – the French, Khmer, Vietnamese, Thai, and Lao dishes are all tasty here. The ambience manages to be classy without being stuffy or overdone. The clientele is equally diverse and includes businessmen, couples, and families.

CENTRAL PHNOM PENH Bougainvillier Restaurant $$$
277C, Sisowath Quay ***Tel** (023)-220-528* **City Map** *E2*

Elegant French dining in the restaurant of Phnom Penh's fine Bougainvillier Hotel *(see p211)*. The white tablecloth formality is toned down by a warm decor, and the food and wines are as good as the service. Royal Cambodian cuisine competes with the imported steaks as house favorites. Popular with businessmen.

CENTRAL PHNOM PENH Comme a la Maison Delicatessen $$$
13, St 57 ***Tel** (023)-360-801* **City Map** *D4*

The chalkboard menu features Western cuisine, ranging from soups and salads to a variety of meat and fish dishes. Meals are served in a pleasant garden patio. The establishment is famous for its bakery and a deli that serves the best charcuterie in the city, and many imported delicacies. Popular at lunch. Staff speaks English and French.

CENTRAL PHNOM PENH Foreign Correspondents' Club $$$
363 Sisowath Quay ***Tel** (023)-724-014* **City Map** *E2*

Far more tourists than real journos here, but the decor and views from this superb third-floor location overlooking the river make the Foreign Correspondents' Club *(see p48)* a good stop, especially for a sundowner. Western food is served here, including great wood-fired pizzas. Regular photo exhibitions and a take-out deli on the first floor.

CENTRAL PHNOM PENH Garden Center Café $$$
4, St 57, between sts 278 & 282 ***Tel** (023)-363-002*

An informal place where the food includes, but is not limited to, things known best to Americans, such as the Sloppy Joe sandwich. The café also serves great steaks and a Sunday roast. Portions are large and the service is efficient and amiable. Also on offer are fresh salads and vegetarian dishes.

CENTRAL PHNOM PENH Green Vespa $$$
95 Sisowath Quay ***Tel** (012)-887-228* **City Map** *E2*

This well-known travelers' restaurant has good breakfasts and British pub grub such as fish and chips and steak and kidney pies. The iconic motor scooter greets diners at the door and the whole place has a friendly and fun atmosphere. Cool tunes on the sound system. Reasonable prices.

CENTRAL PHNOM PENH Romdeng $$$
74, St 174, between sts 51 & 63 ***Tel** (092)-219-565* **City Map** *D2*

Excellent Khmer food is served here in a sophisticated villa setting. Most of the service staff are former street children, rescued and trained in the culinary arts by the local NGO Friends International. The food is based on traditional recipes using healthy local ingredients.

CENTRAL PHNOM PENH Tamarind $$$
31, St 240 ***Tel** (012)-830-139* **City Map** *E3*

The best place in Phnom Penh to enjoy Mediterranean cuisine. Great French and Moroccan dishes, such as cous cous, tagine, and *shawerma* (a sandwich-like wrap with meat), as well as tapas and French favorites. The Tamarind offers a relaxing atmosphere with some of the city's best hookah.

Key to Price Guide *see p232*

CENTRAL PHNOM PENH Tell $$$

13, St 90 ***Tel*** *(023)-430-650* **City Map** *D1*

With its pleasant chalet atmosphere, the Tell is particulary popular with families. The restaurant is a local institution known for fine Swiss and German food, as well as other Western and local favorites, all at moderate prices. The grilled pork leg dinner is renowned. In the evenings, the outdoor beer garden has a more agreeable ambience.

CENTRAL PHNOM PENH Van's Restaurant $$$

5, St 102 ***Tel*** *(023)-722-067* **City Map** *E1*

One of the top French restaurants in the city, Van's occupies the lovely building that housed the former Banque de l'Indochine. The edifice is a Colonial belle bursting with atmosphere. Van's menu is a gourmet's dream, where dishes such as sea perch carpaccio are firm favorites with diners.

CENTRAL PHNOM PENH Le Cedre $$$$

1, St 360 ***Tel*** *(023)-997-965* **City Map** *E4*

The best restaurant in Cambodia for Lebanese food. On offer are stuffed grape leaves, hummus, a variety of mezze hors d'oeuvres, and lots of roasted meats. The dishes are accompanied by either good Lebanese wine or the somewhat potent anise-flavored spirit called arrack.

CENTRAL PHNOM PENH Malis $$$$

136 Norodom Blvd ***Tel*** *(023)-221-022* **City Map** *E4*

A favorite with affluent locals and expats, the sophisticated Malis is set in gardens that have an Angkorian atmosphere. This restaurant is the place to experience Cambodian Royal cuisine at its best. Both traditional and modern interpretations of the great recipes are cooked by reputable Cambodian chef Luu Meng.

CENTRAL PHNOM PENH Pacharan Tapas & Bodegas $$$$

389E1 Sisowath Quay ***Tel*** *(023)-224-394* **City Map** *E2*

Occupying the ground floor of a beautiful Colonial villa, Pacharan Tapas & Bodegas is located on the riverfront, next to the Royal Palace Museum. The interior features authentic Spanish decor and is fully air conditioned. Try the tapas with sangria, followed by the best seafood paella east of Madrid. Excellent selection of Spanish and other wines.

CENTRAL PHNOM PENH Shiva Shakti $$$$

70E Sihanouk Blvd ***Tel*** *(012)-813-817* **City Map** *E3*

Considered the best Indian restaurant in the city, Shiva Shakti serves mainly Mughal cuisine, with all the classic curries and tandoori chicken dishes. Top standards are maintained in the preparation of dishes. Opulent decor and good service, with private dining rooms. The dining experience on the whole is good value for money.

CENTRAL PHNOM PENH Topaz $$$$$

182 Norodom Blvd ***Tel*** *(023)-221-622* **City Map** *E4*

More than deluxe dining in a first-class atmosphere. Chef Alain presents classic French cuisine with hints of Southeast Asian fusion, such as lobster ravioli with green Kampot pepper. Daily specials, great steaks, and a children's menu. The wine cellar is the best in town, and there is a walk-in cigar humidor as well.

ANGKOR

SIEM REAP Blue Pumpkin $

Pithnou St ***Tel*** *(063)-963-574* **Road Map** *C6*

Arguably the most alluring bakery-cum-patisserie in Cambodia, Blue Pumpkin is a haven of air-conditioned cool that tempts with an array of brownies, cakes, sandwiches, salads, fruit shakes, ice creams in local flavors such as star anise and cashew, and comfort food. There is also a cushioned lounging area upstairs. Free Wi-Fi.

SIEM REAP Bopha Angkor Restaurant $

East side of Stung Siem Reap ***Tel*** *(063)-964-928* **Road Map** *C6*

Set in a peaceful location, with beautiful gardens and a terrace ovelooking the river. This traditional Cambodian restaurant serves curries, fried beef with ginger, and chicken and fish *amoks* (meat steamed in a savory coconut-based curry). Also on offer are crêpes, ice creams, cocktails, and fragrantly blended selections of tea.

SIEM REAP Butterflies Garden Restaurant $

535, St 25, near Wat Bo ***Tel*** *(063)-761-211* **Road Map** *C6*

Tranquil location enhanced by tropical butterflies and a koi pond. The establishment has traditional cultural performances, children's parties, and a rich menu featuring Khmer and Western dishes, with a strong vegetarian presence. The breakfasts are good and there is a wide selection of beverages, including healthy shakes.

SIEM REAP Chamkar Restaurant $

Pub St, Old Market area ***Tel*** *(092)-733-150* **Road Map** *C6*

This sidewalk favorite also has indoor seating and is manna from heaven for strict vegetarians. Sweet potato curry, stir-fried egg plant medley, vegetarian oysters, and spring rolls are all on the menu. Additionally, there is no monosodium glutamate (MSG) in the food. Open every day, except on Sundays, when it opens at 5pm.

SIEM REAP Common Grounds $

Behind the Center Market ***Tel*** *(063)-965-687* ***Road Map*** *C6*

A clean, air-conditioned café with modern amenities such as free and speedy Wi-Fi. Also on offer is a dizzying array of cakes, brownies, soups, salads, sandwiches, fresh juices, coffees, and teas. All profits from this excellent eatery directly support NGO projects in Cambodia.

SIEM REAP Hong Kong Restaurant $

Thnou St, Old Market area, opposite the hospital ***Tel*** *(092)-373-682* ***Road Map*** *C6*

Representing terrific value for money, this diminutive restaurant is a local favorite for Chinese food and serves dim sum as the house specialty. The menu features all the usual options, including dumplings, as well as a variety of rice and noodle dishes. Open every day from 9am to 10pm.

SIEM REAP Swensen's $

Pokambor Ave, Old Market area, Angkor Trade Center ***Tel*** *(063)-966-424* ***Road Map*** *C6*

Southeast Asia's favorite ice-cream vendor, Swensen's offers the perfect antidote to Cambodia's hot weather. The myriad flavors of ice cream come in a huge range of scoops, cones, cups, shakes, and sundaes, and are served in a fully air-conditioned parlor.

SIEM REAP The Soup Dragon $

Old Market area ***Tel*** *(063)-964-933* ***Road Map*** *C6*

This hole in the wall has bags of atmosphere and plaudits for its Vietnamese food, particularly its *pho* (noodle soup) and fresh spring rolls. There are also moderately priced entrées and soups, as well as a range of wok-fried dishes. Open-air seating is available on two floors, but the rooftop section offers a cooler place for diners.

SIEM REAP Viroth's $

Wat Bo Rd ***Tel*** *(012)-778-096* ***Road Map*** *C6*

Garnering great reviews for his distinctive *amok* dishes and modern take on Khmer food, Chef Viroth draws a regular crowd of discerning diners to his stylish garden terrace, which also has indoor seating. The restaurant is as well known for its excellent service as it is for its delicious food.

SIEM REAP Amok Restaurant $$

Pub St, Old Market area ***Tel*** *(063)-965-407* ***Road Map*** *C6*

A popular, long-running favorite in Pub Street, Amok is celebrated for its traditional menu of Cambodian dishes, which include staples such as *amok*, beef *lok lak* (marinated beef slices, served with tomatoes and onions, in pepper sauce), fried barbecue skewers, and mango salads. There is also a great balcony overlooking the lively alley below.

SIEM REAP Angkor Café $$

Outside the main entrace of Angkor Wat ***Tel*** *(012)-946-227* ***Road Map*** *C6*

Stocked with delicious pastries, coffees, subs, and salads, the stylish Angkor Café is a great place to stock up on food before exploring the ruins of Angkor Wat. The establishment also offers an air-conditioned area for those who wish to eat here. The cuisine is mainly Western, with a few fine, traditional Khmer dishes.

SIEM REAP Café Central $$

Old Market area ***Tel*** *(017)-692-997* ***Road Map*** *C6*

Siem Reap's most famous café is a great place to unwind with a latte and Western-style sandwich in contemporary, exposed brick surroundings. The menu features many Western favorites: fish and chips, soups and salads, pizzas, pastas, a big selection of burgers, and even a children's menu. Free Wi-Fi.

SIEM REAP Café Indochine $$

Sivatha Blvd ***Tel*** *(012)-804-952* ***Road Map*** *C6*

Set in an old wooden building, this lovely restaurant is popular with tour groups for its consistently tasty cuisine, a blend of Asian and European dishes. On the menu are spring rolls (fresh and fried), savory salads, spicy Thai soups and bouillabaisse, curries, *amok*, and a variety of meat and vegetable dishes.

SIEM REAP Dead Fish Tower $$

Sivatha Blvd ***Tel*** *(063)-963-060* ***Road Map*** *C6*

The restaurant at this guesthouse is an interesting place to sample fine Thai cuisine. The Khmer menu excels with dishes such as *amok* and ginger chicken. The dining area is curiously multitiered, but guests enjoying a cocktail bucket need to be careful, as there is little to break an accidental fall. Open daily from 7am to 1am.

SIEM REAP El Camino Taqueri $$

The Passage, Siem Reap ***Tel*** *(092)-207-842* ***Road Map*** *C6*

This trendy Mexican bar does some very appetizing, authentic Mexican snacks such as tacos, fajitas, nachos, guacamoles, and chimichangas. The decor is more urban chic than rural charm, with mosaic walls to stare at while guzzling deliciously prepared margaritas.

SIEM REAP FCC Angkor $$

Pokambor Ave ***Tel*** *(063)-760-283* ***Road Map*** *C6*

The sister concern of FCC in Phnom Penh, the FCC Angkor has more space and style than its counterpart, but perhaps lacks its effervescence. The building is set amid manicured lawns, beside a swimming pool. Dining upstairs is delightful, with an attractive bar and open kitchen. Food ranges from Western comfort to Asian fusion.

Key to Price Guide *see p232*

SIEM REAP Funky Monkey $$

Pokambor Ave ***Tel** (017)-824-553* **Road Map** C6

This bar-cum-restaurant packs a punch with terrific style-your-own burgers, Pop Art decor, and an extensive cocktail menu. There are also vegetarian burgers on offer. A friendly and fun alternative to more sober dining. The establishment is particularly known for its quiz night, held on Thursdays.

SIEM REAP Joan Yen Lau $$

Angkor Shopping Center ***Tel** (063)-760-269* **Road Map** C6

Located on the third floor of the fabulous expanse of the Angkor Shopping Center, Joan Yen Lau is a great place for shoppers to relax and enjoy some Chinese dishes. The cuisine served here is more Cantonese than Pekinese. The restaurant is also equipped with a full bar.

SIEM REAP Khmer Family Restaurant $$

Pub St, Old Market area ***Tel** (015)-999-909* **Road Map** C6

Inexpensive and cheerful but no less than delicious. Easy-to-read photo menus, outdoor as well as balcony seating, plus a wide selection of tasty and moderately priced fare make Khmer Family Restaurant a great place to eat. Among the best dishes are fish with mango, duck with honey, and the traditional *amok*.

SIEM REAP Khmer Kitchen $$

The Passage, behind Bar St ***Tel** (063)-964-154* **Road Map** C6

Occupying an unpretentious building, the ever-busy Khmer Kitchen offers simple, hearty fare. The eclectic menu of Thai and Khmer staples features a variety of soups, stir-fries, curries, and spring rolls. Try the baked pumpkin or the beef *lok lak*. The staff speaks English and service is friendly. Open from 10am to 10pm daily.

SIEM REAP La Volpaia $$

Charles De Gaulle Blvd ***Tel** (063)-764-184* **Road Map** C6

Occupying a quiet spot on the road to the temples of Siem Reap, Volpaia is set amid lush gardens. The restaurant boasts an impressive kitchen that serves delicious pasta and pizza dishes. The furnishings are minimal, but sufficient for a refined evening outdoors. The owner, who has lived in the US, is a great host.

SIEM REAP Le Grand Café $$

Thnou St, Old Market area ***Tel** (012)-847-419* **Road Map** C6

This street corner restaurant directly opposite the Old Market has kerbside seating and upstairs dining. Located in a graceful old French house, it is a great place to people-watch while eating French and Khmer dishes such as palm pepper scallops, *amok*, and ginger fish. The steaks, imported from Australia, are expertly cooked.

SIEM REAP Le Malraux $$

155, Sivatha Blvd ***Tel** (063)-966-041* **Road Map** C6

With its Art Nouveau-inspired interior, leafy courtyard setting, and Gallic haute cuisine, Le Malraux is a memorable high-end venue. There are also Asian dishes on offer, such as fish *amok*, but traditional French dishes are the highlight. A well-stocked bar, home-made ice creams, and excellent service might persuade you further.

SIEM REAP Madame Butterfly $$

Airport Rd ***Tel** (016)-909-607* **Road Map** C6

Fine dining in a pleasingly traditional house, festooned in silk and with period furniture reminiscent of the Colonial era. Candlelight and warm, diffused lights add to the romantic atmosphere. The vegetarian-friendly menu is versatile, with a range of Western, Asian, Khmer, and French dishes. Popular with diners who enjoy spicy, rich food.

SIEM REAP Rasmei Restaurant $$

Pokambor Ave, Old Market area ***Tel** (063)-964-774* **Road Map** C6

A pleasantly breezy corner restaurant set in a delightful old French Colonial building that houses the Shadow of Angkor I Guesthouse *(see p213)*. The restaurant serves an extensive range of Khmer and Asian dishes, such as *amok* and fried beef with lemongrass, as well as some Western dishes such as pizza and pasta.

SIEM REAP Red Piano Restaurant $$

Pub St ***Tel** (063)-963-240* **Road Map** C6

Patronized by Angelina Jolie during the making of *Tomb Raider*, the Red Piano is set in a lovely old villa. This is a lively place with sidewalk, indoor, and veranda seating. The food is predominantly Western, offering favorites such as pastas and steaks. There is also a selection of Asian dishes on the menu.

SIEM REAP Samot Fine Wine and Cuisine $$

Passage Extension ***Tel** (092)-410-400* **Road Map** C6

Run by a Frenchman with a great sense of humor and a passion for food, Samot Fine Wine and Cuisine is a cosy spot for enticingly prepared fresh seafood. Great Australian meat dishes. The chilli crab is one of the most popular dishes on the menu.

SIEM REAP Selantra Restaurant $$

Wat Bo Rd ***Tel** (012)-569-975* **Road Map** C6

Celebrated for its warm goat's cheese and great sirloin steaks, Selantra Restaurant serves hearty meals, as well as a delicious selection of tapas. The establishment features contemporary decor. A variety of refreshing cocktails are served during happy hour, from 6pm until 8pm every evening.

SIEM REAP Temple Balcony $$

St 8, Old Market area **Tel** *(015)-999-909* **Road Map** *C6*

Set above the lively Temple Bar, this airy balcony restaurant is one of Pub Street's most popular haunts and a meeting point for travelers. Each night, there are traditional *apsara* dances between 7:30pm and 9:30pm. The food comprises tasty Khmer, Thai, and Western dishes. Wi-Fi is available.

SIEM REAP Terrasse Des Eléphants $$

Sivatha Blvd, Old Market area **Tel** *(063)-965-570* **Road Map** *C6*

A hotel restaurant, the Terrasse Des Eléphants is set in a Colonial-style building among gardens bursting with flowers. The menu offers both Khmer and international cuisine, from chicken *amok* and beef curry in coconut milk to burgers and steaks. The bar complements the restaurant and is ideal for an evening cocktail.

SIEM REAP Cambodian BBQ $$$

The Alley **Tel** *(063)-965-407* **Road Map** *C6*

Hidden down the passage running parallel to Pub Street, this place can get rather steamy on a hot night given the smoke rising from its delicious barbecue dishes. The wide menu offers traditional Khmer food for vegetarians and non-vegetarians alike. Journey into a culinary vista of snake, crocodile, and ostrich for an unforgettable meal.

SIEM REAP Hotel De La Paix $$$

Sivatha Blvd **Tel** *(063)-966-001* **Road Map** *C6*

One of the most stylish places to eat in town, this Khmer restaurant is reached via the chic Arts Lounge Bar and ends by a beautiful boddhi tree in the courtyard. On offer is exquisite, seasonal Khmer cuisine presented with great finesse. There is also a range of salads, sandwiches, baguettes, and paninis.

SIEM REAP Shinta Mani $$$

Junction of Oum Khum and 14th St **Tel** *(063)-761-998* **Road Map** *C6*

This polished restaurant takes itself seriously, with its minimalist approach to decor and superb service. The simple menu has diners coming back for its delicious sirloin steak and many of its generic Western dishes such as spaghetti and chicken. Candlelit, charming outdoor area, and peach-colored walls.

SIEM REAP Raffles' Apsara Terrace $$$$

Raffles Grand Hotel d'Angkor **Tel** *(063)-963-888* **Road Map** *D1*

Raffles boasts several restaurants and bars, but the star is the Apsara Terrace on Monday, Wednesday and Friday evenings at 7pm. The sumptuous buffet dinner, served in a candle-lit garden setting, specializes in Asian barbeque and seafood. At 7:45pm the show begins – live traditional music, martial arts and Apsara dancing.

SIEM REAP Chatra $$$$$

Sothea Hotel, Airport Rd **Tel** *(063)-966-788* **Road Map** *C6*

One of the most sought-after restaurants in town, the Chatra is famous for its Asian fusion cuisine. Its dish of the day is designed by the chef around the freshest produce at that day's market. The international menu is also delectable. Decor is particularly elegant and more than compensates for the pricey menu.

NORTHERN CAMBODIA

BAN LUNG Gecko House $

South of Highway 78 **Tel** *(012)-416-234* **Road Map** *E6*

Run by a charming urbanite from Phnom Penh, Gecko House has a dash of internationalism in its wide-ranging menu, which caters to the Western palate. Excellent breakfasts, pizzas, and pasta dishes. Under the low, thatched roof, the dining area is dark and atmospheric; by night, it comes to life with a happy mix of locals and travelers.

BAN LUNG Terres Rouge Lodge $$

Beside Boeng Kansaign Lake **Tel** *(075)-974-051* **Road Map** *E6*

The most refined eating experience in town, Terres Rouge Lodge is jungle chic, surrounded by lush vegetation in an old Colonial house. The sumptuous furnishings match the equally divine menu, be it French, Khmer, or Chinese fare. The staff is delightful. The bar offers cold beer, wine, and cocktails. Closes around 9pm every day.

BAN LUNG Tree Top Ecolodge $$

Phum No.1, Laban Seak-Commune **Tel** *(012)-490-333* **Road Map** *E6*

Tree Top Ecolodge is an unusually rustic-chic dining venue, more typical of Thailand or Laos. The treehouse-style, open-air restaurant and lounge is quite atmospheric, with great views of the small valley below. Fare is Cambodian and Western fusion. Free Wi-Fi.

BATTAMBANG Sunrise Coffeehouse $

Near Psar Nath market **Tel** *(012)-953-426* **Road Map** *C6*

Centrally located, and just opposite the Royal Hotel *(see p215)*, this Western-style bakery has a cornucopia of pies, pancakes, cookies, pastries, and pizzas, as well as finely blended coffees and teas. Makes for a great breakfast stop. The staff is friendly and can help organize tours in and around Battambang.

BATTAMBANG The Bungalow Restaurant $

144 Kamakor, Svaypor ***Tel*** *(012)-916-123* ***Road Map*** *C6*

An unpretentious little eatery west of the Stung Sangker, the Bungalow Restaurant sells standard Western fare such as burgers and pizzas. The photo menu also offers a selection of traditional Khmer and Thai food, prepared by an obliging cook. Good coffee. Quick and friendly service.

BATTAMBANG White Rose $

St 2 ***Tel*** *(012)-693-855* ***Road Map*** *C6*

Often crowded, White Rose is well located in the center of town and a magnet for Westerners gathering to swap stories. The menu is a mix of Khmer and Western dishes. The fried spring rolls with fresh mint leaves are especially delicious. Recommended for breakfast as there is a wide selection of fruit shakes. Variable service.

BATTAMBANG Pomme d'Amour $$

63, St 2 ***Tel*** *(012)-415-513* ***Road Map*** *C6*

Just south of the central market, the Pomme d'Amour is an excellent little restaurant with personable service from its French owner and his Khmer wife. The menu features French, Western, and local fare, with a wealth of well-executed fish, meat, and vegetarian dishes. Serves Italian coffee.

BATTAMBANG Rottanak Resort $$

KO Rd ***Tel*** *(053)-953-255* ***Road Map*** *C6*

A 15-minute walk from the center of town, the restaurant at Rottanak Resort *(see p215)* is one of the best in town, second only to La Villa. Tranquil, atmospheric dining, and impeccably good service. Western and Asian fusion food on the menu. Full bar. Efficient staff.

BATTAMBANG La Villa $$$$$

185 Pom Romcheck 5 ***Tel*** *(053)-730-151* ***Road Map*** *C6*

The restaurant at the beautifully restored, French Colonial La Villa guesthouse *(see p215)* has an air-conditioned interior with a glass roof and cool, tiled floors. Diners can also eat in the courtyard or on the terrace. The Western and Asian cuisine served here features many Italian dishes and a wide choice of barbecue-grilled meat.

KOMPONG CHAM Hao An Restaurant $

Monivong Blvd ***Tel*** *(012)-941-234* ***Road Map*** *C6*

One of the oldest eateries in town, Hao An Restaurant serves a mainly Khmer clientele who use the place as a cross-country pit stop en route to other destinations. The huge menu features a plethora of Chinese and Khmer dishes. A great place to relax and guzzle beer.

KOMPONG CHAM Mekong Crossing $

Preah Bat Sihanouk St ***Tel*** *(012)-432-427* ***Road Map*** *C6*

A firm favorite with locals, and even more so with travelers, this atmospheric retro-feel café is festooned with old movie posters and maps. The food is tasty and fresh, ranging from comfort food such as sandwiches and burgers to more classical Khmer dishes such as fish *amok*.

KRATIE Red Sun Falling $

Rur Preah Suramarit ***Tel*** *(012)-476-528* ***Road Map*** *D6*

By day, this little restaurant, with its pleasant mural and second-hand book stall, is a sleepy place with a dark interior. At night, it becomes a bubbling cauldron of travelers crowded over maps and cheap beer. The food is tasty, with a Western and Asian menu attracting local NGO workers.

KRATIE Star Restaurant and Guesthouse $

West side of the Central Market ***Tel*** *(012)-753-401* ***Road Map*** *D6*

A backpacker favorite, Star Restaurant and Guesthouse has an extensive menu comprising a number of delicious Western favourites and desserts. The staff is friendly and helpful. This is a good place to relax and exchange local information and travel tips with fellow travelers and drink chilled beer.

SOUTHERN CAMBODIA

KAMPOT Akashi Café $$$

Riverfront, opposite the hospital ***Tel*** *(092)-775-900* ***Road Map*** *C7*

Set in a stylish, purple-painted Colonial house near the new bridge, Akashi Café specializes in rich sweets and treats such as coconut-and-lime pie and papaya ice cream. There are also terrific sandwiches, soups, and coffees. The quiche served here is the best in town. A great place to relax and sip beer.

KAMPOT Bamboo Light Café $$$

Riverfront Rd ***Tel*** *(089)-476-578* ***Road Map*** *C7*

An unusual find in provincial Cambodia, this Sri Lankan and Indian restaurant is a hit for its authentic curries, and lamb and seafood dishes. Try the Sri Lankan *kottu roti* dishes (soft, unleavened bread cut up and mixed with potato and curry). There are wholesome Western breakfasts and great smoothies on offer. Internet café upstairs.

KAMPOT Coco House $$$

Riverfront Rd ***Tel** (033)-932-198* **Road Map** *C7*

Occupying a fine Colonial building on the riverfront, this restaurant and bar is run by a Danish couple and managed by local Khmers. The place is kitted out with cane furniture and serves reliably good Khmer and Western food, including pastas and steak. The staff is welcoming and helps visitors choose from the extensive menu.

KAMPOT Epic Arts Café $$$

East of the old market ***Tel** (092)-922-069* **Road Map** *C7*

A small café with a good reputation and ethos (profits aid deaf and disabled Cambodians), Epic Arts Café offers a Western menu featuring Provençal eggplant and tomatos, bagels, omelette, and mezes. The place bakes great cakes and Kep pepper bread on the premises. Wi-Fi available.

KAMPOT Rusty Keyhole $$$

Riverfront Rd ***Tel** (012)-679-607* **Road Map** *C7*

A friendly, scruffy-looking bar-restaurant that is renowned for serving the best ribs in the country. The marinade recipe is a closely-guarded secret. The Western and Asian dishes are tasty and good value, and the seafood specials change on a daily basis. Happy hour at sunset. Outdoor seating in a garden with mountain vistas.

KAMPOT Ta Ouv $$$

New Bridge ***Tel** (033)-932-422* **Road Map** *C7*

This Khmer restaurant is located on a great riverside plot, with tables right next to the water that catch the breeze. Ta Ouv is famous for its seafood, particularly crab, which is served with an aromatic coconut and chili sauce. The eatery is open every day from 10am to 11pm.

KAMPOT Mea Culpa $$$$

44 Sovansokar ***Tel** (012)-504-769* **Road Map** *C7*

Unquestionably the best pizzeria in Kampot, Mea Culpa uses a wood-fired oven and imported ingredients, including mozzarella and pepperoni. It also serves Khmer dishes. The refined garden setting is superb, and service is excellent. The full bar is ideal for a glass of wine or digestif. Free Wi-Fi. Closed on Mondays.

KAMPOT Riki Tiki Tavi $$$$

Riverfront Rd ***Tel** (012)-235-102* **Road Map** *C7*

For the best dining experience in town, head to Riki Tiki Tavi, which enjoys great river views, has elegant seating, and faultless service. Feast on Western dishes such as the Italian wrap with pastrami or Khmer specials such as *kamkoot* Kampot (grilled fish with green mango) or *lok lak*, made with Australian beef. No MSG is used.

KEP Kep Lodge $$$

Pepper St ***Tel** (017)-879-526* **Road Map** *C7*

Set well back from the beach, this large, open-sided hotel-restaurant is an enjoyable place for a Cambodian-style salad or Western cuisine, including some Swiss dishes such as rösti. There is always a daily special and the cooking is healthy and tasty. For dessert, try the fried bananas with honey, or the home-made mango or papaya ice cream.

KEP Breezes $$$$

Kep Beach ***Tel** (097)-675-9072* **Road Map** *C7*

Upscale seafront restaurant with stylish lighting and a nice lounge vibe. The creative pan-Asian menu features Western, Khmer, and fusion dishes such as Japanese noodles, wraps, and plenty of seafood. Outdoor seating on a patio, surrounded by a large garden. Call for a free pick-up from your hotel.

KEP Kimly & Thmorda $$$$

Crab Market ***Tel** (017)-904-077* **Road Map** *C7*

Kep's Crab Market has a strip of near-identical seafood restaurants that back on to the bay. Of these, Kimly & Thmorda is famous for serving the region's signature dish, Kep Pepper Crab, which is wonderfully succulent and accompanied by a rich orange-red spicy sauce. The menu also offers a variety of fish and prawn dishes.

KEP Sailing Club $$$$$

Shoreside ***Tel** (012)-349-742* **Road Map** *C7*

Owned by the boutique hotel Knai Bang Chatt, the Sailing Club is a classy place with a spacious, decked seaside terrace ideal for a long, lazy lunch of prime seafood. Daily specials are chalked up on boards. Extensive wine list with many good French and New World bottles. Seafood barbecues on Saturday evenings. Closed on Mondays.

KOH KONG Baan Peakmai $$$

St 6 ***Tel** (035)-393-906* **Road Map** *B7*

A short hop from the Thai border, Baan Peakmai is a Thai-style garden restaurant and one of the best places to find authentic Siamese cooking in Cambodia. Popular with Thai expatriates, this eatery has a large menu with many vegetarian options, flavorsome seafood, and chili-rich red and green curries.

KOH KONG Café Laurent $$$$

Riverfront Rd ***Tel** (016)-373-737* **Road Map** *B7*

High quality French-owned restaurant boasting an elegant air-conditioned interior replete with rattan seats and smart modern decor. Renowned for its pasta, salads – try the niçoise – and classic Gallic dishes. The café also serves ice cream and fine coffee. Wi-Fi and a large outdoor terrace.

Key to Price Guide *see p232*

KOH KONG Dive Inn $$$$

Riverfront Rd ***Tel*** *(099)-707-434* **Road Map** *B7*

This spacious bar-restaurant on Koh Kong's riverfront has great views, particularly at sunset. The menu features international and Khmer cuisine, plus a good range of snacks. The bar offers cold beer and a variety of cocktails. Dive Inn has a pool table, Wi-Fi, cable TV, and offers good travel advice too.

SIHANOUKVILLE Sandan $$

Sokha Beach Rd ***Tel*** *(034)-452-4000* **Road Map** *C7*

A very popular spot serving traditional Cambodian fare as well as Western favorites, Sandan is located near the center of town. Friendly English-speaking staff perform song and dance shows during meals. Dishes are generous and well presented. Try the seafood *amok* and enjoy delicious cocktails.

SIHANOUKVILLE Café Colonial $$$

Ekareach St ***Tel*** *(092)-529-292* **Road Map** *C7*

One of the best eateries in town, Café Colonial is a modern place with an air-conditioned interior and a patio. On offer are fine espressos, creamy cappuccinos, and fresh fruit juices. Tuck into a burger or club sandwich, and for dessert, savor the delicious Italian ice creams or French pastries.

SIHANOUKVILLE Chi Khmer $$$

Lane to Serendipity Beach ***Tel*** *(034)-934-380* **Road Map** *C7*

This spacious, upscale Cambodian restaurant is renowned for its fine seafood and traditional Khmer cuisine. The dishes are well prepared using fresh ingredients. Enjoy *amok*, *lok lak*, or a banana-flower salad in the wonderful garden setting. Chi Khmer is open daily from 5 to 10pm.

SIHANOUKVILLE Starfish $$$

7 Makura St ***Tel*** *(012)-952-011* **Road Map** *C7*

A café with a cause, Starfish has two locations in Sihanoukville; the central branch, near the market, is larger and has a garden. Both serve Western-style breakfast and lunch, with lots of vegetarian choices. Plenty of baked goodies, plus coffee, tea, and juices. Profits benefit medical and developmental work in Cambodia.

SIHANOUKVILLE Treasure Island Seafood Restaurant $$$

Independence Beach ***Tel*** *(012)-755-335* **Road Map** *C7*

Right by the waves on a lovely stretch of sand, the Treasure Island Seafood Restaurant serves fine Cambodian and Chinese-style fish and seafood. Guests can choose their dinner from the fish tanks. Highly popular with Khmer families on weekends as the eatery is a great spot at sunset.

SIHANOUKVILLE Happa $$$$

81 Ekareach St ***Tel*** *(012)-478-510* **Road Map** *C7*

A very stylish, nicely designed two-story restaurant, Happa is a peaceful place for a snack or a full meal. The interior has comfortable, black-lacquered furniture and lots of art. The Western food served here includes sandwiches, pasta dishes, and soups. There are also Khmer-style salads and curries.

SIHANOUKVILLE Les Feuilles $$$$

Occheuteal Beach ***Tel*** *(034)-933-910* **Road Map** *C7*

A couple of blocks back from the beach, this French/Khmer-owned restaurant is a casual place with tables arranged in a breezy, open-sided dining area. The restaurant serves flavorsome Gallic dishes, including beef with Bordelaise sauce (shallots and red wine) and crêpes. French wines, including Côtes du Rhone, are available.

SIHANOUKVILLE New Sea View Villa $$$$

Lane to Serendipity Beach ***Tel*** *(017)-420-270* **Road Map** *C7*

This restaurant offers an ambitious menu of European classics prepared by a French chef. The setting is terrific, the huge outdoor terrace uses subtle lighting, and the crisp tablecloths and professional service combine to make New Sea View Villa an ideal destination for a romantic dinner. Good desserts and an extensive wine list.

SIHANOUKVILLE Ristorante Marco Polo $$$$

2 Thnou St ***Tel*** *(092)-920-866* **Road Map** *C7*

A well-regarded Italian eatery, Ristorante Marco Polo is ideal for a pizza – made in a wood-fired oven – or home-made pasta, including tortellini, lasagna, and pappardelle. Leave some room for dessert, and a shot or two of limoncello. Open daily from 5 to 10pm.

SIHANOUKVILLE Steak House Swiss Garden $$$$

11 Ekareach St ***Tel*** *(099)-707-155* **Road Map** *C7*

Just inland from the Golden Lion Traffic Circle, this Swiss-owned restaurant has the town's best cuts of steak, broiled on a lava-stone grill. The eatery also offers raclette and fondue dishes. Guests can head to the salad bar – which has around 20 options – for a lighter meal.

SIHANOUKVILLE Luna d'Autunno $$$$$

Ekareach St ***Tel*** *(034)-934-280* **Road Map** *C7*

Probably the classiest restaurant in town, the Italian Luna d'Autunno offers delicious pizzas as well as great pasta, fish, and meat dishes. There is always a daily special and the wine list is comprehensive. Eat in the elegant air-conditioned dining room or out on the terrace.

Choosing a Restaurant in Laos

The restaurants in this guide have been chosen for their food, ambience, and value. In remote areas the focus is on restaurants where visitors will find familiar dishes. Entries are listed alphabetically by region. For map references, see pp138–9 and pp150–51 for Vientiane and Luang Prabang respectively; see the inside back cover for other locations.

PRICE CATEGORIES
The following price ranges are for a meal for two, made up of a range of dishes, including service tax, but no alcohol.

$ Under $5
$$ $5–$10
$$$ $10–$20
$$$$ $20–$30
$$$$$ Over $30

VIENTIANE

CENTRAL VIENTIANE Joma Bakery Café $$
Setthathirat Rd ***Tel*** *(021)-215-265* ***City Map*** *B4*

A popular breakfast venue, Joma makes the best coffee in town, as well as great pastries and sandwiches, which you can create on your own. The café is air conditioned, with newspapers to read, and a strong Wi-Fi connection. Try their blueberry cheesecake and orange pie.

CENTRAL VIENTIANE Lao Kitchen $$
Hengboun Rd, Baan Anou ***Tel*** *(021)-254-332* ***City Map*** *B3*

Set in an open-air shop front in downtown Vientiane, the friendly staff at this popular eatery serve traditional Lao cuisine in a homey atmosphere. Tantalizing dishes are served as tapas or family-style with rice. Recommended are the curries or savoury Lao stews. There are also light bites such as spring rolls and salads.

CENTRAL VIENTIANE Scandinavian Bakery $$
74/1 Pangkham Rd, Nam Phu Square ***Tel*** *(021)-215-199* ***City Map*** *C3*

Vientiane's best-known bakery and breakfast venue is a perennial favorite. It has a nice terrace and a large-screen TV upstairs – good for sporting events. Great pastries, breads, cakes, and sandwiches are on offer. The noticeboard displays upcoming cultural events.

CENTRAL VIENTIANE Istanbul Restaurant $$$
Francois Ngin Rd ***Tel*** *(021)-218-320* ***City Map*** *B4*

Located near the Mekong River, Istanbul Restaurant is owned and managed by a Turkish family. It serves classic Turkish favorites such as delicious doner kebabs and *imam biyaldi*, an eggplant dish. The salads and desserts are equally appetizing. An excellent alternative to European or Lao food.

CENTRAL VIENTIANE Khop Chai Deu $$$
54 Setthathirat Rd ***Tel*** *(021)-251-564* ***City Map*** *B3*

Situated in a Colonial-era villa, and right next to the Nam Phu fountain, Khop Chai Deu is the top evening venue for visiting foreigners and expats. It has a great menu of Lao and international dishes, with everything from pizza to hearty stews. Good buffet at lunch and live music in the evenings.

CENTRAL VIENTIANE Le Banneton $$$
Nokeo Khumman Rd ***Tel*** *(021)-217-321* ***City Map*** *B4*

Offering serious competition to Joma and Scandinavian Bakery for the best pastries in town, Le Banneton also serves fine coffee, scrumptious sandwiches, and other light meals. Fresh country ambience, enhanced by wooden floors, and relaxing music encourage lingering. Popular for both breakfast and lunch.

CENTRAL VIENTIANE Le Central $$$
Setthathirat Rd, near Wat Ong Teu Mahawihan ***Tel*** *(021)-243-703* ***City Map*** *B4*

The ambience in Le Central is both traditional and sophisticated and the food reflects this. The chef prepares some great Asian fusion dishes such as spring rolls with goat's cheese and cashew nuts, but this restaurant is most famous for its mouth-watering cakes and pies.

CENTRAL VIENTIANE Le Vendome $$$
In Paeng Rd, behind Wat In Paeng ***Tel*** *(021)-216-402* ***City Map*** *B3*

Tucked away in a small lane behind Wat In Paeng, Le Vendome is a long-standing Vientiane favorite that serves reasonably priced French and Lao food. Also has a wood-fired pizza oven. Popular among Francophones, it is almost always busy, but the service is good. Try the aubergines stuffed with goat's cheese.

CENTRAL VIENTIANE Red Mekong $$$
Khun Boulom Rd, Ban Vatchan ***Tel*** *(021)-260-905* ***City Map*** *A3*

A two-story building with karaoke on the first floor. Spacious and cool, the Red Mekong has a huge teakwood bar. Serves a good mixture of Western and Lao favorites. There is also a pool table and wide-screen TVs showing the latest sporting events, with soft rock music playing in the background. An expat favorite.

Key to Symbols *see back cover flap*

VIENTIANE Soukviman $$$

89/12 Ban Sisaket, Near That Dam Stupa **Tel** *(021)-214-441* **City Map** *C3*

Open since before the revolution in 1975, Soukviman is famous for using traditional recipes and ingredients, which shows in the food. Also serves Luang Prabang cuisine. This restaurant has a modest ambience and is popular with local businessmen for lunch. The ant egg soup is worth trying.

CENTRAL VIENTIANE Sticky Fingers $$$

10/3 Francois Nginn Rd, opposite Tai Pan Hotel **Tel** *(021)-215-972* **City Map** *B4*

Australian-owned, Sticky Fingers has the feel of a Sydney bistro. Serves good quality Western food at reasonable prices. Though popular, it manages to retain a relaxing environment. The salmon steak, antipasto, and chickpea salads are good. The home-made dips and sauces are guaranteed to cure the homesick Westerner.

CENTRAL VIENTIANE Ty-Na Restaurant $$$

68 Pangkham Rd, off Nam Phu Square **City Map** *B4*

This restaurant is situated near the Nam Phu fountain in a two-story building. The Ty-Na's specialty is Brittany-style buckwheat crêpes, which are famous throughout Vientiane. However, the menu goes far beyond that, into the realm of provincial French food. A charming place to eat and the service is also efficient.

CENTRAL VIENTIANE Khoua Lao $$$$

Samsenthai Rd, near That Dam Stupa **Tel** *(021)-215-777* **City Map** *C4*

This is a good restaurant to sample Lao food for the first time since the dishes are unabashedly tailored to Western tastes. Khoua Lao is located in a huge, restored Colonial mansion and echoes with the sounds of traditional Lao music in the evenings. Extremely clean, with friendly service.

CENTRAL VIENTIANE Le Nadao $$$$

30 Siboungheung Rd, Patuxai **Tel** *(021)-213-174* **City Map** *C3*

A classy restaurant with a lovely ambience, Le Nadao is very popular with the expat community. Serves excellent, yet reasonably priced French cuisine. Try the beef bourguignon, rib-eye steak with green peppercorn sauce, duck breast, or any of the soufflés.

CENTRAL VIENTIANE Makphet $$$$

Setthathirat Rd, behind Wat Ong Teu Mahawihan **Tel** *(021)-260-578* **City Map** *B3*

Established as a project to help former street kids, Makphet trains its students in the English language, cooking, and restaurant operations while they work. The Lao food here is excellent and the kitchen is supremely clean. Has a wide vegetarian selection, but if that does not appeal, the buffalo curry is a great option.

CENTRAL VIENTIANE L'Opera $$$$$

Nam Phu Square **Tel** *(021)-215-099* **City Map** *C4*

The cuisines of both France and Italy are on offer at L'Opera. This classy establishment is famous for its steaks as well as the home-made egg pasta. The ambience is elegant, with soft classical music, and the service is outstanding. Popular with business people.

GREATER VIENTIANE Moon The Night $$$

Fa Ngum Rd, Ban Wattay **Tel** *(021)-217-073* **City Map** *A5*

Located in a stilted house by the Mekong River, en route to the airport, Moon The Night is a bit hard to find, but well worth the effort. It serves great Lao food; especially recommended is the Mekong River sour fish soup. Popular with visitors for the superb sunset views.

GREATER VIENTIANE Nang Kam Bang $$$

Khun Bulom Rd **Tel** *(021)-217-198* **City Map** *A4*

Serves authentic Lao home-style cooking. There is an open kitchen where diners can watch the chef at work. Hygienic, tiled, and has both air-conditioned and non air-conditioned sections. The *laap* (minced meat, poultry, or fish flavored with lime juice, onion, garlic and mint), and deep-fried quail are delicious. Popular with locals.

GREATER VIENTIANE The Spirit House $$$

105 Fa Ngum Rd **Tel** *(021)-262-530* **City Map** *A5*

A great location for a sunset drink on the Mekong River, The Spirit House is much more than a standard bamboo beer bar. It has a touch of class and a wide selection of interesting cocktails and Scandinavian vodkas. The paninis and burgers are delicious. Popular with the expat community.

GREATER VIENTIANE Ton Hom $$$

36/1 Samsenthai Rd **Tel** *(021)-223-113* **City Map** *A5*

A good choice for those seeking excellent Thai food, Ton Hom's location, amid some industrial shops, can appear uninviting at first, but the interior is immaculate and decorated with Thai handicrafts. The *tom kha gai* (chicken with galangale in coconut soup) and the Penang curries are excellent.

GREATER VIENTIANE Aria Italian Culinary Arts $$$$

8 Rue Francois Nginn, Ban Mixai **Tel** *(021)-222-589* **City Map** *B4*

Aria Italian is a real gem, popular with local expats and businesspeople. It boasts a broad and delicious menu of Italian favorites, including pastas, pizzas and soups. The fine wine list is quite good, and highly recommended is dining outside and watching the city's evening activities unfold.

GREATER VIENTIANE Le Silapa $$$$$

17/1 Sihom Rd ***Tel*** *(021)-219-689* **City Map** *A5*

Adorned with original artworks, Le Silapa is a small, cosy restaurant with a pleasant ambience. Serves delectable French dishes such as salmon steak in red wine and grilled shallot sauce. A long-term favorite in Vientiane and considered by the locals to be the best restaurant in town.

GREATER VIENTIANE Tam Nak Lao $$$$$

100 That Luang Rd ***Tel*** *(021)-413-562* **City Map** *A5*

Lao food is cooked to an international standard in Tam Nak Lao. This restaurant has a relaxed and elegant atmosphere, with cultural shows taking place every evening. The specialties here include sour fish soup with lemongrass and coriander root. There is a beer garden, as well as a handicrafts shop.

LUANG PRABANG

CENTRAL LUANG PRABANG Chill Out Café $$

Dara Market, Chao Sisophon Rd ***Tel*** *(071)-261-006* **City Map** *C4*

Located in the quiet Dara Market, Chill Out Café is stylishly designed with comfortable chairs and tables. The café is breezy and ideal for quiet lunches. Sandwiches dominate the menu and the drinks list has lots of espresso-based coffees. Free Wi-Fi.

CENTRAL LUANG PRABANG Joma Bakery Café $$

Chao Fa Ngum Rd ***Tel*** *(071)-252-292* **City Map** *B4*

Located in an air-conditioned, Colonial-style two-story house, Joma Bakery Café serves excellent coffee, pastries, and sandwiches, and even pasta. Has comfortable seating, with an alfresco option, and high-speed Wi-Fi. Lives up to its reputation as the best café in Luang Prabang.

CENTRAL LUANG PRABANG Lao Lao Garden $$

Phou Si Rd, Ban Aphai ***Tel*** *(020)-9997-0106* **City Map** *D3*

Built up the side of a hill, the Lao Lao Garden has a terraced garden setting. It has a lot of barbecue options, both Lao and Western. Patrons can enjoy superb DJ music and dancing in the late evenings. Popular with the young crowd.

CENTRAL LUANG PRABANG Le Banneton Café and Boulangerie $$

Sakkarin Rd, opposite Wat Sop ***Tel*** *(020)-5464-9189* **City Map** *D3*

Close to the row of temples toward the end of the peninsula, Le Banneton Cafe and Boulangerie is a good place for weary tourists. The pastries are superb, and they do a variety of sandwiches for lunch as well. An unpretentious place, popular with resident foreigners as a breakfast stop.

CENTRAL LUANG PRABANG Riverloft Restaurant $$

King Kitsalath Rd ***Tel*** *(030)-200-5228* **City Map** *D3*

One of Luang Prabang's most popular restaurants, Riverloft (formerly the Arthouse Café) serves up traditional Lao cuisine like fried seaweed, *laap* and curries, as well as Western comforts such as burgers, salads and an extensive breakfast menu. Dining is outdoors on the elegant covered veranda.

CENTRAL LUANG PRABANG Vegetarian Buffet $$

Post office parking lot **City Map** *C4*

Every evening at sunset, budget travelers congregate at this impromptu market where folding tables are set up. A variety of vegetarian dishes are on the menu, which is fixed price. The quality is surprisingly good. There is also plenty of barbecued meat and sticky rice, as well as beer served à la carte.

CENTRAL LUANG PRABANG View Khem Kong $$

5/49 Khem Khong Rd ***Tel*** *(071)-212-726* **City Map** *C3*

With a location next to the Mekong River, the main attraction at View Khem Kong is the scenery, but the food is decent and prices reasonable. Both Western food and Lao traditional dishes are on the menu. The Luang Prabang sausage, steamed fish, and *laap* are delicious. The service is good and the place is spotless. Popular with the locals.

CENTRAL LUANG PRABANG Indochina Spirit $$$

Chao Fa Ngum Road ***Tel*** *(071)-252-372* **City Map** *B4*

Located near the fountain across the street from Wat Ho Xieng, the Indochina Spirit serves a variety of Lao, Thai, and Western dishes in an atmospheric, old two-story wooden house. A friendly place with live Lao music. The food is tasty, and the portions are large. This is a good place to try Lao food for the first time.

CENTRAL LUANG PRABANG Malee Lao $$$

Phu Vao Rd ***Tel*** *(020)-7777-2599* **City Map** *B5*

Located on Phu Vao Road, about 2 miles (3 km) downriver from the Old Town, Malee Lao is famous among locals for its traditional Lao cuisine. This restaurant also has a do-it-yourself barbecue, but with special sauces. The food is not fancy, but it is authentic. Try the Luang Prabang rice wine called *lao gaam*.

Key to Price Guide *see p242*

CENTRAL LUANG PRABANG Nazim $$$

78/4 Ban Visoun, Winsunarat Rd **Tel** *(071)-252-263* **City Map** *C3*

A chain of Indian restaurants with a branch in every town in Laos and frequented by foreigners. Its wide selection of northern and southern Indian dishes are delicious and reasonably priced. Slow but reliable service. Standards such as chicken tikka, goat curry, or biryani are all appetizing, as are the *lassis*.

CENTRAL LUANG PRABANG Tamnak Lao $$$

Sakkarin Rd, Ban Wat Sene **Tel** *(071)-252-525* **City Map** *D3*

Located in an old building across the street from Villa Santi *(see p222)*, the Tamnak Lao, also known as the Three Elephants, serves great Lao food at reasonable prices. The staff is friendly and accommodating. Try their steamed fish with local herbs, or the green curry with chicken. The Western and Thai food are worth trying as well.

CENTRAL LUANG PRABANG The Pizza $$$

Sisavang Vong Rd **Tel** *(071)-252-858* **City Map** *C3*

Located in the heart of Luang Prabang's foreign restaurants strip north of the Night Market *(see p156–7)*, The Pizza is a great place to visit after shopping. Popular with travelers, and quite big and busy, but service is efficient. Wide variety of pizzas on offer. It also serves Thai and Lao food.

CENTRAL LUANG PRABANG Utopia $$$

Ban Aphai on the Nam Khan **Tel** *(020)-5589-4394* **City Map** *C4*

A unique restaurant, Utopia has a large vaulted ceiling and an open-air *sala*, which is surrounded by smaller dining areas overlooking the river. Diners are seated on cushions at low tables. They serve good Western and Lao food and excellent cocktails. There is also a volleyball court on the premises.

CENTRAL LUANG PRABANG Arisai $$$$

49–3 Sakkarin Rd **Tel** *(071)-255-000* **City Map** *D3*

A well-conceived and stylish bistro specializing in Mediterranean cuisines, including the best merguez *cous cous* east of Morocco. It has two stories, you can either watch the open kitchen from the first floor, or dine upstairs where it is cool and quiet. The food is reasonably priced and highly recommended.

CENTRAL LUANG PRABANG Blue Lagoon Restaurant $$$$

Ban Choumkhong St **Tel** *(071)-253-698* **City Map** *D3*

Blue Lagoon has an elegant setting, both in the main villa restaurant and the garden pavilion overlooking a small pond and river. Here you'll find a welcome and unusual mix of Lao and European dishes, including imported steak, beef stroganoff and a variety of gourmet desserts.

CENTRAL LUANG PRABANG Tamarind $$$$

Koun Xoa Rd, Ban Vat Nong **Tel** *(020)-7777-0484* **City Map** *D3*

Probably the best place in town to try authentic Lao food cooked to a high standard without any fusion techniques. Tamarind specializes in tasting platters so the diner can get an idea of what to order. The herb barbecued whole fish stuffed with lemongrass is delicious. Open only until late afternoon. Also offers cooking classes.

CENTRAL LUANG PRABANG Apsara $$$$$

Kingkitsarat Rd, Ban Wat Sene **Tel** *(071)-254-670* **City Map** *D3*

Located in the beautifully decorated lobby of the hotel of the same name, Apsara overlooks the Nam Khan. This stylish restaurant offers Asian fusion done to accommodate Western tastes. Indian curries, *cous cous*, Lao dishes, and an excellent selection of salads and vegetarian fare feature on the menu.

CENTRAL LUANG PRABANG L'Elephant $$$$$

Ban Wat Nong, diagonally opposite the School of Fine Arts **Tel** *(071)-252-482* **City Map** *D3*

Widely considered the best restaurant in Luang Prabang, L'Elephant offers Lao, French, and fusion dishes, as well as a tasting menu. The decor is elegant, with white tablecloths and polished brass complemented by Lao antiques. They have their own vegetable and herb garden, which assures fresh and top-quality produce. Advance booking is advised.

CENTRAL LUANG PRABANG Les 3 Nagas $$$$$

Sakkarin Rd, Ban Vat Nong **Tel** *(071)-253-888* **City Map** *C3*

Situated in the hotel of the same name, Les 3 Nagas is managed by the L'Elephant restaurant but focuses on traditional Luang Prabang cuisine done to a high standard. Some of the dishes are based on the recipes of Phia Sing, the royal family's chef. There are also a few fusion dishes on the menu. The buffalo *laap* is delicious.

CENTRAL LUANG PRABANG Nava Mekong Cruise $$$$$

44/03 Suvannakhamphong Rd, Ban Vat Nong **Tel** *(071)-260-319* **City Map** *C3*

Dine aboard a teakwood cargo boat while cruising the Mekong River. The Nava Mekong Cruise offers buffet-style meals served with Lao specialties such as Mekong fish and Thai dishes such as *tom kha ghai*, a mild chicken curry in a coconut sauce flavored with galangal. The boat comfortably seats 40 passengers.

CENTRAL LUANG PRABANG Roots and Leaves $$$$$

Setthathirat Rd, across from The Amantaka **Tel** *(071)-254-870* **City Map** *C3*

Set in a natural garden filled with local fruit trees and a large pond with lotus plants, Roots and Leaves has a tasty set menu of Thai and Lao food. Dinnertime entertainment features everything from Lao folk dancing to classical music and a fashion show. Daytimes are quiet and pleasant, but without any entertainment.

NORTHERN LAOS

HUAY XAI Muang Nuea $$

Saykhong Rd **Road Map** *A2*

Right in the middle of town, next to the Gibbon Experience *(see p183)*, Muang Nuea is the top backpacker option in Huay Xai, and a great place to pick up the latest travel gossip. Both Lao and Western dishes are on offer and they are hearty and hygienically prepared.

HUAY XAI Nut Pop $$

Saykhong Rd **Tel** *(084)-211-037* **Road Map** *A2*

Located down a little dirt road at the northern end of town, Nut Pop does excellent Lao food, which is served in an open-air wooden *sala*. Not surprisingly, their specialty is fish, and the sauces they use are what sets them apart from other similar places.

HUAY XAI Nam Khong View $$$

Saykhong Rd **Tel** *(084)-212-238* **Road Map** *A2*

Situated south of town, this riverside restaurant is where locals go for a big night out. The views on the river are inspiring and the food is fine, with fish being the best choice. Around 9pm, romantic Lao tunes waft through the night air, courtesy of a local band.

LUANG NAM THA Manychan $$

Route 3 **Tel** *(086)-312-209* **Road Map** *B1*

Located in the main area of Luang Nam Tha *(see p180)*, across the street from the Night Market, Manychan is a favorite among foreign visitors, but the food is a step above what one usually finds in tourist-oriented places. Great steaks, pizza, and Lao food feature on the menu. They bake their own bread and make great cappuccino.

LUANG NAM THA Huean Lao $$$

Route 3 **Tel** *(086)-211-111* **Road Map** *B1*

A good place to try local specialties, Huean Lao serves excellent ant egg soup as well as more standard Lao fare such as chicken *laap*. The restaurant is situated in a polished wooden building at the northern end of town. Popular with locals, but offers an English menu too. No Western food served here.

LUANG NAM THA Banana Restaurant $$

Route 3 **Tel** *(086)-212-113* **Road Map** *B1*

A few hundred yards south of the Night Market on Route 3, Banana Restaurant is the place in Luang Nam Tha for a great Western breakfast. Good Lao, Thai, and French food served later in the day. A friendly and lively place, it has a pleasant terrace on the second floor, with sporting events telecast on a big-screen TV.

MUANG KHUA Nam Ou Guest House Restaurant $

Next to the boat landing **Tel** *(088)-210-844* **Road Map** *B1*

This eatery is a good choice for standard Western and Lao fare. The stir-fries made with the town's most important export, *nomai* (bamboo shoot), and chicken *laap*, are especially delicious. This place has nice views of the river and is a good place to exchange information with other travelers.

MUANG NGOI Ning Ning $$

Near the boat docks **Road Map** *B1*

Located in the small lane leading to the boat dock, Ning Ning serves good Lao and Western food. The river fish dishes are the best bet. A cool river breeze and good views make this a pleasant place to relax. The service is good, which in Muang Ngoi means they probably will not forget your order.

MUANG SING Jie Mei Restaurant $$

Route 17 **Road Map** *A1*

Situated across the street from the government tourist office in the center of town, Jie Mei Restaurant is the right choice if you are looking for reasonably priced Chinese food. Try the *yen cai chau ji rou* (minced chicken with pickled cabbage), or the tasty *ru bing* (fried cheese).

MUANG SING Thai Leu Restaurant $$

Route 17 **Tel** *(081)-212-375* **Road Map** *A1*

Located in an attractive, old French-era shophouse in the center of town, Thai Leu Restaurant serves authentic renditions of native cuisine. Thai Leu fare is quite similar to Northern Thai food, and revolves around spicy vegetable dips called *nam prik*, which are eaten with sticky rice. Standard Western and Lao food is also available.

NONG KHIAW Seng Dau Restaurant $

Ban Nong Khiaw **Tel** *(071)-810-001* **Road Map** *B1*

This open-air restaurant is located next to the river, just north of the bridge over the Nam Ou. Seng Dau Restaurant is good for simple Lao food and noodle soup breakfasts. It is a very basic establishment so do not expect anything fancy. Try the local fish *laap*.

Key to Price Guide *see p242*

NONG KHIAW Deen Restaurant $$

Ban Sop Houn **Road Map** *B1*

A wide selection of vegetable and meat curries are on offer at Deen Restaurant, accompanied by home-made naans and chapattis and your choice of *lassi* or cold beer. The open-air wooden structure is a nice place to sit on breezy evenings, which is fortunate because the service is not too rapid.

PAK BENG Khop Chai Deau $$

Facing the river, near the boat docks **Road Map** *A2*

This restaurant has no relation to the similarly named restaurant in Vientiane, but serves great food nevertheless. It specializes in Indian curries, and also offers Lao and Western food, including pizza. It gets lively in the evenings with travelers trading tales of boat trips on the Mekong. Enjoy beautiful views of the river from the outside deck.

PHONGSALI Phou Fa Restaurant $$

NW of the town center ***Tel*** *(020)-5569-5315* **Road Map** *B1*

If Phou Fa Restaurant seems like a fortress, it is because it was the Chinese consulate during the Laotian Civil War. The Lao and Chinese food on offer is decent, and views from the terrace beer garden superb. A fireplace warms the interior on cold nights. It is a steep climb to get here so some might want to take a tuk-tuk from town.

PHONSAVAN Simaly Restaurant $

Route 7 in center of town ***Tel*** *(061)-211-013* **Road Map** *C2*

This restaurant is very popular with local office workers, but attracts its fair share of foreign visitors as well. The cook makes attempts at Western dishes such as hamburgers, however, it is best to stick to the standard Thai/Lao stir-fries such as chicken with cashew nuts. The staff is friendly and the service prompt.

PHONSAVAN Maly Hotel Restaurant $$

Hai Hin Rd ***Tel*** *(061)-312-031* **Road Map** *C2*

Located a little away from the town center, but well known to taxi/tuk tuk drivers, Maly Hotel Restaurant offers both Lao and French food, including seasonal specialties such as wild mushrooms. Call ahead and speak with the owner, Mr Sousath, who can arrange a memorable meal and suggest esoteric itineraries for touring the area.

PHONSAVAN Auberge de Plaine des Jarres $$$

Phou Pha Deng Hill ***Tel*** *(020)-5517-2282* **Road Map** *C2*

Worth a visit even for those not staying at the lodge in which it is located. Excellent classic French food as well as Lao dishes. This lodge offers a cosy fireplace in the winter and a beautiful sundeck in warmer weather. The management can even arrange for you to be taken home at the end of your meal.

SAM NEUA Chittavanh Restaurant $$

Near the Nam Sam, between the bridge and the market ***Tel*** *(064)-312-265* **Road Map** *C2*

Situated on the first floor of the guesthouse of the same name, Chittavanh Restaurant is large by Sam Neua standards, so it is frequented by groups of visitors, but the locals like the tasty Lao and Vietnamese food on offer as well. The service can be uncommunicative, but they seem to get the orders right.

SAM NEUA Dan Nao Restaurant $$

Just north of the bridge ***Tel*** *(064)-314-126* **Road Map** *C2*

Nothing fancy about this establishment, but Dan Nao Restaurant serves clean and tasty food, including Lao and Western fare. Service is friendly and prompt and the menu is in English. They open quite early, which is useful for those heading out on a day trip to the Vieng Xai caves *(see p174)*.

VANG VIENG Arena Restaurant and Bar $$

Ban Savang ***Tel*** *(020)-7818-1171* **Road Map** *B2*

Arena is a welcome respite from the tropical heat, with an air-conditioned downstairs café and an open-air balcony above, offering great views of Vang Vieng nightlife. Open early for breakfast and late into the evening, it serves mainly Western backpacker comfort food, with a few Lao favorites.

VANG VIENG Nokeo $$

Across from the old market ***Tel*** *(020)-2241-1203* **Road Map** *B2*

This long-standing establishment is a perennial favorite, both with travelers and locals. Nokeo is the place to come for good Lao food such as *laap* and *ping paa* (grilled fish). The decor is not anything to write home about, but the food is authentic and hygienically prepared.

VANG VIENG La Veranda Riverside $$$

Inside Villa Nam Song Resort ***Tel*** *(023)-511-637* **Road Map** *B2*

As the name promises, the location affords lovely views of the river, but the quality of the food is what attracts diners. The chef is Thai, and does great Thai curries, such as Penang, as well as credible French cuisine, including a particularly tasty ratatouille for vegetarians. Excellent desserts and a good wine list are also on offer.

VANG VIENG Organic Farm Restaurant $$$

Off Route 13 at km 159 ***Tel*** *(023)-511-220* **Road Map** *B2*

The Organic Farm Restaurant has its own organic vegetable garden. It has an excellent set menu of Lao foods, but good à la carte dishes as well, and the chef spices dishes according to the diner's choice. Tasty goat's cheese and free-range chicken are available too.

CENTRAL & SOUTHERN LAOS

CHAMPASAK Dok Champa Restaurant $$

Ban Wat Amard **Road Map** *D5*

Of all the basic eateries in Champasak, Dok Champa Restaurant gets the best reviews for tasty and hygienically prepared food. They do credible Western food and the Lao dishes, particularly the fish-based ones, are good. The views of the river from this open-air *sala* are superb.

CHAMPASAK Inthira Restaurant & Bar $$$

Ban Wat Amard ***Tel*** *(031)-214-059* **Road Map** *D5*

The atmosphere in this restored Chinese shophouse is quite aesthetic and the bartender knows how to make good cocktails. The chefs are trained in the famous Khop Chai Deu restaurant *(see p242)* in Vientiane and they prepare a wide variety of tasty Western and Lao dishes.

DON DAENG La Folie Lodge $$$$

NW coast of Don Daeng ***Tel*** *(020)-5553-2004* **Road Map** *D5*

For those not staying in Don Daeng, this is an interesting excursion for dinner. The food at La Folie Lodge is exquisite, and includes classic French dishes, a good dessert menu, and a fine wine list. To get here you can hire a boat in Champasak for a roundtrip.

DON KHON Seng Ahloune Restaurant $

Next to Wat Khon Tai ***Tel*** *(030)-534-5807* **Road Map** *D5*

Located just south of the bridge connecting Don Det and Don Khon, this energetically operated place offers good basic traveler's dishes, including Western, Lao, and Vietnamese food. It gets busy at lunch during the high season since it is on the itinerary of day trips to the island.

DON KHONG Phoukhong Restaurant $$

Ban Khangkhong ***Tel*** *(031)-213-673* **Road Map** *D5*

On the river just north of the main central square of Muang Khong, Phoukhong Restaurant seems to try a bit harder than its peers along this strip of guesthouses and restaurants. They do all the backpacker standards of Western food and the Lao food is particularly well spiced.

DON KHONG Auberge Sala Don Khong $$$

Ban Khangkhong ***Tel*** *(031)-212-077* **Road Map** *D5*

Situated by the river, just downstream from the main central square of Muang Khong, this restaurant serves the best Western food on the island and their Lao dishes are also prepared with a special finesse not found in the lesser eateries. It is best to call in advance both for a reservation and dinner suggestions.

PAKSE Delta Coffee $$

Route 13 ***Tel*** *(030)-534-5895* **Road Map** *D5*

A bit out of the town center, Delta Coffee is worth the trip for its excellent Lao and Italian food at reasonable prices. The owners also have a coffee plantation in Paksong, so the coffee served here is reputed to be the best in Pakse. The staff is lively and attentive. They serve good breakfasts and pastries as well.

PAKSE Jasmine $$

Corner of Road 12 and Route 13 ***Tel*** *(031)-251-002* **Road Map** *D5*

A backpacker favorite in Pakse for budget Indian cuisine, Jasmine is in battle for patrons with a rival across the street, which is to the benefit of customers. The menu is long, and pretty much everything is good, although nothing is outstanding.

PAKSE Khem Kong Restaurant $$$

On the Mekong River ***Tel*** *(031)-213-240* **Road Map** *D5*

No trip to Pakse is complete without a visit to a Mekong River boat restaurant and this restaurant is considered the best in terms of food and accessibility for foreigners. There is a good English menu. The views and the breeze are the main attractions, as is the wide variety of fish on offer. Good for families and large groups.

PAKSE Na Dao Restaurant $$$

Just north of the Japanese Bridge **Road Map** *D5*

An air of elegance, not easily found elsewhere in Pakse, permeates the Na Dao Restaurant. The quality of the cuisine, which includes Lao-French fusion dishes, is also very good. It also has a good wine list. Located across the street from the Champasak Grand Hotel *(see p225)*, heading north.

PAKSE Pakse Hotel Roof Garden $$$

St 5 ***Tel*** *(031)-212-131* **Road Map** *D5*

You can enjoy panoramic views from the Pakse Hotel Roof Garden, located in the well-known Pakse Hotel *(see p225)*. A great place for a sundown drink and the barbecue is also good. The French owner's Lao wife does her best to keep the staff active and attentive. Good selection of cocktails and daily specials.

Key to Price Guide *see p242*

SAVANNAKHET Anakhot $$

Ratsawongseuk Rd **Road Map** *C4*

The name means "future" and there is a unique vibe to this little eatery, which serves everything from sushi to Lao food in a pleasant and relaxing atmosphere. Its mission is to support the community, running a project for local women to create handicrafts that are sold in the café. Come for refreshing herbal teas, fruit shakes and Wi-Fi.

SAVANNAKHET Hoongthip Garden Restaurant $$

Phetsarath Rd ***Tel*** *(041)-212-262* **Road Map** *C4*

Located in an attractive open-air *sala* next to the Hoongthip Hotel *(see p225)*, the Hoongthip Garden Restaurant is the best place in Savannakhet to enjoy top-quality Lao, Thai, Vietnamese, and Chinese food. Try the duck *laap* or the steamed fish with herbs, but avoid their attempts at Western food. Popular and sometimes noisy, but fun.

SAVANNAKHET Café Chez Boune $$$

Chaimeuang Rd ***Tel*** *(041)-215-190* **Road Map** *C4*

Popular among locals who wish to experiment with Western food, as well as expats, Café Chez Boune does great pizzas, salads, and steaks (beef, lamb, and salmon). It has a delectable dessert menu as well. Also serves Lao food and delicious Western-style breakfasts. Both the atmosphere and decor are pleasant.

SAVANNAKHET Lao Lao Der $$$

Nakae Village ***Tel*** *(041)-212-270* **Road Map** *C4*

Located a mile upstream from the bridge over the Mekong River, the Lao Lao Der serves Lao and Thai food prepared to international standards, served by the breezy riverside. It is a big place, good for groups and families, and particularly lively in the evenings.

SAVANNAKHET Dao Savanh Restaurant $$$$

Simuang Rd ***Tel*** *(041)-260-888* **Road Map** *C4*

Located on the quiet central square of Savannakhet in an old Colonial mansion, the Dao Savanh Restaurant serves classic French cuisine, including some rather exotic specialties such as lobster flambéed in whiskey. A good fixed-price lunch menu that changes daily and an excellent selection of wines and desserts complete the picture.

TAT LO Tadlo Lodge $$$

Ban Tanglea, Route 20, Lao Ngam District ***Tel*** *(034)-211-089* **Road Map** *D5*

The food here is served in a nice airy *sala* surrounded by trees. Anyone in this part of the Bolaven Plateau *(see p198)*, will probably be staying here, but if not, drop in for some of the best food in the area. They offer Western and Lao dishes and maintain a high standard of cleanliness. The service is amiable if not totally efficient.

THAKHEK Phavilai Restaurant $

Nam Phu Fountain Square **Road Map** *D3*

Located at the downriver Mekong end of the fountain square, the simple Phavilai Restaurant serves a good variety of basic but hygienically prepared Lao, Chinese, and Vietnamese fare. The staff is happy to oblige their customers with barbecued chicken from street-side vendors. Keep a lookout for riverside tables.

THAKHEK Sabaidee Thakhek $$

Nam Phu Fountain Square ***Tel*** *(020) 5654-6690* **Road Map** *D3*

Run by an Englishman and his Lao wife, Sabaidee Thakhek offers a good selection of Western, Lao, and even Vietnamese dishes in a clean and pleasant shophouse looking out on to the usually dry fountain of Thakhek. Book exchange service and BBC on the cable TV are also available.

THAKHEK Inthira Hotel $$$

Chao Anou Rd ***Tel*** *(051)-251-237* **Road Map** *D3*

Located in front of the hotel, this restaurant has its staff trained by the well-known Khop Chai Deu restaurant *(see p242)* in Vientiane, so the quality and presentation is good. Inthira Hotel serves everything from pizza to Lao food, and excellent breakfasts as well. The bar makes good cocktails.

THAKHEK Smile Raft Restaurant $$$

Mekong River ***Tel*** *(051)-212-150* **Road Map** *D3*

This is the best of several floating restaurants on the river in Thakhek and easy to locate by the red neon smiling sign. The food is all Lao, but there is an English menu. If being on the river does not appeal, part of the restaurant is now land-based, across the street from the original.

THAM KONG LO Mu Thuna II $$

Outside park entrance on the left ***Tel*** *(020)-224-0182* **Road Map** *C3*

Now that the road to Tham Kong Lo is sealed, the owners of Mu Thuna II have set up shop here. It has a nice open-air *sala* surrounded by trees, offering Thai and international favorites. It serves the best food in the village. The chicken steak is worth a try.

XE PIAN NPA Kingfisher Ecolodge $$$

Ban Khiet Ngong ***Tel*** *(020)-5572-6315* **Road Map** *D5*

Located in a lovely two-level, wooden, open-air *sala* overlooking a pond, the Kingfisher Ecolodge's restaurant serves a wide variety of Western and Lao food with an emphasis on vegetarian and organic dishes. The owner is Italian so there is a good selection of Italian cuisine, including home-made pasta.

SHOPPING IN CAMBODIA

Cambodia is fast becoming a shopper's paradise with expensive, upscale boutiques and malls sharing space with noisy markets and street stalls. Over the last 15 years, successful jewelry designers and painters, who grew up overseas, have returned, adding to the country's burgeoning growth of arts and crafts. Atmospheric markets offer a wide variety of ceramics, silk *kramas* (scarves), curios, silverware, statuary and carvings, brass rubbings, and paintings. Cambodian silk is prized the world over and shoppers can strike some great bargains in markets where prices are flexible and friendly haggling the norm. Those looking for more exclusive purchases will not be disappointed in the stylish shops that proliferate the shopping districts of major cities.

Ceramic figurine, Russian Market

OPENING HOURS

Most shops in the cities open at 7:30am and usually close by 6pm. They also close for a couple of hours for lunch from 11am. Markets in Phnom Penh and Siem Reap operate from sunrise to sunset and are best visited after the morning rush. Some markets also shut for public holidays. All shops and markets are open through the week and on weekends.

HOW TO PAY

Cash is the most readily accepted means of payment with most upscale stores also accepting credit cards. The US dollar is accepted throughout the country, and many premium shops often quote prices in dollars rather than the local riel. Areas along the eastern border, close to Thailand, also accept the baht.

Haggling is part of Khmer culture and happens everywhere – with vendors, tuk-tuk and *moto* drivers, in local markets, hotels, and shops – but it is unlikely to be the norm in high-end establishments. If bargaining is done in the right manner – with a friendly and calm disposition – you can catch yourself a real steal. Remember that prices are inflated to begin with and the vendor expects you to bargain.

Visitors browsing through the merchandise, Russian Market

RIGHTS AND REFUNDS

As a general rule, once sold, goods are not taken back. In malls, however, where certain items come with a warranty, exchange or refund is possible. Similarly, boutiques owned by foreigners may be more willing to take back damaged goods.

DEPARTMENT STORES AND MALLS

Increasingly popular in Phnom Penh and Siem Reap, department stores and malls offer stiff competition to traditional markets. The capital has three malls, the newest of them being the **City Mall**. **Sovanna**, a department store, and **Sorya**, the oldest and most Western-style mall are located south of the Central Market. Siem Reap's plush **Museum Mall** and **Angkor Trade Shopping Mall** are home to stylish boutiques, electronic shops, and eateries.

SHOPPING STREETS AND DISTRICTS

Phnom Penh's Street 178, running parallel to the road near the National Museum, is known for its sculpture shops and art galleries. There are also a number of handicraft artisans here as well as silk boutiques.

Store selling antique figurines and other carvings, Psar Chaa

Nearby, Sisowath Quay has a rich selection of boutiques, galleries, and bookshops. The charming Boeung Keng Kang area, long considered the foreigner's quarter, has many shops, massage spas, and posh silk boutiques.

Quality boutiques have also blossomed all over Siem Reap, particularly in the old French Quarter, with a wide range of jewelers, tailors, picture galleries, artisans, and shops specializing in luxury home decor. While these shops are not cheap, they reflect the excellence of their artists, many of whom are widely respected outside the country.

MARKETS AND STREET VENDORS

The best places to shop and experience an authentic slice of Cambodian life is in one of its markets. The bustling bazaars of Phnom Penh include the **Russian Market**, **Central Market**, and **Psar Russei**. Siem Reap's well-known markets include **Psar Chaa**, next to the old French Quarter, and the **Angkor Night Market**, which is replete with jewelry stalls, food vendors, and handicrafts, as well as a thatched bar.

ARTS AND CRAFTS

Produced all over the country, Cambodia's arts and crafts include a wide variety of finely wrought silver, gems, *kramas*, wood carvings, stone sculptures, and antiques. **Apsara Art Gallery** has a range of contemporary Southeast Asian art, while **Asasax Art Gallery** celebrates the unique paintings of its contemporary artist Asasax. Silk products can be bought at **CYK Handicrafts**, an NGO, or **Couleurs d'Asie**. **Artisans d'Angkor** make wood and stone carvings worth buying. Visitors can also head to **Mekong Quilts**, for quilts made by rural women.

CLOTHING

Apart from traditional clothes, Cambodia also offers a wide variety of designer garments in outlets such as **Bliss**, which also tailor clothes. Visitors can avail of similar services at **Cherry Blossom Boutique** and **Tom and Alice Tailor**. Attractive T-shirts, sold at **Mulberry Boutique** and **Bambou Company Indochine**, make for memorable souvenirs. Yet another great place to pick up stylish clothes is **Pich Reamker Shop**.

Swatches of silks on display at Artisans d'Angkor

CERAMICS AND LACQUERWARE

Traditional Khmer lacquerware continues to flourish today through organizations such as Artisans d'Angkor where visitors can not only observe the process of making lacquerware, but also buy the finished product. **The National Centre for Khmer Ceramics Revival** is another organization from where visitors can pick up some beautiful souvenirs.

COUNTERFEIT GOODS

Cambodians selling silverware or other silver artifacts in markets are more often than not hawking poor quality products or fakes. If a silver product, for instance, does not weigh much in your hand, it is likely to have a low silver content and should not be priced very high. Visitors should be wary of traders claiming to sell original artifacts from Angkor. This is not only illegal, as it robs the country of its heritage, but also likely to be fake.

DIRECTORY

DEPARTMENT STORES AND MALLS

Angkor Trade Shopping Mall
Pokambor Ave, Old Market area, Siem Reap.
Tel *(063)-766-766.*

City Mall
Monireth Blvd, Phnom Penh. **City Map** B3.
Tel *(023)-883-137.*

Museum Mall
Next to Angkor National Museum, Siem Reap.
Tel *(063)-966-616.*

Sorya
Sts 63 and 154, Phnom Penh. **City Map** D2.
Tel *(023)-883-137.*

Sovanna
Building 307–309, St 271, Phnom Penh. **City Map** B5. ***Tel*** *(023)-883-137.*

MARKETS

Angkor Night Market
Off Sivatha Blvd, Siem Reap. ***Tel*** *(092)-654-315.* **www**.angkornightmarket.com

Central Market
N of St 63, Phnom Penh. **City Map** D2.

Psar Chaa
French Quarter, Siem Reap.

Psar Russei
Between Charles De Gaulle Blvd and St 182, Phnom Penh.
City Map C2.

Russian Market
S of Mao Tse Toung Blvd, Phnom Penh.
City Map B5.

ARTS AND CRAFTS

Apsara Art Gallery
170A, St 450, Phnom Penh. ***Tel*** *(012)-867-390.*

Artisans d'Angkor
Off Sivatha Blvd, near Old Market, Siem Reap. ***Tel*** *(063)-963-330.* **www**.artisansdangkor.com

Asasax Art Gallery
192, St 178, Phnom Penh.
City Map D2.
Tel *(023)-217-793.*
www.asasaxart.com.kh

Couleurs d'Asie
St 240, Phnom Penh.
City Map D3.
Tel *(023)-221-075.*

CYK Handicrafts
67, Sothearos Blvd, Phnom Penh. **City Map** F3.
Tel *(023)-210-849.*

Mekong Quilts
49, St 240, Phnom Penh.
City Map D3.
Tel *(023)-219-607.*

CLOTHING

Bambou Company Indochine
Lucky Mall, Sivatha Blvd, Siem Reap.
Tel *(063)-966-822.*

Bliss
St 240, Phnom Penh.
City Map D3.
Tel *(023)-215-754.*

Cherry Blossom Boutique
St 10, Siem Reap.
Tel *(012)-320-568.*

Mulberry Boutique
On corner of sts 51 and 278, Phnom Penh.
City Map E3.
Tel *(016)-222-750.*

Pich Reamker Shop
Museum Mall, Siem Reap.
Tel *(012)-876-863.*

Tom and Alice Tailor
153, St 278, Phnom Penh.
Tel *(012)-796-286.*

CERAMICS AND LACQUERWARE

The National Centre for Khmer Ceramics Revival (NCKCR)
Charles De Gaulle Blvd, Siem Reap. ***Tel*** *(012)-761-519.* **www**.khmerceramics.com

SHOPPING IN LAOS

In recent years, shopping venues in Laos have increased both in number and variety. Goods on offer range from handwoven rice baskets, commonly found in wet markets, to splendid silk clothing and souvenirs in fancy boutiques. Luang Prabang's Night Market is well known for excellent, locally woven textiles, clothing, and bags. Fair-trade companies help villagers market their goods, although buying direct from a street vendor benefits the local economy. Items, particularly handicrafts, from neighboring countries such as Thailand and Vietnam also find their way here. As a rule, it is best to visit a number of shops selling the same product before going ahead and buying it. Visitors should not expect shopping malls in Laos, nor guarantees or certificates of authenticity.

Bag made of locally woven textiles

Stalls selling goods made by ethnic minorities, Night Market, Luang Prabang

MARKETS AND STREET VENDORS

Every town in Laos has a local market, which is always worth a visit. There are several different markets, some selling dry goods such as textiles and clothing, and others for fresh, local produce. While these markets usually cater to locals and do not have much variety for a visitor, they are good places to find authentic local products. Street markets catering to foreign visitors are often set up in the evening and usually offer products made by Laos's ethnic minorities. Luang Prabang's Night Market, set up along Sisavang Vong Road, is quite popular. In Vientiane, similar markets such as Fa Ngum Quay by the river and Talat Sao sell a variety of products from across the country.

BARGAINING

There are no fixed prices in Laos, but the biggest margin for bargaining is in goods for sale in local markets and boutiques. Bargaining must be done with a smile and buyers can be prepared to walk away as they are sure to find the same thing elsewhere. It is always best to have an idea of an item's price before bargaining. It is also not worth bargaining for small sums since the kip, when converted, is worth very little.

TEXTILES

Laos's handwoven silk and cotton textiles are beautiful, and can be priced quite exorbitantly at times. Each province has its own unique style, with those from Hua Phan in the northeast considered the most delicate. Lao textiles can be tailored into Western-style garments, but they look best in traditional shapes such as a long skirt. Older pieces should be avoided as they are fragile. The geometric appliqué work done by members of the Hmong community on everything, from bedspreads to bedroom slippers, is also attractive and relatively less expensive since it is not handwoven. In Luang Prabang, **Kopnoi** and **Ock Pop Tok** are good sources for innovative designs. **Carol Cassidy Lao Textiles** and **Satri Lao Silks**, in Vientiane, make textiles in more traditional forms.

ANTIQUES

Since fakes abound, it is best to leave the purchase of antiques to experienced buyers who are able to discern an original from a reproduction.

Variety of handwoven silk garments on display at a shop, Ban Xang Khong

Baskets and other goods made of bamboo and rattan, Luang Prabang

Buyers should avoid anything of a religious nature since it may have been stolen from a temple; besides, exporting religious art is illegal in Laos. True antique objects such as porcelain, especially from China, musical instruments, jewelry, wood carvings, and bronze statues are generally illegal to buy and export without a permit. Items such as bank notes, stamps, coins, or medals associated with the previous regime are more likely to be authentic. The best source for buying antiques in Luang Prabang is **Phatana Boupha Antique House**. **Tha Vee Souk** also has an impressive collection of original antiques. Visitors to Vientiane can head to **Indochina Old House** or **Mandalay Furniture**.

HANDICRAFTS

The Lao people are expert weavers of baskets, which they make from both rattan and bamboo. The *tip khaw* (woven rice baskets), used for storing sticky rice, are inexpensive and attractive. Laos is renowned for its wood carvings, which are also worth considering, although visitors should check their quality carefully. Another indigenous product is *sa* paper, which is produced from the bark of mulberry trees. This paper is used to craft beautiful lanterns and other decorative items, which make for great souvenirs. Lacquered parasols made from bamboo, and ceramics are also considered good buys. The upscale **Caruso Lao** in Luang Prabang does fantastic work in carved wood, and **Blue House** has great *sa* paper creations. Shops in Vientiane worth visiting include **Phai Exclusive Crafts**, which sells a wide collection of traditional crafts and **T'shop Lai Gallery**, with its unusual handicraft items.

JEWELRY

Gold and silver jewelry is readily available in the markets of Laos, often sold in brightly lit, red-colored shops. Both are usually sold by weight, with an additional charge depending on the workmanship of the item. Gold is almost always the 24-karat variety with a dull luster popular in Asia, but there are varying qualities of silver with no fixed standard.

Among the best buys are jewelry pieces made by ethnic communities, which though usually rough, are quite unique. Probably the most attractive item is the silver belt, which looks best paired with the traditional *pha sin* wrap-around skirt worn by Lao women. Few gemstones of quality are mined in Laos, so unless you are an expert at recognizing these, avoid buying them. In Luang Prabang, **Naga Creations** is considered to be the place to go to for modern creations, but **Thithpeng Maniphone Silversmiths** is a master silversmith of traditional jewelry of high quality. **Bari Gems & Jewelry** and **Saigon Bijoux**, in Vientiane, offer diverse collections of tempting pieces.

Gemstone-studded earring

DIRECTORY

TEXTILES

Carol Cassidy Lao Textiles
Ban Mixay, Vientiane. **City Map** B3. ***Tel*** *(021)-212-123.* **www**.laotextiles.com

Kopnoi
Across Ban Aphay Primary School, Luang Prabang. **City Map** C4. ***Tel*** *(071)-260-248.*

Ock Pop Tok
Ban Wat Nong, Luang Prabang. **City Map** D2. ***Tel*** *(071)-253-219.* **www**.ockpoptok.com

Satri Lao Silks
Setthathirat Rd, Vientiane. **City Map** B4. ***Tel*** *(021)-219-295.*

ANTIQUES

Indochina Old House
Setthathirat Rd, Vientiane. ***Tel*** *(021)-223-528.*

Mandalay Furniture
Francois Ngin Rd, Vientiane. **City Map** B4. ***Tel*** *(021)-218-738.*

Phatana Boupha Antique House
Across from Wat Visounarat, Luang Prabang. **City Map** D4. ***Tel*** *(071)-212-262.*

Tha Vee Souk
Sisavang Vong Rd, Luang Prabang. **City Map** C3. ***Tel*** *(071)-260-425.*

HANDICRAFTS

Blue House
Sakkarin Rd, Luang Prabang. **City Map** D3. ***Tel*** *(071)-252-383.*

Caruso Lao
Sakkarin Rd, Luang Prabang. **City Map** D3. ***Tel*** *(071)-254-574.* **www**.carusolao.com

Phai Exclusive Crafts
Lao Plaza Hotel, Vientiane. **City Map** C3. ***Tel*** *(020)-547-6700.*

T'shop Lai Gallery
Behind Wat Inpaeng, Vientiane. **City Map** B3. ***Tel*** *(021)-223-178.* **www**.laococo.com

JEWELRY

Bari Gems & Jewelry
Samsenthai Rd, opposite Asian Pavilion Hotel, Vientiane. **City Map** C3. ***Tel*** *(021)-212-680.*

Naga Creations
Sisavang Vong Rd, Luang Prabang. **City Map** C3. ***Tel*** *(020)-777-5005.*

Saigon Bijoux
Samsenthai Rd, Vientiane. **City Map** C3. ***Tel*** *(021)-214-783.*

Thithpeng Maniphone Silversmiths
Ban Wat That, Luang Prabang. **City Map** B4. ***Tel*** *(071)-212-925.*

Entertainment in Cambodia

The country's entertainment industry was destroyed by the Khmer Rouge. However, since the late 1970s, Cambodia has steadily begun to bounce back with a new generation of contemporary artists and a Thai-Chinese influenced pop music scene. Cinema is also making a steady, if slower, return to form. More traditional arts, such as the *apsara* dance closely linked to the artistic zenith of Angkor, are being heavily promoted. Contemporary and traditional music can be heard across the capital and smaller cities, while Cambodia's top new wave of musicians often perform at restaurants situated across the Japanese Bridge in Phnom Penh.

Dancers performing the traditional *apsara* dance, Cambodia

INFORMATION AND BOOKING TICKETS

The city guides published by Canby Publications provide up-to-date information on the best bars, clubs, musical and theatrical events taking place in Phnom Penh, Siem Reap, and Sihanoukville. These guides are also free of charge. The daily English-language newspaper *The Phnom Penh Post* is a useful city guide. *Bayon Pearnik*, a free monthly magazine, also contains listings for local events and places to eat. Booking tickets in advance is not common in Cambodia, but most tour agents and hotels can easily do this for you.

TRADITIONAL DANCE, THEATER, AND FILM

Cambodia's traditional music and dance has seen a poignant return to form. The **Sovanna Phum Arts Association** stages traditional dancing and puppet theater every Friday and Saturday at 7:30pm. Traditional and folk dances can also be seen at the **Apsara Arts Association** every Saturday at 7:30pm. Films are screened at **Cinema Lux** and **Centre Culturel Français**.

CONTEMPORARY MUSIC, NIGHTCLUBS, AND BARS

The capital has a wide range of bars, cafés, and nightclubs. Live music enthusiasts have a couple of options, including the **Art Café** with its blues nights and classical Khmer music, and **Miles**, a rooftop jazz café. Performances of Khmer pop music take place in a number of the large, new hotels in Phnom Penh. **Green Vespa** is a down-to-earth, Irish-owned bar with a friendly atmosphere. Visitors seeking contemporary chic can head to the **Fly Lounge**, which has a cocktail lounge and a boutique pool. On the other hand, the **Foreign Correspondents' Club** has a friendly, yet sophisticated Colonial ambience. **Sharky's Bar** is one of the city's older sports bars with pool tables and a great bar. Siem Reap also has a range of bars and elegant watering holes. **Molly Malone's** is a typical Irish bar selling Guinness for thirsty visitors while **Miss Wong** trades on the nostalgia of 1920s Shanghai. **Angkor What?** has loud music to match its effusive atmosphere. **The Elephant Bar** at Raffles Grand Hotel d'Angkor is the epitome of style and elegance.

DIRECTORY

TRADITIONAL DANCE, THEATER AND FILM

Apsara Arts Association
71, St 598, Phnom Penh. *Tel (023)-990-621.* www.apsara-art.org

Cinema Lux
44 Norodom Blvd, Phnom Penh. **City Map** E2. *Tel (012)-343-498.*

Centre Culturel Français
218, St 184, Phnom Penh. **City Map** D3. *Tel (023)-213-124.* www.ccf-cambodge.org

Sovanna Phum Arts Association
111, St 360, Chamkarmon, Phnom Penh. *Tel (023)-987-564.* www.shadow-puppets.org

CONTEMPORARY MUSIC, NIGHTCLUBS, AND BARS

Angkor What?
Pub St, Siem Reap. *Tel (012)-490-755.*

Art Café
84, St 108, Phnom Penh. **City Map** D1. *Tel (012)-834-517.*

The Elephant Bar
Raffles Grand Hotel d'Angkor, Siem Reap. www.raffles.com

Fly Lounge
St 148, Phnom Penh. **City Map** E2.

Foreign Correspondents' Club
363 Sisowath Quay, Phnom Penh. **City Map** E2. *Tel (023)-210-142.* www.fcccambodia.com

Green Vespa
95 Sisowath Quay, Phnom Penh. **City Map** E1.

Miles
310, St 113, Phnom Penh. **City Map** C4. *Tel (011)-698-470.*

Miss Wong
Passage (behind Pub St), Siem Reap. *Tel (092)-428-332.*

Molly Malone's
Pub St, Siem Reap. *Tel (063)-963-533.* www.mollymalonescambodia.com

Sharky's Bar
126, St 130, Phnom Penh. **City Map** E1. *Tel (012)-228-045.* www.sharkysofcambodia.com

Entertainment in Laos

The entertainment scene in Laos is fairly sedate since the government strictly regulates both closing times and the content of performances. There was a time when any music considered modern or foreign was prohibited. Since 2003, however, the government has relaxed its stance and Lao pop has emerged with a number of home-grown artistes. Vientiane has the widest choice of entertainment venues, followed by Luang Prabang. In smaller towns, things get very quiet after sunset. Performances of Lao classical music and dance, along with Lao folk music are staged in the capital and Luang Prabang, giving visitors a glimpse into Lao culture.

Visitors enjoying the laid-back atmosphere of a popular bar, Laos

INFORMATION

A free local monthly pocket-sized magazine called *Pai Sai*, found in hotels and restaurants in Vientiane, publishes listings of music, sports, drama, and film events. Visitors can even get a daily SMS from the magazine with updates, provided they have a Lao SIM card for their cell phone. The government-owned *Vientiane Times* has a limited but useful selection of upcoming events, as does the monthly magazine *Society Lifestyle*. Other than this, small posters on lampposts around the tourist areas of Vientiane and Luang Prabang can be quite informative regarding upcoming events.

A musician playing a So I

TRADITIONAL DANCE AND THEATER

Both the classical culture represented by the *Phra Lak Phra Lam*, the Lao version of the Hindu epic, *Ramayana*, and the popular culture of Lao folk music, with its hypnotic rhythms, are interesting options. Performances of the *Phra Lak Phra Lam* can be seen at the **Lao National Opera Theatre** in Vientiane, as well as in Luang Prabang at the **Royal Ballet Theatre** within the grounds of the National Museum Complex. Folk music is also staged at these venues, but for a taste of the real thing, travelers should try to visit a temple fair, where audience participation in the form of the *lam wong* dance takes the performance to another level.

FILMS AND ART EXHIBITIONS

Although DVDs have spelled the end of cinemas in Laos, foreign films are still shown by the cultural arms of certain embassies such as the **French Center**, and those of Japan, and Germany, but subtitles are not always in English. It is also worth visiting the **ITECC**, a local trade and convention center. Art exhibitions are found in embassy cultural centers, and there are plenty of private galleries in Vientiane and Luang Prabang displaying the work of Lao artists.

CONTEMPORARY MUSIC, DISCOS, AND BARS

Vientiane and, to some extent, Luang Prabang have a growing nightlife. Although travelers tend to stick to hotel discos, the **Wind West** has good live music. The biggest disco, **Marina Disco**, also has a bowling alley. The **Khop Chai Deu** restaurant in Vientiane also has live music. In Luang Prabang, hotel cocktail lounges trump discos, although **The Hive** offers more upbeat music and an ethnic fashion show.

DIRECTORY

TRADITIONAL DANCE AND THEATER

Lao National Opera Theatre
Khun Bulom Rd, Vientiane.
City Map B3. ***Tel*** *(021)-260-300.*

Royal Ballet Theatre
National Museum Complex, Luang Prabang. **City Map** C3.
Tel *(071)-253-705.*

FILMS AND ART EXHIBITIONS

French Center
Lan Xang Avenue, Vientiane.
City Map D3. ***Tel*** *(021)-214-764.*

ITECC
Khampheng Muang Rd, Vientiane.
City Map B5. ***Tel*** *(021)-415-477.*

CONTEMPORARY MUSIC, DISCOS, AND BARS

The Hive
Across Wat Aphay, Phou Si Rd, Luang Prabang. **City Map** D3.
Tel *(071)-212-880.*

Khop Chai Deu
Setthathirat Rd, Vientiane.
City Map B4. ***Tel*** *(021)-223-022.*
www.khopchaideu.com

Marina Disco
Luang Prabang Rd, Vientiane.
City Map A5. ***Tel*** *(021)- 216-978.*

Wind West
Luang Prabang Rd, Vientiane.
City Map A5. ***Tel*** *(021)-200-777.*

OUTDOOR ACTIVITIES AND SPECIAL INTERESTS IN CAMBODIA

With its natural heritage of rivers, lakes, mountains, and a pristine coastline, Cambodia offers a wide variety of activities. While eco-trekking is developing in the northern wilderness, the western provinces offer wonderful camping excursions in safari-style tents coupled with trekking among ancient ruins. The beaches of the south are perfect for snorkeling, diving, deep-sea fishing, sailing, and windsurfing. Rolling hills and paddy fields also present superb opportunities for cyclists. Ornithologists and marine life enthusiasts can enjoy exploring the natural wonders of the Tonlé Sap Lake, which attracts a rich variety of endangered waterbirds. Those seeking a more relaxed holiday will not be disappointed by the meditation sessions and massages offered at upscale spas.

Sign at a dive shop, Phnom Penh

DIVING AND SNORKELING

Cambodia's fresh and clear waters, home to moray eels, barracuda, scorpion fish, lion fish, parrot fish, octopus, reef shark, dolphins, and whales are a haven for divers. The seaside resort of Sihanoukville is perhaps the best place to undertake these trips, ideally between October and June, when underwater visibility is between 33–82 ft (10–25 m). With their rich, coral-encrusted reefs, the islands of Koh Rong Samloem and Koh Koun, lying a short distance from Sihanoukville, are among the best-known dive sites in Cambodia. Those with more time can venture farther out to Koh Tang, Koh Prins, and Condor Reef. There are several dive centers in Phnom Penh, including a number of authorized PADI (Professional Association of Diving Instructors) centers. All of them organize trips of varying lengths, for different levels of experience. Those not keen on diving can ask centers to arrange day-long snorkeling trips.

Among the better-known centers are **Scuba Nation**, who pioneered diving in the country; **Angkor Dive**, Cambodia's first conservation-based dive center, **Eco Sea Dive**, and **The Dive Shop**.

Snorkeler with a whale shark, Sihanoukville

SAILING, KITESURFING, AND FISHING

Watersports are becoming increasingly popular in Cambodia, and Sihanoukville, with access to four great beaches, is the hub of all water-based activity. Kitesurfing, a relatively new and still evolving sport in the country, is offered by **Hurricane Windsurfing** on Otres Beach. It is one of the few places from where you can hire windsurf boards. **Otres Nautica** rents out catamarans, lasers, and sea kayaks, as well as small fishing speedboats. A number of reliable outfits such as **Sankeor**, **Sun Tours**, and **Trade Winds Charters** also offer fishing of barracudas and marlins in the deep sea. Fishing trips can last for a day or several days, depending on the time available, and the rates are usually quite reasonable.

Sailing in Sihanoukville

KAYAKING

Sea-kayaking is still finding its feet in Cambodia with only a few places offering kayaks for rent. Otres Nautica and **The Golden Sunset**, both on Otres Beach, can organize boat tours to neighboring islands. It is also possible to kayak without too much effort from Otres Beach to nearby Koh Chaluh. It is advisable to use plenty of sunscreen and wear a hat.

TREKKING AND ELEPHANT RIDING

Unlike neighboring Laos, organized walking trips in Cambodia are still a novel activity. The best place to trek is undoubtedly in the remote regions of the northeast, namely Ratanakiri's Virachey National Park. Here, one-day and three-day treks are organized by the **Virachey National Park Headquarters**. The undulating alpine hills of Mondulkiri also provide exciting trekking and elephant-riding trails. **Hanuman Tourism**'s trekking tours take in mountain lakes and some minority villages of the northeast and also include elephant rides. In the south, both Ream and Bokor national parks offer one-day treks to the Cardamom Mountains with their picture-perfect waterfalls. Both parks are accessible from Koh Kong.

Tour organizers in Siem Reap also organize treks to remote Angkorian temples. **Terre Cambodge**, for instance, organizes interesting three-day safaris, on foot or elephant back, to isolated temples.

It is best to use the services of an experienced guide for these trekking trips and never venture alone, since UXO (Unexploded Ordnance) continues to pose a threat.

CYCLING

Cambodia's flat terrain is perfect for cycling and many travelers are now bringing their own bikes, rather than renting a cheap one on arrival. Mountainbiking in Ratanakiri and Mondulkiri provinces is particularly popular owing to challenging roads, bounteous countryside, and the rugged appeal of the area. A number of companies specializing in motorcycle and bicycle tours, including **Pepy Ride** and **Terre Cambodge**, organize regular excursions in these areas.

Cyclists, however, should be careful of rash driving by locals, unexpected obstacles in the form of cattle or children running across roads, and UXO on fresh or unexplored terrain. It is also better to bring your own supply of inner tubes and other spares as these are not readily available, especially for expensive foreign bicycle models.

GOLF

Long associated with the Khmer elite, golf has always been popular in Cambodia. While major cities such as Siem Reap and Phnom Penh have some good courses, **Cambodia Golf and Country Club**, situated some distance from Phnom Penh off Highway 4, was the country's very first course. **Phokeethra Country Club** is

Braving a tough trail through the thick forests of northeast Cambodia

Siem Reap's first international standard 18-hole golf course. **Angkor Golf Course**, also in Siem Reap, has been rated by the Professional Golfers' Association of America (PGA) and is equally popular.

BIRD-WATCHING

Cambodia is an ornithologist's paradise, thanks to the Tonlé Sap Lake and the host of migratory birds that nest there each year. These include the milky stork, black-headed ibis, grey-headed fish eagle, spot-billed pelican, and greater and lesser adjuncts. These birds depend on the nutrient-rich water of the lake. The Prek Toal Bird Sanctuary, located in the heart of the Tonlé Sap Biosphere Reserve, is known to be the most important breeding ground for globally threatened large waterbirds in Southeast Asia. The biosphere, which covers an area of 120 sq miles (311 sq km), is best visited during the dry season when the water recedes and there are large numbers of migratory birds. Day trips can easily be arranged by your hotel or guesthouse in Siem Reap, as can overnight stays at the **Prek Toal Environment Research Station**, which is superb for viewing the birds at sunset and sunrise. In cooperation with the locals, **Sam Veasna Center**, based in Siem Reap, organizes full- and half-day trips to remote places such as Chepp, to see birds such as the Saurus crane and giant and white-shouldered ibis.

View of Hole 13, Angkor Golf Course, Siem Reap

MARTIAL ARTS

Kbach kun pradal, better known as kickboxing, is very popular across the country and can prove to be quite an interesting pastime. Although a Thai might disagree, kickboxing in its purest form is said to have its roots from Khmer fighters. For thousands of years, senior figures in the military were expected to be proficient in martial arts, the oldest of which is *bogotao*. Unfortunately, this martial art is all but obsolete today with only one local, an octogenarian, still alive with knowledge of this form. Many martial arts masters were also prosecuted under the Khmer Rouge. Since the end of their regime, efforts have been made to restore these ancient traditions. Kickboxing events are held regularly in Sihanoukville and Siem Reap, but most notably at the **Phnom Penh National Olympic Stadium**. Those interested in learning the art can visit **Paddy's Fight Club and Gym**, also in Phnom Penh, which is renowned for its excellent training sessions.

COOKING COURSES

Cambodian cuisine is fast becoming popular with international visitors who are keen to take back some of its culinary secrets. You can enrol in **Cambodia Cooking Class** in Phnom Penh or **The River Garden Guesthouse** and **Le Tigre De Papier** in Siem Reap, which offer cooking classes.

SPAS

Once a byword for refinement, comfort, and panache under the French Colonialists, traditional spa treatments are regaining popularity in the country. Developers keen to cater to increasing numbers of visitors are restoring antique Gallic villas and turning them into chic spa boutiques providing excellent service. There are several such spas in both Phnom Penh and Siem Reap where you can not only enjoy a relaxing spa treatment, but also taste the finest of wines. The treatments at **Spa Indochine** at Hotel De La Paix in Siem Reap are well regarded as are those at **Amara Spa** in Phnom Penh. Those on a tighter budget can try the **Seeing Hands Massage** run by blind people.

Cooking class in progress at Le Tigre De Papier, Siem Reap

DIRECTORY

DIVING AND SNORKELING

Angkor Dive
Serendipity Beach, Sihanoukville.
Tel *(097)-799-3395.*

The Dive Shop
Serendipity Beach Rd, Sihanoukville. ***Tel*** *(034)-933-664.* **www**.diveshopcambodia.com

Eco Sea Dive
Serendipity Beach, Sihanoukville.
Tel *(012)-654-104.*
www.ecoseadive.com

Scuba Nation
Mohachai Guesthouse, Serendipity Beach Rd, Sihanoukville.
Tel *(012)-604-680.*
www.divecambodia.com

SAILING, KITESURFING, AND FISHING

Hurricane Windsurfing
Otres Beach, Sihanoukville.
Tel *(017)-471-604.*

Otres Nautica
Otres Beach, Sihanoukville.
Tel *(092)-230-065.*

Sankeor
Sihanoukville.
Tel *(099)-905-430.*

Sun Tours
Sihanoukville.
Tel *(016)-396-201.*
www.suntours-cambodia.com

Trade Winds Charters
Fisherman's Den Sports Bar, Sihanoukville.
Tel *(012)-702-478.*

KAYAKING

The Golden Sunset
Golden Sunset Beach Restaurant, end of Otres Beach, Sihanoukville.
Tel *(012)-812-087.*

TREKKING AND ELEPHANT RIDING

Hanuman Tourism
12, St 310, Phnom Penh.
City Map C4.
Tel *(023)-218-396.*
www.hanumantourism.com

Terre Cambodge
Hup Guan St, Siem Reap. ***Tel*** *(077)-448-255.* **www**.terrecambodge.com

Virachey National Park Headquarters
Department of Environment, Ban Lung, Ratanakiri.
Tel *(077)-965-196.*
www.viracheyecotourism.blogspot.com

CYCLING

Pepy Ride
PO Box 93220, GPO Siem Reap.
Tel *(017)-737-519.*
www.pepyride.org

GOLF

Angkor Golf Course
Kasekam village, Siem Reap.
Tel *(063)-767-688.*
www.angkor-golf.com

Cambodia Golf and Country Club
Sang Kreach Tieng, St 222, Phnom Penh. **City Map** D3. ***Tel*** *(023)-363-666.*

Phokeethra Country Club
Angkor Wat, Siem Reap.
Tel *(063)-964-600.*
www.phokeethragolf.com

BIRD-WATCHING

Prek Toal Environment Research Station
Osmose Tonlé Sap, Siem Reap. ***Tel*** *(063)-965-574.* **www**.osmosetonlesap.net

Sam Veasna Center
552, Group 12, Wat Bo, Siem Reap.
Tel *(063)-963-710.*
www.samveasna.org

MARTIAL ARTS

Paddy's Fight Club and Gym
63, St 294, Phnom Penh.
City Map D5.
Tel *(012)-217-877.*
www.paddysgym.com

Phnom Penh National Olympic Stadium
Blvd Samdech Preah Sihanouk, Phnom Penh.
City Map C3.

COOKING COURSES

Cambodia Cooking Class
67, St 240, Phnom Penh.
City Map E3.
Tel *(012)-524-801.*
www.cambodiacooking-class.com

The River Garden Guesthouse
113 Mondul, 111 Phoum Treang, Siem Reap.
Tel *(063)-963-400.*
www.therivergarden.info

Le Tigre de Papier
La Residence, Siem Reap.
Tel *(063)-760-930.* **www**.letigredepapier.com

SPAS

Amara Spa
Sisowath Quay, Phnom Penh. **City Map** E1.
Tel *(023)-998-730.*

Seeing Hands Massage
6Eo Ph 94, central Phnom Penh. **City Map** D1.
Tel *(023)-680-934.*

Spa Indochine
Hotel De La Paix, Sivatha Blvd, Siem Reap.
Tel *(063)-966-000.*

OUTDOOR ACTIVITIES AND SPECIAL INTERESTS IN LAOS

With its stunning landscape and remote getaways, Laos is any adventure traveler's dream destination. Visitors can choose from a variety of itineraries, which include trekking, cycling, kayaking, and elephant riding, in a single day. Many prefer focused trips, especially for trekking, the most popular activity here. It is not necessary to join a tour either – those keen to go cycling or kayaking can import their own gear and set off independently. Those looking for relaxed pastimes will find plenty of activities to fill their days – from cooking courses to traditional techniques of weaving and dyeing. Laos is one of the few places where visitors can take a course in elephant tending. Studying with a master *mahout*, visitors can learn the basics of feeding, bathing, controlling, and taking care of these beasts.

Cyclist with camping gear, Laos

Trekkers negotiating a path through the wilderness in Luang Nam Tha

TREKKING

The Lao government has established 20 National Protected Areas (NPAs), some of which are open to trekkers. Tour companies employ the services of local guides and trekkers usually spend the night at a local village. Such community-based tourism, an excellent way to pump money into local communities and involve them in environment protection, is being increasingly encouraged. While trekking is possible throughout the country, certain areas, such as the Nam Ha National Protected Area, have earned a reputation for being particularly diverse and fascinating. Treks are organized by **Vientiane Orchidées**, based in Vientiane, and **Green Discovery** and the **Nam Ha Eco-Guide Unit**, which have offices in Luang Nam Tha.

CYCLING

With its low vehicular traffic and spectacular scenery, Laos is an ideal destination for cycling. Mountain bikes are particularly suitable, since most of the best routes still include unpaved sections. Local tour operators offer either one-day rides or several-day tours, but serious cyclists usually arrive with their own bikes and set out independently. Particularly popular is the route from the northern port of entry at Huay Xai on the Thai border to Luang Prabang, a several-day ride through mountains and forests involving some serious climbs. From Luang Prabang, Route 13 extends farther south to Vang Vieng, Vientiane, and eventually to the Cambodian border. These are demanding rides, but if things get too arduous, it is always possible to continue the rest of the way on a bus. For fully supported countrywide tours, **Spice Roads**, in Thailand, is by the far the best operator. In Luang Prabang, **Tiger Trail** organizes trips lasting a day or longer.

KAYAKING AND RAFTING

The many rivers in Laos also provide great opportunities for kayaking and rafting. Like the other outdoor activities in Laos, it is possible to undertake this independently, although taking advantage of local knowledge, logistical support, and equipment is recommended. All major rivers are navigable and the areas east of Thakhek in Khammuan province get particularly good reviews. The Green Discovery office in Thakhek provides all necessary information. It also has an office in Luang Prabang.

Kayakers beginning their journey on the Nam Song, Vang Vieng

An adventure sports enthusiast trying an exciting zip line over a waterfall in the forests of southern Laos

SPELUNKING AND ROCK CLIMBING

The limestone karsts of Laos offer world-class opportunities for spelunkers. Except for those who are expert at it, spelunking is best done with the help of a local guide for it can prove to be very dangerous, even life threatening. Besides this, many caves still remain relatively unexplored and are known only to locals. Vang Vieng is regarded as the national center for this activity since the caves here are superb and well explored. Experienced spelunkers can also try the area around Phu Hin Pun NPA in Khammuan province, which is deemed to be the best in the country.

The karst formations of Laos also lend themselves well to rock climbing. Again, the area around Vang Vieng sees the most activity. Here, dozens of bolted and mapped routes of varying difficulty await the climber. Some climbing is also done around Luang Prabang. **Green Discovery** and **Adam's Rock Climbing School** in Vang Vieng organize spelunking and rock-climbing tours.

ZIP LINING

Not as physically demanding as other outdoor adventures, zip lining can be a lot of fun. Typically, zip lines run above the jungle canopy and are a great way to spend a day. The most popular zip line tour is offered by **Flight of Nature** at the Tat Sae Waterfalls near Luang Prabang. Flight of Nature also offers elephant trekking. At Nam Lik, between Vang Vieng and Vientiane, is another zip line. Those who prefer a longer, more thrilling experience with excellent zip line facilities and the opportunity to spy on the elusive Laotian black gibbon, should try **The Gibbon Experience**, near Huay Xai. The place also provides night stays in a fascinating treehouse deep within the jungle.

ELEPHANT ACTIVITIES

Riding an elephant has now become an almost mandatory part of a visit to Laos. Tours are available throughout the country, particularly in the north. For those interested in gaining a deeper knowledge of the subject, *mahout* courses teach the basics of tending to these giant mammals. Quite popular among visitors, the best courses are usually offered in Luang Prabang by **Elephant Village** and the **Mahout Lodge**. An alternative is a multi-day safari through the jungles of Sainyabuli province, usually starting from the town of Hong Sa to the Mekong River. This safari is offered by the well-known **ElefantAsia**.

COOKING COURSES

A great way for visitors to gain insight into the culture and traditions of the country, cooking courses are usually a full day affair and begin with a visit to the market to buy ingredients. This is followed by the actual hands-on cooking of the meal, and finally enjoying the fruits of your labor. For true aficionados, however, several-day courses are usually a better choice. Luang Prabang is the best place to try out your culinary skills. Courses are offered by the **Tamarind Cooking School** and the **Tamnak Lao Restaurant**. **Villa Lao Guesthouse** also runs several good cooking courses.

TEXTILE COURSES

The hand-woven textiles of Laos are an important aspect of the country's culture. Visitors can enrol in courses that

Visitors undergoing *mahout* training at a camp near Mohout's Tomb

explore the traditional arts of silk weaving and dyeing. But these are not vocational training classes; rather they confer an appreciation for the skill and the patience this ancient art requires. Course attendees get to keep a sample of their own work. Courses are offered at the workshops of **Ock Pop Tok** in Luang Prabang and **Houey Hong Vocational Training Centre for Women**, an NGO working to reinvigorate traditional skills among local women, in Vientiane.

Spectators enjoying a match of *kataw* in the evening

SPECTATOR SPORTS

There are two unique sports worth looking out for in Laos. The first, *kataw*, is better known as *sepak takraw*, and is similar to volleyball, but it only allows the use of the feet and head. The ball is made from rattan, and is half the size of a volleyball. Informal matches are usually held in temple compounds in the evenings, but for serious competition, contact the **Lao Kataw Federation**. *Muay lao*, or Lao boxing, differs from Western versions of the sport in that the feet are also used. Matches are held at the **Sok Sai Boxing Stadium**. It is also hard to miss the games of *pétanque*, a French legacy, played by the roadside in the evenings all over Laos.

DIRECTORY

TREKKING

Green Discovery
Route 7, Luang Nam Tha.
Tel *(086)-211-484.*
www.greendiscovery laos.com

Nam Ha Eco-Guide Unit
Behind the Night Market, Luang Nam Tha.
Tel *(086)-312-047.*

Vientiane Orchidées
642/37, Ban Phonethong Tchomany, Vientiane.
Tel *(021)-560-444.*

CYCLING

Spice Roads
14/1-B Soi Promsi 2, Sukhumvit, Bangkok, Thailand.
Tel *(066)-0271-25305.*

Tiger Trail
Sisavang Vong Rd, Luang Prabang. **City Map** C3.
Tel *(071)-252-655.*

SPELUNKING AND ROCK CLIMBING

Adam's Rock Climbing School
Route 13, N of Wat Kang, Vang Vieng.
Tel *(020)-501-0832.*

Green Discovery
Route 13, next to Xayoh Restaurant, Vang Vieng.
Tel *(023)-511-230.*

ZIP LINING

Flight of Nature
Tat Sae Waterfalls, Luang Prabang.
Tel *(020)-434-8748.*

The Gibbon Experience
Main road, S of Sabaidee Guest House, Huay Xai.
Tel *(084)-212-021.*
www.gibbon experience.org

ELEPHANT ACTIVITIES

ElefantAsia
Ban Khunta, Vientiane.
City Map A5.
Tel *(020)-541-8730.*
www.elefantasia.org

Elephant Village
Xieng Lom village, Luang Prabang.
Tel *(071)-212-311.*

Mahout Lodge
Ban Nonsavath (near Mouhot's tomb), Luang Prabang. **City Map** C3.
Tel *(071)-254-547.*
www.mahoutlodge.com

COOKING COURSES

Tamarind Cooking School
Kounxoa Rd, opp Wat Nong, Luang Prabang.
City Map C3.
Tel *(020)-777-0484.*
www.tamarindlaos.com

Tamnak Lao Restaurant
Sakkarin Rd, across from Villa Santi, Luang Prabang.
City Map D3.
Tel *(071)-252-525.*
www.tamnaklao.net

Villa Lao Guesthouse
Near Northern Bus Station, Vientiane.
City Map A4. ***Tel*** *(021)-242-292.* **www**.villa-lao-guesthouse.com

TEXTILE COURSES

Ock Pop Tok
Next to L'Elephant Restaurant, Ban Wat Nong, Luang Prabang.
City Map C3.
Tel *(071)-253-219.*
www.ockpoptok.com

Houey Hong Vocational Training Centre
Lane 19, Houey Hong village, Vientiane.
Tel *(021)-560-006.*
www.houeyhong centre.com

SPECTATOR SPORTS

Lao Kataw Federation
National Stadium, Vientiane.
City Map C3.
Tel *(020)-569-4355.*

Sok Sai Boxing Stadium
Thong Khan Kham Rd, Vientiane.
Tel *(021)-212-459.*

SURVIVAL GUIDE

PRACTICAL INFORMATION

Both Cambodia and Laos are rapidly developing tourist destinations. New and improved road networks and better facilities have made access possible even to the remote parts of these countries. Old Colonial villas in cities such as Siem Reap, Phnom Penh, Vientiane, and Luang Prabang have been restored as trendy boutique hotels, while restaurants in even the most isolated places are beginning to offer a variety of cuisines. Unlike Laos, tour operators in Cambodia, with a few exceptions, have been slow to develop. However, savvy customer-focused companies, specializing in ecotourism and sightseeing in and around Angkor, are now burgeoning. Laos, on the other hand, is regarded as an ecotourism blueprint for the developing world, with vast protected areas open for responsible trekking companies.

Cambodia Ministry of Tourism logo

Colorful umbrellas lining the seafront at Occheuteal Beach

WHEN TO GO

Cambodia and Laos are both tropical countries and generally hot year round. The temperature during the hot season, from March to May, usually exceeds 40° C (104° F) and exploring temples, especially in Cambodia, can be an unpleasantly humid affair. A few mountainous regions in Laos, however, have cool weather throughout the year.

It is possible to visit during the rainy season, from May to August, since the downpours usually last only a few hours in the late afternoon, and visitors can make the most of deserted beaches and archaeological ruins; besides, accommodations are cheaper and easily available. However, most unpaved roads are washed away by flooding and heavy rain during this time.

The best time to visit is during the cool season, from October to February, soon after the monsoon, when both countries glimmer with verdant paddy fields, wooded mountains, and a welcome breeze that caresses the land. The ideal months are December and January since by mid-February the temperatures are already rising.

WHAT TO TAKE

Although most necessary items can be bought in major cities such as Siem Reap and Luang Prabang, as well as the capital cities of both countries, it is best to bring your own supply of important items. Wide-brimmed hats are highly recommended, as is a good quality sunscreen. For those planning trekking trips in the remote Cardamom Mountains or Northern Laos, a sturdy pair of walking boots are a must as is insect repellant. Dengue and malaria are quite common in both these countries and a mosquito repellent as well as anti-malaria pills are strongly recommended. Those traveling during the rainy season can buy rain ponchos in most towns. For the cooler months, a sweatshirt is usually advisable because the evenings can be chilly, especially in the north.

VISAS AND PASSPORTS

It is essential to have a visa when entering Cambodia by land, air, or sea. While a tourist visa is the preferred choice, a business visa is also an option. Visitors disembarking at Siem Reap and Phnom Penh airports, or entering Cambodia by land, automatically receive a one-month visa. This can be applied for in advance, since the formalities are minimal and the visa is processed surprisingly swiftly. Those applying for a visa on arrival should carry a passport-sized photograph, failing which they will be charged an additional fee (although it is quite nominal). Those planning to extend their stay by a couple of months should apply for

Trekkers interacting with a local guide during a trek in Luang Nam Tha

◁ Tuk-tuks, a convenient mode of transport, plying the main road in Luang Prabang a business visa, which can be extended for long periods with multiple entries; tourist visas only provide the option of extending the stay once, and for a single month. Those overstaying their visa are usually charged an additional fee for each extra day.

The cost of a visa to Laos depends on the visitor's nationality and can be acquired on arrival at Vientiane, Luang Prabang, and Pakse airports, as well as the land borders at Nong Khai, Chiang Khong (on the Thailand-Laos border), and Savannakhet. Visitors must bring along two passport-sized photographs, since there are no provisions for getting one taken. Visa extensions are painless affairs and cost a few dollars for every extra day up to a maximum of 30 days. The immigration office in Vientiane is well equipped to handle visa proceedings, although they can also be done through a travel agency.

IMMUNIZATION

Medical facilities in Cambodia and Laos are not very dependable. Visitors suffering from a serious injury or from an illness that requires specialized treatment, may need to be evacuated to neighboring Thailand for help. Getting immunized against some of the widespread diseases is therefore advisable. These include Hepatitis A and B, rabies, tuberculosis, typhoid, yellow fever, polio, diptheria, tetanus, and Japanese B encephalitis. Malaria can be a problem in remote parts of these countries, but taking a dose of prophylactics during the stay is not required unless traveling to such areas.

Medical treatment for foreign visitors in Cambodia and Laos is expensive and visitors need to have medical insurance, while ensuring that their travel documents are on hand in the event of an emergency.

CUSTOMS INFORMATION

Customs regulations in both Cambodia and Laos are relatively relaxed compared to neighboring countries. Visitors can officially enter and exit both countries with one bottle of spirits, a carton of 200 cigarettes, as well as a moderate amount of perfume or aftershave. Cigarettes in both Cambodia and Laos are quite inexpensive and a carton of 200 usually costs around US$10. However, the authorities are quite tough on the import of drugs, guns, and pornography. A maximum of US$10,000 in cash can be brought into the countries.

TOURIST INFORMATION

There are very few tourist offices in Cambodia apart from those in cities such as Phnom Penh and Siem Reap. The staff in the tourist offices in Phnom Penh are usually not very helpful and may not always be fluent in English. While the best source of information is usually the local listings guide or your hotel information desk, visitors can also consult the helpful **Canby Publications** website for the latest offerings. Siem Reap has plenty of tourist offices that can help visitors plan their itinerary to the temples of Angkor, but even here, the best source of information is usually your hotel or even a busy guesthouse.

Tourist information in Laos, however, is easier to come by with the helpful **Lao National Tourism Administration**, which has offices in most major cities. The staff is usually eager and helpful, and will have brochures and other handy information about trekking and other activities, although they may not be very fluent in English or other languages.

Travelers outside a tour agency in Huay Xai, Laos

ADMISSION CHARGES

Most museums, zoos, and botanical gardens in Cambodia and Laos charge an entry fee between US$1–5. Entry to the countries' active *wats* is usually free. However, it is customary to make a donation toward the upkeep of the temple.

Entrance tickets to Angkor and the National Museum and Silver Pagoda

TIME AND CALENDAR

Cambodia and Laos are 7 hours ahead of Greenwich Mean Time (GMT), 15 hours ahead of Pacific Standard Time (PST), and 12 hours ahead of Eastern Standard Time (EST). Although the Western Gregorian calendar is used for official and commercial purposes in these countries, the lunar calendar is still used for religious purposes and for calculating the dates of festivals.

MEASUREMENTS

Both countries have been using the metric system since the Colonial era.

Imperial to Metric

1 inch = 2.54 centimeters
1 foot = 30 centimeters
1 mile = 1.6 kilometers
1 ounce = 28 grams
1 pound = 454 grams
1 US quart = 0.947 liter
1 US gallon = 3.6 liters

Metric to Imperial

1 millimeter = 0.04 inch
1 centimeter = 0.4 inch
1 meter = 3 feet 3 inches
1 kilometer = 0.6 mile
1 gram = 0.04 ounces
1 kilogram = 2.2 pounds
1 liter = 2.1 pints

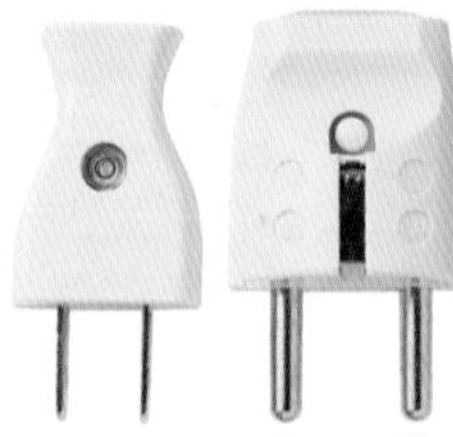

Two-prong electric plugs used in Cambodia and Laos

ELECTRICITY

The electric current for both Cambodia and Laos is 220 volts. While flat, American-style pins and French-style rounded pins are most commonly used, multi-prong plugs are also in use. It is advisable to buy a multi-purpose adaptor beforehand. Power cuts are the norm, and visitors should ensure that they keep a flashlight handy by the bed or in their pocket.

FACILITIES FOR THE DISABLED

Unfortunately, Cambodia and Laos are ill-equipped for disabled travelers, with unkept pavements, poor quality roads, high curbs, and crowded buses. Although much of Cambodia is flat and major tourist attractions such as Angkor Wat *(see pp68–9)* are easily accessible by wheelchairs, the more remote provinces can prove to be quite a challenge, since hotels are not usually equipped with elevators, nor are there any toilet facilities for the disabled. Laos is even more difficult with its mountainous roads and lack of facilities for the disabled.

FACILITIES FOR CHILDREN

Khmer and Lao people love children, be it their own or other peoples's. Children can expect to be treated with affection wherever they go. However, facilities for children leave a lot to be desired anywhere outside of major hotels and in the capital cities. Separate beds and high chairs are only available in upscale establishments, nor are there any special meals for children. Hired cars rarely have seats for strapping infants and parents need to be especially vigilant about letting children walk the streets in the capitals unattended – tuk-tuk drivers can be careless and accidents are not uncommon. Despite these shortcomings, there is enough to keep children amused and occupied. The Phnom Tamao Wildlife Rescue Center *(see p59)* in Phnom Penh, for instance, and the city's many swimming pools offer enough opportunities for fun. Alternatively, boat trips down the Mekong River are enjoyed by most children, as are visits to the ancient Angkorian ruins such as Ta Prohm *(see pp80–81)*. An aerial view of Angkor Wat in a hot air balloon would also be appealing to most kids. This can be followed by shadow puppets at the Sovanna Phum Arts Association *(see p254)* in Phnom Penh.

Provinces such as Ratanakiri have waterfalls and offer elephant rides, which make for many lasting memories. In the south, there are plenty of gently shelving beaches, including Otres *(see p107)*, which are child-friendly, although parents need to keep a watch since the current can get dangerously strong at times.

In Laos, Xieng Khuan *(see p146)* is a quirky place; children love the variety of statues. Vientiane also offers several opportunities for a refreshing swim with its many clean swimming pools. For children who enjoy the outdoors, trekking in the north is an excellent option. A visit to the Tat Kuang Si Falls *(see p167)* in Luang Prabang is a wonderful experience, as are the resident sun bears rescued from poachers. Elephant rides can also be organized in Luang Prabang and children often enjoy the magical Night Market *(see pp156–7)* with its authentic Oriental feel and delectable food.

A family enjoying a meal at a restaurant in Phnom Penh

LANGUAGE

Khmer is the official language of Cambodia, spoken by almost 90 percent of its population, while the official language of Laos is Lao. Used since the 7th century AD, Khmer script appears similar to Thai but is in fact much older, originating in India. It is not an easy language to learn, but its non-tonality makes it easier than Thai or Vietnamese. English is widely spoken in most major hotels, restaurants, and tour offices. French is also spoken by the older generations, a hangover from the days of French Colonialism.

TAKE OFF YOUR SHOES

Sign outside a temple in Laos

PHOTOGRAPHY

Among Southeast Asia's most photographically rewarding countries, Cambodia and Laos offer visitors abundant opportunities to take good pictures. However, there is certain etiquette to be followed when photographing monks – photographers must seek their permission before capturing them on camera and never get in their way. Followers of animism may not react well to having their portrait taken as they believe it steals a part of their soul. Recent measures to protect children from Western paedophiles have also raised awareness and suspicion. Visitors should be careful of photographing children.

Western-standard hardware, from tripods to digital cameras, is available in major cities such as Phnom Penh, Siem Reap, Vientiane, and Luang Prabang, as are memory cards and batteries. Although digital photography is burgeoning, film rolls are also widely available.

Shooting panoramic views from Mt Phou Si

Printing of photographs is easy and quite inexpensive, especially in Cambodia, and shops and Internet cafés will readily burn a CD or DVD for a charge.

ETIQUETTE

Cambodians and Lao are very polite and placid people. Cambodians can get easily offended, but more often than not, they will refrain from confrontation. It is best to keep a few things in mind when interacting with the locals.

The traditional greeting in both countries is offered by pressing the hands together as if in prayer and bowing slightly, and it is polite to return the greeting in the same way. Losing one's temper is seen as a loss of face, indeed Lao people use the term *jai yen* (cool heart) to describe their preferred state of equilibrium. The fastest way for a foreigner to exacerbate any situation is to lose his or her temper, and such behavior should be avoided.

When entering a temple, visitors must remove their hat and shoes, and turn their feet away from any sacred statue when sitting down. Visitors must also be appropriately dressed in a long-sleeved shirt or T-shirt; women should avoid showing too much skin when entering a *wat*. The top of the head is regarded as the repository of the soul and you must avoid touching anyone, child or adult, on the head.

Visitors to Laos should take special care to respect the allowed atmosphere of calm while observing the morning almsgiving ceremony (*tak bat*). Flash photography is not allowed, and it is best to maintain an appropriate distance.

Visitors at a temple, sitting with feet facing away from Buddha statues

Sunbathing in bikinis is considered offensive, except in Southern Cambodia where it is viewed as acceptable. Lastly, when offered a drink or something to eat, it is polite to take at least a sip or a bite to prevent the host from losing face.

RESPONSIBLE TRAVEL

Owing to their slow rate of development, Laos and Cambodia are not yet in a position to consider carbon emissions as an environmental priority. Less polluting fuels, such as gasohol and Liquid Petroleum Gas (LPG), have not yet found their way into these countries, which use benzene and diesel to power vehicles. Hopefully, the many hydroelectric dams being built, especially in Laos, will provide a cleaner source of fuel in the future.

There are, nevertheless, a few choices that an informed traveler can make to lessen the ecological impact of a trip. In general, shared transport, such as buses or ferries, emit less carbon per person than private vehicles. When renting a motorcycle, visitors should avoid the highly polluting two-stroke engine bikes. Water transport, such as the speedboats that ply the Mekong River are not only dangerous, but also polluting and should be avoided. Visitors should consider hiring a bicycle for long excursions and walking for shorter distances.

DIRECTORY

EMBASSIES

Australia
16B, National Assembly St, Phnom Penh. **City Map** E3. ***Tel*** *(023)-213-470.*

Nehru Blvd, Ban Phonxai, Vientiane. **City Map** D3. ***Tel*** *(021)-413-600.* **www**.cambodia.embassy.gov.au

China
156 Mao Tse Toung Blvd, Phnom Penh. **City Map** C5. ***Tel*** *(023)-720-920.*

Ban Wat Nak, Vientiane. **City Map** A5. ***Tel*** *(021)-315-105.*

France
1 Monivong Blvd, Phnom Penh. ***Tel*** *(023)-430-020.*

Setthathirat Rd, Vientiane. **City Map** D4. ***Tel*** *(021)-215-258.*

Germany
76–78, St 254, Phnom Penh. **City Map** D3. ***Tel*** *(023)-216-381.*

Sok Pa Luang Rd, Vientiane. **City Map** A5. ***Tel*** *(021)-312-111.*

Thailand
196 Norodom Blvd, Phnom Penh. **City Map** E5. ***Tel*** *(023)-726-306.*

Kuvoravong Rd, Vientiane. **City Map** E2. ***Tel*** *(021)-212-373.*

UK
27, St 75, Phnom Penh. ***Tel*** *(023)-427-124.*

USA
1, St 96, Phnom Penh. **City Map** D1. ***Tel*** *(023)-728-000.*

That Dam Rd, Vientiane. **City Map** C3. ***Tel*** *(021)-267-000.*

TOURIST INFORMATION

Canby Publications
www.canbypublications.com

Lao National Tourism Administration
Lan Xang Ave, Chanthabuli, Vientiane. **City Map** D3. ***Tel*** *(021)-212-248.* **www**.tourismlaos.org

Personal Health and Security in Cambodia

Cambodia is a relatively safe country to travel in. The primary dangers visitors might face are posed by pickpockets, motorcycle thieves, or crafty tuk-tuk drivers overcharging them. Visitors should refrain from wearing flashy jewelry and using expensive gadgets in public. Healthcare facilities are quite poor, except in main cities, and visitors should ensure that their health insurance makes provision for a medical evacuation.

A well-stocked pharmacy in Siem Reap

GENERAL PRECAUTIONS

The days of impoverished, war-torn Cambodia, especially in Phnom Penh, are long over. Even though there is a concentration of arms in the capital, it rarely affects foreigners. Visitors should keep an eye out for pickpockets, bag-snatchers on motorcycles, and con artists. It is also advisable to take a licensed taxi at night to avoid getting mugged. Visitors should also be wary of the fact that prostitution is on the rise, and the country has one of the highest incidences of HIV infection in Southeast Asia.

Cambodia is one of the most mined countries in the world, with UXO (Unexploded Ordnance) still scattered in the remote northeast, and Khmer Rouge-laid mines in the west around Battambang and Pailin. It is recommended that visitors exercise caution in these areas, use a guide, and never stray from marked paths.

A general travel insurance, which covers theft, accident, and illness is also vital.

POLICE

Cambodia has a limited number of tourist police in cities that are frequented by foreigners, such as Phnom Penh, Siem Reap, and Sihanoukville. Tourist police officials speak English and may help with general questions, but can be reluctant to fill in insurance details should you suffer theft or other criminal offences. Visitors should be careful in cities such as Sihanoukville, where gun mugging and pickpocketing are common after dark. In remote areas, where tourist police officials are not available, visitors have to contact the regular police station.

MEDICAL FACILITIES

Standards of hygiene are not always high in Cambodia and the most common ailment contracted by travelers is diarrhoea, which affects a staggering 30–50 percent of visitors within the first couple of weeks. It is best dealt with by resting and drinking plenty of water. Diseases such as giardiasis and amoebic dysentery, commonly contracted through food, can be prevented by washing hands before each meal and avoiding roadside eateries. Water-borne diseases such as typhoid and cholera are not uncommon either; it is advisable to avoid consuming tap water or ice.

Over exposure to the sun can be prevented by wearing a hat during the day, taking breaks while sightseeing, and drinking plenty of water.

Mosquito bites are another nuisance. Most mosquitoes do not carry malaria or dengue, but visitors should exercise caution by using a mosquito net or repellent.

Hospitals such as **Calmette Hospital** and **International SOS Medical Center** in Phnom Penh and **Royal Angkor International Hospital** and **Angkor Hospital for Children** in Siem Reap are equipped to handle minor health problems such as an upset stomach or a fever. In case of serious illness or injury, however, visitors should head to Bangkok. It is advisable to visit a private clinic rather than provincial hospitals, which are usually under-equipped. Antibiotics and anti-malaria medication can be bought over the counter in most well-stocked pharmacies in urban areas.

Visitors wearing hats to escape the scorching heat

DIRECTORY

EMERGENCY NUMBERS

Fire Service ***Tel*** *(063)-760-133.*

Police ***Tel*** *(011)-997-296.*

Tourist Police
Tel *(012)-942-484* (Phnom Penh).
Tel *(012)-402-424* (Siem Reap).

MEDICAL FACILITIES

Angkor Hospital for Children
Achar Maen St, Siem Reap.
Tel *(063)-963-409.*
www.angkorhospital.org

Calmette Hospital
3 Monivong Blvd, Phnom Penh.
Tel *(023)-723-840.*

International SOS Medical Center
161, St 51, Phnom Penh.
City Map D2. ***Tel*** *(023)-216-911.*

Royal Angkor International Hospital
Airport Rd, Siem Reap.
Tel *(063)-761-888.*
www.royalangkorhospital.com

Personal Health and Security in Laos

Visitors to Laos do not need to worry about safety, but a few general precautions should be taken to avoid petty crime such as pilfering and bag snatching in larger towns. Road travel is safe, with the armed attacks on buses that generated much publicity having ceased. Food is also generally safe, although bottled water is a must. UXO still pose a problem, but only in the most remote areas. However, medical facilities are quite poor and visitors should have traveler's insurance that includes medical evacuation.

Street food, best avoided by those with a delicate stomach

GENERAL PRECAUTIONS

Violent crime against visitors is unheard of in Laos, but theft is not. It is best to keep an eye on your baggage, especially when using public transport, and look out for bag snatchers who operate in pairs on motorcycles. Ideally, large sums of money should be kept in the hotel safe, and visitors should be wary of bystanders when changing money or using an unguarded ATM.

Although UXO continues to pose a problem, statistically, the chances of a visitor suffering injuries caused by these are quite low. Nevertheless, it is best to stick to marked paths or follow guides closely in rural areas. Visitors are also cautioned to never pick up anything that remotely resembles a grenade.

Drug trafficking is another danger visitors need to be wary of. Foreigners are often approached as potential customers for illegal drugs, but they should be aware that the Lao government is anxious to ensure that the country is not known as a drug tourist destination. Those found dealing in drugs usually face severe penalties and the government has no qualms about prosecuting foreigners.

Visitors should also take precautions against accidents on roads. Sidewalks in Vientiane, in particular, have large holes. Speedboats on the Mekong River are also best avoided as they can be quite dangerous.

POLICE

A lingering suspicion about foreign spies still prevails in the country and it is best not to take pictures of soldiers or military bases. Although attempts to pull scams on foreigners are not common, visitors need to take care of their own safety since police officials in Laos do not speak English, and may not be very helpful if anything goes wrong.

Laos does not have any designated tourist police officials. In case of a mishap with a foreign national, a local English teacher is usually called in to translate.

MEDICAL FACILITIES

The most common ailments that affect visitors are usually food or water-borne diseases such as diarrhoea, mild dysentery, or intestinal parasites. These illnesses are usually not serious and can be treated locally. In case of a serious infection, however, visitors should head to a hospital or medical center in a larger city. A wide range of imported medicines is available at pharmacies in Vientiane.

Foreign visitors report good care for minor medical matters at the **Mahosot International Clinic** in Vientiane, but a serious illness is best addressed across the border in Thailand. The **Aek Udon Hospital** in Udon Thani, Thailand, about 50 miles (80 km) from Vientiane, can dispatch an ambulance to Laos. For information on any current disease outbreaks or recommended vaccinations, foreign nationals should consult the websites of the **US Centers for Disease Control** as well as that of the **UK Department of Health**.

Typical police vehicle, common in the streets of Vientiane

DIRECTORY

EMERGENCY NUMBERS

Ambulance
Tel 195.

Fire
Tel 190.

Police
Tel 191.

MEDICAL FACILITIES

Aek Udon Hospital
Udon Thani, Thailand. ***Tel** (042)-342-555.* **www**.aekudon.com

Mahosot International Clinic
Fa Ngum Rd, Vientiane.
City Map C4. ***Tel** (021)-214-022.*

US Centers for Disease Control
www.cdc.gov

UK Department of Health
www.doh.gov.uk

Banking and Currency in Cambodia

ANZ Royal ATM, Phnom Penh

Travelers should carry a fair amount of riel or US dollars at all times. Although the US dollar is readily accepted, it is worth keeping a few riel on hand. ATMs are common in Phnom Penh and Siem Reap but absent in rural areas. Visitors must be aware that there are no banks near Cambodian land borders. Traveler's checks can be cashed at all major banks in Phnom Penh, Siem Reap, Sihanoukville, and a few banks in Battambang. Visa and MasterCard are accepted in upscale restaurants, boutiques, hotels, and travel agents. The exchange rate hovers at 4,200 riel to a US dollar.

BANKS AND BANKING HOURS

Cambodia's leading banks are **SBC Bank**, **Acleda Bank**, **Cambodia Commercial Bank**, **Cambodia Asia Bank**, and **Canadia Bank**. **ANZ Royal Bank** is the most well-known international bank. All these banks have an ATM presence across the major cities and withdrawing money from them is safe, quick, and more efficient than going into the bank itself. Travelers will of course be charged for withdrawals, with the exception of Canadia Bank.

While timings can vary from bank to bank, most remain open Monday to Saturday from 7:30 to 11:30am and from 2 to 5pm or 6pm. Bureau de change in international chain hotels are usually open through the weekend.

CHANGING MONEY

The Thai baht is often accepted in towns such as Poipet and Battambang. However, travelers should keep in mind that the riel is not accepted or changed in Thailand. The US dollar can be used everywhere but getting change for higher denomination notes can prove difficult unless it is in a top hotel or restaurant. Banks may refuse to change US dollar notes with a slight rip or tear. However, this is not the case with ragged riel notes. Changing any non-dollar currency will result in a poor exchange rate; however, money-changers in the markets will give better rates. Markets usually operate from around 6am till sundown. Western Union and Moneygram money transfer services are represented by a number of banks such as Cambodia Asia Bank. Changing money with black market operators waiting at borders yields a very poor conversion.

CREDIT AND DEBIT CARDS

Visa and **MasterCard** are accepted by hotels, airlines, and upscale restaurants, as is **JCB** and, to a lesser extent, **American Express**. However, shops, restaurants, and hotels in smaller towns do not accept credit cards and it is best to carry the local currency or US dollars to make payments. Using a credit or debit card often means a 3 percent charge on the spot.

Western Union counter at Cambodia Asia Bank, Phnom Penh

DIRECTORY

BANKS

Acleda Bank
61 Preah Monivong Blvd, Phnom Penh. **City Map** D2. ***Tel*** *(023)-430-999.*
www.acledabank.com.kh

ANZ Royal Bank
265 Sisowath Quay, Phnom Penh. **City Map** F2. ***Tel*** *(023)-726-900.*
www.anzroyal.com

Cambodia Asia Bank
St 271 (next to Sovanna Shopping Center), Phnom Penh. **City Map** D3. ***Tel*** *(023)-216-426.*
www.cab.com.kh

Cambodia Commercial Bank
26 Preah Monivong, Phnom Penh. **City Map** D1. ***Tel*** *(023)-426-245.*

Canadia Bank
265, St 110, Phnom Penh. **City Map** D1. ***Tel*** *(023)-215-286.*

SBC Bank
68, St 214, Phnom Penh. **City Map** D3. ***Tel*** *(023)-990-688.*
www.sbc-bank.com

CREDIT CARDS

American Express
Tel *001-800-528-4800.*

JCB
Tel *001-800-366-4522.-*

MasterCard
Tel *001-636-722-7111.*

Visa
Tel *001-410-581-9994.*

Credit card advances are available at Battambang, Phnom Penh, Sihanoukville, Siem Reap, Kampot, and Kompong Cham. All banks, apart from Canadia Bank, which offers free advances, levy a US$5 charge.

TRAVELER'S CHECKS

Traveler's checks can be cashed in most banks, major hotels, and upscale restaurants. American Express, although not the most useful credit card to have, is the most widely accepted traveler's check. Acleda Bank, with branches throughout the country, even in far-flung northeast provinces such as Mondulkiri and Ratanakiri, now accepts traveler's checks. The standard commission rate for exchanging checks is about 2 percent and checks should be in US dollars rather than other international currencies.

CURRENCY

The official unit of currency in Cambodia is the riel, however, the US dollar is the de facto currency and the one travelers will find it most useful to carry. The riel cannot be exported, so it must be spent or exchanged before leaving the country. 500 and 1,000 riel notes are the most convenient denominations to have when paying for tuk-tuk rides. There is no coinage in Cambodia, only notes.

Bank Notes

The riel comes in denominations of 100, 200, 500, 1,000, 2,000, 5,000, 10,000, 20,000, 50,000 and 100,000.

5,000 riel

100 riel

10,000 riel

500 riel

20,000 riel

1,000 riel

50,000 riel

2,000 riel

100,000 riel

Banking and Currency in Laos

Siam Commerical Bank logo

The unit of currency in Laos is the kip, although the US dollar and the Thai baht are widely accepted and at times prices for more expensive items are quoted in dollars. Financial services in Laos are efficient and easily available, at least in major towns. Travelers rarely encounter problems while changing currency, cashing traveler's checks, getting a cash advance on a credit card, or when using an ATM. With an exchange rate hovering at about 8,500 kip to a US dollar, many visitors to the country will feel like multimillionaires. Even small purchases can seem more expensive than they actually are. It is best to keep both kip and dollars on hand while traveling around Laos.

Money exchange counter, Banque Pour le Commerce Exterieure Lao

BANKS AND BANKING HOURS

Most banks in Laos are open Monday to Friday from 8:30am to 3:30pm. The bank most foreigners will deal with is the government-owned **Banque Pour le Commerce Exterieure Lao (BCEL)**, which has numerous red and yellow streetside exchange kiosks. These are open from morning till night and can be used for all standard exchange transactions. Apart from BCEL the best local bank is **ANZ Laos**, which is a joint venture between ANZ, International Finance Corporation, and Vientiane Commercial Bank. In addition to the Thai-owned **Bangkok Bank** and **Siam Commercial Bank**, a few small privately owned Lao banks, such as **Phongsavanh Bank**, also offer useful services to travelers. Thai banks are a better choice for transactions other than exchanging money, since the Lao banks are geared more toward catering to the needs of the local population.

CHANGING MONEY

Although the US dollar and the Thai baht are the most commonly traded currencies, all major international currencies are exchangeable in Laos. In addition to banks, there are also private money changers. Gold shops in small towns, or the biggest store in a village, often exchange money, but these are cash transactions only. Rates change daily and are posted. However, it is best to change enough money before embarking on any trips through smaller towns and provinces. Visitors should be aware that the kip is not convertible into other currencies outside Laos.

Entry to Phongsavanh Bank, Vientiane

DIRECTORY

BANKS

ANZ Laos
33 Lan Xang Avenue (across Talat Sao), Vientiane. **City Map** D3. ***Tel*** *(021)-222-700.* **www**.anz.com

Bangkok Bank
Khun Bulom Rd, Vientiane. **City Map** C3. ***Tel*** *(021)-213-560.* **www**.bangkokbank.com

Banque Pour le Commerce Exterieure Lao (BCEL)
1 Pangkham Rd, Vientiane. **City Map** B4. ***Tel*** *(021)-223-190.* **www**.bcellaos.com

Phongsavanh Bank
147 10 Samsenthai Rd, Vientiane. **City Map** B3. ***Tel*** *(021)-212-666.* **www**.phongsavanhbank.com

Siam Commercial Bank
117 Lan Xang Avenue, Vientiane. **City Map** C3. ***Tel*** *(021)-213-501.* **www**.scb.co.th

CREDIT CARDS

MasterCard
Tel *001-636-722-7111.*

Visa
Tel *001-410-581-9994.*

Visitors withdrawing money from an ATM, Luang Prabang

ATMS AND CREDIT CARDS

Both BCEL and ANZ Laos have Automatic Teller Machines (ATMs) in major towns, although the rate is about 7 percent less favorable than other exchange transactions. Added to it is a fixed transaction fee of about 50,000 kip. This is in addition to a foreign transaction fee that most US and European banks charge. Debit cards and bank cards using the Cirrus or Plus systems should work in Laos, but if they are not accepted in ATMs, making a cash withdrawal from an exchange counter or a bank is a good alternative. Credit cards such as **MasterCard** and **Visa** are most readily accepted in major hotels, upscale boutiques, and restaurants. In all other places, they are grudgingly accepted and a service charge of 3 percent is often added. Travelers who encounter any credit card-related problems can call the home company for assistance.

TRAVELER'S CHECKS

As ATMs accepting all major credit cards become more common, traveler's checks are becoming less popular, but they can be exchanged at Lao banks, and the rate is in fact better than ATM-based transactions. Upscale hotels will also exchange them, but most merchants will not. If traveler's checks are lost in Laos, a collect call to a representative office abroad will suffice to have replacement checks sent via courier.

CURRENCY

The currency of Laos is the Lao kip, abbreviated as LAK. Denominations are displayed in Arabic numerals on one side of the notes only. All notes bear the portrait of Kaysone Phomvihane, and the 20,000 and 50,000 kip notes are both red. It is better to pay with small bills when buying from vendors as they often lack sufficient change.

Bank Notes

The kip comes in denominations of 500, 1,000, 2,000, 5,000, 10,000, 20,000, and the fairly recent 50,000 kip note. Coins are not in use.

5,000 kip

500 kip

10,000 kip

1,000 kip

20,000 kip

2,000 kip

50,000 kip

Communications and Media in Cambodia

Cambodia's communication facilities have improved vastly over the past few years. Cell phones and laptops are a common sight. It is easy to make a call and 3G Internet is fast and cheap in Phnom Penh and Siem Reap. Most hotels and cafés have Internet or Wi-Fi access. Major newspapers are available across Siem Reap and Phnom Penh. The postal system is also fairly reliable although it is advisable to use a courier service for valuables.

A swanky Internet café offering several facilities, Phnom Penh

INTERNATIONAL AND LOCAL TELEPHONE CALLS

Cambodia uses the GSM mobile telephone system and cell phone coverage is strong in most parts of the country. Phone cards are usually a good way of making a local or international call. They can be used in phone kiosks on the street or in hotel lobbies. Personal cell phones automatically connect to a local network but calls can prove to be fairly expensive. Calls placed from hotel rooms can also be exorbitant as a surcharge is applied over and above the cost of the call. Using a prepaid SIM card with a local number on your cell phone is usually a good option, but using Skype from an Internet café is usually the cheapest.

If dialing from a local SIM card-operated cell phone or if using a card phone, replace the 001 country code with 007, for cheaper rates. Numbers starting with 01 or 09 are cell phone numbers.

INTERNET FACILITIES

Internet connections are widely available in most hotels, mid-range guesthouses, as well as in bars, restaurants and cafés. Siem Reap and Phnom Penh boast excellent cafés with Internet, good menus and air conditioning. Broadband is widely available, though it can be slow, with many customers on the same line. Now normally free, Wi-Fi is a standard feature in many tourism venues.

POSTAL SERVICES

Cambodia's postal system is fairly reliable. Post offices are open from 7am–7pm and closed on Sundays. There is also a *poste restante* service at the main post office in Phnom Penh. Letters and postcards take one to two weeks to reach countries outside of Asia, although the service is usually inexpensive. Valuable items should preferably be sent by courier companies such as **DHL**, **TSP Express Cambodia**, and **UPS**, which operate in Siem Reap and Phnom Penh.

NEWSPAPERS AND MAGAZINES

There are two major English-language newspapers in Cambodia – *The Cambodia Daily*, which carries a good round up of local and international affairs, and the excellent *The Phnom Penh Post*, published on weekdays, which carries local and international articles. *Time, Newsweek, The Bangkok Post*, and *Herald Tribune* are all sold in Phnom Penh, Sihanoukville, and Siem Reap, apart from other major cities. A number of glossy magazines, published periodically, offer a calendar of upcoming events. *Phnom Penh Asia Life Guide* has colorful features on food and drink, shopping, and fashion. *Touchstone Magazine*, which features restaurant reviews, is also popular. The free periodicals published by Canby Publications, which include maps, local features, temple guides, and restaurant and hotel listings, are very useful for visitors.

Streetside kiosks selling newspapers and magazines, Phnom Penh

TELEVISION AND RADIO

While Cambodia ranked 85th among 169 countries in the press freedom index released by Reporters Without Borders in 2008, it slipped several slots to reach the 117th position in 2011. There have been repeated incidents of journalists and their families being harassed or murdered after highlighting issues of corruption and illegal logging.

Most hotels have cable TV where you can access BBC or CNN news as well as sports channels covering major events. Among the radio channels, most people prefer the BBC World Service to state-run channels.

DIRECTORY

COURIER SERVICES

DHL
353, St 110, Phnom Penh.
City Map C1. ***Tel*** *(023)-427-726.*
Sivatha St, Siem Reap. ***Tel*** *(063)-964-949.* **www**.dhl.com

TSP Express Cambodia
701, Monivong Blvd, Phnom Penh.
City Map D4. ***Tel*** *(023)-211-278.*

UPS
30E, St 274, Phnom Penh. ***Tel*** *(023)-219-213.* **www**.ups.com

Communications and Media in Laos

Laos has kept abreast of the latest developments in communications, in particular the Internet and mobile telephony. Barring remote areas, cell phones are widely used. Public phones are not common and few venture to the Lao Telecom offices. The postal system is outdated and it is better to use international courier companies. Cable TV is available in most hotels, and international newspapers arrive regularly, although a few days late.

Popular brand of phone card and cell phone SIM used in Laos

INTERNATIONAL AND LOCAL TELEPHONE CALLS

Although the offices of Lao Telecom can make overseas calls for you, it is better to use either a VOIP system, available in Internet cafés, or to bring along a cell phone. Laos uses the GSM system, so those who have an unlocked tri-band phone can simply buy a local SIM card from any cell phone shop or street kiosk. This will allow you to make and receive calls locally and internationally. Those whose phones are locked can consider using the service provider's roaming system, which is usually good enough for staying connected, although the service is expensive and does not permit making or receiving local calls. When making a local call in Laos, you must always remember to include the city code before the phone number.

INTERNET FACILITIES

Internet cafés abound in Laos. Their prices are moderate and connection speeds are generally adequate for checking e-mail and surfing the Internet. Wi-Fi is also a common feature in numerous hotels, cafés, and restaurants in Vientiane as well as Luang Prabang. However, the service is rarely free of charge. Those traveling with a laptop or smart phone will find Wi-Fi more convenient than using an Internet café.

POSTAL SERVICES

The Lao postal system is not always reliable and visitors should avoid using it, especially for mailing valuables or other important items. A safer alternative is to use a courier company such as **DHL** or **FedEx**, which also have domestic operations, although the service is usually expensive. Travelers who are continuing on to Thailand or Vietnam could consider posting their packages from there.

Variety of stationery, books, and publications at Monument Books, Vientiane

DIRECTORY

COURIER SERVICES

DHL
031, Nongno St, Ban Wattay Noy, Vientiane. **City Map** D4. ***Tel*** *(021)-214-868.*

FedEx
Lan Xang Ave, Vientiane. **City Map** D4. ***Tel*** *(021)-223-278.*

Ocher-colored postbox, typically seen throughout Laos

NEWSPAPERS AND MAGAZINES

The government-published English-language *Vientiane Times* is the most commonly available newspaper in Laos. Although Communist in its leanings, it offers an insider's view of the country. Besides vernacular publications, there is also the popular French-language *Le Renovateur*. Some international publications are available at large bookstores in Vientiane, as well as Luang Prabang and in hotel shops. There are also a few cultural magazines such as *Vannasin Magazine* and *Sinxay Weekly*, which are published in Lao, and *Wattanatham (Culture) Magazine*, which is published in both English and Lao.

TELEVISION AND RADIO

The government controls the television and radio channels and there are no programs in English. The satellite systems found in hotels vary widely, and often focus on Thai programs. But there is usually some English-language news, as well as financial and sports coverage.

TRAVEL INFORMATION IN CAMBODIA

The most convenient way of getting to Cambodia is by air from Bangkok. Connections are short, and there are a number of carriers servicing Phnom Penh from Bangkok's Suvarnabhumi International Airport. The country's internal air transport system is reasonably well developed with regular flights between major towns. Remote provinces such as Ratanakiri, however, are no longer serviced by air.

Logo of Vietnam Airlines

Visitors can also enter Cambodia by rail, bus, or ferry from Laos, Thailand, or Vietnam. Traveling within the country varies from easy to grueling depending on the roads. While many highways have been greatly improved, making journeys by bus fairly comfortable, reaching remote places may not always be a pleasant experience. For commuting within cities, visitors can choose from tuk-tuks, *motos*, and taxis.

Shops and cafés inside Phnom Penh International Airport

ARRIVING BY AIR

There are two major airports: Phnom Penh International Airport and Siem Reap-Angkor International Airport, which operate flights from Ho Chi Minh City, Vientiane, Kuala Lumpur, Seoul, Shanghai, and most major cities in the US, UK, and Australia. International carriers, such as **Thai Airways**, **Bangkok Airways**, **Vietnam Airlines**, **Eva Airways**, **Air Asia**, **Lao Airlines**, **Malaysia Airlines**, and **Cathay Pacific**, operate flights from Cambodia. Flying from the US takes more than 20 hours, while flying from Europe takes around 13 hours.

AIR FARES

The cost of flying to Cambodia varies depending on the airline, season, and travel agent used. Fares are usually high during holidays and the cool season (Nov–Feb), when the country gets most of its visitors. However, air fares fall considerably during the rainy season (Jun–Oct). Visitors are advised to book tickets well in advance.

ARRIVING BY LAND OR WATER

There are at least 12 border crossings into Cambodia from Thailand, Vietnam, and Laos. The most popular crossing from Thailand is Arayprathet to Poipet. Due to recent trouble with Thailand over the ownership of Prasat Preah Vihear temple *(see pp94–5)*, however, the northeastern border is sometimes closed. Veun Kham to Dom Kralor from Laos and Moc Bai to Bavet from Vietnam are also used regularly. These places are accessible only by car since none of the borders are linked by a rail service. Besides, improved highways have now cut journey time significantly.

A Bangkok Airways plane standing at Siem Reap-Angkor Airport

Tuk-tuks waiting outside Phnom Penh International Airport

Travel by water is becoming increasingly rare with few waterways linking the borders.

ON ARRIVAL

Cambodia provides the facility of visa on arrival, though it can also be applied for in advance. An evisa can be obtained from the website http://www.mfaic.gov.kh/evisa. Visitors are handed an immigration form in-flight, which must be presented on arrival, along with a passport-sized photograph. The procedure is swift, provided there are at least six months left before your passport expires. A one-month business visa is slightly more expensive than a tourist visa. At Siem Reap and Phnom Penh airports, visitors automatically receive a one-month visa.

GETTING TO AND FROM AIRPORTS

Departures and arrivals are handled with courtesy and efficiency at international airports, although visitors must be prepared for security checks during arrival and departure. Tuk-tuks and air-conditioned taxis can be hired from outside the terminal at both airports. Taxis and minibuses can also be organized in advance from upscale hotels. While the journey time from Siem Reap's airport to the town center is 10–15 minutes, traveling through Phnom Penh's over-crowded streets can take up to an hour.

DEPARTURE TAX

All visitors leaving Cambodia are expected to pay a departure tax, which costs US$25 at international airports and US$18 at domestic airports. Fees are now included in the original price of airline tickets, as airport tax.

GREEN TRAVEL

While travel around Cambodia is becoming increasingly convenient with improved road networks and a growth in the transport infrastructure, it is far from eco-friendly. Many cars and mopeds still use leaded fuel, which is sold on the roadside in second-hand plastic and glass bottles, because unleaded fuel is expensive. Added to this, cities such as Phnom Penh are crowded with numerous outdated, polluting vehicles.

Visitors, however, can help by taking measures such as avoiding excessive use of air conditioning in the car, especially during the cool season; using bicycles or walking for sightseeing trips wherever possible; and careful disposal of litter. When participating in activities such as eco-trekking, visitors should check the credentials of the company they are considering using, including details of how long they have been operating, how they contribute to the local community, and what they do to minimize their carbon footprint.

Visitors cycling out of the eastern gate, Angkor Thom

DIRECTORY

ARRIVING BY AIR

Air Asia
179, St Sisowath, Phnom Penh.
Tel *(023)-890-035.*
www.airasia.com

Bangkok Airways
61A, St 214, Phnom Penh. **City Map** D3. ***Tel*** *(023)-426-624.*
www.bangkokair.com

Cathay Pacific
168 Monireth Blvd, Phnom Penh. **City Map** B3. ***Tel*** *(023)-424-300.*
www.cathaypacific.com

Eva Airways
11-14B, St 205, Phnom Penh. **City Map** B4. ***Tel*** *(023)-210-303.*
www.evaair.com

Lao Airlines
111 Sihanouk, St 274, Phnom Penh. **City Map** D3. ***Tel*** *(023)-222-956.* **www**.laoairlines.com

Malaysia Airlines
35–37 Samdech Pan, St 214, Phnom Penh. **City Map** D3.
Tel *(023)-426-688.*
www.malaysiaairlines.com

Thai Airways
294 Mao Tse Toung, St 245, Phnom Penh. **City Map** B4. ***Tel*** *(023)-890-292.* **www**.thaiairways.com

Vietnam Airlines
41 Samdech Pan, St 214, Phnom Penh. **City Map** D3.
Tel *(023)-215-998.*
www.vietnamairlines.com

Getting Around Cambodia

Bus ticket for Mekong Express

Transportation is finally coming of age in Cambodia, after years of stagnation. The last few years have seen major investment in roads and highway networks, with water-resistant surface roads connecting major towns such as Phnom Penh, Siem Reap, Sihanoukville, and Battambang. Boat travel is often very slow, although enjoyable, but it is not recommended for visitors on a short trip. The internal airways network is also quite efficient although visitors traveling to remote locations will have to make use of local transportation such as a bus service, or hire a car and driver. Driving alone, however, can be quite challenging, especially in the provinces, where few locals speak English and road signs are in the Khmer script.

New inter-city, air-conditioned buses at a bus station, Phnom Penh

DOMESTIC AIRLINES

Cambodia is served by one domestic airline – **Cambodia Angkor Air** in collaboration with Vietnam Airlines. Cambodia Angkor Air offers flights to Sihanoukville, Siem Reap, Phnom Penh, and Ho Chi Minh City.

PLANE TICKETS, FARES, AND RESERVATIONS

Tickets can be purchased at the airlines' reservation offices at the airport, in their offices in Phnom Penh, online, or through a reputable tour agent. Agents are usually a good choice because they are often able to get discounts on ticket prices, especially on long-distance flights. Prominent agents such as **Exotissimo** and **Hanuman Tourism** are located in Phnom Penh, while others, including **All Concierge Services** have offices in Siem Reap. Some of the larger hotels will also be happy to deal with your onward travel at no extra cost. A one-way ticket from Phnom Penh to Siem Reap will usually cost under US$100. Tickets may not be easily available during Christmas, major festivals, or at any time during the peak season from November to February. Visitors are therefore advised to book their flights well in advance during these times. Ticket prices generally drop during lean periods, especially in the months of February, June, and October.

BUSES

Bus journeys have improved immeasurably, with newer air-conditioned buses and vastly upgraded roads on major routes. As a result, travel time between places such as Siem Reap and Battambang have more than halved. Among the principal bus companies that operate decent services out of the capital are **Phnom Penh Sorya Transport Company**, which runs services to Sihanoukville, Siem Reap, Bangkok, Battambang, and other provincial towns, and **Mekong Express**, which follows similar routes, but offers greater luxury. For remote places, it is necessary to hire a car with a driver or catch a local minibus, which can be uncomfortable and dangerously overcrowded and the seating space is quite constricted. It is usually advisable to hire a minibus and driver if there are sufficient passengers. Buses and minibuses take regular breaks en route.

BUS TICKETS AND FARES

Tickets can be bought through tour agents, organized from your hotel, or on arrival at the bus terminus – from where most buses operate. If traveling on a busy route, such as Phnom Penh to Siem Reap, it is advisable to make reservations in advance as buses fill up very quickly. Bus fares are usually very reasonable.

RENTING A CAR OR MOTORBIKE

Renting a motorbike is a great way to see the country, and if you are an experienced rider, it can be a terrific way to tackle the roads in isolated regions such as Mondulkiri and Ratanakiri. Motorbikes also have the advantage of allowing travelers to move at their own pace, as well as interact with locals. However,

Counter at a travel agency selling bus tickets, Phnom Penh

Motorcycles for rent outside a dealer's office in Kep

bikers must keep in mind that traveling this way may not always be a pleasant experience, especially since many of the roads in remote areas, barring the highways, are in very poor condition. Besides, locals often speed along the wrong side of the road, especially on hairpin bends, and riders also need to keep an eye out for wandering livestock and children running across their path.

Renting a car is generally quite easy and affordable, but only recommended if you plan to take a local driver who knows the road and the locations of temples and other sights. Driving on one's own is not advisable for visitors who do not speak the local language. However, should you wish to do so, bear in mind that driving without a license may warrant a fine from the Cambodian police.

BOATS AND FERRIES

Cambodia's many rivers are a great way to travel from one place to another while observing the fantastic wildlife, as well as local cultures en route. Travel companies such as **Angkor Express** offer boat trips between Siem Reap and Battambang, which usually take around 5 to 8 hours. Boat tours between Phnom Penh and Siem Reap can take up to 5 hours. Although both routes take in the Tonlé Sap Lake, the latter is less rewarding as there is little to see except vast expanses of water.

Travelers coming from Laos now have the option of the rocket boat, which can be a dangerous way to travel due to rocks hidden below the surface of the river, particularly during the wet season. These longtail boats ply the route between the Lao border and Cambodia's Stung Treng, but in the dry season, when the river is low, the route can be fraught with danger. In Laos, similar vessels have met with accidents that have killed people every year. If traveling on these boats, visitors must carry earplugs as the noise from the engines can be deafening. They must also never agree to travel when the light is fading and visibility is poor. Sun block and a hat are essential, especially if traveling on the roof.

DIRECTORY

DOMESTIC AIRLINES

Cambodia Angkor Air
206A, Preah Norodom Blvd, Phnom Penh. **City Map** E5. ***Tel*** *(023)-666-6786.*
www.cambodiaangkorair.com

BUSES

Mekong Express
87 Sisowath Quay, Phnom Penh. **City Map** E1. ***Tel*** *(023)-427-518.*

Phnom Penh Sorya Transport Company
Corner of Sts 217 and 67. **City Map** D2. ***Tel*** *(023)-210-359.*
www.ppsoryatransport.com

BOATS AND FERRIES

Angkor Express
Beside the Titanic Restaurant, Sisowath Quay, Phnom Penh. **City Map** E1. ***Tel*** *(012)-789-531.*

TRAVEL AGENCIES

All Concierge Services
051, Stung Thmei Village, Siem Reap. ***Tel*** *855-89-855-855.*

Exotissimo
66 Norodom Blvd, Phnom Penh. **City Map** E2. ***Tel*** *(023)-218-948.*
www.exotissimo.com

Hanuman Tourism
310, St 12, Phnom Penh. **City Map** E4. ***Tel*** *(023)-218-396.*
www.hanumantourism.com

Tourists crossing the Tonlé Sap Lake on a ferry, Chong Kneas

Local Transportation

The last five years have seen some rapid development in Cambodia, with improved road networks and better transportation facilities. However, this has also led to an increase in traffic and jams are common in major cities such as Phnom Penh and Siem Reap, particularly in the morning and evening. The quickest way of getting around bigger cities is on *motos* (motorcycle taxis), which weave effortlessly through congestion. Leisurely *cyclos*, motorized tuk-tuks, and metered taxis are also readily available.

Locals riding on a *cyclo*, Siem Reap

Visitors enjoying the sights of Phnom Penh from a tuk-tuk

GETTING AROUND PHNOM PENH

A small city, Phnom Penh is easy to get around despite the absence of a local bus system. Perhaps the most charming means of navigating the city streets is on a *remorque-moto*, better known as the tuk-tuk. Another gentle, albeit time-consuming way of getting through the traffic is the *cyclo*, tried by most visitors to the city. A *cyclo* can easily accommodate two to three passengers and is pedalled by the driver who sits at the back. While a ride on a *cyclo* may not cost much, tuk-tuk drivers often hike their prices for foreigners, particularly if they see them exiting an expensive hotel. It is recommended that visitors negotiate prices before taking the ride.

Those keen to explore the city at their own pace can also hire a bicycle for the purpose. Bicycles are usually available at most guesthouses for a few dollars per day. Cyclists, however, are advised to be careful, when riding, of the heat and pollution in larger cities. Motorcycles are another way to explore the city, but riders must wear helmets. Riders should also possess a local license, or else they run the risk of being stopped by the police and fined a few dollars.

BUSES AND MINIBUSES

Although there is no centralized bus service in Cambodia yet, the country is well served by buses heading to all provinces. These buses, run mostly by private operators, are usually air-conditioned and cover most major towns. Minibuses also operate in the provinces and are an inexpensive, if overcrowded, way to get around. Visitors are advised to book tickets in advance to ensure a seat.

METERED TAXIS

With improved transportation facilities, metered taxis are available in Phnom Penh. **Global Taxis** is the only official metered taxi service, running air-conditioned, modern cars at reasonable prices. Although a certain minimum amount is charged to all visitors, the service is usually quite inexpensive. Upscale hotels, guesthouses, and most travel agents can also arrange for taxis, especially if hiring one for the entire day, or for traveling long distances. There are also non-official taxi drivers eager to ferry visitors, though sometimes they are hard to spot. It is essential to settle on a price before getting into these cars in order to avoid disagreement or arguments later on.

RULES OF THE ROAD

With rapidly increasing traffic and little concern for safety, driving in large cities

Metered taxis operated by different companies in Phnom Penh

Group of visitors on an organized tour of Ta Prohm, Siem Reap province

such as Phnom Penh and Siem Reap is quite a dangerous proposition. Rules are seldom followed and pedestrians have no right of way.

While driving in Cambodia is on the right-hand side of the road, there are few traffic lights at junctions and most vehicles do not follow traffic rules. Drivers must be careful not to turn left on a "No left turn" sign and to use headlights at night. Pedestrians should remain vigilant when crossing roads; the ideal way to do this is to walk at a regular pace with purpose, ensuring that drivers can see you and swerve around you accordingly.

Road sign in Kampot

Renting a self-drive car, especially in Phnom Penh, is not advisable because in case of an accident, foreigners will find the local police difficult to deal with, not to mention the red tape and the language barrier. Besides, traffic police officials in the capital, although lax with locals, are quite strict with foreigners.

If traveling on a motorcycle, drivers must wear a helmet. Although this rule is hardly followed by locals, foreigners are fined for the same offence.

ORGANIZED TOURS

Considering the number of sights worth visiting, not just in and around Phnom Penh and Siem Reap, but also other major towns in Cambodia. Taking an organized tour is usually a great idea. These range from one- to several-day trips. Besides being convenient, they are often less time consuming and usually work out to be less expensive. As a rule, the more people there are in a group, the cheaper the individual price will be. At the same time, prices for the same trip can vary a lot, so visitors should ask in several offices before settling for any one agent, in order to get the best deal. There are several good tour companies in Phnom Penh, mostly around the Sisowath Quay area, as well as in Siem Reap. Companies such as **Exotic Angkor Travel** in Siem Reap and **Diethelm Travel** in Phnom Penh are great for package tours and cover all major sights in and around these towns. They are also helpful for organizing flight bookings, accommodation facilities, and transportation. Hanuman Tourism, among the best known in the business, and **Hola Travel**, based in Phnom Penh, also organize comprehensive tour packages for visitors. **Sun Tours** arranges unique one- and two-day boat cruises to the verdant islands off Sihanoukville.

Cruise taking visitors on a trip to the Sihanoukville Islands

DIRECTORY

METERED TAXIS

Global Taxis
Phnom Penh International Airport, Phnom Penh.
Tel *(023)-222-788.*

ORGANIZED TOURS

Diethelm Travel
65, St 240, Phnom Penh.
City Map D3.
Tel *(023)-219-151.*
www.diethelmtravel.com

Exotic Angkor Travel
Psar Damkralahn Rd, N of Route 6, Siem Reap.
Tel *(063)-965-326.*
www.exoticangkor.com

Hola Travel
415 Sisowath Quay, Phnom Penh. **City Map** F3.
Tel *(023)-221-091.*
www.holacambodia.com

Sun Tours
Sihanoukville.
Tel *(016)-396-201.*
www.suntours-cambodia.com

TRAVEL INFORMATION IN LAOS

Most visitors arrive in Laos by air. Since there are no direct flights into the country from Europe or the Americas, many travelers make the final leg of their trip via Bangkok, which has the highest number of connecting flights to Laos. Lao Airlines, the national carrier, serves eight cities within the country. There are also international air connections from China, Vietnam, Malaysia, and Cambodia.

Logo of Lao Airlines

There are 15 border crossings open from all the countries bordering Laos with the exception of Myanmar. The road network connecting Laos to its neighbors is rapidly improving and the roads are plied by modern buses and minivans. Boat travel is an interesting option, particularly on the wide and navigable Mekong River. Within the towns and cities tuk-tuks are a convenient mode of transportation.

ARRIVING BY AIR

Most visitors to Laos arrive at Wattay International Airport in Vientiane since it has flights to and from Bangkok in Thailand, Ho Chi Minh City in Vietnam, Phnom Penh and Siem Reap in Cambodia, Kuala Lumpur in Malaysia, as well as Kunming in China. The international airport at Luang Prabang serves Bangkok, as well as Hanoi and Siem Reap. Pakse International Airport has flights to Bangkok, Siem Reap, and Phnom Penh. **Lao Airlines** has the most flights in and out of the country, followed by **Thai Airways**, **Vietnam Airlines**, **China Eastern Airlines** and **Air Asia**.

Lao Airlines plane stationed on the tarmac, Savannakhet airport

AIR FARES

The cost of getting to Laos by air fluctuates depending on the season. Fares can double during the peak season. Most of the discount flights from Europe and the US are usually via Bangkok. Online travel companies and travel agents can assist travelers in finding the best deals.

ON ARRIVAL

There are two official forms that need to be filled out upon arrival. The first is a visa application form and the second is an immigration form. These forms are distributed on all flights landing in Laos. Visitors can apply for a visa at the port of entry with a passport-sized photograph and the completed forms along with a fee. The fee varies with nationality and payment is always in foreign currency, usually US dollars. The formalities required are minimal and generally involve only a stamp in the passport. Visas can also be applied for in advance. The immigration form that is placed in the passport is an important document and must be kept carefully since losing it can result in a fine. Customs checks are cursory, although the standard limits on the import of alcohol and tobacco should be observed.

Arrival terminal, Pakse International Airport

GETTING TO AND FROM AIRPORTS

The three international airports in Laos are located fairly close to the cities they serve and as a result there are no shuttle bus services between the airports and the cities. However, taxi tickets are sold within the arrivals terminal in Vientiane.

In Luang Prabang and Pakse, tuk-tuks are readily available outside the airport. Hotels usually offer pick-ups from airports for a small fee. Upscale hotels, however, offer free airport transfer for all guests.

ARRIVING BY LAND

Laos has 15 international land-border crossings. The main crossing from Thailand is via the Friendship Bridge from the Thai town of Nong Khai to Tha Deua in southern Laos, linked to the capital by bus and rail. The boat crossing from the Thai town of Chiang Khong in Chiang Rai province to Huay Xai in Bokeo province allows travelers to cruise down the Mekong River to Luang Prabang. Another crossing in Mukdahan province leads to the town of Savannakhet via the Friendship Bridge. A crossing near Loei in Thailand leads to the Lao village of Nam Heuang; however, no visas are issued here. There is a crossing from the Thai town of Chong Mek to Vang Tau, which is 27 miles (43 km) from Pakse, where visas are available on arrival.

The border between Laos and Cambodia is also open. Boats and minibuses operate between Stung Treng and the crossing in Laos. The immigration point at Vueng Kham in Laos may or may not issue visas on arrival. Visitors need to check with travel agents in Phnom Penh.

Pick-up car, Lao Plaza Hotel

A Lao visa is available on arrival at all the border crossings from Vietnam. There is a remote entry point at Bo Y, about 60 miles (100 km) east of Attapeu town. Buses and taxis ply the route. The Vietnamese village of Lao Bao is connected to Dan Savan in Laos, a popular crossing. From here a good road leads to Savannakhet, 140 miles (230 km) west. Buses originating in Da Nang ply the route regularly. The crossing from Cau Treo to Nam Phao puts the traveler within striking distance of the beautiful Phu Hin Pun National Protected Area. The border crossing at Nam Can into Nam Kahn can be used to get to the Plain of Jars, which is a 5-hour bus journey farther west. From Tay Trang a crossing leads to Sop Hun, which is 36 miles (60 km) southwest of the town of Muang Khua. Buses to Muang Khua originate in Dien Bien Phu in Vietnam.

A crossing from the Chinese town of Mohan leads to the village of Boten in Luang Nam Tha province. Public transport is available to the provincial capital Luang Nam Tha.

GREEN TRAVEL

The Lao National Tourism Administration, working in conjunction with foreign governments and NGOs, has been seriously promoting the country as an ecotourism destination. The Lao people are being educated about the advantages of sound environmental practices, in order to preserve the resources that attract visitors. Preserving the environment will, in turn, be economically beneficial for them as opposed to slash and burn agriculture, logging, and trapping wildlife. Community-based treks, which promote village homestays and involve villagers by hiring them as guides, are popular.

However, old practices still persist. Visitors should steer clear of items such as deer, often featured on restaurant menus, and wildlife products such as tooth necklaces, bags made from animal skins, and alcohol containing snakes.

DIRECTORY

ARRIVING BY AIR

Air Asia
www.airasia.com

China Eastern Airlines
Luang Prabang Rd, Vientiane.
City Map A5. ***Tel*** *(021)-212-300.*
www.flychinaeastern.com

Lao Airlines
2 Pangkham Rd, Vientiane.
City Map B4. ***Tel*** *(021)-212-051-54.* www.laoairlines.com

Thai Airways
Luang Prabang Rd, Vientiane.
City Map A5. ***Tel*** *(021)-222-527.*
www.thaiair.com

Vietnam Airlines
Lao Plaza Hotel, Samsenthai Rd, Vientiane. **City Map** C3.
Tel *(021)-217-562.*
www.vietnamairlines.com

Passengers waiting at the terminal, Wattay International Airport, Vientiane

Getting Around Laos

A popular river cruise company

Road conditions in Laos have improved, but dirt roads are still common in remote areas and road repairs are never immediate. The Russian flat-bed truck with wooden seats and a zinc roof has given way to double-decker air-conditioned buses. Minivans are also popular and more comfortable and faster than buses. The *songthaew* (literally meaning two rows) is common in rural areas. Due to the improved road network, boat travel is less common, although still possible, and necessary, in some areas. Laos's only railway ends just after crossing the Friendship Bridge from Thailand. Two domestic airlines reach all the major cities in Laos.

DOMESTIC AIRLINES

Laos's national carrier, **Lao Airlines**, has regular domestic flights between cities, such as Vientiane, Luang Prabang, Pakse, and Luang Nam Tha, covering most regions of the country. **Lao Capricorn Air**, a private company, operates flights from Vientiane to areas such as Phonsavan in Xieng Khuang province and Sam Neua in Hua Phan province. Lao Capricorn Air also flies to Phongsali and Sainyabuli, although these flights are seasonal. The destinations covered by both carriers seem to change quite frequently, so it is best to check locally for the latest information. Both carriers use modern turbojet aircraft and have good safety records.

PLANE TICKETS, FARES, AND RESERVATIONS

While it is possible to purchase tickets at the offices of Lao Airlines, an efficient e-ticketing service makes it much simpler to stop in at any travel agent, who can issue the ticket

Passengers waiting to buy tickets at a bus ticket counter in Savannakhet

immediately at the same price as the airline itself. Top hotels also offer this service. Domestic airfares are usually under US$100 per flight, but not all are direct. For example, flights from Luang Prabang to Pakse would entail a change in Vientiane. Lao Capricorn flights, which cover the less-traveled routes, do not provide the facility of an e-ticket and are more expensive. However, a travel agent can book tickets for a small fee. In the peak season, from November to February, demand for flights always exceeds supply, and it is advisable to book resonably far in advance.

Air-conditioned, double-decker VIP luxury bus

BUSES

A wide variety of buses ply the roads of Laos. These range from the sleek, new air-conditioned VIP coaches that ply Route 13 along with the international routes, to the rattletrap blue- and white- government-run buses that serve the environs of Vientiane and other cities. There are also a variety of mid-range options to choose from. As a rule, the longer and more well-traveled the route, the better the vehicles serving it will be. Travelers should find out about the kind of vehicle they are boarding in order to avoid arduous road journeys. A local bus will probably stop at every village, while an express bus will make fewer stops. Ascertaining this is not always easy, although the fare is usually the best indication of the quality of the ride.

BUS TICKETS AND FARES

Most long-distance buses depart from a station located on the outskirts of town rather than city-center bus stations. Additionally, most major cities have two or more bus stations, depending on the direction and distance of travel. For example, Vientiane has three bus stations: the **Southern Bus Station** on Route 13 situated on the southern edge of town; the **Northern Bus Station** en route to the airport; and the Talat Sao Bus Station in the center of town for short journeys and trips to Thailand. Luang Prabang makes do with two bus stations – a northern and a southern bus terminal.

It is worth making a trip to the bus station on the day before a long journey in order to buy a ticket. This will allow travelers to see the types of buses that are available as well as get the most accurate information on departure times. If time does not permit this, it is also possible to buy VIP bus tickets from travel agents, but travelers must be specific about their requirements in order to avoid misunderstandings about the types of buses and departure times.

MINIVANS AND SONGTHAEWS

Air-conditioned minivans are an excellent way for small groups to travel. They are usually designed to take about 10 passengers and seats are sold individually. However, it is possible for travelers to charter the vehicle, often at a negotiable price, and also arrange rest or sightseeing stops en route at their convenience. Minivans run between all major cities and also stop in the city centers, thereby avoiding the inconvenience of suburban bus stations.

At the other end of the mid-sized vehicle spectrum lies the *songthaew*, which is basically a pick-up truck fitted with two benches. Passengers usually sit facing each other or on the roof of the vehicle. These are a common sight in rural Laos as they ply the routes between cities and are used for short-to-medium distance trips in rural areas. They are usually tightly packed with passengers and their belongings. *Songthaew* follow fixed routes and stop whenever a potential passenger flags them down or when someone wishes to disembark. These vehicles are generally slower and dustier compared to buses, but they are an excellent way to observe local life in rural Laos.

Visitors riding rented motorcycles, a convenient mode of transport

RENTING A CAR OR MOTORCYCLE

Most rental cars come with a driver, although self-drive options are available; neither is cheap. Cars can be rented from **Europcar**, but driving within cities can be dangerous because of darting motorcycles, stray cattle and water buffaloes, and pedestrians. Once out of town, the relative lack of traffic makes it less of a challenge, especially for those used to driving. Renting a motorcyle is quite popular, especially in Vientiane, from companies such as **Jules Classic Bikes.** Travelers should rent motorcycles only if they have prior riding experience and it is advisable to wear long pants, and shoes instead of sandals.

BOATS AND FERRIES

The improved road network in Laos has resulted in a reduction in the number of riverboats that once carried travelers along scenic if slow routes on the Mekong and other rivers. However, boats still ply the upper Mekong, the Si Phan Don region *(see pp202–3)*, and the Nam Ou in Northern Laos. The Luang Say Mekong Cruise from Luang Prabang to Huay Xai *(see pp184–5)*, or vice versa, remains the highlight of many a visitor's trip to Laos. Mekong riverboats are large wooden-hulled motor launches with a roof to protect passengers from the sun, and are capable of carrying dozens of passengers. The so-called speedboat is a light, narrow, shallow-draft vessel with a huge gimbal-mounted engine. These operate on the upper Mekong, but are dangerous and should be used in emergency situations only. Riverboats on the Nam Ou are smaller and faster versions of the Mekong cruisers, and chartering one is a viable option, especially if traveling in a group. Small motorized pirogues are used to get between the islands in the Si Phan Don region.

Massive wooden riverboat plying the scenic Mekong River

DIRECTORY

DOMESTIC AIRLINES

Lao Airlines
2 Pangkham Rd, Vientiane. **City Map** B4. **www**.laoairlines.com

Lao Capricorn Air
Wattay Airport Domestic Terminal, Vientiane. **City Map** A4. **www**.laoscapricornair.net

BUS STATIONS

Northern Bus Station
Evening Market Rd 12, Vientiane. **City Map** A4. ***Tel*** *(021)-260-094.*

Southern Bus Station
Dongdok Rd, Vientiane. **City Map** D4. ***Tel*** *(021)-740-521.*

CAR AND MOTORCYCLE RENTAL

Europcar
354 Samsenthai Rd, Vientiane. **City Map** C3. ***Tel*** *(021)-223-867.*

Jules Classic Bikes
Setthathirat Rd, Vientiane. **City Map** C3. **www**.bike-rental-laos.com

Local Transportation

Visitor on a bicycle

Laos lacks a reliable intra-city public transportation system that travelers can realistically use. There are shared tuk-tuks that ply fixed routes in Vientiane, but destinations are not written in English and this can be a handicap for travelers without knowledge of the local language. Moreover, tuk-tuk drivers often quote exorbitant fares and can be difficult to deal with, especially in Vientiane. It is better to use metered taxis, which are easily available in the capital and are often cheaper than tuk-tuks. Motorcycles and bicycles are also good options, but walking is sometimes the easiest way to explore a particular region.

GETTING AROUND VIENTIANE AND LUANG PRABANG

Given the absence of public transportation, and the extortionate fares charged by tuk-tuk drivers, many visitors find themselves happier getting around Vientiane and Luang Prabang on foot or on a bicycle. While Vientiane consists of a fairly large urban and suburban sprawl, the area where most visitors will spend their time is in fact quite small. The areas lying between the Mekong River and Samsenthai Road, and between Lan Xang Avenue and Chao Anou Road are only about a mile (2 km) from one end to the other and can be covered on foot. In Luang Prabang, the peninsular Old Town is about the same size as central Vientiane and can also be explored on foot. However, Luang Prabang is better suited to bicycles than Vientiane, since there is less vehicular traffic on the roads. It is easy to rent motorcycles in both Vientiane and Luang Prabang and they are a good option for those with some experience on these machines. Visitors should not attempt to learn to ride a motorcycle while in Laos as traffic conditions are challenging and medical facilities basic. Motorcycle rental shops usually ask for a passport as a deposit; an international driving permit is technically required but rarely asked for. Warnings to use the extra lock supplied and to park in designated motorcycle parking areas, where an attendant is on duty, should be taken seriously. Motorcycle theft is rife in Vientiane, and the renter will be held responsible if this happens. Travelers should also inspect the condition of the vehicle (brakes in particular) and check for any damage, even small scratches, which should be noted on the contract in order to avoid being charged for damaging the bike later.

Bicycles available for rent on the roadside, Vientiane

Walking, however, is the best option and also provides visitors with a chance to interact with the locals while taking in the sights. It should be kept in mind, though, that the sun shines brightly most of the time so a hat and sun block are essential. Drinking plenty of fluids is vital and walkers should try and keep to the shade. Mornings and late afternoons are best for strolls.

TUK-TUKS AND TAXIS

Since tuk-tuk drivers mainly serve foreign travelers, the ones in major tourist centers have also evolved into self-appointed guides offering tours of local sights, particularly those out of town, such as waterfalls. If travelers chance upon a reliable tuk-tuk driver, it is advisable to obtain his cell phone number and use his services regularly. Several types of tuk-tuk *(see p142)* ply the streets of Vientiane and other towns

Shared tuk-tuks lined up, waiting for passengers, Vientiane

Typical rush-hour traffic, Vientiane

and cities. These three-wheeled vehicles are usually brightly painted and can be useful to get between towns and bus stations, which are often located far from the town center. Most commonly, tuk-tuks are hired for one-way trips to a specific destination. They can also be engaged for a round trip with waiting time included. Travelers should expect a serious amount of bargaining before boarding. In Vientiane, metered taxi services, such as **TVLG**, offer air-conditioned, dust-free rides at reasonable prices. Older, unmetered taxis are also available but travelers should settle on a price before boarding.

RULES OF THE ROAD

Observing local traffic etiquette is vital, even for pedestrians. In Vientiane, particularly, the once quiet streets are now filled with new cars, especially at rush hour. In provincial towns, motorcycles weave through the downtown thoroughfares without any consideration for road safety. Most riders are inexperienced, and many do not even have a license. Traffic rules are seldom followed, with the larger vehicles usually getting right of way. Pedestrian crossings are also ignored by drivers, although the recently installed stop lights garner more respect, especially with a policeman ready to give chase and extract a fine from miscreants. Although cars keep to the right side of the road, it is wise to look both ways while crossing a street, since motorcycles will go against the flow of traffic if it means a shortcut. Only about half the motorcyclists on the road will use headlights after dark. Travelers will find it easier to get around once they are familiar with and learn to expect these local ways.

Tourist taxi logo

ORGANIZED TOURS

Organized tours are available in all the major towns and cities of Laos. Single-day excursions and several-day trips are easy to book. In Vientiane and Luang Prabang, travelers can contact any one of the numerous tour operators, such as **Green Discovery**, **Exotissimo**, and **Diethelm Travel Laos**, while in other cities the local tourist office can provide information. These government-run services are excellent, and focus on trekking and community based ecotours. In Vientiane, a typical itinerary would take in the Haw Phra Kaew *(see p140)*, Wat Si Saket *(see p141)*, the Patuxai, and the Talat Sao *(see p142)*. In Luang Prabang, the National Museum Complex *(see p156)*, Wat Xieng Thong *(see pp160–61)*, the Santi Chedi *(see p166)*, and sometimes a Mekong River cruise, are covered in a day.

DIRECTORY

TAXI SERVICE

TVLG
Tel *(021)-454-168.*

ORGANIZED TOURS

Diethelm Travel Laos
Nam Phu Square, Setthathirat Rd, Vientiane. **City Map** C4. ***Tel*** *(021)-213-833.*
Phu Vao Rd, Luang Prabang. **City Map** B5. ***Tel*** *(071)-261-011.*
www.diethelmtravel.com

Exotissimo
Pangkham St, Vientiane. **City Map** B4. ***Tel*** *(021)-241-861.*
Khemkhong Rd, Luang Prabang. **City Map** D2. ***Tel*** *(071)-252-879.*
www.exotissimo.com

Green Discovery
Setthathirat Rd, Vientiane. **City Map** B3. ***Tel*** *(021)-251-524.*
Sisavang Vong Rd, Luang Prabang. **City Map** C3. ***Tel*** *(071)-212-093.*
www.greendiscoverylaos.com

River cruise boat on the Mekong River from the Thai border to Luang Prabang

General Index

Page numbers in **bold** refer to main entries

A

B

T

Acknowledgments

Dorling Kindersley would like to thank the many people whose help and assistance contributed to the preparation of this book.

Main Contributors

Peter Holmshaw has lived in Asia for 25 years and now makes his home in Chiang Mai, Thailand where he raises his family, rides a mountain bike, and works in publishing.

Iain Stewart first visited Cambodia and Laos in 1991 as a backpacker. Now an author and journalist, he has written over 30 guidebooks to destinations as diverse as Ibiza and Indonesia. He lives in Brighton, UK.

Richard Waters has had a long association with Southeast Asia and writes for a number of British newspapers, magazines, and other guidebooks. He lives in the Cotswolds with his family.

Fact Checker Adam Bray

Proofreader Janice Pariat

Indexer Hilary Bird

Khmer and Lao Translations Andiamo! Language Services Ltd

Editorial Consultants Ros Belford, Claire Boobyer

Design and Editorial

Publisher Douglas Amrine
List Manager Vivien Antwi
Project Editor Michelle Crane
Junior Editor Vicki Allen
Editorial Assistance Adam Bray, Scarlett O'Hara
Project Art Editor Shahid Mahmood
Senior Cartographic Editor Casper Morris
Senior DTP Designer Jason Little
Senior Picture Researcher Ellen Root
Production Controllers Vicky Baldwin, Linda Dare

Revisions Team

Neha Dhingra, Caroline Elliker, Catherine Palmi, Erin Richards

Cartography Credits

Base mapping supplied by Kartographie Huber, www.kartographie.de and Lovell Johns Ltd, www.lovelljohns.com
The maps on pages 46/47, 60/61 and 138/139 are derived from © www.openstreetmap.org and contributors, licensed under CC-BY-SA, see www.creativecommons.org for further details.

Additional Photography

Max Alexander; Edward Allwright; Jane Burton; Ian O'Leary; Bethany Dawn; Tim Draper; Christopher and Sally Gable; Steve Gorton; Frank Greenaway; Amisha Gupta; David Henley; Barnabas Kindersley; Dave King; Stephen Oliver; Rough Guides: Simon Bracken, Tim Draper; Rob Shone; Michael Spencer.

Photography Permissions

Dorling Kindersley would like to thank the following for their assistance and kind permission to photograph at their establishments:
The Apsara Hotel; Artisans d'Angkor; The Battambang Provincial Museum; The Foreign Correspondents' Club; Khmer Ceramics Centre; Saun Kham at The Laos National Museum; Hab Touch at The National Museum of Cambodia; Raffles Hotels & Resorts; Santuk Silk Farm; The Traditional Arts and Ethnology Centre; Wat Ong Teu Mahawihan; Wat Pa Huak; Wat Si Muang; Wat Si Saket; Wat Xieng Thong; Xieng Khuan.

Picture Credits

Key: a-above; b-below/bottom; c-centre; f-far; l-left; r-right; t-top.

The publisher would like to thank the following individuals, companies, and picture libraries for their kind permission to reproduce their photographs:
4CORNERS IMAGES: SIME/Kaos03 162-163. ALAMY IMAGES: Alan Copson City Pictures 277br; Alan Howden - Cambodia Stock Photography 281tl; Alan King engraving 9c, 29c; Victor Paul Borg 181cra; G P Bowater 16cr; Jon Bower Cambodia 24clb; Thomas Cockrem 21ca; Ian Cruickshank 18cr; Danita Delimont 19tr, 135crb; David Myers Photography 26cl; David Noton Photography 230cla; DBImages 19cl; Adam Deschamps 79br, 86; Dreamtours 167tc; Shaun Edwards 154br; F1online digitale Bildagentur GmbH 276b; Philip Game 193tc; David Gee 25cr, 183tr; Mike Goldwater 175br; Micah Hanson 13b, 23tl, 23bl, 124cr, 179cl, 191br; Henry Westheim Photography 16fclb, 49br, 127bc, 250bl, 262-263; Roger Hutchings 18clb; Imagebroker 125c; ITPhoto 187b; Alistair Laming 31tr; Lonely Planet Images 153cra ,153bc; Neil McAllister 168; neilsetchfield.com 90crb; Douglas O'Connor 231cl; Paul Gisby Photography 153crb; The Photolibrary Wales 102; Photos-12 21cr; Prisma Bildagentur AG 52bl; Robert Harding Picture Library Ltd 121c, 263c; Bert de Ruiter 174bc; Yaacov Shein 123bl; Michael Sparrow 229c; Dave Stamboulis 181bl; Stephen Frink Collection 117br; Bjorn Svensson 183bl; Travel Ink 124bl; travelib prime 120-121; Peter Treanor 59tr, 276cl; Ian Trower 198c; Tom Vater 279tl; Volvox Inc 203tl; Whitehead Images 181bc; Terry Whittaker 84tl, 183br, 199cla, 199br; Andrew Woodley 283b. JERRY ALEXANDER: 127c, 167b. ANGKOR GOLF RESORT: 257bc. ANGKOR NATIONAL MUSEUM: 66tl, 66b. ARDEA.COM: D. Parer & E. Parer-Cook 16cb; Masahiro Iijima 199c; Thomas Marent 16bl; M. Watson

16clb; Wardene Weisser 17bl. ASIAN EXPLORERS: Timothy Tye 71cla. ANNA BOYSON: 193bl. THE BRIDGEMAN ART LIBRARY: Standing statue of Harihara, Phnom Da Style, from Angkor Borei (sandstone), Cambodian, (7th century)/Musee Guimet, Paris, France/Giraudon 37c, View of the Ho Chi Minh Trail in Laos (b/w photo),/Private Collection/Peter Newark Military Pictures/191tr. CAMBODIAN LIVING ARTS, A PROGRAM OF THE MARION INSTITUTE: Daniel Rothenberg 114bl. CENTRE CULTUREL FRANÇAIS DU CAMBODGE: 26bl, 26br. CORBIS: Bettmann 133t; Michael Freeman 94clb; National Geographic Society/ Gervais Courtellemont 55cra; Kevin R. Morris 108bl; Keren Su 52tl; Sygma/Robert Patrick 146bl. CPA MEDIA: 36, 37bc, 38crb, 39crb, 39bl, 40ca, 130tr, 130c, 131tc, 131crb, 131bc, 132tc, 132clb, 132bc, 133br; Joe Cummings 126br; Oliver Hargreave 19bl, 126cl, 181cla; David Henley 37br, 38br, 43br, 125b, 130bc, 133crb. DANITA DELIMONT STOCK PHOTOGRAPHY: Inger Hogstrom 44. DK IMAGES: Bethany Dawn 42cl, 72br; Courtesy of Ashley Leiman/Dave King 48clb; Courtesy of The National Birds of Prey Centre, Gloucestershire/Frank Greenaway 117tc; Courtesy of the Natural History Museum, London/Frank Greenaway 117cb. DUTCH CO & CO: Rik Hendriks 43cr, 257tr, 271br. ELEFANTASIA: Yves Bernard © 2008 185br. FLPA: Minden Pictures/Hiroya Minakuchi 17cb; Terry Whittaker 17fbr. GETTY IMAGES: AFP/Eric Feferberg 40bc,/Jimin Lai 41tr, 41cb,/Claude Juvenal/Staff 40clb,/Stringer 155c,/Tang Chhin Sothy 33cr, 33bl, 34bl, 41bc; DigitalGlobe 14bl; Hulton Archive/Alex Bowie 40cb; Roger Viollet/Francoise De Mulder 41c; Stringer/Tang Chhin Sothy 94br, 95cla; Time Life Pictures/Larry Burrows 39tl. GREEN DISCOVERY LAOS: 260t, Inthy Deuansavanh 147tr. PETER HOLMSHAW: 192tr. HÔTEL DE LA PAIX: 226cl. KEITH KELLY: 111br. THE KOBAL COLLECTION: Enigma/Goldcrest 119br; Lawrence Gordon/Mutual Film/Paramount/Bailey, Alex 81bc. LE TIGRE DE PAPIER: 258tc. LONELY PLANET IMAGES: Rachel Lewis 228cla, 229tl; Aldo Pavan 231tr; Carol Wiley 20bl. MARINE CONSERVATION CAMBODIA: 117crb. MASTERFILE: 41crb, 133bc, 174tl; Horst Herget 20cr; J. A. Kraulis 65tl; Robert Harding Images 21cla; Jeremy Woodhouse 199bl. MONUMENT BOOKS & TOYS CO., LTD: 275bl. NATUREPL.COM: Roberto Rinaldi 17br; Rod Williams 17ca, 17bc. PHOTOLIBRARY: Age fotostock/Eric Baccega 199cr,/R Matina 24tr,/Morales Morales 17cla, /Juan Carlos Munoz 30c,/Jose Fuste Raga 76-77; Asia Images RM/Gareth Jones 4br, 10br; Stefan Auth 2-3, 70crb, 112-113; F1 Online/Rozbroj Rozbroj 227tl; Hemis/Body Philippe 13tr, 28-29, 96-97,/Gotin Michel 22-23c; Per-Andre Hoffmann 53b; Imagebroker.net/ Stefan Auth 179br; Imagestate/Pisit Jiropas 176-177; jspix jspix 199cra; JTB Photo 27tr, 95tc, 144-145; Juniors Bildarchiv 17clb, 199cb; Jean Kugler 21tr; Lonely Planet Images/Juliet Coombe 45b,/Mark Kirby 103b,/Peter William Thornton 23cr; Mary Evans Picture Library 21clb; R Matina 85cl; Louis Meulstee 71cr; Oxford Scientific (OSF)/David Courtenay 17tc; Robert Harding Travel 35c,/Tim Hall 56-57; Still Pictures/Stuart Chape 16cl; Claire Takacs 62; The Travel Library/Paul Strawson 52tr, 83tr, 142cr; Ticket/Thien Do 54tr; Tips Italia/Luca Invernizzi Tettoni 136, 148; WaterFrame-Underwater Images/Franco Banfi 117bl,/Borut Furlan 16bc. SUNTOURS CAMBODIA: 11br, 17cr, 42br, 108cla, 109c, 256bl, 281br. SUPERSTOCK: Robert Harding Picture Library 205c. TRAVEL-IMAGES.COM: M. Torres 54bc. XE PIAN NATIONAL PROTECTED AREA: Phillipe Coste 198b.

Front Endpaper: ALAMY: Adam Deschamps tr, Neil McAllister tl, The Photolibrary Wales br; DANITA DELIMONT STOCK PHOTOGRAPHY: Inger Hogstrom tc; PHOTOLIBRARY Claire Takacs cr, Tips Italia/Luca Invernizzi Tettoni cl, cb.

JACKET IMAGES Front Cover: Getty Images: Photographer's Choice/John W Banagan main. Back Cover: DK Images: Linda Whitwham tl, cla, bl, Photolibrary: Pisit Jiropas clb. Spine: Getty Images: Photographer's Choice/John W Banagan t

For further information see: www.dkimages.com

Phrase Book for Cambodia

Khmer or Cambodian is the language of the Khmer people and the official language of Cambodia. It is a widely spoken Austroasiatic language. Khmer has been considerably influenced by Sanskrit and Pali, especially in the royal and religious registers, through the vehicles of Hinduism and Buddhism. It is also the earliest recorded and written language of the Mon-Khmer family, predating Mon and, by a significant margin, Vietnamese. Khmer has influenced and also been influenced by Thai, Lao, Vietnamese, and Cham many of which form a pseudo-sprachbund in peninsular Southeast Asia, since most contain high levels of Sanskrit and Pali influences. Additionally, during and after the French occupation, Khmer was strongly influenced by French. Hence, some of the medical, legal, and technical terminology is borrowed from it. The Khmer alphabet consists of 28 consonants and about 38 vowels. Unlike English, Khmer has a vowel for almost every sound and is a phonetic language in both oral and written forms. It consists of long and short vowels with distinctive pronunciation. Unlike its Southeast Asian counterparts, Khmer does not have intonation.

GUIDELINES FOR PRONUNCIATION

The consonants are pronounced as follows:

k is equivalent to the French pronunciation of k

kh is equivalent to the English pronunciation of k

c is a sound that is between c and j in English

ch is equivalent to the English pronunciation of ch

ng is equivalent to the English ending sound of ng

ny is equivalent to the Spanish pronunciation of ñ

t is equivalent to the French or Spanish pronunciation of t

th is equivalent to the English pronunciation of t

p is equivalent to the French or Spanish pronunciation of p (bi-labial, nonfricative)

ph is equivalent to the English pronunciation of p

អ is a representation of a consonant that has a vowel-like sound. Unlike English, Khmer cannot begin any word with a vowel. Hence this consonant "អ" is used

Vowels are pronounced as follows:

/**a**/ or /**aa**/ is equivalent to the French or Spanish pronunciation of /a/. The single /a/ is short while the double /aa/ is long.

/**i**/ or /**ii**/ is equivalent to the French or Spanish pronunciation of /i/. The single /i/ is short while the double /ii/ is long.

/**o**/ or /**oo**/ as in "zone", "cone", or "bone". The single /o/ is short while the double /oo/ is long.

/**u**/ or /**uu**/ as in "tune", "soon", or "cube". The single /u/ is short while the double /uu/ is long.

/**aw**/ as in "saw" or "thaw"

/**y**/ or /**yy**/ is a sound that does not exist in the English language. It is made in the epiglottis; a high sound made in the back of the oral cavity.

/**ɛ**/ or /**ɛɛ**/ is equivalent to the short /a/ or /ă/ of the English language. The single /ɛ/ is short while the double /ɛɛ/ is long.

/**uh**/ as in "doctor", "master", or "pasture"

/**u**/ as in the English sound "schwa"

A single vowel is a short vowel using the glottal stop to distinguish it from the long vowel.
A double or two vowels make a long vowel.
Akhosa is any consonant that ends with (aw) while khoosa is any consonant that ends with (oo).
The former has a low sound while the latter is high. Hence, the tones change depending upon which of the two consonants is used.

In an Emergency

Help!	ជួយផង!	*Cuay phawng!*
Fire!	ភ្លើងឆេះ!	*Phluhng cheh!*
Where is the nearest hospital?	តើមន្ទីរពេទ្យក្បែរនេះនៅទីណា?	*Tau montii peet kbae nih nuv tii naa?*
Call an ambulance!	សុំហៅឡានពេទ្យ	*Som hau laan peet*
Call the police!	សុំហៅប៉ូលីស!	*Som hau poolis!*
Call a doctor!	សុំហៅវេជ្ជបណ្ឌិត	*Som hau wiceabawndit*

Communication Essentials

Hello!	សួស្តី	*Sua sdey*
Goodbye!	លាសិនហើយ	*Lia senhauy*
Yes	បាទ / ចាស	*Baat / caas*
No	ទេ	*Tee*
Please	សូម	*Soom*
Thank you	សូមអរគុណ	*Soom awkun*
No, thank you	មិនអីទេ	*Min ey tee*
I don't understand	ខ្ញុំមិនយល់ទេ	*Khnyom min yul tee*
I don't know	ខ្ញុំមិនដឹងទេ	*Khnyom min dung tee*
Sorry/excuse me	សូមអភ័យទោស!	*Soom abpheytoos*
What?	អ្វី?	*Aawey aawey?*
Why?	ហេតុអ្វី?	*Haet aawey?*
Where?	នៅទីណា?	*Nuv tii naa?*
How?	ដោយរបៀបណា?	*Doay roobiab naa?*

Useful Phrases

How are you?	តើអ្នកសុខសប្បាយជាទេ?	*Tau neak sok sabaay cia tee?*
Very well, thank you – and you?	សប្បាយជាទេ អរគុណ ចុះអ្នកវិញ?	*Sabaay cia tee awkun coh neak vinya?*
What is this?	តើនេះជាអ្វី?	*Tau nih cia aawey?*
How do I get to...?	តើខ្ញុំអាចទៅឯ...?	*Tau khnyom aac tuv ae...?*
Where is the restroom/toilet?	តើ...នៅទីកន្លែងណា? បន្ទប់ទឹក?	*Tau...nuv tii kawnlaeng naa? bawntub tyk?*
Do you speak English?	តើអ្នកនិយាយភាសាអង់គ្លេសទេ?	*Tau neak niyiay phiasaa awngkles ryy tee?*
I can't speak Khmer/Lao	ខ្ញុំមិននិយាយភាសាខ្មែរ / លាវទេ	*Khnyom min niyiay phiasaakhmae/ liaw tee*

Useful Words

woman/women	ស្ត្រី	*satrey*
man/men	បុរស	*boraws*
child/children	កុមារ	*komaa*
hot	ក្តៅ	*kdaw*
cold	ត្រជាក់	*trawceak*
good	ល្អ	*l-aw*
bad	អាក្រក់	*aakrawk*
open	បើក	*bauk*
closed	បិទ	*bet*
left	ខាងឆ្វេង	*khaang chweeng*
right	ខាងស្តាំ	*khaang sdam*
straight ahead	ខាងមុខ	*khaang muk*
near	ក្បែរនេះ	*kbae nih*

far ឆ.ងាយ *chngaay*

entrance ផ.លវូចលូ *phlow cool*

exit ផ.លវូចពេញ *phlow cenya*

Money

I want to change US$100 into 100 Cambodian/Lao currency. ខ.ញចុំងប់.តរូលយុ ១០០ដលុ.លា ទេ ៅក.នងុ ១០០ លយុខ.មរែ/លាវ *Kbnyom cawng bdoo luy muayrooy dollaa tuv knong luy kbmae/ liaw.*

exchange rate តលំនៃកោរប.តរូ *dawmlay ney kaabdoo*

I'd like to cash these traveler's checks. ខ.ញចុំងប់.តរូសកែទសេ ចរទេ ៅជាលយុ *Kbnyom cawng bdoo saek tesacaw tuv cia luy.*

bank ធនាគា *thooniakia*

money/cash លយុ / លយុសទុ.ធ *luy/ lut sot*

credit card កាតគ.រឌេតិ *kaatkreedit*

Keeping in Touch

I'd like to make a telephone call. ខ.ញចុំងប់.រើទរូសព.ទ *Kbnyom cawng prau tuurosap.*

I'd like to make an international phone call. ខ.ញចុំងទរូសព.ទចញេក.រ ៅប.រទសោ *Kbnyom cawng tuurosap cenya tuv prawteh.*

mobile phone ទរូសព.ទដៃ *tuurosap day*

public phone booth ទកីន.លងែទរូសព. ទសាធារណរដ.ឋ *tii kawnlaeng tuurosap saathiaronaroad*

address អាសយ័ដ.ឋាន *aasaythaan*

street វថិ *witbey*

town ស.រកុ *srok*

village ភមូ *phuum*

Shopping

Where can I buy…? តើខ.ញអុំាចទញិ... ទកីន.លងែ? *Tau kbnyom aac tii kawnlaeng?*

How much does this cost? តើនេះមានតម. លបៃន៉ុមាន? *Tau nib mian dawmlay ponmaan?*

I would like… ខ.ញចុំង... *Kbnyom cawng…*

Do you have…? តើអ.នកមាន...? *Tau neak mian…?*

Do you take credit cards? តើអ.នកយកគ.រឌេតិកាតរទើ? *Tau neak yook kreedit kaat ryy tee?*

What time do you open/close? តើពេលណាអ.នកបើកទ.វា របើទិទ.វា? *Tau peel naa neak bauk twia ryy but twia?*

How much? តលំបៃន៉ុមាន? *Dawmlay ponmaan?*

expensive ថ.លណែាស់ *thlay nab*

cheap ថោកណាស់ *thoak nab*

to bargain តថ.លៃ *dawmlay*

size ទហំ *tumbum*

color ពណ៌ *poa*

black ពណ៌ខ.មៅ *poakhmau*

white ពណ៌ស *poasaw*

red ពណ៌ក.រហម *poakrawhawm*

market ផ.សារ *phsaa*

pharmacy ឱសថស.ថាន *oasawtthaan*

souvenir shop ហាងលក់អនសុ.សាវរយី *haang luk abnubsaawoorii*

souvenirs អនសុ.សាវរយី *abnubsaawoorii*

lacquer painting គនំរូ.ក់សណាទ.មក *kumnuu msahsankhuk*

painting on silk គនំរូទៅលើសត្ធ *kumnuu nuv lub soot*

wooden statue របូចម.លាក់ *ruub cawmlak*

silk scarf កន.សងែបងក់សត្ធ *kawnsaeng bawng kaw soot*

Sightseeing

beach មាត់សមទុ.រ *moat sawmut*

cave, grotto រង្គភ.នំ *roongphnom*

festival ពធិបីណ.យ *pitbii bon*

forest ព.រៃ *prey*

island កោះ *koh*

lake បងឹ *bung*

mountain ភ.នំ *phnom*

museum សារមន.ទរី *saamontii*

pagoda វត.ត *wat*

river ស.ទងឹ *nam, stung*

tourist office ការយិាលយ័ទសេចរណ៍ *kaariyaalay tebsacaw*

travel agent ភ.នាក់ងារទសេចរណ៍ *phneak ngia tebsacaw*

Transportation

When does the train for…leave? តើរទេះភ.លើងចាក ចញេ...ពលេណា? *Tau rootehphlubng caakcenya…peel naa?*

A ticket to…please. សមូទញិសបំត.រទេ ៅ... *Soom tinya sawmbot tuv.*

How long does it take to get to…? តើត.រវូចណំាយពលេបនុ៉ មានដើម.បទីទ ៅ...? *Tau trow cawmnaay peel ponmaan daumbey tuv?*

I'd like to reserve a seat, please. ខ.ញចុំងក់.សាកៅអទីកុ *Kbnyom cawng reaksaa kaw-ey tuk.*

Which platform for the…train? តើណាមយួគជឺទវេកិា សំរាប់រទេះភ.លើង? *Tau naamuay kyycia weetikaa sawmrab rooteh phlubng?*

Where is the bus stop? តើវទេកិាសំរាប់បស៊ី នៅទណីា? *Tau weetikaa sawmrab bus nuv tii naa?*

Where is the bus station? តើស.ថានយីបស៊ី នៅទណីា? *Tau sthaanii bus nuv tii naa?*

arrivals ការមកដល់ *kaamook dawl*

train station ស.ថានយីរទេះភ.លើង *sthaanii rootehphlubng*

airport វាលយន.តហោះ *wial yunhawb*

bus station ស.ថានយីបស៊ី *sthaanii bus*

ticket សបំត.រ *sawmbot*

one-way ticket សបំត.រឯកទសិ *sawmbot aektys*

return ticket សបំត.រត.រឡប់មកវញិ *sawmbot trawlawb niik winya*

taxi តាកស៊ី *taksii*

car rental ការជលួឡាន *kaacual laan*

car ឡាន *laan*

train រទេះភ.លើង *rootehphlubng*

plane យន.តហោះ *yunhawb*

plane ticket លខិតិយន.តហោះ *likhet yunhawb*

motorcycle មតូ៉ *mootoo*

bicycle កង់ *kawng*

Accommodations

Do you have a vacant room? តើមានបន.ទប់ទនំេរទើ? *tau mian bawntub tumnee ryytee?*

I have a reservation ខ.ញចុំងធ់.វើកា របរំងុទកុជាមនុ *Kbnyom cawng thwubkaa bawmrong tuk cia mun*

double/twin room បន.ទប់សំរាប់មនសុ. សពរីនាក់ *bawntub sawrab moonub pii neak*

single room បន.ទប់សំរាប់មនសុ. សម.នាក់ *bawntub sawrab moonub mneak*

hotel សណ.ឋាគារ *sawnthaakia*

guesthouse បន.ទប់ទលួភ.ញៀវ *bawntub tootual phnyiaw*

air conditioning ម៉ាសុីនត.រជាក់ *maasin trawceak*

bathroom បន.ទប់ទកឹ *bawntub tyk*

passport number លខេប៉ាស់ប័រ *leek pabboa*

Eating Out

A table for two please. តុសរំាប់ពរីនាក់ *Tob sawmrab pii neak.*

May I see the menu? ខ.ញសុំមុើលបញ. ជរីមុខម.ហូបបានទេ? *Kbnyom som mubl aabaa baan tee?*

Can I have the bill, please? តើខ.ញអុំាចមានលខិតិ លយុរទើ? *Tau kbnyom bann likbut luy ryy tee?*

Do you have any special dishes today?	តើមានមុខអាហារពិសេសសំរាប់ថ្ងៃនេះទេ?	Tau mian muk aahaa pises sawmrab thngay? nih ryy tee?
baguette	នំបុ័ង	num pang
beef	សាច់គោ	sac koo
beer	បៀរ	bia
bottle	ដប	dawb
breakfast	បាយព្រឹក	baay pryk
butter	ប៊ឺ	bub
chicken	សាច់មាន់	sac moan
chilli	ម្ទេស	mteeh
chopsticks	ចង្កឹះ	cawngkus
coconut	ដូង	doong
coffee	កាហ្វេ	kaafee
crab	ក្តាម	kdaam
dessert	បង្អែម	bawng aem
egg	ពងមាន់	poongmoan
fish	សាច់ត្រី	sactrey
fork	សម	sawm
fruit	ផ្លែឈើ	plaechuh
glass	កែវ	kaew
ice	ទឹកកក	tykkawk
ice cream	ការ៉េម	kaarm key
knife	កាំបិត	kambut
lime	ក្រូចឆ្មា	krooc chmaa
mandarin orange	ក្រូចតូចៗ	krooc tooc tooc
mango	ស្វាយ	swaay
meat	សាច់	sac
milk	ទឹកដោះគោ	tyk dawhkoo
mineral water	ទឹកសាប	tyk saab
mushrooms	ផ្សិត	phset
noodles	គុយទាវ	kuytiaw
onion	ខ្ទឹមបារាំង	khtum barang
papaya	ល្ហុង	lhong
paté	សាច់ប៉ាតេ	sac paatee
pepper	ម្ទេស	mtees
pork	សាច់ជ្រូក	sac crook
prawn	បង្គា	bawngkia
restaurant	ភោជនីយដ្ឋាន	phooconiithaan
rice	អង្ករ / បាយ	awngkaw/ baay
salad	សាឡាដ	saalad
salt	អំបិល	awmbel
soft drinks	ទឹកក្រូច	tyk krooc
soup	ស៊ុប	sub
spicy (hot)	ហឹរណាស់	hel nas
sour	ជូរ	cuu
soy sauce	សុីអុីវ	tyk sii-iw
spoon	ស្លាបព្រា	slaappria
stir-fried	ឆា	chaa
sugar	ស្ករ	skaw
tea	ទឹកតែ	tyk tae
vegetables	បន្លែ	bawnlae
water	ទឹកសាប	tyk saab
western food	អាហារអាមេរិកាំង	aahaa aameerikang
wine	ស្រា	sraa

Health

I do not feel well	ខ្ញុំមិនស្រួលខ្លួន	khnyom min srual khluan
It hurts here	ឈឺកន្លែងនេះ	chyy kawnlaeng
I have a fever	ខ្ញុំគ្រុន	khnyom krun
I'm allergic to	ខ្ញុំមិនត្រូវធាតុ	khnyom min toas
antibiotics	ថ្នាំរំងាប់មេរោគ	thnam rumngoab meerook
blood	ឈាម	chiam
blood pressure (high/low)	ឈាម (ឡើង / ចុះ)	chiam (laum/cos)
cough	ក្អក	k-awk
diabetes	ជំងឺទឹកនោមផ្អែម	cumngyy tyknoomph-aem
diarrhea	រាគ	riak
dizzy	វិលមុខ	wilmyk
doctor	គ្រូពេទ្យ	kruupeet
ear	ត្រចៀក	trawceak
flu	ជំងឺគ្រុនញាក់	cumngyy krun nyeak
food poisoning	ការពុលអាហារ	kaapul aabaa
headache	ការឈឺក្បាល	kaachyy kbaal
heart	បេះដូង	behdoong
hospital	មន្ទីរពេទ្យ	muntii peet
illness	ជំងឺ	cumngyy
injection	ការចាក់ថ្នាំ	kaa cakthnam
malaria	ជំងឺគ្រុនចាញ់	cumngyy krun canya
operate	ជួសជុល	cuascul
prescription	សំបុត្រថ្នាំពេទ្យ	sawmbot thnam peet
temperature	ធាតុអាកាស	thiat aakas
toothache	ឈឺធ្មេញ	chyy thmenya

Time and Day

minute	នាទី	niatii
hour	ម៉ោង	moang
day	ថ្ងៃ	thngay
week	អាទិត្យ	aatit
month	ខែ	khae
year	ឆ្នាំ	chnam
Monday	ថ្ងៃចន្ទ	Thngay can
Tuesday	ថ្ងៃអង្គារ	Thngay awngkia
Wednesday	ថ្ងៃពុធ	Thngay put
Thursday	ថ្ងៃព្រហស្បតិ៍	Thngay prooboas
Friday	ថ្ងៃសុក្រ	Thngay sok
Saturday	ថ្ងៃសៅរ៍	Thngay sau
Sunday	ថ្ងៃអាទិត្យ	Thngay aatit
What time is it?	តើម៉ោងប៉ុន្មានហើយ?	Tau moong ponmaan hauy?
8:30	ម៉ោងប្រាំបីកន្លះ	moong prambay kawnlah
10:15	ម៉ោងដប់ដប់ប្រាំនាទី	moong dawbpiipram niatii
12:00	ម៉ោងដប់ពីរ	moong dawbpii
morning	ព្រឹក	pryk
midday	ថ្ងៃត្រង់	thngay trawng
afternoon	ថ្ងៃរសៀល	thngay roosial
evening	ល្ងាច	lngiac
night	យប់	yub

Numbers

1	មួយ	muay
2	ពីរ	pii
3	បី	bey
4	បួន	buan
5	ប្រាំ	pram
6	ប្រាំមួយ	prammuay
7	ប្រាំពីរ	prampii
8	ប្រាំបី	prambey
9	ប្រាំបួន	prambuan
10	ដប់	dawb
11	ដប់មួយ	dawbmuay
12	ដប់ពីរ	dawbpii
13	ដប់បី	dawbbey
15	ដប់ប្រាំ	dawbpram
20	ម្ភៃ	muayphey
30	សាមសិប	saamseb
40	សែសិប	saeseb
50	ហាសិប	haaseb
60	ហុកសិប	hokseb
70	ចិតសិប	cetseb
80	ប៉ែតសិប	paetseb
90	កៅសិប	kawseb
100	មួយរយ	muayrooy
200	ពីររយ	piirooy
1,000	មួយពាន់	muaypoan
10,000	មួយម៉ឺន	muaymubn
1,000,000	មួយលាន	muaylian

Phrase Book for Laos

Lao or Pasa Lao, the official language of Laos, is a tonal, generally monosyllabic language. Thus having good pronunciations and tonal sounds is essential for communication. It is a part of the Tai sub-group of the Sino-Tibetan group of languages and its written form evolved from an ancient Indian script called Pali. Just like English, Lao is read from left to right and follows the subject-verb-object word order. In addition, most Lao letters are pronounced just like the sounds that exist in English. However, Lao differs from English in that it has little grammar, no plurals, few articles, and regularly omits the subject pronouns (I, he, she) when the context is understood.

GUIDELINES FOR PRONUNCIATION

Lao consonants below have been divided into three groups according to the tone in which they are spoken. The consonants are pronounced as follows:

Aksone sung (high sounding consonant)

- ຂ **kh** like 'c' in "cat" (aspirated)
- ສ **s** like 'ss' in "hiss"
- ຖ **th/t** like 't' in "top"
- ຜ **ph** like 'p' in "pig" (aspirated)
- ໝ **m** similar to 'm' in "mother"
- ຫຼ **l** similar to 'l' in "long"
- ຫວ **w** like 'w' in "weight"

Aksone kang (middle sounding consonant)

- ກ **k/g** like 'k' in "skate" (unaspirated)
- ຈ **ch/j** like 'ch' in "chop"
- ດ **d/t** like 'd' in "dog"
- ຕ **t** like 't' sound in "stab"
- ບ **b** like 'b' in "bed"
- ປ **p** like 'p' in "spit" (unaspirated)
- ຢ **y** like 'y' in "yes"
- ອ **o** like 'o' in "top"

Aksone tum (low sounding consonant)

- ງ **ng** like 'ng' in "sing"
- ຊ **s/x** like 'z' in "zoo"
- ຍ **nh/y** like 'y' in "yes"
- ຟ **f** like 'f' in "fan"
- ມ **m** like 'm' in "mother"
- ຣ **r** like 'r' in "room"
- ລ **l** like 'l' in "love"
- ວ **v** like 'v' in "vacant"
- ຫ **h** like 'h' in "help"
- ນ **n** like 'n' in "nice"

Lao vowels are pronounced as follows:

- ◌ິ **i** like 'i' in "nit"
- ◌ີ **ii** like 'ee' in "beer" or "feet"
- xະ **a** like 'u' in "gum"
- xາ **aa** like 'a' in "father"
- ແxະ **ae** like 'a' in "fat"
- ແx **e** like 'e' in "fence"
- ເx **eh** like in 'ai' in "bait"
- xຸ **u** like 'u' for "fruit"
- xູ **ou** like 'oo' in "mood"
- xາວ **aw** like 'aw' in "saw"
- xໍາ **am** like 'um' in "drum"
- xົ **oe** similar to the 'uh' in "huh"
- ເ◌ື **eu** like 'eu' in the French *"deux"*

In an Emergency

Help!	ຊ່ວຍແດ່!	*Suoy dae*
Fire!	ໄຟໄໝ້!	*Fai mai*
Where is the nearest hospital?	ໂຮງໝໍໃກ້ສຸດຢູ່ໃສ?	*Hong Mor Kai Sud Yu sai?*
Call an ambulance!	ໂທຫາລົດຂົນສົ່ງຄົນເຈັບແດ່!	*Towha lod khonsong khonchep dae!*
Call the police!	ໂທຫາຕໍາຫຼວດແດ່!	*Towha tum luot dae!*
Call a doctor!	ໂທຫາທ່ານໝໍແດ່!	*Towha thanmor dae!*

Communication Essentials

Hello!	ສະບາຍດີ!	*Sabaidee*
Goodbye!	ລາກ່ອນ!	*Lakhon*
Yes	ແມ່ນ	*Maen*
No	ບໍ່	*Bauw*
Please	ກະລຸນາ	*Kaluna*
Thank you	ຂອບໃຈ	*Khobjai*
No, thank you	ບໍ່, ຂອບໃຈ	*Bauw, Khobjai*
I don't understand	ຂ້ອຍບໍ່ເຂົ້າໃຈ	*Khoy Bauw Khaojai*
Sorry/excuse me	ຂໍໂທດ!	*Khauwthod*
What?	ແມ່ນຫຍັງ?	*Maen yang?*
Why?	ຍ້ອນຫຍັງ?	*Yonyang?*
Where?	ຢູ່ໃສ?	*U sai?*

Useful Phrases

How are you?	ເຈົ້າສະບາຍດີບໍ?	*Jaw Sabaidee Bor?*
Very well, thank you – and you?	ຂ້ອຍສະບາຍດີ, ຂອບໃຈ - ເຈົ້າເດ?	*Khoy sabaidee, Khobjai – Jawdei?*
How do I get to...?	ຂ້ອຍຈະໄປ... ໄດ້ແນວໃດ?	*Khoychapai ....ai neo day?*
Where is the restroom/toilet?	ຫ້ອງນໍ້າຢູ່ໃສ?	*Hongnam u sai?*
Do you speak English?	ເຈົ້າເວົ້າພາສາອັງກິດບໍ?	*Jaw Vaw Pasa Anggit Bor?*
I can't speak Khmer/Lao	ຂ້ອຍບໍ່ສາມາດເວົ້າພາສາກໍາປູເຈຍ/ພາສາລາວໄດ້	*Khoy bor sa mart vaw pasa gampuchia/ pasa Lao dai.*

Useful Words

woman/women	ແມ່ຍິງ	*mae ying*
man/men	ຜູ້ຊາຍ	*phu xai*
child/children	ເດັກນ້ອຍ	*dek noy*
open	ເປີດ	*peurt*
closed	ປິດ	*pit*
left	ຊ້າຍ	*sai*
right	ຂວາ	*khoua*
near	ໃກ້	*kai (high falling short)*
far	ໄກ	*kai (mid – long)*
entrance	ເຂົ້າ	*khao*
exit	ອອກ	*ork*

Money

I want to change US$100 into 100 Cambodian/Lao currency.	ຂ້ອຍຕ້ອງການປ່ຽນ 100 ໂດລາເປັນເງິນກໍາປູເຈຍ/ເງິນກີບລາວ	*Khoy tong kan pien neung hoy do la pen ngeun kampuchia/ngeun kip lao*
exchange rate	ອັດຕາແລກປ່ຽນ	*aat ta laek pien*
I'd like to cash these traveler's checks.	ຂ້ອຍຕ້ອງການແລກໃບເຊັກທ່ອງທ່ຽວເຫຼົ່ານີ້ເປັນເງິນສົດ	*Khoy tong kan laek bai sek thong thieu nee pen ngeun sot*
bank	ທະນາຄານ	*thanakhan*
money/cash	ເງິນ/ເງິນສົດ	*ngeun/ngeun sot*
credit card	ບັດເຄດິດ	*bat khe dit*

Keeping in Touch

I'd like to make a telephone call.	ຂ້ອຍຢາກໂທລະສັບ	*Khoy yark tow la sap*
mobile phone	ໂທລະສັບມືຖື	*tow la sap meu theu*
public phone booth	ຕູ້ໂທລະສັບສາທາລະນະ	*tu tow la sap sa tha la na*

Shopping

How much does this cost?	ອັນນີ້ລາຄາເທົ່າໃດ?	*An nee la kha thao dai?*
What time do you open/close?	ເຈົ້າເປີດ/ປິດເວລາຈັກໂມງ?	*Jaw peurt/pit vei la chak moung?*
size	ຂະໜາດ	*kha nat*
market	ຕະຫຼາດ	*ta lat*
pharmacy	ຮ້ານຂາຍຢາ	*han khai ya*
souvenir shop	ຮ້ານຂາຍຂອງທີ່ລະນຶກ	*han khai khong tee la neuk*

Sightseeing

cave, grotto	ຖ້ຳ	*tham*
lake	ໜອງ	*nong*
mountain	ພູເຂົາ	*phu khao*
river	ແມ່ນ້ຳ	*nam*
tourist office	ຫ້ອງການທ່ອງທ່ຽວ	*hong kan thong thieu*
travel agent	ຕົວແທນທ່ອງທ່ຽວ	*tou thaen thong thieu*

Transportation

A ticket to…please.	ເອົາປີ້ໄປ.... ໃຫ້ແດ່.	*Aw pii pai ... hai dae*
Where is the bus stop?	ບ່ອນຈອດລົດເມຢູ່ໃສ?	*Bon chot lot mei u sai?*
arrivals	ຂາເຂົ້າ	*kha khao*
airport	ສະໜາມບິນ	*sa nam bin*
one-way ticket	ປີ້ຂາໄປ	*pii kha pai*
return ticket	ປີ້ໄປກັບ	*pii pai kub*
taxi	ລົດແທັກຊີ	*lot taek xee*
car rental	ການເຊົ່າລົດ	*kan sao lot*
plane ticket	ປີ້ຍົນ	*pii nhon*
motorbike	ລົດຈັກ	*lot chak*
bicycle	ລົດຖີບ	*lot theep*

Accommodations

Do you have a vacant room?	ເຈົ້າມີຫ້ອງຫວ່າງບໍ?	*Jaw mee hong vang bor?*
I have a reservation	ຂ້ອຍໄດ້ຈອງຫ້ອງໄວ້ແລ້ວ	*Khoy dai chong vai laeo*
double/twin room	ຫ້ອງຕຽງຄູ່/ສອງຕຽງ	*hong tieng khou/ song tieng*
single room	ຫ້ອງຕຽງດ່ຽວ	*hong tieng dieu*
hotel	ໂຮງແຮມ	*hoong haem*
guesthouse	ເຮືອນພັກ	*heuan pak*
air conditioning	ເຄື່ອງປັບອາກາດ	*kheuang pap aakard*
bathroom	ຫ້ອງອາບນ້ຳ	*hong arb nam*
passport number	ເລກທີໜັງສືຜ່ານແດນ	*Leik tee nang su phan daen*

Eating Out

May I see the menu?	ຂ້ອຍຂໍເບິ່ງເມນູໄດ້ບໍ?	*khoy khor beung mei nu dai bor?*
Can I have the bill, please?	ກະລຸນາ ເອົາບິນໃຫ້ແດ່?	*Ka lu na ao bin hai dae?*
baguette	ເຂົ້າຈີ່ກ້ອນຍາວ	*khao chii kon yao*
beef	ຊີ້ນງົວ	*xeen ngua*
chopsticks	ໄມ້ທູ່	*mai thu*
chicken	ໄກ່	*gai*
coffee	ກາເຟ	*ka fei*
crab	ປູ	*pu*
egg	ໄຂ່	*khai*
fish	ປາ	*pa*
fork	ສ້ອມ	*som*
fruit	ໝາກໄມ້	*mark mai*
meat	ຊີ້ນ	*xeen*
mineral water	ນ້ຳແຮ່	*nam hae*
milk	ນົມ	*noom*
noodles	ໝີ່	*mee*
pepper	ພິກໄທ	*pik thai*
pork	ຊີ້ນໝູ	*xeen mou*
prawn	ກຸ້ງ	*kung*
restaurant	ຮ້ານອາຫານ	*han aa han*
rice	ເຂົ້າ	*khao*
salt	ເກືອ	*keua*
spicy (hot)	ເຜັດ	*fet*
spoon	ບ່ວງ	*boang*
sugar	ນ້ຳຕານ	*nam tan*
tea	ຊາ	*xaa*
vegetables	ຜັກ	*fak*
water	ນ້ຳ	*nam*
western food	ອາຫານຕາເວັນຕົກ	*aa han ta ven tok*

Health

I do n[illegible] well	ຂ້ອຍຮູ້ສຶກບໍ່ສະບາຍ	*Khoy h[illegible] seuk bor sa bai*
It hurts h[illegible]	ມັນເຈັບຢູ່ບ່ອນນີ້	*Man cheb bon nee*
I have a [illegible]	ຂ້ອຍເປັນໄຂ້	*Khoy pen khai*
I'm allergic [illegible]	ຂ້ອຍແພ້	*Khoy pae*
antibiotics	ຢາຕ້ານເຊື້ອ	*ya tan xeua*
blood pressur (high/low)	ຄວາມດັນເລືອດ (ສູງ/ຕ່ຳ)	*khoam dun luot (sung/tum)*
cough	ໄອ	*i*
diabetes	ເບົາຫວານ	*bao wan*
diarrhea	ຖອກທ້ອງ	*thok thong*
food poisoning	ອາຫານເປັນພິດ	*aa han pen pit*
headache	ເຈັບຫົວ	*cheb hua*
illness	ການເຈັບປ່ວຍ	*kan cheb puoy*
malaria	ໄຂ້ມາລາເຣຍ	*khai ma la ria*
prescription	ໃບສັ່ງຢາ	*bai sang ya*
toothache	ເຈັບແຂ້ວ	*cheb khaeo*

Time and Day

minute	ນາທີ	*na tii*
hour	ຊົ່ວໂມງ	*xou mohng*
day	ມື້	*meuh*
week	ອາທິດ	*aa thit*
month	ເດືອນ	*deuan*
Monday	ວັນຈັນ	*Van chan*
Tuesday	ວັນອັງຄານ	*Van ang khan*
Wednesday	ວັນພຸດ	*Van phut*
Thursday	ວັນພະຫັດ	*Van pa hat*
Friday	ວັນສຸກ	*Van suk*
Saturday	ວັນເສົາ	*Van sao*
Sunday	ວັນອາທິດ	*Van aa thit*
What time is it?	ເວລາຈັກໂມງແລ້ວ?	*Vei la chak mohng laeo*
morning	ຕອນເຊົ້າ	*ton xao*
afternoon	ຕອນບ່າຍ	*ton baii*
evening	ຕອນແລງ	*ton laeng*
night	ກາງຄືນ	*kang keun*

Numbers

1	ໜຶ່ງ	*neung*
2	ສອງ	*song*
3	ສາມ	*saam*
4	ສີ່	*sii*
5	ຫ້າ	*ha*
6	ຫົກ	*hok*
7	ເຈັດ	*jet*
8	ແປດ	*paet*
9	ເກົ້າ	*kao*
10	ສິບ	*sip*
20	ຊາວ	*xao*
30	ສາມສິບ	*saam sip*
40	ສີ່ສິບ	*sii sip*
50	ຫ້າສິບ	*ha sip*
60	ຫົກສິບ	*hok sip*
70	ເຈັດສິບ	*jet sip*
80	ແປດສິບ	*paet sip*
90	ເກົ້າສິບ	*kao sip*
100	ໜຶ່ງຮ້ອຍ	*neung hoy*
1,000	ໜຶ່ງພັນ	*neung pan*
10,000	ສິບພັນ	*sip pan*
1,000,000	ໜຶ່ງລ້ານ	*neung laan*